T0301406

A Research Agenda for Brand Management in a New Era of Consumerism

Elgar Research Agendas outline the future of research in a given area. Leading scholars are given the space to explore their subject in provocative ways, and map out the potential directions of travel. They are relevant but also visionary.

Forward-looking and innovative, Elgar Research Agendas are an essential resource for PhD students, scholars and anybody who wants to be at the forefront of research.

For a full list of Edward Elgar published titles, including the titles in this series, visit our website at www.e-elgar.com.

A Research Agenda for Brand Management in a New Era of Consumerism

Edited by

CERIDWYN KING

White Lodging Services Head and Professor, White Lodging-J.W. Marriott, Jr. School of Hospitality and Tourism Management, Purdue University, USA

ENRIQUE MURILLO

Professor of Marketing, Facultad de Ciencias Económicas y Empresariales, Universidad Panamericana, Mexico

Elgar Research Agendas

Cheltenham, UK • Northampton, MA, USA

Published by
Edward Elgar Publishing Limited
The Lypiatts
15 Lansdown Road
Cheltenham
Glos GL50 2JA
UK

Edward Elgar Publishing, Inc.
William Pratt House
9 Dewey Court
Northampton
Massachusetts 01060
USA

A catalogue record for this book
is available from the British Library

Library of Congress Control Number: 2023940690

This book is available electronically in the **Elgar**online
Business subject collection
http://dx.doi.org/10.4337/9781803925516

ISBN 978 1 80392 550 9 (cased)
ISBN 978 1 80392 551 6 (eBook)

Printed and bound in Great Britain by TJ Books Limited, Padstow, Cornwall

Contents

Figures

Tables

Contributors

M. Billur Akdeniz is a Professor of Marketing at the University of New Hampshire. Billur's research encompasses empirical modeling of marketing strategy problems. Her areas of interest are new products, sustainable innovation strategies, brand management, and international marketing. Her research has appeared in the *Academy of Management Journal*, *Journal of the Academy of Marketing Science*, *International Journal of Research in Marketing*, and *Journal of Product Innovation and Management*, among others. In addition, Billur is an Associate Editor at the *Journal of Business Research* and on the Editorial Review Boards of *Journal of the Academy of Marketing Science*, *Journal of Product Innovation and Management*, *Industrial Marketing Management*, and *International Business Review*.

Daniela Andreini, Ph.D., is Full Professor in Marketing and Prorector for Innovation and Digitalization at the University of Bergamo (Italy). Her scientific research focuses mainly on the innovation and digitization of business models, on digital brands, digital marketing, and social media marketing. She is consulting editor of *International Journal of Management Reviews*, and a member of the editorial board of *Journal of Business Research*, *Journal of Product & Brand Management*, *Italian Journal of Marketing*, and *International Journal of Information Management*. Her research has appeared in international journals such as *Journal of Advertising*, *Journal of Business Research*, *Industrial Marketing Management*, *Organization Studies*, *Journal of Advertising Research*, *Family Business Review*, *Journal of Business and Industrial Marketing*, *Journal of Business Ethics*, and *Journal of Service Theory and Practice*.

Beatriz Itzel Cruz-Megchun is an Assistant Professor of Design and Innovation at the Dr. Robert B. Pamplin, Jr. School of Business at the University of Portland, US. Her research focuses on the role and value of design in organizations from the strategic to the operational level and the role of design in technological innovations, social innovations, and responsible innovations. She has over 15 years of experience consulting in the creative, manufacturing, and new technology industries. She also participates in projects with non-governmental organizations and governmental institutions addressing social inequalities.

Salvador del Barrio-García holds a Doctoral Degree in Economics and Business Studies from the University of Granada (UGR), and is a Full Professor at the UGR's Department of Marketing and Market Research. His areas of expertise include integrated marketing communications (IMC), cross-cultural communication, brand management, and tourism marketing. He has published over 60 peer-reviewed papers in prestigious journals in these fields, as well as several books as author and co-author. He has also undertaken research and teaching stays at the University of Texas at Austin (USA), Burgundy School of Business (France), and University of San Andrés (Argentina), among others.

Andreas B. Eisingerich is Professor of Marketing and Head of Analytics, Marketing and Operations at Imperial College Business School in London, UK. He studies consumer–brand relationships, consumer usage and adoption of new technologies and wellbeing, mobile health solutions, consumer psychology, and service innovation. He has numerous research publications in top business journals including *Journal of Marketing*, *Journal of Consumer Psychology*, *Journal of Service Research*, *Journal of International Marketing*, *Journal of the Academy of Marketing Science*, *Harvard Business Review*, *European Journal of Marketing*, *Journal of Retailing and Consumer Services*, *Research Policy*, *California Management Review*, and *Journal of Services Marketing*.

Yujia Huang is a Lecturer at the University of Dundee, UK. Drawing upon her extensive industry experiences and academic development in design, she adopts a systematic and transdisciplinary approach that critically addresses individual, organizational, and social issues and innovation demands through design research. Her expertise lies in Design for Business and Leadership, Design for Services and Experiences, Socially Responsible Design, and Design for Education and Creativity. Her textbook *Design Thinking for New Business Contexts* (Springer, 2022) interweaves academic theory with contemporary industry practice and proposes design thinking as organizational philosophy instead of a simple problem-solving tool.

Nicholas Ind is a Professor at Kristiania University College, Oslo. He is the author of 16 books that have been published in nine different languages, and articles in *California Management Review*, *Journal of Brand Management*, *Journal of Product & Brand Management*, and *Business Horizons*. Nicholas is a member of the scientific committee of the Global Brand Conference and the editorial board of the *Journal of Brand Management.* Since 2009 he has been a Visiting Professor at ESADE, Barcelona and Edinburgh Napier University.

Hyunsu Kim, Ph.D., is Assistant Professor in the Department of Management, Mihaylo College of Business and Economics, California State University, Fullerton, USA. He was awarded his Ph.D. in Hospitality Management at the University of South Carolina. His research interests focus on service management and services marketing, with an emphasis on customer experience, customer engagement, and service and technological innovations in hospitality and tourism. His research has appeared in top tourism and hospitality and journals including *Journal of Travel Research, International Journal of Hospitality Management, Tourism Management, International Journal of Contemporary Hospitality Management*, and *Cornell Hospitality Quarterly.*

Ceridwyn King is a Professor and White Lodging Services Head of the White Lodging-J.W. Marriott, Jr. School of Hospitality and Tourism Management at Purdue University. An internationally renowned scholar, her research focuses on service management and marketing, emphasizing the internal stakeholder's role in realizing marketing strategies to create competitively sustainable service experiences. With a particular passion for hospitality brand management, she is regularly engaged as an expert witness in this field. She is the Editor-in-Chief of *Services Marketing Quarterly*, Associate Editor of *Journal of Hospitality and Tourism Research*, and Co-ordinating Editor of *International Journal of Hospitality Management.* Additionally, she serves on the editorial boards for *International Journal of Contemporary Hospitality Management, Cornell Hospitality Quarterly*, and the *Journal of Service Management.*

Samuel Kristal gained his Ph.D. from the University of Twente, the Netherlands. His research mainly focuses on brand management and branding in B2C and B2B. His research has been published in international journals, such as *Journal of Product and Brand Management, Journal of Business Research*, and *International Journal of Sports Marketing and Sponsorship.* He was Assistant Professor at the Chair of Product–Market Relations of the University of Twente, the Netherlands. Currently, he holds a full Professorship for Business Administration with a focus on Marketing at the Brandenburg University of Applied Sciences, Germany.

Charles Aaron Lawry, Ph.D., is an Assistant Professor of Marketing at Hult International Business School in Cambridge, MA. His research agenda focuses on the adoption and use of Industry 4.0 technologies in high-touch retail environments, namely art, fashion, and luxury goods. He examines these issues through the theoretical lenses of human–computer interaction, cultural production, and mediatization. His empirical research and conceptual work have been published in leading journals, including the *International Journal of Advertising, Fashion Marketing and Management, Frontiers in Psychology*, and *Psychology & Marketing*.

Zoe Lee is a Senior Lecturer of Marketing at Cardiff Business School, Cardiff University, UK. She is an Associate Editor of the *Journal of Strategic Marketing* and a member of the Editorial Review Board for the *Journal of Philanthropy and Marketing*. She has published in top ranked peer-reviewed academic journals including the *Journal of Business Research*, the *Industrial Marketing Management*, the *Journal of Business Ethics*, the *European Journal of Marketing*, and the *Journal of Brand Management*. Her research focuses on contemporary branding issues (including corporate brand and rebranding & brand activism), sustainability (including communication strategies and inclusivity) and nonprofit marketing strategy.

Catarina Lelis is a Senior Lecturer at the University of Aveiro, Department of Communication and Art, in Portugal. She began her professional experience in 1997 as a graphic designer. Whilst in industry, she co-founded a technology-based company, a publishing start-up, and the Portuguese Association for Innovation and Creativity in Organisations. She won two entrepreneurship contests and was semi-finalist of MIT-Portugal Innovation & Entrepreneurship Competition. As an academic, she spent six years in London, dedicating her efforts to Brand Design and to Service Innovation, and being awarded a teaching fellowship with her project *The Impact Plan* (www.impact-plan.com). Catarina's research interests include Brand Design, Smartness in Visual Identities, Design Literacy, and Anticipation of Impact.

Jing Li, Ph.D., is Assistant Professor in the Department of Hospitality and Retail Management at Texas Tech University. She received her Ph.D. from the University of South Carolina. Her research interests lie primarily in service marketing and management, with emphases on the customer experience, branding, service and technological innovation. She also has interests in advanced quantitative and qualitative methods. Her research can be found in leading international journals such as *Journal of Travel Research*, *International Journal of Contemporary Hospitality Management*, *International Journal of Hospitality Management*, and *Journal of Destination Marketing & Management*.

Filip Lievens is Lee Kong Chian Professor of Human Resources at the Lee Kong Chian School of Business of Singapore Management University. In 1999, he obtained his Ph.D. at Ghent University, Belgium. His main interests deal with talent acquisition, talent assessment, and adaptability. He has published over 60 papers in top-tier journals, including *Annual Review of Psychology*,

Journal of Applied Psychology, *Personnel Psychology*, *Journal of Management*, and *Organizational Behavior and Human Decision Processes*. Recently, he was ranked among the top 1% of scientists in the world in the field of Business & Management.

Deborah J. MacInnis is Professor Emerita at the Marshall School of Business, University of Southern California (USC). She is a Fellow of the American Marketing Association, Association for Consumer Research, and Society for Consumer Psychology. She is also the recipient of the AMA-Irwin-McGraw Hill Distinguished Educator Award. She has received the Lifetime Achievement Award from the AMA's Consumer Behavior Special Interest Group and the Faculty Lifetime Achievement Award from USC. She has received numerous awards for her research. Debbie has been Coeditor and Associate Editor for the *Journal of Consumer Research*, and Associate Editor for the *Journal of Marketing* and the *Journal of Consumer Psychology*.

Ady Milman is a Professor at Rosen College of Hospitality Management at the University of Central Florida. His expertise areas include tourism planning and development, airline management, travel agency management, theme park and attraction management, consumer behavior and consumer experience. Dr. Milman was the recipient of the Martin Oppermann Memorial Award for Lifetime Contribution in Tourism Education. Dr. Milman has served on the editorial boards of the Journal of Hospitality and Tourism Research, Journal of Travel Research, Journal of Teaching and Travel and Tourism, and other key publications in hospitality and tourism.

Michela Mingione is Professor of Marketing at the University of Rome Tor Vergata, Italy. Her current research interests are in corporate marketing, corporate identity and branding. Her work has been published in the *Journal of Business Research*, *Industrial Marketing Management*, *Journal of Marketing Management*, *Journal of Brand Management*, *Journal of Product & Brand Management*, and the *Journal of Marketing Communications*, among others. Moreover, she is an editorial board member of the *Journal of Marketing Analytics*.

Susan M. Mudambi is Professor of Marketing at the Fox School of Business, Temple University, with a secondary appointment in Management Information Systems. Her research addresses digital technology, B2B branding, customer and supplier relationships, and international business strategy. Her work has appeared in prestigious journals including *MIS Quarterly*, *Journal of Management Studies*, *Journal of Product Innovation Management*, *Industrial Marketing Management*, and *Journal of International Management*. She serves on the Editorial Review Boards of multiple journals in marketing and management. She holds a B.A. from Miami University, an M.S. from Cornell University, and a Ph.D. from the University of Warwick (UK).

Enrique Murillo is Professor of Marketing at Universidad Panamericana in Mexico City. He has a Management Ph.D. from the University of Bradford (UK), and a postdoc in Organizational Behavior from Tulane University. He is a member of Mexico's National System of Researchers (SNI). His research focuses on Internal Branding, examining the drivers of employees' positive attitudes toward the service brand, a prerequisite for brand-aligned service encounters. In pursuit of this topic he has conducted studies in various organizations in Latin America, including restaurants, airlines, universities, fashion retailers, drugstore chains, and ride-sharing platforms. His work has appeared in the *Journal of Product & Brand Management*, *Journal of Service Management*, *International Journal of Contemporary Hospitality Management*, *Review of Business Management*, *International Journal of Hospitality Management*, and *Journal of Business Research*.

C. Whan Park is Robert E. Brooker Professor of Marketing at the University of Southern California's Marshall School of Business. Dr. Park has published numerous articles in leading journals, including the *Journal of Marketing Research*, *Journal of Consumer Research*, *Journal of Marketing*, *Journal of Retailing*, and *Harvard Business Review*. He was the editor of the *Journal of Consumer Psychology* (2008–2012), and serves on the editorial board of the *Journal of Marketing* and the *Journal of Consumer Psychology*. Professor Park is currently Director of the Global Branding Center at the Marshall School of Business.

María Eugenia Rodríguez-López holds a Ph.D. in Business Administration from the University of Granada (Spain). She is Assistant Professor at the Department of Marketing and Market Research, Faculty of Education, Economics and Technology of Ceuta (University of Granada). Her areas of research interest are advertising effectiveness, tourism marketing and cross-cultural marketing. She has published in prestigious journals such as the *Journal of Business Research*, *International Journal of Hospitality Management*, *International Journal of Contemporary Hospitality Management*, and *European Journal of Marketing*, among others.

Álvaro J. Rojas-Lamorena holds a Ph.D. in Business Administration from the University of Granada (Spain). He is Assistant Professor at the Department of Marketing and Market Research, Faculty of Education, Economics and Technology of Ceuta (University of Granada). His areas of research interest are consumer behavior, brand management, and cross-cultural marketing. He has published various peer-reviewed articles in prestigious journals such as *Journal of Business Research* and *Journal of Marketing Communications*, among others.

Gordhan K. Saini is Professor at the School of Management & Labour Studies in the Tata Institute of Social Sciences, Mumbai. His areas of research interest include employer branding, social marketing and pricing. He has published more than 40 research papers in international journals including *Career Development International, Asia-Pacific Journal of Human Resources, Journal of Brand Management, Journal of Consumer Marketing, Social Marketing Quarterly, International Journal of Nonprofit and Voluntary Sector Marketing,* and *Journal of Global Marketing*. In addition, he has consulting experience of research projects for corporates, and research projects for government and non-government organizations.

Kevin Kam Fung So, Ph.D., is William S. Spears Chair in Business and Full Professor at the School of Hospitality and Tourism Management, Spears School of Business, Oklahoma State University. An award-winning scholar in his field, Dr. So's research expertise lies at the intersection of hospitality and tourism marketing and service management with emphases on branding, customer engagement, social media marketing, electronic word of mouth, and the rise of the sharing economy. He has published extensively in the top-tier journals in his discipline, including *Journal of Travel Research, Tourism Management, Annals of Tourism Research, International Journal of Hospitality Management, Journal of Hospitality and Tourism Research, International Journal of Contemporary Hospitality Management*, and *Cornell Hospitality Quarterly*, as well as *Journal of Business Research* and *Journal of Service Management*.

Mukta Srivastava is an Associate Professor, and Chairperson of the Marketing Area at T A Pai Management Institute, Manipal Academy of Higher Education, India. She has years of academic and research experience. Her research interests have been in the domain of customer engagement, eWOM, and branding. Her articles have been published in reputed international journals such as *International Marketing Review, Journal of Product & Brand Management, Marketing Intelligence & Planning*, and *Journal of Consumer Marketing*. She has also contributed case studies and chapters in books from reputed publication houses.

M. Berk Talay is a Professor of Marketing at the University of Massachusetts Lowell. He studies strategic marketing problems about competitive co-evolution of products, brands, companies, and industries. He is currently involved in a set of large-scale projects, which examine the drivers of new product success in different markets with particular emphasis on competition, sustainability, and portfolio management. His work has appeared in top-tier scholarly business journals such as the *Journal of International Business Studies*, *Journal of the Academy of Marketing Science*, *Journal of Product Innovation Management*, *Journal of International Marketing*, and *Industrial Marketing Management*, among others.

Asli D.A. Tasci is a Professor of Tourism and Hospitality Marketing in the Department of Tourism, Events & Attractions in the Rosen College of Hospitality Management at the University of Central Florida. Her research interests include tourism and hospitality marketing, particularly consumer behavior. She completed a number of studies measuring destination image and branding with a cross-cultural perspective. Her work has appeared in highly reputed journals such as *Journal of Travel Research*, *International Journal of Contemporary Hospitality Management*, and *Journal of Destination Marketing & Management.*

Janell D. Townsend is a Professor of Marketing and International Business, and Chair of the Management & Marketing Department at Oakland University in Rochester, Michigan, USA. She has also taught at Michigan State University, Technical University of Vienna, Wayne State University and the University of Zurich. Dr. Townsend earned her Ph.D. from Michigan State University, with current research falling within the nexus of branding, product design and innovation, in a global marketplace. Her work has appeared in top-tier business journals such as the *Journal of International Business Studies*, *Journal of Product Innovation Management*, and *Journal of International Marketing*, among others.

Cleopatra Veloutsou is Professor of Brand Management in the Adam Smith Business School of the University of Glasgow (UK), Visiting Professor at the University of Bari (Italy), University of Bergamo (Italy), President University (Indonesia), Hellenic Open University (Greece) and University of Coimbra (Portugal) and Head of the Marketing Research Unit of the Athens Institute of Education and Research (ATINER) (Greece). Her primary research interest is on Brand Management, and she has published over 60 articles in international journals, and presented over 100 papers in international academic conferences. She is Co-Editor-in-Chief of the *Journal of Product & Brand Management*, Associate Editor of the *Journal of Business Research*, and serves on the editorial board of several academic journals.

Lina Xiong is an Associate Professor in the Department of Human Dimensions of Natural Resources at Colorado State University. Dr. Xiong is an accomplished researcher who focuses on internal branding and destination marketing research with an internal stakeholder perspective. She has published many papers in top tourism, hospitality and marketing journals. She teaches tourism strategic management and tourism marketing classes. She is also the director for two collaborative Master's programs in tourism and park and protected area management. She emphasizes a sense of purpose and wellbeing in her work and life.

Lia Zarantonello is Professor of Marketing at Roehampton University, Faculty of Business & Law, UK. Her research interests are in the field of brand management and consumer psychology. She has published in international journals including *Journal of Marketing*, *Journal of Consumer Psychology*, and *International Journal of Research in Marketing*. In 2015 she co-authored, for Routledge, the first *Handbook of Brand Management Scales*. She is Associate Editor of the *Journal of Business Research* and the *Italian Journal of Marketing*, and sits on the editorial boards of several journals including the *Journal of Brand Management* and the *Journal of Product & Brand Management*.

Introducing *A Research Agenda for Brand Management in a New Era of Consumerism*

Enrique Murillo and Ceridwyn King

When Edward Elgar Publishing reached out to us to commission a new book in their popular series *A Research Agenda*, we were excited to learn that our own field of work, brand management, would be the focus of the volume. We have been active in this scholarly space for some time now, and thus found the scope of the project to be an interesting challenge, particularly in light of the emergence, since the turn of the century, of important branding topics.

From the outset, being mindful of several exemplary research volumes on brand management recently published or forthcoming, we have been very intentional in striving to offer scholars interested in this field a compelling read. Accordingly, we decided our chief aim would be to curate an up-to-date overview of the extensive field of brand management research for a target audience who might be unfamiliar with the depth and breadth of its offerings. Specifically, the book offers PhD students and their dissertation advisors, as well as scholars considering a new line of enquiry, a theoretical and methodological roadmap of key brand management research topics, as well as potential routes for further research development.

We strongly believe there is a need for such a volume. In what Kantar Consulting has named The Third Age of Consumption, where challenges of cognitive, economic and resource capacity have redefined the aspirations and expectations of consumers, a new era has emerged whereby value is defined by experiences, relationships, and algorithms (Kantar Consulting, 2018). Consumerism is characterized by a new imperative, that can aptly be described as Live Large–Carry Little. While consumers still want enjoyment, convenience and enrichment, they no longer take for granted that owning "things" is indispensible for consumption (Walker Smith, 2018). As a result, brand management has had to evolve to ensure what defines a brand's value proposition today reflects these seismic shifts in consumerism. In response to this shift, the field of brand management has experienced exponential growth in the number of publications, driven in part by the emergence of several novel perspectives. Brand co-creation (Iglesias et al., 2013), conscientious brands (Ind & Horlings, 2016), online brand communities (Dessart & Veloutsou, 2021), nonprofit branding (Lee & Davies, 2021), and internal brand management (King & Grace, 2010) are among the more recent topics that afford both PhD students and established scholars a plethora of opportunities for groundbreaking and impactful research.

To facilitate this process, and to ensure future research reflects original contributions to the field of brand management that builds on extant knowledge, this Elgar Research Agenda identifies and illuminates topics that are at the forefront of the field. For each chapter, a subject matter expert with a strong publication record in their chosen topic, was commissioned. As Editors we encouraged authors to think of their chapter as trying to win the hearts and minds of new researchers – make them want to contribute to the field of the author's expertise.

The chapters in this book have been written by 32 international scholars from 27 different universities, hailing from North America, Latin America, Europe and Asia. During this project, we have been lucky and privileged to collaborate with a talented and enthusiastic roster of contributors, each of them committed to the book's goal and with the desire to make a difference in the development of their chosen field of research, by communicating their enthusiasm to the next generation of scholarly researchers.

The book provides excellent coverage of foundational brand management topics. Additionally, it illuminates more contemporary contributions to the field, with every chapter designed to articulate the latest research directions and opportunities. Readers are provided with a holistic understanding of the state of each dynamic area of knowledge and practice.

The chapters are structured to provide a theoretical roadmap of the topic and a synthesis of the methodological approaches that have previously been used in the field. The experts also offer their personal take on the most interesting avenues for future research, in effect providing a compelling research agenda to move the theme forward. Authors were encouraged to write their chapters from the perspective of motivating doctoral students and emerging scholars to undertake innovative research in a topic that, in several cases, the authors have personally pioneered (e.g., Ind, King, Lievens, Veloutsou, Zarantonello). As a bonus, the chapters are all compact and accessible, with most being around 6000 words, not counting the list of references. They thus provide an efficient roadmap to the current state-of-the-art of distinct themes within brand management.

The outline of this book

This book is organized into two parts: Part I is titled Foundations of Brand Management Research and includes ten chapters that address the theoretical taxonomy of the field, with coverage of all major topics in branding research, such as brand design, brand architecture and portfolios, corporate brands, brand equity, internal brand management, and consumer responses to brands. Special Interest Branding Research is the focus of Part II of the book, comprising five chapters that examine in greater detail the application of branding principles and best practices in common business contexts, such as B2B branding, destination branding, nonprofit branding, and luxury brands.

Chapter 1, which leads the Foundations of Brand Management, is titled "Design-led brand management: a new territory". In this ambitious chapter, Lelis, Cruz-Megchun and Huang effectively communicate their deep knowledge of the design discipline, to convey to business readers how brand management can and should draw inspiration from design theories, methods and practices. They do this by following a structure that is mostly inspired by the "brand thinking canvas", divided into three main areas: brand core, brand identity and brand interactions. This division is used to present the current challenges, gaps, and future possibilities of brand design research. By addressing the epistemological issues of branding, the authors cover a considerable range of topics, raising questions around authenticity, dynamic identities, brand narrative design and audience participation, proxemics in branded spaces, design thinking and hybrid business models, and finally, the concept of smart brands and how these must prepare for a future that includes machine learning, the metaverse, bots and extended realities. The authors are explicit about their position to the effect that there is no brand to be managed if it is not being "designed" in the first place. Hence, they discuss throughout the chapter what design entails in the context of brands, and how design and its human-centeredness contributes to brand management.

Chapter 2 focuses on corporate branding, a classic theme of brand management. In "The emergence and evolution of corporate branding", Ind provides a concise review of the emergence and evolution of the topic in academic research since its origins in the mid-1990s. The author identifies three inter-connected evolutionary paths: The first has been the shift in perspective away from the idea that brand meaning is fixed by the organization to one that recognizes the fluidity that accompanies greater connectivity within business ecosystems. The second path, which flows from the first, is the opportunity, that has been seized by some organizations, to enrich the corporate brand by facilitating the active involvement of diverse stakeholders through co-creation. The third is the response of corporate brands to the pressure from investors, government, NGOs, consumers, partners and citizens, to take a broader view of their responsibilities to society and the environment. Each of these major and ongoing changes has spawned numerous issues worthy of further investigation. Thus, Ind compiles in the second part of the chapter, a rich agenda for future research on the three themes of organic corporate brands, brand co-creation and brand conscience.

Brand architecture and by implication brand portfolios is the focus of Chapter 3, which bears the title "Brand architecture: a literature review and future research directions". Since organizations rarely use a single brand for all their different products and services, designing a coherent architecture that defines the number and nature of common and distinctive brand elements across the firm's products and services, is vital for its marketing strategy. To examine this important topic, Talay, Akdeniz and Townsend perform an extensive review of the marketing strategy literature since 2000, with a specific focus on the brand architecture research stream, detecting five key themes: (i) brand hierarchy, (ii) brand portfolios, (iii) brand–finance interface, (iv) brands and innovation management, and (v) global branding. Within each theme, the authors present the evolution of the topic, current thinking, and offer outstanding questions and future research avenues. As a chapter bonus, the authors provide a comprehensive perspective on best practice methodology considerations in researching this topic.

Chapter 4, titled "How does brand equity work? A review of theory and a research agenda" addresses a foundational topic that has attracted the attention of brand management researchers for nearly four decades, and yet important questions remain. Del Barrio-García, Rodríguez-López and Rojas-Lamorena briefly describe the evolution of brand equity research through a bibliometric analysis, presenting the two major prisms through which brand equity has been studied, namely the financial perspective and the customer perspective. Against this backdrop, the chapter centers on customer-based brand equity (CBBE) to explore the conceptual definition of the term, examining the seminal works of Aaker and Keller. It also addresses the measurement of CBBE, its component dimensions, and scholarly attempts to develop multidimensional and unidimensional measurement scales. The authors close their chapter with a research agenda on the construct of CBBE focusing on the one hand on measurement and dimensionality, and on the other hand on underexplored drivers of CBBE, such as consumers' geographical environment, consumer-perceived brand authenticity, and companies' marketing investment and corporate reputation.

Brand co-creation, among the more recent topics in the literature, is the focus of Chapter 5, titled "Brand value co-creation: field emergence, applications, measurement and future research directions". Mingione and Kristal open their review by pointing out that the emergence of the co-creation construct at the start of the millennium shifted brand management and branding from a unilateral, managerially controlled creation of value to a new logic whereby brands co-create value with their customers, an issue already explored by Ind in Chapter 2. Indeed, the modern conceptualization of brand co-creation expands the traditional duality of customers and company, to include a multitude of stakeholders who are all potentially co-creators of the brand and who are in large measure enabled by the interactive capabilities of web-based technologies. As a result, a brand is seen as a dynamic social process constructed through multiple networked interactions and relations between the company, the brand, and various stakeholders. The concept of co-creation is thus regarded as a dominating paradigm shift in contemporary brand research in the business-to-consumer as well as in the business-to-business context. Several chapters in the book mention the impact on their field of research that the co-creation perspective has brought about, including nonprofit branding, B2B branding, destination branding, and employer branding. Mingione and Kristal provide a compact roadmap of the emergence of brand value co-creation research and practice, its different areas of application, possible measurement constructs, outcomes that can be achieved when companies apply brand value co-creation strategies, and potential avenues and impulses for future research.

Chapter 6 by So, Li and Kim, provides a succinct yet thorough review of the most important "Consumer responses to branding" that have been researched in the literature to date. The chapter covers an extensive repertoire of consumer-based constructs, including relationship quality, emotional brand attachment, customer brand identification, brand equity (examined in greater detail in Chapter 4), brand switching, and brand loyalty. The list is further augmented with brand trust and brand satisfaction which are conceptualized to build the second order construct of relationship quality in Crosby et al.'s (1990) widely used approach. In their recommendations for future research, the authors note that technological advances and a rapidly changing consumer environment have spawned a hyperconnected world which calls for a reassessment of existing research that gives due consideration to these new circumstances. Additionally, they review three emergent brand constructs that further expand the list of consumer responses, namely brand coolness, customer engagement and psychological brand ownership. For each of them, seminal studies are identified, applications in different branding contexts are reviewed, and a substantial number of still-open research questions are provided to outline a future agenda for researchers and graduate students who wish to push the boundaries of branding research.

The foundational concept of brand experience is covered in Chapter 7, coauthored by one of the seminal authors in this line of research. In "A roadmap of brand experience", Zarantonello and Andreini analyze the origins of the construct within the framework of experiential marketing (Schmitt, 1999) and the context of the experience economy (Pine & Gilmore, 1998). Brand experience is conceptualized as a multidimensional phenomenon, defined as "subjective, internal consumer responses (sensations, feelings, and cognitions) and behavioral responses evoked by brand-related stimuli that are part of a brand's design and identity, packaging, communications, and environments" (Brakus et al., 2009, p. 53). Having described its origins, the chapter then moves to further conceptualizations and measurements of brand experience in specific business contexts, such as service organizations, retail, and omnichannel retail. The authors conclude with an overview of emerging areas of importance for research, such as brand experience in relation to new technologies and with respect to broader societal goals including individual and social well-being. Each of these directions provide opportunities for future research, which Zarantonello and Andreini have organized into a generous list of open research questions.

The topic of brand communities has attracted much researcher attention in the two decades since the publication of the pioneering article by Muñiz and O'Guinn (2001). In Chapter 8, Veloutsou offers an insightful critique of this literature under the title "Reflections on brand communities academic research". Given the size of this research corpus, the author organizes the chapter into three categories of problematic issues named "definitional", "context" and "method and focus". In turn, each category groups several current debates around brand communities that offer promising directions for future research. For instance, the very first definitional issue centers on the ongoing debate over the definition of brand community, and what is the difference between brand community and other brand-centered groups such as brand tribes or brand fan pages. Lack of clarity over what a brand community is implies lack of clarity about who is and who is not a member of the brand community, another topic in need of further research. For instance, few of the previous studies take into consideration, or attempt to obtain data from "lurkers", that is, brand community members who engage through non-visible behavior such as reading online content. Within the "context" category, Veloutsou points out that extant studies have mostly emphasized company-initiated and managed communities, and little is known about the birth, growth, and structure of consumer-run communities. As for the "method and focus" category, an exciting avenue for future studies is to exploit some of the new methods, such as big data, text-mining and sentiment analysis of such online data as customer reviews.

The focus of Chapter 9 is the concept of brand attachment. The title "A theoretical framework exploring three foundational benefits of brand attachment" hints how Eisingerich, MacInnis and Park take a different approach from other chapters in the book. Rather than recounting what the literature on brand attachment has already covered, the authors seek to illuminate previous work by identifying how it informs a novel or new way of thinking. From this novel perspective they are then able to derive future research directions. The chapter first defines brand attachment as the strength and salience of the bond connecting the brand to the self and describes the positive outcomes that follow from this consumer attitude, such as difficult-to-perform pro-brand behaviors. The authors then advance a framework of three brand benefits that drive brand attachment: enabling, enticing, and enriching benefits, which they label the 3 Es. Subsequently, each of these are examined in detail, placing a particular emphasis on the processes that connect each of these brand benefits to brand attachment. The interactions of the three benefits acting together are also discussed, as is the critical role of enriching benefits in forming brand attachment compared to enabling and enticing benefits. The chapter closes with a discussion presenting a number of managerially relevant open research questions concerning the novel 3 Es perspective. While for each question the authors are not shy to advance their best conjecture and rationale, they clarify that the questions remain open to empirical research, and together they outline a complete research agenda on these novel drivers of brand attachment.

Internal Brand Management (IBM), which emphasizes aligning employee attitudes and behavior with the organization's brand values to deliver the brand promise to customers, is the topic of Chapter 10. Under the title "The coming of age of internal brand management research: looking back to look forward", King, Murillo and Xiong present a systematic literature review complemented with a bibliometric cluster analysis of this literature. While most IBM studies have been undertaken in service industries, where employees are critical in bringing the unique brand values to life because of the intangibility and heterogeneity characteristics of service products, the insights illuminated in this chapter are relevant for all contexts where human capital is key to brand success. The authors provide a roadmap of the theories, methods and contexts that have been used in past studies. Based on their review, the authors conclude that IBM studies appear to have reached a bottleneck, where newer studies are often repetitions of previous studies, only in different contexts or under different terms. Hence, they dedicate a section of the chapter to advocate for truly novel and meaningful research. Specifically, they call for strong theoretical underpinning of future IBM studies, as their review showed that half of published studies either lack theory or are based on the cognate field of study (e.g., IBM theory). They also encourage future researchers to use methods such as focus groups, experiments, and longitudinal designs, which are quite scarce in the extant literature. Lastly, in the context of contemporary workforce trends, they suggest examining IBM in organizations that do not rely on traditional employees to deliver their brand promise (e.g., Uber and Airbnb), and to investigate how and to what extent the brand can address the needs and expectations of employees, as a means to counter the workforce disruption that has been amplified in the aftermath of the COVID pandemic.

Chapter 11 opens the second part of the book, dedicated to Special Interest Branding Topics. Business-to-business brands is the first of these topics, with the chapter title "B2B branding: a review and research agenda for turbulent times". As with other chapters in the book, Mudambi provides a roadmap for future B2B branding research by first curating an up-to-date review of the key themes in extant literature. Foremost among these is identifying the sources of value for B2B brands. Montgomery and Wernerfelt (1992) identified two, quality guarantees and risk reduction. For Chitturi and Mudambi (2009) it was two different sources, relationship building and differentiation. For Homburg et al. (2010), brand value was connected to the reduction of information costs and of perceived risk of decision makers. Leek and Christodoulides (2012) distinguished two sources of brand value leading to lasting relationship value, namely functional (technology, infrastructure, innovation) and emotional (risk, trust, reassurance, credibility). In looking forward to future research directions, Mudambi reflects that businesses must consider present-day economic turbulence as the new reality, and therefore prioritizes three directions for future enquiry: First, B2B branding and digital platforms, including both ecommerce and social media platforms, where B2B brands have shown to be as competent content creators as B2C brands. Second, supply chains, as the COVID pandemic elevated customer concerns about their resilience and effectiveness, B2B branding must address these concerns head-on. Finally, in the current era of heightened concern about societal issues, the chapter calls for consideration of increased transparency in supply chains to limit the risk to B2B brands of negative associations from third parties with questionable business practices, such as slave labor, or operating within pariah nation states.

The next special interest topic is "Destination branding", covered in Chapter 12. It is defined as the purposeful actions of destination authorities, manifested in consistent marketing communications, to differentiate and position their destination against their competitors. However, Tasci and Milman point out that destination brands are not solely the product of the purposeful actions of authorities, because other influencers also affect a destination's brand including the media, word-of-mouth, and even competitors' branding activities. Moreover, a destination's brand is influenced also by the branding activities of its individual attractions and businesses. Therefore, consistent with the co-creation perspective, a destination brand can never fully be controlled by destination authorities. Much of the extant literature has focused on the construct of destination brand equity, from both a financial perspective and a consumer-perceptual perspective. For the former, the chapter notes the challenge of compiling relevant and objective consumption metrics for destinations, which are conglomerate and complex products, resulting in a scarcity of empirical studies centered on the financial perspective. By contrast, since customer-based brand equity of destinations relies on visitor surveys, there is a plethora of studies investigating the perceptual perspective, and a variety of multidimensional scales have been proposed, which the chapter summarizes in tabular form. Based on their review, the authors identify several gaps in the literature and opportunities for future research. The chapter also contrasts destination branding with the concept of place branding, which is typically concerned with the perceptions of locals/residents of the location as an attractive place to move and live in. Destination and place branding have evolved in parallel with little communication, even using different indicators of brand equity. Hence, the integration of the two research streams is advocated, to achieve a more comprehensive understanding of the brand equity of a location (Tasci, 2020); this consolidation in itself outlines another research agenda.

The topic of employer branding is covered in Chapter 13 which bears the title "Third-party employment branding: current status and future directions". Lievens, Srivastava and Saini examine one of the newer topics in brand management, third-party employment branding (TPEB), which owes its rapid growth to the popularity of independent workplace rankings, such as Fortune's 100 Best Companies to Work For, and the emergence of company review websites such as Glassdoor, Kununu and Indeed. Defined as communications, claims, or status-based classifications generated by parties outside of direct company control that shape, enhance, and differentiate organizations' images as favorable or unfavorable employers (Dineen et al., 2019), TPEB is used to refer to several types of workplace branding that escape control by employing organizations. This is a dramatic evolution of the original concept of employer branding (Backhaus & Tikoo, 2004) whereby organizations attempted to build a differentiated image as an attractive employer. Nowadays the company's employer image is co-created by company employer branding but also by current/former employees and other external stakeholders such as applicants and customers. The authors perform a bibliometric analysis of the literature with data obtained from the Scopus database between 1996 and 2021, compiling up-to-date results regarding most cited articles, influential authors, and keywords. Through a cluster analysis, current themes in the literature are identified, and future research directions suggested within the top articles in each cluster are summarized in an overview table. As a capstone for the chapter, Lievens, Srivastava and Saini provide their own detailed suggestions, as longtime subject matter experts, on the most promising directions for future TPEB research.

Another branding topic which has become increasingly relevant in recent times is nonprofit branding, the subject of Chapter 14 under the title "Building brands for nonprofit organisations: a review of current themes and future research directions". In the introductory section, Lee points out the historical reluctance of nonprofit organizations to adopt for-profit branding tools and practices in their sector, seeing them as too profit-driven and commercialized. The author contrasts this with the current societal demand for all organizations to be more purpose-driven, noting too how the brand can effectively communicate this intent and provide direction. The chapter refers to nonprofit branding as a set of tools developed for fundraising purposes as well as for driving broad, long-term social goals while strengthening the internal identity, cohesion and capacity. Much of the early work in nonprofit branding adopted a narrow approach to brand management, focused heavily on donors' giving behavior and fundraising issues. Research has been energized more recently by adopting a social constructionist approach that suggests brand value is co-created through continuous social interactions and practices among multiple, networked stakeholders (Merz et al., 2009), beyond the dyadic relationship between nonprofit managers and supporters. Echoing a theme from other chapters in the book, this shift emphasizes that nonprofit managers are no longer the sole authors and custodians of brand identity. Rather, embracing interactions with multiple stakeholders in shaping the meanings of nonprofit brands is necessary to ensure the survival of nonprofit organizations. The chapter also explores two key contemporary research avenues: activist brand positioning and heritage management. Brand activism, whereby organizations take a stand on a social, environmental, or political issue, is becoming more common in the nonprofit sector, even as it risks damaging the traditional image of nonprofits as warm and compassionate. The notion of brand heritage is also increasingly adopted by nonprofits that engage in rebranding exercises as a way to return to their roots and stay authentic to their brands. The risk is that stakeholders' perceptions may diverge, such as young supporters who feel no connection with the history versus old-timers who are strongly attached to the brand's heritage.

Consumers' fascination with brands is especially salient within luxury branding, the final topic addressed in Part II of the book. In "Luxury brand research: four decades of innovation", Lawry puts together a concise yet detailed roadmap of the evolution of luxury research organized into four phases labeled Luxury 1.0, 2.0, 3.0 and 4.0. In the first phase, covering the 1990s, researchers identified three traits of luxury brands: desirability indicated their coveted, yet exclusive, status; polysensoriality referred to their ability to stimulate multiple senses through creative strategies that involved brand storytelling and unique offerings; and temporality, or standing the test of time. This era also yielded pioneering studies about consumers' luxury motivations, with both intrinsic and extrinsic motives identified. The Luxury 2.0 phase, which spanned the first decade of the 21st century, was marked by widespread availability and exploding sales of luxury brands. Among researchers, this democratization of luxury spawned concerns about brand dilution, which were further exacerbated by the uncertainties of digital disruptions and the Great Recession (2007–2009). To counteract the ill effects of democratization, studies examined the limits of vertical and horizontal brand extensions. Research in Luxury 3.0 (2010–2020) was characterized by two major themes: the mediatization and the artification of luxury. The former examines luxury consumers that interact with digital media in pursuit of convenience, self-fulfillment, and emotional gratification (e.g., Yoo & Park, 2016). The latter chronicles brands' efforts to connect with the art world to rekindle their status as tastemakers in society. Luxury 4.0 comprises Lawry's synthesis of open research questions within each of the previous phases, such as how luxury brands can contribute to tackle current social issues, or how they can capitalize on the phygital trend, which blends immersive mobile experiences with physical servicescapes (Lawry, 2022). The chapter closes with a call for luxury researchers to keep pace with the innovation in this fast-moving industry in order to stay relevant and develop meaningful work in this fascinating field.

In conclusion, curating this collection of chapters chronicling the wide field of brand management has been illuminating for us as Editors, as we have been struck by the fast pace of publication and the quality of recent work in each of the specialized topics our Contributors have expertly reviewed. To all of them we convey our heartfelt gratitude. And to the graduate students, dissertation advisors and scholars that this book is dedicated to, we truly believe you will find it a useful reference to begin your own research journeys in brand management.

References

Backhaus, K.B., & Tikoo, S. (2004). Conceptualizing and researching employer branding. *Career Development International*, *9*(5), 501–517.

Brakus, J.J., Schmitt, B.H., & Zarantonello, L. (2009). Brand experience: What is it? How is it measured? Does it affect loyalty? *Journal of Marketing*, *73*(3), 52–68.

Chitturi, P., & Mudambi, S.M. (2009). Building brand value in business markets, in *B-to-B Brand Management: Fundamentals, Concepts, and Best Practices*, edited by Carsten Baumgarth (pp. 181–198). Istanbul: Gabler Verlag Publishing.

Crosby, L.A., Evans, K.R., & Cowles, D. (1990). Relationship quality in services selling: An interpersonal influence perspective. *Journal of Marketing*, *54*(3), 68-81.

Dessart, L., & Veloutsou, C. (2021). Augmenting brand community identification online to increase brand loyalty: A uses and gratification perspective. *Journal of Research in Interactive Marketing*, *15*(3), 361-385.

Dineen, B.R., Van Hoye, G., Lievens, F., & Rosokha, L.M. (2019). Third party employment branding: What are its signaling dimensions, mechanisms, and sources? *Research in Personnel and Human Resources Management*, 173-226. Research Collection Lee Kong Chian School Of Business.

Homburg, C., Klarmann, M., & Schmitt, J. (2010), Brand awareness in business markets: When is it related to firm performance? *International Journal of Research in Marketing*, *27*(3), 201-212.

Iglesias, O., Ind, N., & Alfaro, M. (2013). The organic view of the brand: A brand value co-creation model. *Journal of Brand Management*, *20*, 670–688.

Ind, N., & Horlings, S. (Eds.) (2016). *Brands with a Conscience: How to Build a Successful and Responsible Brand*. London: Kogan Page.

Kantar Consulting (2018). Coming of age: The coming E.R.A. of value & growth in the third age of consumption. https://sites.kantar.com/thought_leadership/Growth/Kantar_Coming_of_Age.pdf

King, C., & Grace, D. (2010). Building and measuring employee-based brand equity. *European Journal of Marketing*, *44*(7-8), 938-971.

Lawry, C.A. (2022). Blurring luxury: The mediating role of self-gifting in consumer acceptance of phygital shopping experiences. *International Journal of Advertising*, *41*(4), 796–822.

Lee, Z., & Davies, I. (2021). Nonprofit brand and managing nonprofit rebranding strategy, in *Charity Marketing*, edited by Fran Hyde and Sarah-Louise Mitchell (pp. 46-58). London: Routledge.

Leek, S., & Christodoulides, G. (2012). A framework of brand value in B2B markets: The contributing role of functional and emotional components. *Industrial Marketing Management*, *41*(1), 106-114.

Merz, M., He, Y., & Vargo, S. (2009). The evolving brand logic: A service-dominant logic perspective. *Journal of the Academy of Marketing Science*, *37*, 328-344.

Montgomery, C.A., & Wernerfelt, B. (1992). Risk reduction and umbrella branding. *Journal of Business*, *65*(1), 31-50.

Muñiz, A.M., & O'Guinn, T.C. (2001). Brand community. *Journal of Consumer Research*, *27*(4), 412-432.

Pine, B.J., & Gilmore, J.H. (1998). Welcome to the experience economy. *Harvard Business Review*, *76*, 97-105.

Schmitt, B. (1999). Experiential marketing. *Journal of Marketing Management*, *15*(1-3), 53-67.

Tasci, A.D.A. (2020). Exploring the analytics for linking consumer-based brand equity (CBBE) and financial-based brand equity (FBBE) of destination or place brands. *Place Branding and Public Diplomacy*, *16*(1), 36–59.

Walker Smith, J. (2018). Live large–carry little. *Research World*, *2018*(68), 10–13.

Yoo, J., & Park, M. (2016). The effects of e-mass customization on consumer perceived value, satisfaction, and loyalty toward luxury brands. *Journal of Business Research*, *69*(12), 5775–5784.

PART I

Foundations of brand management research

1 Design-led brand management: a new territory

Catarina Lelis, Beatriz Itzel Cruz-Megchun and Yujia Huang

1. Introduction

Defining design is complex. When we talk about design, we need to be specific since we can refer to a theory (methods and philosophies), an action (as in a verb), a process, or an artefact (the outcome). Its understanding and application vary according to the context and area of application. Design in business focuses on materialising core competences, producing intellectual property, raising awareness about the product and service lifecycle, considering environmental, social, and economic dimensions, among other strategic activities. Businesses apply design to create symbolic and visual communication outcomes, produce material objects, organise activities and services, conceive environments for living, playing, and learning, and devise complex systems (Buchanan, 1997). However, in this context, managers may know what would sell and make a profit but do not understand good design, and designers often lack broader commercial awareness. To integrate design and business, both parties must understand what design in a business context is and how it links to overall business effectiveness. When designing and managing brands, managers and designers need to secure strategic alignment from top to bottom of the organisation, and from inside to outside, connecting the brand to the end-user (Cooper and Press, 1995).

The concept of "brand" has a plethora of definitions and an evolving theory. De Chernatony and Dall'Olmo Riley (1998) identified 12 main themes: (1) legal instrument; (2) logo; (3) company; (4) shorthand; (5) risk reducer; (6) identity system; (7) image in consumers' mind; (8) value system; (9) personality; (10) relationship; (11) adding value; and (12) evolving entity. The brand concept addresses multiple assets that are essential to convey brand intentions, principles, values, attributes, and promises. Hence, brand management becomes essential in helping to connect and deliver the essence of a brand to their target's needs through strategies, tools, and orchestrated performances. Kapferer (2012) defined brand management as a fulfilment in customer expectations and consistent customer satisfaction. Customer expectations are fulfilled when their experiences are positive and meaningful, and consistency comes with order. According to Papanek, "design is the conscious and intuitive effort to impose meaningful order" (2019, p.4). Thus, brands need to design relatable and authentic core principles, meaningful and recognisable brand identities, and engaging and emotional touchpoints that reassure consumers in each of their encounters with the brand's value proposition (Motta-Filho, 2020).

The goal of this chapter is to guide the reader through the several mechanisms design uses/promotes/generates to create meaningful order for brands. Our position is that there is no brand to be managed if it is not being "designed" in the first place. Throughout this chapter we will discuss what design entails in the context of brands, and how design and its human-centredness can contribute to brand management. The chapter also provides future research directions which are needed to further solidify the increasing relevance and contribution of design in brand strategy and management.

2. Brand design

The role of design can be significant in brand strategy development. The top strategic level is the highest and most powerful form of decision making or influencing, impacting upon every aspect of design touchpoints within the brand. Design recognition and advocacy at the boardroom level is fundamentally connected to driving the brand's overall vision in terms of long-term direction, brand goals, management structure, finance, and human resources. In this context we introduce the concepts of "design leadership", "design management", and "design thinking".

Design Leadership helps in defining what the future looks like by aligning people with a vision, and inspiring them to make it happen (Kotter, 1996). It aims to lead design and to lead business by design. Design Management focuses on managing design activities and deploying resources throughout the organisation (Martin, 2009) to influence its internal and external performance (de Mozota, 2006). It shapes the broader design context, such as the market situation and branding decisions. Design Thinking is a "human-centred approach to innovation that draws from a designer's toolkit to integrate the needs of people, the possibilities of technology, and the requirements for business success" (Brown, 2009, p.115). It facilitates the analysis, synthesis, and evaluation of process development using different thinking styles (convergent and divergent, serial and holistic, or linear and lateral), and draws evidence through appropriate design research methods (such as How-Might-We questions, user journey maps, personas, prototypes, etc.) to address commercial and non-commercial "wicked problems" (Buchanan, 1992).

Design is recognised as a strategic resource of brand innovation. It plays a vital role in reducing the distortion between what the brand wants to convey (its identity) and what the audience perceives (its image) (Karjalainen, 2004), but also between what the brand may offer and what the audiences need. The challenge is that identity (both brands' and audiences') is abstract and dynamic (Neumeier, 2016). It is shaped by the realities of our world and evolves as the world around us changes and forces us to encounter new experiences.

Furthermore, design supports brands to generate value through offerings that meet or exceed the functional value of products or services (what they do), and the symbolic or experiential value (what they mean) (Holbrook and Hirschman, 1982). Therefore, brands are expected to design functional, usable, intuitive, aesthetic, and emotional products/services that are compelling and memorable (Berry et al., 2002). Additionally, brands design physical and digital means that consider emotional responses, expectations, and motivations before, during, and after the audiences' interaction with the brand (Lee et al., 2013).

Undoubtedly, designing a brand is a conscious process that requires different design specialisations at project/operational level:

- For the visual presentation of a brand, *graphic design* is critical for creating a brand's visual identity, tone, style, and visual language. To deliver the brand identity and values to the audiences, *communication design* provides a strategic plan to communicate these messages.
- For brand offerings, *product* and *service design* allow a brand to concretise its brand value proposition in responding to the target customer needs. Based on the type of products, specialisations like *industrial*, *fashion*, and *interior design* help a brand gain competitive advantages through concept, shape, material, aesthetic, meaning, and more. For digital presence, *UI* (user interface) and *UX* (user experience) *design* serve users with clear visual touchpoints to brand services and a pleasant journey through all aspects of brand interactions.
- For creating an immersive brand experience, *experience design* considers the brand as an ecosystem and the holistic integration of all brand assets,

including brand philosophy, values, and culture (the core), and uses design tools to achieve a full sense of brand interaction.

Despite having to be carefully designed, such a plethora of resources, assets, expertises, and elements will have to be adequately managed, in tandem with the design premisses and parameters.

To articulate the different levels in which design and its specialisations contribute to brand management, Miltenburg's "Brand Thinking Canvas" (2017) offers a comprehensive representation of a designable brand's anatomy. It identifies the elements that make a strong brand and what it takes to successfully direct how people think and feel about it. It is divided into three groups:

1. *Brand core* embodies the character, beliefs, and personality of the brand and captures its essence, mission, vision, values, and brand promises (further described in Section 3).
2. *Brand identity* consists of the visual and verbal expression communicated to, with, and by every stakeholder. It deals with the sense-making and semantic tactics that are used to crystallise the core (described in Section 4).
3. *Brand interactions* guide all the points of contact that are built to connect with said stakeholders. It encompasses not only people, talent, and behaviour, but also technology, products and services, places and events, communication and channels, and partnerships and collaborations (described in Section 5).

In the following sections, essential design theories and design research are showcased to illustrate how design empowers brands at their core, identity, and interactions.

3. Design for brand core

Resorting to Plato and his analogy of the "segmented line of knowledge", Guzman and Lelis (2021) suggest that existing branding models (e.g. mind-share branding, Customer-Based Brand Equity (CBBE) model) have been paying little attention to design and its role in the brand's core, which is mostly experience-led. These models resort to the identification and reaching of homogeneous segments (Beverland, 2018), therefore requiring a stable subject/object of knowledge. Hence, the authors argue that these methods tend to objectify the brands' targets, making it difficult to find space for a different understanding of audiences – which are increasingly heterogeneous. In fact, these approaches tend to follow a scientific realist methodology, which is supported by deductive thinking. This is greatly opposed to regular design practice, mostly grounded on abductive reasoning, which is about making a probable conclusion from what one observes and infers (Dorst, 2011), underpinned by qualitative and empathy-based research. By conceiving brands from a design thinking and human-centred perspective, Guzman and Lelis (2021) propose that brands are also a subject-matter of the human sciences, and, for that reason, their core (grounded on human propositions and human experience-orientation) cannot be studied in the same ways as we study exact sciences.

These authors' supposition is that brands should be managed based on the elements of reality that are in permanent change, such as the everyday social, political, economic, and any other mundane practices – since these define the brands' audiences and, consequently, the core of a brand. Outdoor brand Patagonia's newest statement in September 2022, "Earth is now our only shareholder" (Chouinard, 2022) is the perfect example of linking the core value of a brand to urgent environmental responsibility. With a rather different business model and proposition, Apple's products, communications, and experiences have all been designed. The brand departs from a very precise and strong core, strongly defined by a desired experience. For decades, Apple has been relying on the anticipation of everydayness to design these experiences – the iPhone paved the way to the current mundane necessity of relying on a smartphone.

When brands are constructed and analysed with the support of design practice, it is plausible to easily relate to the most basic field of human imagination and the most authentic (and yet subjective, hardly quantifiable) personal experiences. Participatory storytelling is particularly successful here: when the brand narrative is left open, it leads to high levels of brand customisation that can successively represent both the audience and the brand. Social networks have been particularly relevant in promoting this mundane, authentic, and participatory approach. This is how brand managers can nudge users/consumers to participate in a brand's narrative: by providing them with the feeling that they can, even if just partially, contribute to the brand's story, with content that is genuinely meaningful to them. It ensures the outcome meets key stakeholders' (users, customers, or investors) needs, increasing their sense of ownership, which can lead to higher brand loyalty. For example, Guzman and Lelis (2021) show how being true to the brand's core has had an impact on the UK's most recognised spreadable brand: Marmite®. Its success does not rely on whether the public likes its taste or not (their slogan is "You either Love it or Hate it"); rather, it depends mostly on being true to itself. The expression "Like

Marmite" is, in fact, regularly used to describe anything considered divisive. Hence, Marmite's labels include bold approaches such as a tribute to Margaret Thatcher (who was either loved or hated by the British and was a popular topic in most family households), and customisable ones, linked to popular celebrations – that you either love or hate.

Considering factors such as human existence, reason, knowledge, and values, is the first step for brands to establish their own right inner core and to establish authentic human-centric relationships with the audiences. Guzman and Lelis' (2021) work is grounded on an initial supposition, opening the doors for future research opportunities: not only on new branding models and on how a brand's core elements can be managed to address heterogeneous audiences, but also on mapping the ways marketers and designers can work together to best design and strategise on the central elements that define a brand.

4. Design for brand identity

Recently, we witnessed the emergence of non-conventional narratives, in which the story can virtually unfold into infinite possibilities, and where the reader/user becomes an active participant (Lelis & Kreutz, 2022; 2023). This has been most common in the contexts of literature, film, hypertext websites, and other narratives, such as the performative ones, of which Cirque du Soleil is a great example. Likewise, contemporary brands allow a level of flexibility to accompany a constantly evolving and participatory world (e.g. MTV and Google), acknowledging that identity is not a fixed condition, and that brands can have dynamic brand identities (Van Nes, 2012).

Martins et al. (2019) propose a model for the analysis of these brand identities, based on visual variation mechanisms (colour variation, content variation, varying positioning of graphic elements, shape transformation, etc.) used to attain dynamism. For example, OCAD University's visual identity uses content variation within their logo, whilst the Brooklyn Museum resorts to shape transformation. The authors developed an interactive web-based visualisation tool[1] to demonstrate the application of their model, using a group of successful and established dynamic visual identities in which variation mechanisms have been employed. Such a tool can be used by brand managers in mapping the alignment of such logo variation mechanisms against both the brand core (the purpose) and the brand interactions (for example, how the variations are expected to be incorporated in the store design and product performance). Further research is needed on these mechanisms' performance, when visual identities are animated and when these variations become dependent on movement and time. It would also be important to understand the demographic that is more receptive to these dynamic approaches.

Younger generations are becoming increasingly aware of and sensible towards societal issues, and how the brands they consume act towards those issues. Some brands invite their audiences to co-design the tangible components of their identity, such as logotypes and symbols (which used to be finished, untouchable, and proprietary resources), thus establishing stronger emotional bonds with the public. Later, audiences can observe their own designs displayed in merchandise, advertising, and promotional materials.

Rio450 is one such example. The brand was created and designed by Brazilian agency Crama Design to celebrate the 450th anniversary of Rio de Janeiro as a city. The brand's visual identity is composed of two elements that, together, reinforce its informal and inviting attitude: (1) the logotype, stating "Rio450" and resorting to a script-like typeface; and (2) the numbers 4, 5, and 0 displayed in a way that resembles a smiley human face. The second element is the empty profile of Rio's native individuals (known as "Cariocas"), accepting graphic interferences in both planned or completely unrestrained ways. The audience is free to co-design and customise the logo, provided these creations are used to represent the Cariocas's many identities, idiosyncrasies, and expressions (Figure 1.1). An excellent example of a dynamic brand identity, Rio450 is open to shaping its visual identity according to the ones of its audiences, a challenge for both communication and graphic design, but loyal to the brand's core which is: "Rio is multifaceted, and one face only is not enough".

Lelis and Kreutz (2021) propose the existence of different levels of audience participation in the design of brands' visual narratives, in the context of dynamic or flexible brands. The authors map brand identities within two dimensions (Narrative Design Strategy and Audience's Interaction), leading to the identification of four different realms of participation. These must be thoroughly planned at the time of designing the brand core, namely due to the two realms in which the audience's interaction is higher, both when planned (Engaged) and when it is out of a brand's intentions (Deviated):

- *Engaged*: the realm in which participation is expected to be meaningful for both the brand and the audiences, and where co-creation in the brand's visual and verbal identity are strategically defined and adequately managed. Rio450 belongs to this realm. Crama developed a 50-page brand manual where users can learn how to adopt and utilise the visual identity without distorting or misusing it.[2]

- *Deviated*: the realm in which uncontrolled and reactive audiences decide they should participate without following any pre-existing identity rules or participation briefs. They recreate a brand's story, often by means of unfavourable narratives, leading to the "culture jamming" of anti-branding actions. These are illicit designs, created by the public, namely to express depreciative views of large international and capitalism-based corporations. McDonald's, BP, Starbucks, and Coca-Cola are just a few of those that have been targeted by jammed, pun-like versions of their logos that rapidly spread and became popular.

Figure 1.1 The customisable brand identity of Rio450, by Crama Design

Hence, Lelis and Kreutz (2021) provide a framework for the anticipation and evaluation of the degree of participation a brand may want to develop. It is also a bi-dimensional model that supports the planning of the level of contribution the audiences can have in a brand's storytelling, which should always be subject to some degree of management. It opens a great range of opportunities for new research, namely regarding the exploration of each of the realms individually, paying special attention to these two opposing realms. On the one hand, brand design can focus on what the brand wishes to communicate, and how it sees audiences being motivated towards participating in their storytelling. On the other hand, brand design may need to act in the context of a communication crisis, when the brand suddenly discovers their audiences' interventions are reactive counternarratives, motivated by the public's perception of hypocrisy, covert political orientation, greenwashing, or basically, a twisted inauthentic brand core. In this sense, it is reasonable to suggest that further research is needed on mapping this model against, for example, the levels of audiences' heterogeneity, which can include variables that go beyond the obvious demographic ones – such as design literacy (which influences the quality of contributions), education (which may lead to a taxonomy of interactions), or geography (since some regions/countries are known for being more vocal than others).

5. Design for brand interactions

Global branding's approach is a subject of debate in international marketing theory, as these brands are much more than single entities. They have unique historical, geographical, and social contexts. They have a set of symbols and perceptions ubiquitous in global popular culture and local appropriations (Miller and Berry, 1998). Therefore, it is vital to explore how people use, act, and behave in their natural and cultural environment to design meaningful consumer experiences in global brands. According to Doorley and Witthoft (2012), spatial characteristics can be adjusted and calibrated to radically alter the mood in a situation, fundamentally altering the nature of an interaction. Williams (2013) suggests three sensory foundations: the Aristotelian senses (taste, smell, touch, sight, and sound); the neurological senses (spaciousness and movement); and the Steinerian senses (speech, thinking, life, and I). However, these sensory foundations do not regard the cultural, behavioural, and sociological aspects of spatial differences between individuals with different identities (gender, ethnicity, race, sex, sexual orientation, age, and physical ability).

Cruz-Megchun (2018, 2020) argues the need for studying the relationship between design, brand, and proxemic behaviour in commercial spaces to provide sensory, cognitive, and emotional stimuli relevant to consumers' context. Proxemics is a field of knowledge that studies the cultural, behavioural, and sociological aspects of spatial distances between individuals (Sorokin, 1943; Lewin, 1948). It analyses humans' perceptions of space and their use in a behavioural complex set of activities. Studying the physical distance between interacting people is key to shaping the quality and tone of their encounter and helping maintain a level of intimacy that is comfortable, appropriate, and safe in social interactions. These encounters represent the core of everyday experiences because they provide the context in which social capabilities evolve and develop. Significant work has been done in ethnography, anthropology, and human ecology to generate design methods for noting and describing the experience of space. Hall (1963) discusses eight different and relevant dimensions in this matter: (1) postural (sex identifiers); (2) sociofugal (sociopetal orientation); (3) kinesthetic factors; (4) touch code; (5) retinal combinations; (6) thermal code; (7) olfaction code; and (8) voice loudness scale. However, designers (architects) do not have methods to note proxemic behaviours in retail.

Cruz-Megchun and Istanbuli (2016) researched proxemic behaviours in retail space from a global brand immersed in a multicultural context. They noted the proxemic behaviours between person-to-person in a space to explore users' traffic patterns, their position in the space, and their movements over time. They found that proxemic behaviours can help brands influence consumers' reactions to the space atmosphere. Designers can address the physical (furniture, products, and equipment available in the space), the cognitive (space layout and organisation of furniture and equipment), and the emotional (materiality, lighting, and sensorial qualities of the space) aspects of the space. They can also increase traffic spots, identify areas affected by human factors, and facilitate the user's purchase journey (intuitive pathways). Hence, developing research instruments that support design decisions beyond anthropometric indicators is vital and, currently, necessary. Anthropometry is a scientific discipline that addresses human body measurements and physical characteristics of different regional populations, and the application of these data sets in various systems.

Cruz-Megchun (2016) also investigated how user-oriented brands address their audiences through physical, cognitive, emotional, and contextual elements. The researcher found that when brands consider a user-centred approach, they engage in aspects from the physical interaction to the cognitive stimuli. Brands study users through understanding their aesthetic impressions and their symbolic and semantic identification of the product and service offered. They concentrate on users' emotional relations, affects, and behaviours towards the brand. In addition, they analyse the context that engulfs the users' cultural, situational, and social reality. For example, Tommy Hilfiger Adaptive designs a series of clothes collections that offer thoughtful, discreet solutions, accessible to everyone that needs to dress. Their research allowed them to focus on empathy, to tackle users' situational and social realities and their emotional relation and effect on fashion. Tommy Hilfiger's clothing enables users to complete an activity (dressing) with dignity, while breaking the stigma that disability is not only a medical condition but a societal action. Design supports brands to address and consider the individual, and build an emotional attachment to the brand.

Man-made disasters, such as environmental accidents, health emergencies, and social injustice, dictate future research. For example, COVID-19 altered to various extents our use, understanding, and behaviour of space in public spaces, especially for vulnerable groups. Researchers previously studied culture and gender as variables that influence individual proxemic behaviour. Now, we need to regard variations associated with environmental, sociopsychological, and neurobiological variables. According to Franco-Pérez (2021), it can be plausible to hypothesise that during the COVID-19 pandemic, fear responses modified the individual proxemic behaviours by avoiding interaction in specific proxemic zones and increasing social isolation. Future studies will be necessary to determine if the pandemic stresses impacted our brain, specifically the amygdala. It is a structure of the limbic system that is an integrative centre for emotional responses, including feelings like pleasure, fear, anxiety, or anger. Hence, it is of the utmost importance that the development of noting tools and methods inform (and educate) designers about proxemics and sociocultural identity variables in the design (postmodern subject) of inclusive spaces. Furthermore, it is also important to adopt consumer-centred approaches in every interaction (physical, cognitive, emotional, and contextual elements) with the brand to create products, services, and systems that reflect the reality of society and the environment.

Regarding practising human-centred principles and involving experience design at a strategic level, Huang and colleagues investigated how design thinking could guide city-based physical retailers to evolve their strategic brand planning to reshape experiences (Huang and Hands, 2018, 2020; Huang et al., 2021). To achieve all levels of physio-, socio-, psycho-, and ideological pleasures, brands need multiple channels working together, simulating users/consumers' full senses (Maslow, 1943; Jordan, 2000). Brands must integrate tools and "communication techniques" (Morschett et al., 2006) at a strategic level to deliver the brand message to the audience, and by doing that, brands can improve customer satisfaction and loyalty, and promote economic gain. Through the research of physical retail stores, the results indicated that design could capture demographic and social environment changes to drive brand innovation through different levels of human needs based on Maslow's Hierarchy (1943).

Huang et al.'s (2021) study on the Chinese retailers' hybrid business model proposed a full-spectrum human-needs-based branding strategy that design has used to explore new channels for customer engagement, based on brand values and social innovation (Figure 1.2). From the bottom up, design can support the brand's product (or service) innovation (1) by changing the visible presentation and engaging formats to satisfy the customers' physiological

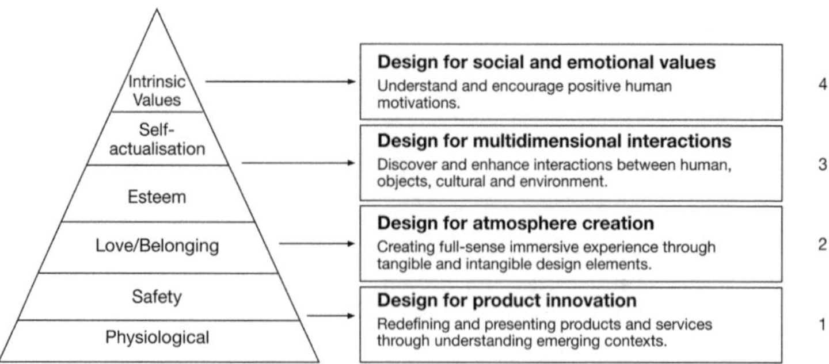

Source: Huang et al. (2021).

Figure 1.2 Four design value principles

needs – such as Kioskafe, a newsstand and coffee bar in London that tailored its business model to provide products and services that travellers need. Further above, a purposely designed brand store atmosphere (2) can stimulate consumers' deeper emotional responses and brand associations. For example, Morioka Shoten in Tokyo, "a single room with a single book", transforms the space every week for each book of that week to complement the story, and elaborate the feeling of the literary world, that provides customers with a direct visual description of the book content, making it more attractive and easier for them to make a purchase decision. Many brand's showrooms (such as Dyson Demo) might not generate direct profits for the brand; however, channelling the brand story to mass audiences could reach potential consumers and create word-of-mouth marketing. At the esteem level, meaningful interactions (3) in real and everyday life dominate the overall personal wellbeing and satisfaction. Design helps brands to identify and create meaningful and different terms of interactions: *human–human* interactions that bring closer both families and communities; *human–social* interactions that introduce the heritage and characteristics of a place to its citizens and visitors; and *human–culture* interactions that provoke in browsers the possibility of serendipity to meet and interact with new knowledge. At the top level, to reach self-actualisation and intrinsic values, design provides methods and tools for brands to understand fundamental human motivations (4), and helps brands to explore possibilities by redefining its "citizen roles". HUANYUE Art Space in Guangzhou, China, practises their brand core value of "allowing everyone to become an artist of life" by providing art and handcraft experience services for residential communities, regional libraries, schools, and disability support institutions.

Further research on the topic can use design and design thinking to guide brand strategy transformation, for example, with the identification of levels of self-efficacy (considering the diverse stakeholders) in the process of experiencing the different brand touchpoints, and in the definition of clear brand design taxonomies, typologies, parameters, and even performance indicators, to support the articulation with brand management.

6. The future may be in smart(er) brands

The global pandemic pushed businesses to discover tools to connect virtual worlds with the real one, showing that brands must plan their future business territory in this new area. Technological developments and big data have certainly changed the way brands design experiences for their multifaceted publics. Advanced technologies are always a significant force, pushing brands to evolve the format to present their products and the engaging methods and contexts of interaction with stakeholders. Alibaba showcases a future "Smart Business" model to coordinate multiple business players to achieve a common business goal (Zeng, 2018). For example, Taobao benefited from the technical support of Alibaba, its mother company: machine learning algorithms allow Taobao to tailor the user interface and product list to everyone's needs, and an AI-powered chatbot can quickly respond to customer queries in various aspects. Moreover, the internet has become the main battlefield for brands to engage and impress their customers – not to mention the metaverse which is on its way to challenging the physical world. Design supports the creation of these new worlds through Extended Reality (XR) – including Virtual Reality (VR), Augmented Reality (AR), and Mixed Reality (MR). The virtual city ELECTRICCITY,[3] created by Charli Cohen with Selfridges, allows visitors to use a customisable digital AR avatar to explore the space and shop for exclusive physical and digital fashionwear. Gamification and gameful design are non-negligible areas for branding in continuously discovering XR. Gamification is the way to add playful in-game mechanics (e.g. collecting points, badges, upgrade levels, and getting rewards) into brand experiences (Deterding et al., 2011). These create a fun atmosphere of competition in customer interactions – and never-ending possibilities of brand-related narratives in which audiences can participate (Lelis, 2021; Nobre and Ferreira, 2017). Gameful design, instead, is emphasised on the psychological impacts to create ever-engaging and enjoyable experiences. For example, luxury brand Louis

Vuitton created a game-based app called "Louis: The Game" to celebrate the brand's 200th birthday. Through the main mascot, players can collect NFT candles that unlock the stories of Louis and the brand history (Northman, 2021).

Related and future research can draw on the advantages of speculative design (creating fictional worlds, building different scenarios, and solving future problems), and co-design methods to discover alternative and preferable contexts for brands, where these actually and authentically meet global and humanity-level challenges, such as the United Nations' Sustainable Development Goals.

7. Concluding remarks

Throughout the chapter, we introduced key design concepts and frameworks to support brand management. We focused on discussing the design values for brand core, brand identity, and brand interactions. We used different research cases to raise awareness of a new research territory for brand management scholars and students. Design is what connects the brand to consumers, stakeholders, and shareholders. It is a powerful medium to transform strategies into tactics, to communicate and deliver all the positive attributes, both tangible and intangible, around the brand name. Regardless of size, brands that understand the "value" of design, and that invest in it as a vital ingredient and source of both inspiration and opportunity, can separate from the competition. When carefully managed and orchestrated, design has the innate ability to offer a distinct range of authentic value propositions that brands can use to better align their identities with those of their audiences and, therefore, win their trust and love. The audiences will engage and play an active role in the brand's story and development.

Design plays a fundamental role in paving the way for brands to operate in a simplified and humanised way, considering users/customers' emotions that amplify brand satisfaction. Hence, as a final suggestion towards further research that brings together design and brand management, we should mention the relevance of Don Norman's Emotional Design Framework (2005) to explore the interplay between logical and emotional aspects of everydayness through design. This framework is split into three levels: (1) visceral design, to appeal to the senses through sensorial stimuli (appearance, form or shape, proportion, and colour); (2) behavioural design, to make evident the brand promise (through function, understandability, usability, and physical feel);

and (3) reflective design, to address message, culture, and the meaning of a product/service.

We would argue that designing and managing the visceral, alongside the behavioural and the reflective components of a brand, with a deeper understanding of emotional design, is precisely what has been missing in brand management – being a huge gap in (and opportunity for) research.

Therefore, brands must pay greater attention to their products, services, spaces, and experiences in consideration of their audiences' identities, behaviours, needs, and desires, namely by making space for those things that affect us all – in this chapter we touched on ageing and diversity, but certainly (mental) health and circular economy are aspects to consider as well. Overall, design helps brands to respond to societal, economic, and environmental changes with suitable technology tools, exploring alternative business models, in order to guarantee their sustainability in the future world. Brands need design, and its inductive and abductive methodologies, to guarantee their relevance in, and responsibility towards, the future and a fairer world.

Much more of the value of design for brands is waiting to be unfolded because surely without design interfering with, and contributing to an entity's philosophy, goals, insights, functions, resources, experiences, messages, and touchpoints, there is no brand at all, and consequently, no need for brand management. That is the reason why there is so much work and research to be done, as the relevance of design in brand management is to be increasingly acknowledged.

Notes

1. https://cdv.dei.uc.pt/2018/dynamic-identities/.
2. http://www.rio.rj.gov.br/dlstatic/10112/169617/4131016/Rio450_manual.pdf.
3. https://electriccity.co.

References

Berry, L. L., Carbone, L. P., & Haeckel, S. H. (2002). Managing the total customer experience. *MIT Sloan Management Review*, *43*, 85–89.

Beverland, M. (2018). *Brand management: Co-creating meaningful brands*. London: Sage.

Brown, T. (2009). *Change by design: How design thinking transforms organizations and inspires innovation*. New York: HarperCollins.

Buchanan, R. (1992). Wicked problems in design thinking. *Design Issues*, *8*, 5–21.

Buchanan, R. (1997). Education and professional practice in design. Remarks presented at the Plenary session of the International Council of Graphic Design Association XVII World Congress, Uruguay.

Chouinard, Y. (2022). Earth is now our only shareholder. Patagonia. https:// eu .patagonia.com/gb/en/home/ (accessed: 19 September 2022).

Cooper, R., & Press, M. (1995). *The design agenda: A guide to successful design management*. Chichester, UK: John Wiley and Sons.

Cruz-Megchun, B. I. (2016). Retail design: Brand experiences through merging art, design and science. In L. Crispi (Ed.), *Design innovations for contemporary interiors and civic art* (pp. 209–224). Hershey, PA: IGI Global.

Cruz-Megchun, B. I. (2018). *Rethinking the design of brand experience in multicultural spaces in the experience economy*. 1st International Brand Design Conference, London, UK.

Cruz-Megchun, B. I. (2020). Rethinking retail in the experience economy. In L. Crispi (Ed.), *Cultural, theoretical, and innovative approaches to contemporary interior design* (pp. 174–190). Hershey, PA: IGI Global.

Cruz-Megchun, B. I., & Istanbuli, M. (2016). *Rethinking the design of multicultural spaces*. DMI: Academic Design Management Conference. Inflection point: Design research meets design practice, Boston, US.

de Chernatony, L., & Dall'Olmo Riley, F. (1998). Defining a "brand": Beyond the literature with experts' interpretations. *Journal of Marketing Management*, *14*(5), 417–443. doi:10.1362/026725798784867798

de Mozota, B. B. (2006). The four powers of design: A value model in design management. *Design Management Review*, *17*(2), 44–53.

Deterding, S., Dixon, D., Khaled, R., & Nacke, L. (2011). From game design elements to gamefulness: Defining "gamification". In *Proceedings of the 15th International Academic MindTrek Conference: Envisioning Future Media Environments, MindTrek 2011* (pp. 9–15). Tampere: MindTrek.

Doorley, S., & Witthoft, S. (2012). *Make space: How to set the stage for creative Collaboration*. Chichester, UK: John Wiley & Sons.

Dorst, K. (2011). The core of "design thinking" and its application. *Design Studies*, *32*(6), 521–532.

Franco-Pérez, J. (2021). COVID-19 and the brain regulation of the new proxemics. *Salud Mental*, *44*(1), 1–2.

Guzman, B. M., & Lelis, C. (2021). Everyday social practices as a source of design-led branding. In N. Martins & D. Brandão (Eds.), *Advances in design and digital communication* (pp. 489–497). Cham: Springer. https://doi.org/10.1007/978-3-030-61671-7_45

Hall, E. T. (1963). A system for the notation of proxemic behavior. *American Anthropologist*, *65*(5), 1003–1026.

Holbrook, M. B., & Hirschman, E. C. (1982). The experiential aspects of consumption: Consumer fantasies, feelings, and fun. *Journal of Consumer Research*, *9*(2), 132–140.

Huang, Y., & Hands, D. (2018). Design for future retailing: An investigation into the changing status of city-based retailers in the UK. In C. Storni et al. (Eds.), *DRS 2018 International Conference: Catalyst* (pp. 461–476). Limerick: Design Research Society.

Huang, Y., & Hands, D. (2020). Experience design in city-based future retail innovation: A bookstore case study approach. In *ADMC 2020: Impact The Future By*

Design. Academic Design Management Conference (pp. 870–884). Toronto: Design Management Institute.

Huang, Y., Hands, D., Cooper, R., & Dunn, N. (2021). Evolving future city-based retailing via design thinking: A Chinese hybrid model approach. In L. Di Lucchio et al. (Eds.), *Design Culture(s) CUMULUS Conference Proceedings Roma 2021* (pp. 2846–2861). Rome: Cumulus: The Global Association of Art and Design Education and Research.

Jordan, P. W. (2000). *Designing pleasurable products: An introduction to the new human factors*. London: Taylor & Francis.

Kapferer, J.-N. (2012). *The new strategic brand management: Advanced insights and strategic thinking*. London: Kogan Page.

Karjalainen, T-M. (2004). Semantic transformation in design: Communicating strategic brand identity through product design references. University of Art and Design, Helsinki.

Kotter, J. P. (1996). *Leading change*. Cambridge, MA: Harvard Business School Press.

Lee, K., Chung, K., & Nam, K.-Y. (2013). Orchestrating designable touchpoints for service businesses. *Design Management Review, 24*(3), 14–21. https:// doi .org/ 10 .1111/drev.10246

Lelis, C. (2021). Smart brands and identities: Building friendly bridges between design and smartness. *International Journal on Interaction Design & Architectures*, Special Issue "Pedagogical Approaches, Ludic and Co-Design Strategies & Tools supporting Smart Learning Ecosystems and Smart Education".

Lelis, C., & Kreutz, E. (2021). The realms of participation in visual identity design. *Corporate Reputation Review*, Special Issue "Design, Branding and Marketing: Experience and Value Creation in Design, Branding, Marketing, Corporate Reputation and Identity". https://doi.org/10.1057/s41299-021-00134-4.

Lelis, C. & Kreutz, E. A. (2022). The HOW behind the story: a framework for the design of brand narratives. In D. Raposo (Ed), *Design, Visual Communication and Branding* (pp. 132–159). Newcastle: Cambridge Scholars Publishing.

Lelis, C. & Kreutz, E. A. (2023). Mapping out the narrative dimensions of visual identities: a typological classification. In N. Martins & D. Raposo (Eds.), *Communication Design and Branding: A Multidisciplinary Approach*, Springer (in press).

Lewin, K. (1948). *Resolving social conflicts*. Washington, DC: American Psychological Association.

Martin, R. (2009). *The design of business: Why design thinking is the next competitive advantage*. Cambridge, MA: Harvard Business School Press.

Martins, T., Cunha, J. M., Bicker, J., & Machado, P. (2019). Dynamic visual identities: From a survey of the state-of-the-art to a model of features and mechanisms. *Visible Language, 53*(2), 4–35.

Maslow, A. H. (1943). A theory of human motivation. *Psychological Review, 50*(4), 370–396. doi:10.1037/h0054346.

Miller, S., & Berry, L. (1998). Brand salience versus brand image: Two theories of advertising effectiveness. *Journal of Advertising Research, 38*(5), 77–78.

Miltenburg, A. (2017). *Brand the change: The branding guide for social entrepreneurs, disruptors, not-for profit and corporate trouble makers*. Amsterdam: BIS Publishers.

Morschett, D., Swoboda, B., & Schramm-Klein, H. (2006). Competitive strategies in retailing: An investigation of the applicability of Porter's framework for food retailers. *Journal of Retailing and Consumer Services, 13*, 275–287. doi:10.1016/j.jretconser.2005.08.016.

Motta-Filho, M. (2020). Brand experience manual: Bridging the gap between brand strategy and customer experience. *Review of Managerial Science, 15*, 1173–1204. https://doi.org/10.1007/s11846-020-00399-9

Neumeier, M. (2016). *The brand gap*. San Francisco, CA: New Riders.

Nobre, H., & Ferreira, A. (2017). Gamification as a platform for brand co-creation experiences. *Journal of Brand Management, 24*(4), 349–361. doi:10.1057/s41262-017-0055-3.

Norman, D. A. (2005). *Emotional design: Why we love (or hate) everyday things*. New York: Basic Books.

Northman, T. (2021). Louis Vuitton's new game is better than "Fortnite". *Highsnobiety*. https:// www .highsnobiety .com/ p/ louis -vuitton -nft -game/ (accessed: 11 March 2022).

Papanek, V. (2019). *Design for the real world*. London: Thames & Hudson.

Sorokin, P. A. (1943). *Sociocultural causality, space, time: A study of referential principles of sociology and social science*. Durham, NC: Duke University Press.

Van Nes, I. (2012). *Dynamic identities: How to create a living brand*. Amsterdam: BIS Publishers.

Williams, A. (2013). *A grammar of creative workspaces*. PhD Thesis, University of East London.

Zeng, M. (2018). Lessons from China's innovative digital giant: The future of business. *Harvard Business Review, 96*(5), 88–96. https://www.gra.world/wp-content/uploads/2018/09/12/00010025.pdf.

2 The emergence and evolution of corporate branding

Nicholas Ind

Introduction

In 1997, I wrote a book called *The Corporate Brand.* At the time the joining together of 'Corporate' and 'Brand' was rare. Branding was seen to be dominantly about promoting fast-moving consumer goods through marketing communications. The logic behind the fusion of corporate and brand was driven by diverse factors including the need to explain the purpose of a corporation to financial audiences, the growing importance of employees as determinants of value in a services-oriented landscape, and the increase in the intangible component of corporate value – including the value that a brand conferred. Prior to the mid-1990s the language that was used was that of corporate identity, and in 1995 John Balmer noted in an article on corporate branding that 'the strategic importance of corporate brand management (or what is more appropriately called strategic corporate identity management) would appear to be irrefutable' (Balmer, 1995, p. 24).

Balmer's article expressed the idea that a corporate brand was an expression of an organization's identity, while corporate branding was seen here as a management process concerned with developing the firm's reputation with a diverse set of stakeholders by building relationships and communicating the identity. In essence the distinctions from product branding were a close connectedness to business strategy, a long-term perspective and a stakeholder orientation that drew in employees, investors, suppliers, partners and media. This diversity of stakeholders and their potentially competing interests, alongside the structure of the corporate brand which might have numerous businesses and brands contained within it, suggested a degree of complexity beyond that experienced in the management of product brands. This meant that control of the brand was difficult: 'With a physical brand and to a lesser extent a service brand, continuity of experience is achievable. Within a corporate brand it is much harder to attain' (Ind, 1997, p. 9). The solution to this problem was to build clarity by using the cohesion of the firm's identity (its mission, philosophy and values) to integrate actions and communications.

In addition to the requirement to be profitable and to meet the expectations of investors, it was also argued that a corporate brand had a responsibility to its stakeholders and society. This countered the then prevailing belief in shareholder primacy: 'In addition to interacting effectively with all its audiences and balancing their often countervailing needs, the corporate brand also has a broader social responsibility, an ethical imperative' (Ind, 1997, p. 11).

Since corporate branding emerged in the mid-1990s its influence has grown as the role of the corporation has come to embrace an important and vital role in tackling social and environmental problems, alongside the traditional commitment to wealth creation. Managers now have to listen to, understand and meet the expectations of an increasingly fragmented group of stakeholders that include activists (employees, consumers, investors, citizens), influencers and governments. Firms are under pressure on all sides and they need to become adept at maintaining the corporate brand, while adapting to a more fluid environment where many stakeholders shape it. In this chapter, we will explore how corporate branding has evolved and the implications this has for future research.

Three evolutionary paths

Since its emergence, corporate branding has evolved along three inter-connected evolutionary paths. The first has been the shift in perspective away from the idea that brand meaning is fixed by the organization to one that recognizes the fluidity that accompanies greater connectivity. The second path, which flows from the first, is the opportunity, that has been seized by some organizations, to enrich the corporate brand by facilitating the active involvement of diverse stakeholders through co-creation. The third is the evolution of a broader sense of corporate responsibility.

1. Fluidity: how corporate brands became organic

The early perspective on corporate branding largely followed the traditions of product branding in viewing the corporate brand as a managerial creation (Balmer, 1995; Harris & de Chernatony, 2001; Hatch & Schultz, 2002). It took the view that the corporate brand was constructed by the conscious choices made by managers, and that it was then communicated to stakeholders through mainstream advertising and public relations activity and somewhat tailored direct marketing. Within a company, the process was run by a cadre of professionals, who used traditional research to build insights into their stakeholders, and to fashion effective campaigns. This perspective links to the idea of a corporate brand promise (Argenti & Druckenmiller, 2004) or a corporate brand covenant (Balmer, 2001; Balmer & Gray, 2003). Balmer and Gray argue that 'A corporate brand may be viewed as a contract in that the company needs to articulate its accord with its key stakeholders by demonstrating, unceasingly and over time, that it has kept true to its corporate branding pledge' (Balmer & Gray, 2003, p. 982). However, the idea of a corporate brand promise or covenant becomes problematic as interactions between an organization and the outside world shift from being one-way to multi-directional. A promise or covenant is a relational action designed to bring about a future state that is valuable to the one to whom it is made (Anker, 2009), which indicates that the promise or covenant can only be realized through the actions of the recipient, which is where value is created (Grönroos & Voima, 2013). It might also be noted that once stakeholders move from being seen as largely passive recipients of corporate brand communications to active participants engaged in social and communicative processes, then also the meaning of the promise or covenant becomes more fluid (Kärreman & Rylander, 2008).

The catalyst for the move to greater stakeholder participation was the growing orientation towards online media and its interactive potential (Ind & Riondino, 2001). The emergence of online communications diminished managerial control as different departments and individuals within organizations began to express their ideas and opinions. Companies could still police the visual expression of the corporate brand, but increasingly they found it hard to control the conversational space in which employees and external stakeholders expressed themselves (Merz et al., 2009; Vallaster & Lindgreen, 2011; Golant, 2012). One implication of the rapid growth in contact points between the inside and the outside, was to elevate the importance of having a pellucid and engaging idea of the brand that could inspire employees and enable them to reflect it in their daily actions and communications (Roper & Davies, 2007; Brodie et al., 2009). This was no guarantee though of a unified presentation of the corporate brand, because, while the process of articulation can be performative in itself, it cannot ensure that individuals adhere to the intended meaning. We might also note that as companies and their consultants weighed up the words they used to describe a corporate brand, the meaning attributed to them would shift over time as the abstraction of language met the reality of peoples' interpretations and their actions (Eco, 1999).

The implication of this fluid, organic perspective is that corporate brands should understand that heterogeneity is inevitable (De Landa, 2003) and potentially enriching, when individuals explore and negotiate meaning, and help develop the brand through organic social processes (Iglesias et al., 2017). Yet, while the blurring of organizational boundaries has positive attributes in the way it connects a corporate brand to its stakeholders and allows for the development of brand meaning, it is not without some difficulties. Sometimes external inputs can be threatening to the identity of those inside the organization, especially if outsiders manage to solve problems that those inside have struggled to resolve. Resistance can then threaten the gains of involvement (Lifshitz-Assaf, 2015). Also, managers can find that the identities that they have carefully designed are pushed in new directions by users who construe and experience the brand in different but not necessarily conflictual ways (Kornberger, 2010; Kornum et al., 2017). However, at the extreme it can lead to a loss of clarity. In their study of the Statens Museum for Kunst (SMK) – the National Gallery of Denmark – Schmeltz and Kjeldsen (2019) note that the diversity of interacting voices (e.g., user, marketing, corporate, expert) creates considerable variability. The ideal of a harmonious polyphony, where each voice connects to and builds on the other (Belova et al., 2008) begins to fracture and blurs the intended idea of the brand. Left untended, the result is stakeholder confusion. The recommendation from this study is to encourage diverse expression, but to do so within a framework that ensures an appropriate level of coherence: 'seen through the metaphor of polyphony, there needs to be a common acceptance of a shared chord to create productive polyphony rather than destructive cacophony' (Schmeltz & Kjeldsen, 2019, p. 263). In practice this means that managers must recognize the inherent fluidity of the corporate brand, but also work to ensure the intention is clear.

2. Co-creation: decentering and democratizing

As control of the corporate brand was seeping away, so some organizations saw the opportunity to adopt a more open mindset and they began to reach out, first through building direct relationships with stakeholders and then through the creation of online communities. This co-creative approach drew on some interesting antecedents in the form of literary theory (Barthes, 1977), participatory design – particularly in software development (Bødker & Grønbæk, 1990; Grønbæk et al., 1997), the open source movement (Raymond, 1999), lead user innovation (von Hippel, 2005) and the pioneering work of the early management thinker, Mary Parker Follett and her conception of 'power with' – 'a jointly developed power, a co-active, not a coercive power' (Graham, 1995, p. 103). The incipient idea of co-creation accelerated with the rapid growth of Internet usage during the dot-com boom years of the 1990s, which led to the emergence of online brand communities (Muniz & O'Guinn, 2001) and the recognition that brand value could be created together with stakeholders. The growing pervasiveness of the Internet enabled a more decentered and democratized approach to emerge (Ramaswamy & Ind, 2021), that was articulated in the foundational work of CK Prahalad and Venkat Ramaswamy (2000, 2004).

The essence of Prahalad and Ramaswamy's work was to move beyond the linear process of the value chain, which perceived value creation as something managed by the firm (Porter, 1985) to the idea that experience value was co-created through the interaction of stakeholders and organizations. This changed the idea of value creation beyond user experience to a way of thinking that embraced the active involvement of stakeholders as partners. The co-creational perspective began to impact the practices of organizations (Antorini et al., 2012; Ind et al., 2012; Ramaswamy & Ozcan, 2014) and saw the emergence of purpose-built digital platforms to enable interaction. This spawned entirely new platform-based businesses such as Netflix and Airbnb in what Ramaswamy and Pieters (2021) call I2N2I (Individual-to-Network-to-Individual) interactions that used artificial intelligence to augment human capabilities and also changed the way well-established companies operated.

For example, the software company SAP moved from a purpose rooted in efficient systems – *To help the world run better* – to a co-creative purpose – *To help the world run better and to improve people's lives* – that embraced the latent and transformative power of its ecosystem that comprises 440,000 customers, 21,000 commercial partners, 2.5 million community users and a network of co-innovation labs. SAP's purpose is the framework within which it works to realize the ever-changing meaning of its corporate brand together with others. Similarly, Unilever's purpose *To make sustainable living commonplace,* requires a co-creative approach involving employees, farmers, suppliers, partners, investors and consumers. Unilever sets the direction through adherence to its purpose, but the company then works together with its internal and external stakeholders to explore and then enrich the Unilever brand (Polman & Winston, 2021).

One of the notable impacts of the co-creation shift has been to redefine the role of managers. In the traditional corporate brand management perspective, the brand was designed and delivered by managers. This implied thinking through the purpose, vision and values of a company (or however the company phrased its *raison d'être* and its way of working) and trying to ensure that the brand delivered on what was intended. However, as soon as the walls of the organization become more permeable, the role of the manager began to move away from that of controller to one of a conductor (Michel, 2017) – or perhaps an improviser (Hatch, 1999). This role involves listening, partnering and building relationships. It is a way of working that is more complex and can create challenges (as we saw with SMK), but it has three important virtues. First, it enables managers to become closer to their stakeholders, and to better understand their needs and desires. Second, it provides companies with the agility that they need to respond to an ever-changing environment. Third, it creates an approach to corporate branding that is less instrumental. Instead of doing things to stakeholders, the co-creative approach is predicated upon a more democratized philosophy that thinks of value creation in human-centric terms that aims to benefit the organization and its stakeholders: 'stakeholders are increasingly seen as contributing intrinsically to value creation rather than as entities to be merely managed by the enterprise' (Ramaswamy & Ozcan, 2014, p. 249).

3. From CSR to conscience

In *The Corporate Brand* the idea was put forward that brands have a social role that involved meeting the needs of diverse stakeholders and the environment. In doing so, it ran counter to the dominant credo of shareholder primacy, that had been popularized by Milton Friedman, most notably in his 1970 article in *The New York Times* – 'The social responsibility of business is to increase its profits' – and developed by agency theory (Jensen & Meckling, 1976). Friedman argued that everything should be sacrificed to the needs of shareholders. In this view the owners of the business should expect the executives who ran the company to meet their expectations and that any additional activities, such as social responsibility, were only permissible if there were resulting business benefits. Any deviation from this, he argued, was 'pure and unadulterated socialism'.

The era of shareholder primacy spawned the concept of Corporate Social Responsibility (CSR), and led to firms establishing CSR departments and programs, both to burnish their corporate reputation and to reduce risks (Walsh & Beatty, 2007; Lyon et al., 2018). The limitation in the practice of CSR, however, has been that all too often it has been poorly integrated into the strategy and operations of the business (Maon et al., 2017). It remains at the margins rather than being at the core because it is largely a tactical activity. The downside of this is that corporate brands' commitment can wax and wane as circumstances change (Schmidt et al., 2021), and there is a temptation to over-claim achievements in communications which has led to charges of greenwashing and wokewashing (Kim & Lyon, 2015; Lyon & Montgomery, 2013; Marquis et al., 2016). The glossing over of failures and trumpeting of successes can be seen not only in public relations activity, but also in the way corporate brands communicate with financial audiences (Boiral, 2013; Hess, 2019).

However, with the recognition that businesses can play a vital role in social and environmental issues (Scheyvens et al., 2016), there has been a move towards a more stakeholder-oriented view that is cognizant of the connectivity of different stakeholders. This change means going beyond CSR and its limitations to a more deeply rooted approach. This can be framed in terms of corporate conscience, which is concerned with how a firm integrates its social and environmental commitments into its purpose and uses them to guide its actions. It is instructive that purpose-driven conscientious firms such as Patagonia, Unilever and SAP do not generally refer to CSR, but rather focus on how to use their belief systems to guide sustainable actions. Defining corporate conscience is however complex. Drawing on Immanuel Kant (2004) and Adam Smith (2009) it can be argued that a business with a conscience combines critical thinking and the power of acting together (Ind & Iglesias, 2022). It can both guide firms in their actions and help evaluate actions already performed. It encourages a long-term perspective and a balanced multi-stakeholder approach. While there is some skepticism as to whether firms can have a conscience (Velasquez, 2003; Köllen, 2016), others have argued that firms have a degree of unity that is more than the sum of their constituent parts and that they can act intentionally (Goodpaster & Matthews, 1982; Sulmasy, 2008). Individuals bring their own purposes and beliefs to organizations, and the purpose and beliefs of the organization influence the moral life of individuals as part of their social identity (Ellemers & Van der Toorn, 2015).

A research agenda for the future

Within the three discussed themes there is still considerable research potential:

Organic corporate brands

That corporate brands have become more organic, creates a challenge for both the process of articulating the corporate brand itself and bringing it to life. A lot of attention has been paid to the words that define a corporate brand, as if the process of articulation somehow pins down the brand once and for all. Here, it would be fascinating to conduct some longitudinal studies into how the meaning of the corporate brand changes over time as it is used in decision making and influenced by the actions of external partners. The temporal dimension here is particularly interesting, due to the way in which a corporate brand's history has the potential to create strategic legitimacy for internal and external stakeholders (Howard-Grenville et al., 2013; Hatch & Schultz, 2017; Iglesias et al., 2020). It may be the case that a well-rooted corporate brand that connects with its past and provides inspiration for the future is able to provide both continuity and change, not so much by fixing the corporate brand and its intended meaning but by creating a framework within which interpretations of the corporate brand's past and the future ebb and flow (Schultz & Hernes, 2013). By exploring how different stakeholders view the evolution of the corporate brand meaning over time, researchers would be able to acquire insights as to how organic corporate brands can best be managed. Finally, while it is interesting to hear about successes, as various cases show, e.g., LEGO (Schultz & Hernes, 2013), Adidas (Iglesias et al., 2020) and SMK (Schmeltz & Kjeldsen, 2019), corporate brands that have problems can be very instructive.

Co-creation

Since the emergence of co-creation, there has been much research conducted into the field, both in terms of the motivations of firms and stakeholders. However, there is still a lack of understanding as to how corporate brands can manage the interplay between promoting a co-creative approach that encourages the active involvement of stakeholders while still maintaining corporate brand cohesion. It would be particularly valuable to investigate firms that have used co-creation, and to better understand how they have navigated the tensions between openness and the need for brand direction. These tensions apply to the way managers and employees have been re-thinking their approach and behaviors in a more fluid stakeholder environment.

For managers there is a need for a nuanced approach that recognizes while there are some common desirable attributes to leading in a co-creative environment such as humility and openness, different roles co-exist along a continuum that demonstrates different beliefs and attitudes (Riedmeier & Kreuzer, 2022). In turn employees are placing greater demands on corporate brands to be relevant and impactful and there is a growing expectation that their needs will be met. A 2021 study of 7000 employees in seven countries, not only showed employees have an increasing concern with personal empowerment and social impact, but that they are also willing to challenge the companies they work for, with half the respondents agreeing with the statement 'A large group of employees exerting strong pressure within our organization can get it to change almost anything about itself' (Edelman, 2021). The changing nature of leadership in a multi-stakeholder, activist world with heightened expectations makes it important that we understand how companies can utilize the knowledge, creativity and desire of stakeholders to contribute in a productive way to enriching the corporate brand.

Conscience

Conscience is less well developed relative to co-creation, although there have been studies exploring the construct (Ind & Horlings, 2016; Ind & Iglesias, 2022; Rindell et al., 2011; Olsen & Peretz, 2011; Hutchinson et al., 2013). A challenge with conscience is to pin down what it means, because it is difficult to put into words. We only become aware of conscience when a belief system meets specific events, and where managers have to make a choice. We can use the proxy of purpose and principles as a way to think about conscience, but it is not exactly the same thing. In our research, we have found that expert audiences such as business managers and marketing and brand professionals understand the construct and can comment on it, but it is far harder to research with consumers, who lack insight into the processes that determine the way corporate brands act.

However, there are different opportunities to further deepen the understanding of conscience and how it can contribute to firms' success. First, is to explore through in-depth case studies, how firms make and implement decisions, especially when different moral choices are possible, and choosing one argument over another brings with it economic and moral cost. How such dilemmas are played out in practice would provide insight as to how to balance the needs of different stakeholders, as well as how implementation is managed in a conscientious way. Second, there are specific audiences, who form part of a corporate brand's ecosystem, that possess knowledge as to how a firm's conscience influences their actions. As noted above, employees play an increasingly influential role on the organization's conscience – and have the ability to deliver on the firm's purpose and principles, if they understand its impact (Gast et al., 2020). There is an opportunity here to research the way in which individual purpose (as a reflection of one's own conscience) and corporate purpose connect, and what the tensions between the two might be. Externally there would be value in researching such audiences as suppliers, partners and investors. The relationship between the corporate brand and its suppliers and partners, indicates how the corporate brand views its relationship with others. Does it have a view that is transactional, or does it see mutually beneficial relationships in which partners and suppliers contribute towards the development of a conscientious corporate brand, while enabling them to survive and thrive by enhancing their capabilities and well-being (Longoni & Luzzini, 2016)? Similarly, how is the relationship with investors managed? Increasingly, investors are becoming a force for change as they push firms to provide accurate and transparent reporting of their performance in terms of Environment, Social and Governance (ESG) factors. While there is a clear suggestion that embedding ESG into strategy and operations is valuable, not least because it reduces risk and delivers strong financial returns (Serafeim, 2020), there is evidence that a desire to enhance corporate reputation can lead to a lack of candor in ESG reporting. This suggests that research into the relationship between firms and investors would be valuable as a means of understanding how ESG reporting requirements impact the firm and the need for conscientious choices that meet both its, and society's, long-term needs (Geradts & Bocken, 2019).

A third emergent area of research is to better understand the way in which artificial intelligence (AI) is increasingly having an impact on the corporate brand – and the implications of this in terms of conscience. AI is posited to provide four benefits for brand management practice: (i) it provides superior and more accurate insights into stakeholder behavior; (ii) it fosters the development of brand relationships; (iii) it can support marketing operations; and (iv) it delivers greater efficiency and consistency. Yet, in spite of the value of AI in brand building, there is a note of caution. AI can reduce the biases of humans in their stakeholder interactions, but it can also treat people as objects, especially if the orientation in AI is towards efficiency and consistency rather than to enhance the stakeholder experience (Mangio et al., 2022). While firms are powering ahead in their use of AI, academic research has hardly kept pace. The research opportunity here is to not only understand the uses that AI is being put to, but to also evaluate how firms are applying their conscience in making choices where there is a lack of precedent to guide their decisions.

Conclusion

Overall, there has been some continuity in corporate branding, but also considerable change, due primarily to the increase in influence and activism of diverse stakeholder groups. As a consequence, corporate brands have become more open and some have seized the opportunity to embrace the input and creativity of others. As corporate branding continues to evolve this will have implications for the definition of corporate brands, how they are managed to the benefit of investors, but also to society and the environment, and how human-centric leadership styles can support the needs of internal and external stakeholders – all areas worthy of research.

References

Anker, M. (2009). *The Ethics of Uncertainty: Aporetic Openings.* New York: Atropos Press.

Antorini, Y. M., Muñiz Jr, A. M., & Askildsen, T. (2012). Collaborating with customer communities: Lessons from the LEGO Group. *MIT Sloan Management Review, 53*(3), 73–79.

Argenti, P., & Druckenmiller, B. (2004). Reputation and the corporate brand. *Corporate Reputation Review, 6*, 368–374.

Balmer, J. M. T. (1995). Corporate branding and connoisseurship. *Journal of General Management, 21*(1), 24–46.

Balmer, J. M. T. (2001). Corporate identity, corporate branding and corporate marketing: Seeing through the fog. *European Journal of Marketing, 35*(3–4), 248–291.

Balmer, J. M. T., & Gray, E. R. (2003). Corporate brands: What are they? What of them? *European Journal of Marketing, 37*(7/8), 972–997.

Barthes, R. (1977). The death of the author. In *Image-Music-Text* (pp. 142–148). London: Fontana Press.

Belova, O., King, I., & Sliwa, M. (2008). Introduction: Polyphony and organization studies: Mikhail Bakhtin and beyond. *Organization Studies, 29*(4), 493–500.

Boiral, O. (2013). Sustainability reports as simulacra? A counter-account of A and A+ GRI reports. *Accounting, Auditing & Accountability Journal, 26*(7), 1036–1071.

Brodie, R. J., Whittome, J. R., & Brush, G. J. (2009). Investigating the service brand: A customer value perspective. *Journal of Business Research, 62*(3), 345–355.

Bødker, S., & Grønbæk, K. (1990). Cooperative prototyping: Users and designers in mutual activity. Draft paper submitted for *International Journal of Man-Machine Studies*, special issue on CSCW.

De Landa, M. (2003). *A Thousand Years of Nonlinear History.* New York: Swerve.

Eco, U. (1999). *Kant and the Platypus: Essays on Language and Cognition* (Kant e L'ornitorinco, 1997, Trans. Alastair McEwen). London: Secker and Warburg.

Edelman. (2021). *Edelman Trust Barometer. Special Report: The Belief-Driven Employee.* https:// www .edelman .com/ sites/ g/ files/ aatuss191/ files/ 2021 -09/ 2021 %20Edelman %20Trust %20Barometer %20Special %20Report %20The %20Belief -Driven%20Employee%20Global%20Report%20Full%20w%20Talk%20Track.pdf

Ellemers, N., & Van der Toorn, J. (2015). Groups as moral anchors. *Current Opinion in Psychology, 6*, 189–194.

Gast, A., Illanes, P., Probst, N., Schaninger, B., & Simpson, B. (2020). Corporate purpose: Shifting from why to how. *McKinsey Quarterly.* https:// www .mckinsey .com/ business -functions/ organization/ our -insights/ purpose -shifting -from -why -to -how#.

Geradts, T. H., & Bocken, N. M. (2019). Driving sustainability-oriented innovation. *MIT Sloan Management Review, 60*(2), 78–83.

Golant, D. (2012). Bringing the corporate brand to life: The brand manager as practical author. *Journal of Brand Management, 20*(2), 115–127.

Goodpaster, K. E., & Matthews, J. B. (1982). Can a corporation have a conscience? *Harvard Business Review, 6*(1), 132–141.

Graham, P. (Ed.) (1995). *Mary Parker Follett: Prophet of Management.* Washington, DC: Beard Books.

Grönroos, C., & Voima, P. (2013). Critical service logic: Making sense of value creation and co-creation. *Journal of the Academy of Marketing Science, 41*(2), 133–150.

Grønbæk, K., Kyng, M., & Mogensen, P. (1997). Toward a cooperative experimental system development approach. In M. Kyng & L. Mathiassen (Eds.), *Computers and Design in Context* (pp. 201–238). Cambridge, MA: The MIT Press.

Harris, F., & de Chernatony, L. (2001). Corporate branding and corporate brand performance. *European Journal of Marketing, 35*(3/4), 441–456.

Hatch, M. J. (1999). The jazz metaphor for organizing: Historical and performative aspects. Paper presented to the Critical Management Studies Conference, *Popular Culture and Critical Management Stream*, Manchester, July, 1–17.

Hatch, M. J., & Schultz, M. (2002). The dynamics of organizational identity. *Human Relations, 55*(8), 989–1018.

Hatch, M. J., & Schultz, M. (2017). Toward a theory of using history authentically: Historicizing in the Carlsberg Group. *Administrative Science Quarterly, 62*(4), 657–697.

Hess, D. (2019). The transparency trap: Non-financial disclosure and the responsibility of business to respect human rights. *American Business Law Journal, 56*(1), 5–53.

Howard-Grenville, J., Metzger, M. L., & Meyer, A. D. (2013). Rekindling the flame: Processes of identity resurrection. *Academy of Management Journal, 56*(1), 113–136.

Hutchinson, D. B., Singh, J., Svensson, G., & Mysen, T. (2013). Towards a model of conscientious corporate brands: A Canadian study. *The Journal of Business and Industrial Marketing, 28*(8), 687–695.

Iglesias, O., Ind, N., & Alfaro, M. (2017). The organic view of the brand: A brand value co-creation model. In J. M. T. Balmer, S. M. Powell, J. Kernstock, & T. O. Brexendorf (Eds.), *Advances in Corporate Branding* (pp. 148–174). London: Palgrave Macmillan.

Iglesias, O., Ind, N., & Schultz, M. (2020). History matters: The role of history in corporate brand strategy. *Business Horizons, 63*(1), 51–60.

Ind, N. (1997). *The Corporate Brand.* London: Palgrave Macmillan.

Ind, N., & Horlings, S. (Eds.). (2016). *Brands with a Conscience: How to Build a Successful and Responsible Brand.* London: Kogan Page.

Ind, N., & Iglesias, O. (2022). *In Good Conscience: Do the Right Thing while Building a Profitable Business.* London: Palgrave Macmillan.

Ind, N., & Riondino, M. C. (2001). Branding on the web: A real revolution? *Journal of Brand Management, 9*(1), 8–19.

Ind, N., Fuller, C., & Trevail, C. (2012). *Brand Together: How Co-creation Generates Innovation and Re-energizes Brands.* London: Kogan Page.

Jensen, M. C., & Meckling, W. H. (1976). Theory of the firm: Managerial behavior, agency costs and ownership structure. *Journal of Financial Economics, 3*(4), 305–360.

Kant, I. (2004). *Kant's Groundwork of the Metaphysics of Morals* (Trans. Mary Gregor). Cambridge: Cambridge University Press.

Kärreman, D., & Rylander, A. (2008). Managing meaning through branding: The case of a consulting firm. *Organization Studies, 29*(1), 103–125.

Kim, E. H., & Lyon, T. P. (2015). Greenwash vs. Brownwash: Exaggeration and undue modesty in corporate sustainability disclosure. *Organization Science, 26*(3), 705–723.

Köllen, T. (2016). Acting out of compassion, egoism, and malice: A Schopenhauerian view on the moral worth of CSR and diversity management practices. *Journal of Business Ethics, 138*(2), 215–229.

Kornberger, M. (2010). *Brand Society: How Brands Transform Management and Lifestyle.* Cambridge: Cambridge University Press.

Kornum, N., Gyrd-Jones, R., Al Zagir, N., & Brandis, K. A. (2017). Interplay between intended brand identity and identities in a Nike-related brand commu-

nity: Co-existing synergies and tensions in a nested system. *Journal of Business Research*, *70*, 432–440.
Lifshitz-Assaf, H. (2015). From problem solvers to solution seekers: Knowledge boundaries permeation at NASA. In *Academy of Management Proceedings* (Vol. 2015, No. 1, p. 14234). Briarcliff Manor, NY: Academy of Management.
Longoni, A., & Luzzini, D. (2016). Building social capital into the disrupted green coffee supply chain: Illy's journey to quality and sustainability. In *Organizing Supply Chain Processes for Sustainable Innovation in the Agri-Food Industry* (Organizing for Sustainable Effectiveness, Vol. 5, pp. 83–108). Bingley: Emerald.
Lyon, T. P., & Montgomery, A. W. (2013). Tweetjacked: The impact of social media on corporate greenwash. *Journal of Business Ethics*, *118*(4), 747–757.
Lyon, T. P., Delmas, M. A., Maxwell, J. W., Tima Bansal, P., Chiroleu-Assouline, M., Crifo, P., et al. (2018). CSR needs CPR: Corporate sustainability and politics. *California Management Review*, *60*(4), 5–24.
Mangio, F., Pedeliento, G., & Andreini, D. (2022). Brand experience co-creation at the time of artificial intelligence. In O. Iglesias, N. Ind, & M. Schultz (Eds.), *The Routledge Companion to Corporate Branding* (pp. 195–210). Abingdon: Routledge.
Maon, F., Swaen, V., & Lindgreen, A. (2017). One vision, different paths: An investigation of corporate social responsibility initiatives in Europe. *Journal of Business Ethics*, *143*, 405–422.
Marquis, C., Toffel, M. W., & Zhou, Y. (2016). Scrutiny, norms, and selective disclosure: A global study of greenwashing. *Organization Science*, *27*(2), 483–504.
Merz, M. A., He, Y., & Vargo, S. L. (2009). The evolving brand logic: A service dominant logic perspective. *Journal of the Academy of Marketing Science*, *37*(3), 328–344.
Michel, G. (2017). From brand identity to polysemous brands: Commentary on 'Performing identities: Processes of brand and stakeholder identity co-construction'. *Journal of Business Research*, *70*, 453–455.
Muniz, A. M., & O'Guinn, T. C. (2001). Brand community. *Journal of Consumer Research*, *27*(4), 412–432.
Olsen, L. E., & Peretz, A. (2011). Conscientious brand criteria: A framework and a case example from the clothing industry. *Journal of Brand Management*, *18*(9), 639–649.
Polman, P., & Winston, A. (2021). *Net Positive: How Courageous Companies Thrive by Giving More than they Take*. Brighton, MA: Harvard Business Review Press.
Porter, M. (1985). *Competitive Advantage*. New York: The Free Press.
Prahalad, C. K., & Ramaswamy, V. (2000). Co-opting customer competence. *Harvard Business Review*, *78*(1), 79–90.
Prahalad, C. K., & Ramaswamy, V. (2004). *The Future of Competition: Co-creating Unique Value with Customers*. Brighton, MA: Harvard Business Press.
Ramaswamy, V., & Ind, N. (2021). Company brands as purpose-driven lived-experience ecosystems. *The European Business Review*, May–June, 37–45.
Ramaswamy, V., & Ozcan, K. (2014). *The Co-creation Paradigm*. Redwood City, CA: Stanford University Press.
Ramaswamy, V., & Pieters, M. K. (2021). How companies can learn to operate as co-creational, adaptive, 'living' enterprises. *Strategy & Leadership*, *49*(2), 3–8.
Raymond, E. S. (1999). *The Cathedral and the Bazaar: Musings on Linux and Open Source by an Accidental Revolutionary*. Sebastopol, CA: O'Reilly.
Riedmeier, J., & Kreuzer, M. (2022). Me versus we: The role of luxury brand managers in times of co-creation. *Journal of Business Research*, *145*, 240–252.

Rindell, A., Svensson, G., Mysen, T., Billström, A., & Wilén, K. (2011). Towards a conceptual foundation of 'conscientious corporate brands'. *Journal of Brand Management*, *18*(9), 709–719.

Roper, S., & Davies, G. (2007). The corporate brand: Dealing with multiple stakeholders. *Journal of Marketing Management*, *23*(1–2), 75–90.

Scheyvens, R., Banks, G., & Hughes, E. (2016). The private sector and the SDGs: The need to move beyond 'business as usual'. *Sustainable Development*, *24*(6), 371–382.

Schmeltz, L., & Kjeldsen, A. K. (2019). The case of SMK: Co-creation in the context of the Danish National Gallery. In N. Ind & H. J. Schmidt (Eds.), *Co-creating Brands: Brand Management from a Co-creative Perspective* (pp. 257–263). London: Bloomsbury Publishing.

Schmidt, H. J., Ind, N., Guzmán, F., & Kennedy, E. (2021). Sociopolitical activist brands. *Journal of Product and Brand Management*, *31*(1), 40–55.

Schultz, M., & Hernes, T. (2013). A temporal perspective on organizational identity. *Organization Science*, *24*(1), 1–21.

Serafeim, G. (2020). Social-impact efforts that create real value. *Harvard Business Review*, *98*(5), 38–48.

Smith, A. (2009). *The Theory of Moral Sentiments* (first published 1759). London: Penguin Books.

Sulmasy, D. P. (2008). What is conscience and why is respect for it so important? *Theoretical Medicine and Bioethics*, *29*, 135–149.

Vallaster, C., & Lindgreen, A. (2011). Corporate brand strategy formation: Brand actors and the situational context for a business-to-business brand. *Industrial Marketing Management*, *40*(7), 1133–1143.

Velasquez, M. (2003). Debunking corporate moral responsibility. *Business Ethics Quarterly*, *13*(4), 531–562.

von Hippel, E. (2005). *Democratizing Innovation*. Cambridge, MA: MIT Press.

Walsh, G., & Beatty, S. (2007). Customer-based corporate reputation of a service firm: Scale development and validation. *Journal of the Academy of Marketing Science*, *35*(1), 127–143.

3 Brand architecture: a literature review and future research directions

M. Berk Talay, M. Billur Akdeniz and Janell D. Townsend

1. Introduction

Brands are among a firm's most valuable intangible assets as they are a means to identify, define, and differentiate an organization from its competitors. A brand reflects the value associated with its products and services, and perceptions of the brand are a function of the sum of a person's experiences with it. Organizations rarely use a single brand for all their different products and services. Defining the number and nature of common and distinctive brand elements across a firm's products or services, and implementing a well-crafted brand architecture, are vital for its marketing strategy. The resulting structure, a brand's architecture, determines what brand elements a firm should apply across new and existing products and services, providing the firm with a strategic roadmap (Brexendorf & Keller, 2017). A brand architecture strategy establishes the brand's breadth or boundaries and its depth or complexity across and within marketplaces.

The foundations of brand architecture and portfolio management research in the marketing strategy literature are well established (e.g., Keller & Lehmann, 2006; Kirca et al., 2020; Rego et al., 2009; Morgan & Rego, 2009). However, there have been critical shifts in brand management research in response to changing dynamics in the business environments. For instance, recent research by Swaminathan et al. (2020) identifies two distinct changes: the first from a single to shared ownership of brands; and the second from a limited geographic reach and impact on societies to a greater geographic reach and a larger impact on societies. These dynamics allow future researchers to expand the knowledge that will benefit theory, methodology, and practice. Previous research and prospects for future research in the brand architecture domain fall naturally into distinct areas with their own theoretical lenses and methodological approaches.

In the remainder of this chapter, first, we discuss the progression of brand architecture research in light of the literature review we conducted. Next, we organize the literature review across five main themes where we present the theme, discuss previous research in this space, and provide future research avenues related to it. Following that, we elaborate on the methodological considerations unique to the brand architecture area, and we conclude with a further emphasis on emerging topics and future research directions.

2. The progression and the key themes of the brand architecture research

We performed an extensive review of the marketing literature since 2000, explicitly focusing on marketing strategy and empirical modeling research streams and the leading marketing journals. We identified 48 articles using select keywords such as brand architecture, brand portfolio, brand management, and brand performance. Table 3A.1 displays a representation of the articles in chronological order, and delineates the key findings, theoretical and methodological approaches, and future research directions of each study to convey the progression of brand architecture research over time.

The discussion of the criticality of brands for a firm's marketing strategy emanated from the 1980s (Aaker & Shansby, 1982; Keon, 1983; Park et al., 1986; Trout & Ries, 1986). These early papers mainly focus on positioning and brand image management. Later, in the 1990s, the branding literature became more concerned with topics such as brand equity, quality, and extensions (Aaker & Keller, 1990; Boush & Loken, 1991; Dacin & Smith, 1994; Erdem, 1998). At the turn of the millennium, with the rising importance of the value of brands as an intangible asset of a company, research shifted to a more systematic examination of brand architecture and its various components. Brand architecture strategy mainly consists of (i) whether one or multiple levels of brands are used; (ii) whether and how individual brands within the company's portfolio are clustered and related to each other, and (iii) the role of corporate branding within this structure (e.g., Aaker & Joachimsthaler, 2000; Hsu et al., 2016; Kapferer, 2012). In addition, brand architecture and portfolios are examined by marketing strategy scholars to understand their impact on company performance.

Over the last 20 years, innovation has led to the proliferation of products, services, and brands. Accordingly, designing and implementing a successful brand architecture as part of a company's marketing strategy has become highly critical for brand managers. Firms typically use multiple brands for different products or services, or multiple brands combined differently for a single product. Yet, they are challenged in configuring a brand architecture strategy that manages and maximizes the brand value and ensures long-term financial prosperity. In our literature review, we observed five key themes within the brand architecture research in the marketing strategy field: (i) brand hierarchy; (ii) brand portfolios; (iii) brand–finance interface; (iv) brands and innovation management; and (v) global branding.

2.1 Brand hierarchy

Regarding the structure of how a firm's products and services are branded, brand hierarchy is a critical tool within brand architecture strategy (Keller, 2012). Systematically investigating brand hierarchies, Rao et al. (2004) propose a three-category brand architecture strategy (e.g., corporate branding, house of brands, and mixed strategy) and examine their effects on the financial value of a company. Following Rao et al. (2004), Völckner and Sattler (2006) look deeper into a more focused category within brand hierarchies, namely brand extensions within and beyond the original product category. They follow a more comprehensive framework with ten different factors of success, and test moderating and mediating relationships to account for the possibilities that some success factors can also be dependent variables, and that some boundary conditions to the relationships exist.

Later, studies such as Kapferer (2012) and Keller (2012) note that brand hierarchies have a strong influence on the performance of a company, and govern the efficiency and effectiveness of marketing resources. Hsu et al. (2016) propose a more detailed view of brand architecture strategy, adding the dimensions of sub-branding and endorsed branding, to Rao et al.'s (2004) model, and empirically examine how a five-category brand architecture strategy affects the company's value and risk. Rao et al. (2004) conclude that corporate branding is associated with a higher value of Tobin's Q (i.e., the market value of a firm divided by its book value), whereas the house of brands and mixed branding architectures are associated with a lower value of Tobin's Q due to their distributing risk on other brands. Hsu et al. (2016), via a more detailed view of brand architecture on both firm value and risk, add that (i) endorsed branding lowers risk relative to sub-branding, and (ii) hybrid architecture, which constitutes a mix of branded house and house of brands, does not offer consistent performance improvements over the house of brands and branded house (i.e., corporate branding) strategies of which it is comprised.

As marketing becomes more digital and a brand's stakeholders get more connected geographically, we expect that brand hierarchies still constitute an important component of an organization's brand architecture strategy. Accordingly, we suggest three avenues for future research. First, future research needs to examine more comprehensive and relevant brand architecture strategies in the context of the digital revolution. Second, given the increase in technology and channels where consumer information about brands is disseminated in a broader and faster fashion, research should provide further knowledge on what type of brand hierarchy strategies are the most inclusive for different consumer segments. Third, aside from brand managers and consumers, it will be important to identify what other stakeholders have a say in the future of brand hierarchies that increase firm performance and reduce risk.

2.2 Brand portfolios

Referring to the set of all brands and product lines that a firm offers to its consumers, the brand portfolio is a related theme to brand hierarchy in brand architecture research. Building on some of the earlier studies on brand portfolio characteristics and dynamics (i.e., Aaker, 2004; Anand & Shachar, 2004), Morgan and Rego (2009) dissect brand portfolio strategy into five components (i.e., brand scope, competition, positioning, perceived quality, perceived price). This study demonstrates that brand portfolios with a high perceived quality enjoy a superior financial performance. In addition, more brands marketed across a smaller number of segments that enjoy a low level of competition and high perceived quality drive up consumer loyalty. These findings paved the way for more recent studies on brand portfolios.

For instance, recently, Nguyen et al. (2018) and Kirca et al. (2020) propose new typologies to the brand portfolio literature, namely brand portfolio coherence (BPC) and brand–product portfolio (BPP) matrix. These are both managerially and scholarly relevant tools to understand the impact of brand portfolios on performance measures such as loyalty and market share. Specifically, Nguyen et al. (2018) develop the BPC construct, describing consumers' perceptions that sub-brands in a brand portfolio share a common underlying logic of features reflected in the design, personality, and status, and BPC is positively associated with brand loyalty within a portfolio. Kirca et al. (2020), on the other hand, contribute to prior research that examines the impact of product and brand portfolio characteristics on market performance in silos (e.g., Barroso & Giarratana, 2013; Bordley, 2003; Grewal et al., 2008; Morgan & Rego, 2009; Rao et al., 2004). They present the BPP matrix, and examine the interactions between portfolio depth, breadth, and innovativeness, along with their effects on brand performance. Findings indicate that positive brand positioning enhances brand performance only when considered jointly with product portfolio breadth, depth, and innovativeness.

As brand portfolios continue to hold strategic importance for brand management, future research will continue to address its various components. First, as more brand stakeholders such as social media influencers and brand communities emerge in the digital economy, a firm's control over the brand identity shifts from marketers to those stakeholders. Future research needs to investigate the new drivers of brand portfolio decisions in terms of increasing and decreasing the breadth and depth of brand portfolios. Second, there has been an increasing trend towards building brands that support sustainable business models, social causes, and political activism. Some brands strive to do this to put social change before company profitability, and some merely try to stay relevant by taking a stance. Future research should investigate the consequences of such actions from both consumer-related and market-related performance metrics. Potentially, a related area for study is developing and validating metrics for brand authenticity in social causes and its effect on the consumer base.

2.3 Brand-finance interface

Marketing professionals have been challenged to explain the value of strategic brand management for firm performance. In addressing this, one research stream has specifically focused on establishing a relationship between brand extensions within a brand architecture and the financial value of a company as early as the 1990s (e.g., Aaker & Jacobson, 1994; Kerin & Sethuraman, 1998). Later, studies such as Madden et al. (2006) compare the stock market performance of brand-focused companies (i.e., Interbrand list) to all firms in the CRSP (Center for Research in Security Prices). This study provides compelling empirical evidence that strategically managing brands creates higher shareholder value.

Following these early studies, research has focused on understanding the financial value implications of more specific actions of brand management such as brand architecture decisions, brand endorsements, and rebranding (e.g., Cao & Sorescu, 2013). Later, in the brand portfolio field, Nguyen et al. (2018) point out that brand portfolio coherence affects firm performance due to the economies of scale and scope that can be achieved through synergies between brands and marketing mix variables. Kirca et al. (2020) also suggest research should examine the interactive effects between marketing mix variables and brand portfolio characteristics (e.g., breadth, depth) on sales.

Although important insights have been established to understand the value of a firm's brand architecture and portfolio as well as their characteristics on firm valuation (Barroso & Giarratana, 2013; Grewal et al., 2008; Morgan & Rego, 2009; Rao et al., 2004), much remains to be learned about the impact of those characteristics on the short-term and long-term financial performance of brands. It is essential for future research to understand how a change in brand hierarchy and portfolios impacts various financial metrics, and the trade-offs among them. This balance of both top-line and operational considerations with respect to brand architecture management has practical implications, and can be guided by the extension of theoretical frameworks to help improve managerial decision making. Hence, future studies should elucidate these complex and multifarious relationships.

2.4 Brands and innovation management

Along with many of their functions and identities, brands constitute growth platforms for organizations (Keller & Lehmann, 2006). Developing new products, generating new markets for existing products, and innovation in general, are primary strategic tools for sustainable brand growth and profitability. Brands are valuable signals for consumers to evaluate new products, as well as to reduce risk and set expectations. Hence, strategies for growing or pruning brands (e.g., co-branding, ingredient branding, acquiring/selling brands, creating/eliminating new product lines) have an influence on the size, quality, and congruency of the brand architecture and portfolios. In fact, how new products and innovation affect brand equity has been among the most frequently researched topics, as organizations rely on both strong brands and innovation to increase their competitive advantage and profitability (e.g., Keller & Lehmann, 2006). Some of the earliest work in this research stream appeared in the 1980s and 1990s with the branding decisions of new products. Wernerfelt (1988) presented the concept of umbrella branding, where firms use their brand name and reputation to signal the quality of a new product introduced to the market. Later, Erdem (1998) empirically investigated how consumers' quality perceptions of a brand in a product category were affected by their experience with the same brand in a different product category.

Brand and innovation management have become popular, synergistic research streams in studies focusing on brand architecture and portfolio management. Brexendorf et al. (2015) suggest a three-pronged framework to understand the interplay and mutual dependence between brand and innovation management of an organization: (i) brands provide strategic focus to new products and innovation; (ii) brands support the introduction of new products; and (iii) successful innovations improve brand equity and attitude. As far as the provision of a strategic focus is concerned, the brand architecture that a firm adopts is a critical ingredient in defining the boundaries of a brand name, designing the launch of incremental versus radical innovations, and influencing the success of innovations (Chandy & Tellis, 1998; Rao et al., 2004). Brands and innovation can reinforce each other. Strong brands help with the introduction and adoption of new products through enhancing their visibility and communication (e.g., Keller & Lehmann, 2006), and successful innovations improve brand credibility, value, and competitive advantage (Aaker & Jacobson, 2001; Beverland et al., 2010).

As brands become more purpose-driven in the marketplace, future research needs to provide knowledge on the type of new product and innovation strategies that help versus hurt brand growth and architecture. Equally important is the role of different brand associations (e.g., political stance, environmental friendliness) and affiliations (e.g., sponsorships to certain events, sports games) to enable versus prevent the introduction of new products. In addition, researchers can examine whether shifts in brands, such as from single to shared ownership (e.g., multiple stakeholders), or from permanent to temporary ownership (e.g., sharing economy), lead to more incremental or radical innovation, and also how this varies across industries (e.g., products versus services).

2.5 Global branding

As a company expands to international markets it faces several questions in terms of its international branding strategy, such as whether to use powerful domestic brands abroad (e.g., Coca-Cola), or to develop brands specific to regional and national preferences. A rational global brand architecture is an imperative component of the firm's international marketing strategy, as it provides a structure to leverage strong brands into other markets, integrate brands purchased in other markets, and convey the firm's international branding strategy. Douglas et al. (2001) propose a conceptual model of the market-, product-, and firm-based drivers of international brand architecture. Implementing a version of this structure, where brands are classified as local, regional, multi-regional, and global, Townsend et al. (2009) find that market attractiveness, experiential learning, and mimetic behavior impact on a brand's position in a global brand architecture. Talay et al. (2015) conceptualize brand multi-nationality as a hierarchical continuum based on the dispersion of brands across geographies, and empirically demonstrate that brands in the architecture that are more global perform better.

Another approach to managing global brand architectures is to balance domestic, foreign, and global positioning strategies for different brands in the company's portfolio. Erdem et al. (2006) provide evidence that brands serve as signals of product positions across markets. Ozsomer and Altaras (2008) suggest the degree and scope of a global brand is also a signal of quality to the marketplace. Brand positioning in a global environment provides mediation between brand strategies and market-based performance. Future research should incorporate consumers' perceptions of a brand's image into a model of actual market-based performance to test for these mediation effects.

The interaction of other brand characteristics with categories of brand dispersion in a global brand architecture, as well as the relationships between each layer within the portfolio are areas for future research. For example, country-of-origin (COO) is an important extrinsic cue for consumer perceptions of brands, and interacting this with brand architectures is a stream of research that could be developed. Furthermore, the operationalization of what constitutes a global brand from a geographic dispersion perspective may need to be updated to reflect broader revenue generation from foreign markets, and the increased importance of emerging markets. Finally, a germane area of consideration for future research is the exploration of how consumers' preferences for global brands are driven by the interaction between cultural and institutional variations among countries.

3. Methodological approaches in brand architecture studies

In this section, we provide a synopsis of the methodological approaches used in the recently published articles on brand architecture (Table 3A.1) with regard to the types of data (i.e., primary versus secondary), units of analysis (i.e., individual, brand, company), geographic scopes (i.e., single- versus multi-country), and other aspects of methodological rigor (i.e., controlling for endogeneity and/or common method bias and robustness checks) followed by recommendations for future research.

3.1 Data types and units of analysis

We have observed a strong correlation with the type of data (i.e., primary versus secondary) and unit of analysis (individuals versus brands, companies) such that most studies with primary data have individuals (e.g., consumers, managers, etc.) as their unit of analysis (i.e., Desai & Keller, 2002; Nguyen et al., 2018; Sood & Keller, 2012; Steenkamp et al., 2003; Völckner & Sattler, 2006), and most studies that collected secondary data analyze brands or companies as their unit of analysis (i.e., Aribarg & Arora, 2008; Hsu et al., 2016; Kirca et al., 2020; Madden et al., 2006; Morgan & Rego, 2009; Rao et al., 2004; Strebinger, 2014; Talay et al., 2015). Aurier and Mejía (2021) is a notable exception in that they use household panel data to analyze the link between the impacts of brand-line breadth and depth on customers' repurchasing behavior. Moreover, only one of the articles (i.e., Strebinger, 2014) used a combination of primary and secondary data to shed light on the drivers of branding strategy selection. These findings reveal that there has been a dearth of studies that rely on both primary and secondary data. Considering the well-established strengths and weaknesses of these data types, we invite multi-method research that can provide a comprehensive view of the causal mechanisms within the brand architecture domain. While multi-method research projects require more resources, time commitment, and – by definition – proficiency in the implementation of different techniques; they help the researchers to triangulate their findings, gain a more complete understanding of the phenomena, and even lead to new insights; they are well worth the effort. As such, we believe that adopting a multi-method approach can be especially feasible and beneficial for a team of scholars.

3.2 Geographic scope

All but two (i.e., Steenkamp et al., 2003; Talay et al., 2015) articles we reviewed used data collected in a single country. Among the studies with data from a single country, the United States has been the most popular with nine articles (i.e., Aribarg & Arora, 2008; Desai & Keller, 2002; Hsu et al., 2016; Kirca et al., 2020; Madden et al., 2006; Morgan & Rego, 2009; Nguyen et al., 2018; Rao et al., 2004; Sood & Keller, 2012) while Austria (Strebinger, 2014), France (Aurier and Mejía, 2021), and Germany (Völckner and Sattler, 2006) were the others. Steenkamp et al. (2003) collected data from consumers in South Korea and the United States to examine the link between perceived brand globalness and brand value. The cultural differences between the two countries notwithstanding, the results of their cross-cultural analyses reveal that consumers in the U.S. and South Korea are, in general, similar in terms of their likelihood of purchase of a brand with high perceived globalness. On the other hand, Talay et al.

(2015) report, based on their analysis using a panel data set of 165 automotive brands operating in 65 countries from 2002 to 2008, that cultural differences moderate the link between a brand's locus in the global brand architecture and its market performance. In light of our review of the geographic scope of the articles in this domain, we have two recommendations for future research. First, we invite scholars to conduct studies in countries that haven't been focused on before (e.g., emerging and/or developing markets), since they have the potential to identify new boundary conditions for the extant literature. For instance, countries with higher degrees of consumer ethnocentrism may exhibit a less favorable attitude towards global brands (e.g., Akdeniz & Talay, 2013), contrary to the findings of the previous studies. Second, we believe that more cross-cultural/multi-country research is warranted, since incorporating socio-economic variations across countries will expand our understanding of the drivers and outcomes of brand architecture.

3.3 Methodological rigor

Unambiguously, all of the articles included in this review meet the bar for contemporaneous methodological rigor as they have been published in the most reputable journals in their fields. However, in an attempt to provide suggestions for future research, we highlight a few articles that went the extra mile. Among the studies that use survey data only Nguyen et al. (2018) controlled for common method bias. As suggested by Podsakoff et al. (2003), common method bias can be caused by (i) using a single source for both independent and dependent variables (e.g., due to social desirability bias), (ii) various characteristics of the questions (e.g., positive and negative wording), (iii) context of the questions (e.g., scale length), and (iv) measurement context (e.g., predictor and criterion variables measured at the same point in time), and can lead to spurious results. On the other hand, endogeneity has been controlled for in the analyses of seven articles (i.e., Aribarg & Arora, 2008; Aurier & Mejía, 2021; Hsu et al., 2016; Kirca et al., 2020; Morgan & Rego, 2009; Nguyen et al., 2018; Strebinger, 2014). Endogeneity refers to situations where an independent variable correlates with the error term, leading to inconsistent and biased estimates (Rutz & Watson, 2019). We invite all researchers to develop research designs that minimize, if not avoid completely, the common method bias and endogeneity. If this is not possible, they should demonstrate that their effects are not detrimental to their findings. Finally, pre- and post-estimation analyses provide additional support for the internal and external validity of findings for any study. Most articles we reviewed have conducted standard pre-estimation checks (e.g., reliability, convergent validity etc.) while only six presented the results of their post-estimation analysis (i.e., Desai & Keller, 2002; Hsu et al., 2016; Kirca et al., 2020; Madden et al., 2006; Morgan & Rego, 2009; Steenkamp et al., 2003). Research should conduct, and preferably present the findings of, multiple tests to illustrate the robustness of their findings to variations in several aspects of their analyses including, but not limited to, variable operationalizations, model estimations, subsamples, etc.

4. Conclusion: nascent issues in brand architecture research

Brand architecture has been a central component of branding and brand management. In the past 20 years, academic research has covered various topics in a multitude of studies that have advanced both scholars' and managers' understanding of the complex issues regarding brand architectures. In this chapter, we identify five key themes that have emerged in previous research from the top journals within the field of marketing strategy that provide the foundations of knowledge and guidance for future research. These five themes span the importance of brand structures from the specific perspectives of *strategic brand management*, *brands as growth engines*, and *brand–performance relationships*. Along with discussing these themes and their foundations, we also present the methodological characteristics of brand architecture research with a specific focus on data, methods, and research contexts.

Based on these foundations, we discuss the future of brand architecture research given the changing dynamics of the business environments due to technological advancements, digital transformation, and increased connectivity worldwide. Due to those changing dynamics, several factors emerge related to brand management and structures. In setting nascent issues in brand architecture research that have not yet been considered in the literature but are essential for future studies to consider, we focus on three of those factors: (i) the stakeholders that partake in the evolution of brands have increased and diversified; (ii) the brand roles and meanings have expanded to the frontiers of societal and political issues; and (iii) the meaning of globalization has changed with increased nationalistic sentiments (Swaminathan et al., 2020).

We expect the key themes of brand architecture (i.e., brand hierarchy, brand portfolios, brand–finance interface, brands and innovation management, and global branding) to provide fertile ground for future research in the transformed business environments from a number of perspectives. Having discussed these perspectives under each theme, below, we provide specific future research questions:

- Are the existing brand hierarchy strategies effective in digital business platforms (e.g., sharing economy businesses)? If not, what other strategies could address the needs of various brand stakeholders of digital businesses?
- Who are the prominent stakeholders that have an impact on the brand hierarchies in digital business platforms?
- What are the drivers of brand portfolio decisions for companies that are at the forefront of supporting social causes (e.g., sustainable manufacturing, social justice, political activism)?
- How should companies measure the value of brands with their newly emerging roles and identities in a brand architecture?
- How does a change in brand architecture or brand portfolio impact customer-based, market-based, and financial-based performance of brands? Are there different implications in the short versus long term?
- What are some new product development strategies that help brand architecture and growth for more socially responsible and purpose-driven companies?
- How are global brand architectures affected in a more connected world given that nationalistic sentiments are rising?
- Do we expect an increase versus decrease in consumer preferences for global brands in the future? What type of cultural and institutional factors play a role in such trends?

Given the complexity of the business environments and brand architectures, we hope this chapter illustrates the next steps for future scholars to expand brand knowledge and performance in the global marketplace.

References

Aaker, D. A. (2004). Leveraging the corporate brand. *California Management Review, 46*(3), 6–18.

Aaker, D. A., & Jacobson, R. (1994). The financial information content of perceived quality. *Journal of Marketing Research, 31*(2), 191–201.

Aaker, D. A., & Jacobson, R. (2001). The value relevance of brand attitude in high-technology markets. *Journal of Marketing Research, 38*(4), 485–493.

Aaker, D. A., & Joachimsthaler, E. (2000). The brand relationship spectrum: The key to the brand architecture challenge. *California Management Review, 42*(4), 8–23.

Aaker, D. A., & Keller, K. L. (1990). Consumer evaluations of brand extensions. *Journal of Marketing, 54*(1), 27–41.

Aaker, D. A., & Shansby, J. G. (1982). Positioning your product. *Business Horizons, 25*(3), 56–62.

Akdeniz, M. B., & Talay, M. B. (2013). Cultural variations in the use of marketing signals: A multilevel analysis of the motion picture industry. *Journal of the Academy of Marketing Science, 41*(5), 601–624.

Anand, B. N., & Shachar, R. (2004). Brands as beacons: A new source of loyalty to multiproduct firms. *Journal of Marketing Research, 41*(2), 135–150.

Aribarg, A., & Arora, N. (2008). Research note: Interbrand variant overlap: Impact on brand preference and portfolio profit. *Marketing Science, 27*(3), 474–491.

Aurier, P., & Mejía, V. D. (2021). The differing impacts of brand-line breadth and depth on customers' repurchasing behavior of frequently purchased packaged goods. *Journal of the Academy of Marketing Science, 49*(6), 1244–1266.

Barroso, A., & Giarratana, M. S. (2013). Product proliferation strategies and firm performance: The moderating role of product space complexity. *Strategic Management Journal, 34*(12), 1435–1452.

Beverland, M. B., Napoli, J., & Farrelly, F. (2010). Can all brands innovate in the same way? A typology of brand position and innovation effort. *Journal of Product Innovation Management, 27*(1), 33–48.

Bordley, R. (2003). Determining the appropriate depth and breadth of a firm's product portfolio. *Journal of Marketing Research, 40*(1), 39–53.

Boush, D. M., & Loken, B. (1991). A process-tracing study of brand extension evaluation. *Journal of Marketing Research, 28*(1), 16–28.

Brexendorf, T. O., Bayus, B., & Keller, K. L. (2015). Understanding the interplay between brand and innovation management: Findings and future research directions. *Journal of the Academy of Marketing Science, 43*(5), 548–557.

Brexendorf, T. O., & Keller, K. L. (2017). Leveraging the corporate brand: The importance of corporate brand innovativeness and brand architecture. *European Journal of Marketing, 51*(9), 1530–1551.

Cao, Z., & Sorescu, A. (2013). Wedded bliss or tainted love? Stock market reactions to the introduction of cobranded products. *Marketing Science, 32*(6), 939–959.

Chandy, R. K., & Tellis, G. J. (1998). Organizing for radical product innovation: The overlooked role of willingness to cannibalize. *Journal of Marketing Research, 35*(4), 474–487.

Dacin, P. A., & Smith, D. C. (1994). The effect of brand portfolio characteristics on consumer evaluations of brand extensions. *Journal of Marketing Research, 31*(2), 229–242.

Desai, K. K., & Keller, K. L. (2002). The effects of ingredient branding strategies on host brand extendibility. *Journal of Marketing, 66*(1), 73–93.

Douglas, S. P., Craig, C. S., & Nijssen, E. J. (2001). Executive insights: Integrating branding strategy across markets: Building international brand architecture. *Journal of International Marketing, 9*(2), 97–114.

Erdem, T. (1998). An empirical analysis of umbrella branding. *Journal of Marketing Research, 35*(3), 339–351.

Erdem, T., Swait, J., & Valenzuela, A. (2006). Brands as signals: A cross-country validation study. *Journal of Marketing, 70*(1), 34–49.

Grewal, R., Chakravarty, A., Ding, M., & Liechty, J. (2008). Counting chickens before the eggs hatch: Associating new product development portfolios with shareholder expectations in the pharmaceutical sector. *International Journal of Research in Marketing, 25*(4), 261–272.

Hsu, L., Fournier, S., & Srinivasan, S. (2016). Brand architecture strategy and firm value: How leveraging, separating, and distancing the corporate brand affects risk and returns. *Journal of the Academy of Marketing Science*, *44*(2), 261–280.

Kapferer, J.-N. (2012). *The new strategic brand management: Advanced insights and strategic thinking*. Kogan Page.

Keller, K. L. (2012). Brand strategy. In V. Shankar & G. S. Carpenter (Eds.), *Handbook of marketing strategy* (pp. 289–305). Edward Elgar Publishing.

Keller, K. L., & Lehmann, D. R. (2006). Brands and branding: Research findings and future priorities. *Marketing Science*, *25*(6), 740–759.

Keon, J. W. (1983). Product positioning: TRINODAL mapping of brand images, ad images, and consumer preference. *Journal of Marketing Research*, *20*(4), 380–392.

Kerin, R. A., & Sethuraman, R. (1998). Exploring the brand value–shareholder value nexus for consumer goods companies. *Journal of the Academy of Marketing Science*, *26*(4), 260–273.

Kirca, A. H., Randhawa, P., Talay, M. B., & Akdeniz, M. B. (2020). The interactive effects of product and brand portfolio strategies on brand performance: Longitudinal evidence from the US automotive industry. *International Journal of Research in Marketing*, *37*(2), 421–439.

Madden, T. J., Fehle, F., & Fournier, S. (2006). Brands matter: An empirical demonstration of the creation of shareholder value through branding. *Journal of the Academy of Marketing Science*, *34*(2), 224–235.

Morgan, N. A., & Rego, L. L. (2009). Brand portfolio strategy and firm performance. *Journal of Marketing*, *73*(1), 59–74.

Nguyen, H. T., Zhang, Y., & Calantone, R. J. (2018). Brand portfolio coherence: Scale development and empirical demonstration. *International Journal of Research in Marketing*, *35*(1), 60–80.

Ozsomer, A., & Altaras, S. (2008). Global brand purchase likelihood: A critical synthesis and an integrated conceptual framework. *Journal of International Marketing*, *16*(4), 1–28.

Park, C. W., Jaworski, B. J., & MacInnis, D. J. (1986). Strategic brand concept-image management. *Journal of Marketing*, *50*(4), 135–145.

Podsakoff, P. M., MacKenzie, S. B., Lee, J.-Y., & Podsakoff, N. P. (2003). Common method biases in behavioral research: A critical review of the literature and recommended remedies. *Journal of Applied Psychology*, *88*(5), 879–903.

Rao, V. R., Agarwal, M. K., & Dahlhoff, D. (2004). How is manifest branding strategy related to the intangible value of a corporation? *Journal of Marketing*, *68*(4), 126–141.

Rego, L. L., Billett, M. T., & Morgan, N. A. (2009). Consumer-based brand equity and firm risk. *Journal of Marketing*, *73*(6), 47–60.

Rutz, O. J., & Watson, G. F. (2019). Endogeneity and marketing strategy research: An overview. *Journal of the Academy of Marketing Science*, *47*(3), 479–498.

Sood, S., & Keller, K. L. (2012). The effects of brand name structure on brand extension evaluations and parent brand dilution. *Journal of Marketing Research*, *49*(3), 373–382.

Steenkamp, J.-B. E., Batra, R., & Alden, D. L. (2003). How perceived brand globalness creates brand value. *Journal of International Business Studies*, *34*(1), 53–65.

Strebinger, A. (2014). Rethinking brand architecture: A study on industry-, company- and product-level drivers of branding strategy. *European Journal of Marketing*, *48*(9), 1782–1804.

Swaminathan, V., Sorescu, A., Steenkamp, J.-B. E., O'Guinn, T. C. G., & Schmitt, B. (2020). Branding in a hyperconnected world: Refocusing theories and rethinking boundaries. *Journal of Marketing, 84*(2), 24–46.

Talay, M. B., Townsend, J. D., & Yeniyurt, S. (2015). Global brand architecture position and market-based performance: The moderating role of culture. *Journal of International Marketing, 23*(2), 55–72.

Townsend, J. D., Yeniyurt, S., & Talay, M. B. (2009). Getting to global: An evolutionary perspective of brand expansion in international markets. *Journal of International Business Studies, 40*(2), 301–320.

Trout, J., & Ries, A. (1986). *Positioning: The battle for your mind.* McGraw-Hill New York.

Völckner, F., & Sattler, H. (2006). Drivers of brand extension success. *Journal of Marketing, 70*(2), 18–34.

Wernerfelt, B. (1988). Umbrella branding as a signal of new product quality: An example of signalling by posting a bond. *The RAND Journal of Economics, 19*(3), 458–466.

Appendix

Table 3A.1 Recent studies on brand architecture

Authors (Year)	Key Findings	Theoretical Approaches	Data Source/ Research Context	Method	Future Research Directions
Aurier & Mejía (2021)	Repurchasing is broken down into: intensification (repurchasing the same product) vs. diversification (cross-purchasing); and inter-trip (over shopping trips) vs. intra-trip (during purchasing trips). Breadth demonstrates only positive effects on the repurchasing components and has no protective effect against brand-switching. Depth has a negative impact on inter-trip product repurchasing, but offers a protective negative impact against brand-switching. There are significant moderating impacts of brand-line quality, brand-line alignability, and household size on these relationships.	Prior literature on brand management and repurchasing literature (e.g., behavioral loyalty, repeat purchasing, brand-switching).	Marketing Scan household panel data/ The category of chocolate bars sold in supermarkets, in a Western European market over a 36-month period between 2008 and 2010.	Multivariate logit model.	Investigate the same model for other product categories.

Authors (Year)	Key Findings	Theoretical Approaches	Data Source/ Research Context	Method	Future Research Directions
Kirca, Randhawa, Talay, & Akdeniz (2020)	Product and brand portfolio characteristics interact to affect brand performance such that while brand portfolio scope augments the positive effects of portfolio depth and innovativeness on brand performance, it attenuates the positive effects of product portfolio breadth on brand performance. Brand positioning in the auto industry enhances brand performance only when considered jointly with product portfolio breadth, depth, and innovativeness. There are critical managerial trade-offs between product and brand portfolio decisions, as product and brand portfolio decisions are intertwined.	Prior literature on brand management, brand and product portfolios, and innovation.	Secondary panel data collected from multiple sources/All passenger cars and light trucks sold in the U.S. automotive industry between 2007 and 2013.	Dynamic panel generalized method of moments estimation.	(1) Examine other industries with varying innovation cycles and brand portfolio strategies. (2) Examine how the change in product and brand portfolios impacts other financial metrics that account for the cost component of marketing operations, firm value, and customer metrics. (3) Investigate how product and brand portfolios emerge and develop further as a function of heterogeneous customer preferences or competitive industry dynamics. (4) Examine the interactive effects of other marketing mix variables with the product portfolio characteristics on sales.

Authors (Year)	Key Findings	Theoretical Approaches	Data Source/ Research Context	Method	Future Research Directions
Nguyen, Zhang, & Calantone (2018)	The study develops and validates a multi-dimensional measure of a new construct, brand portfolio coherence (BPC) to describe consumers' perceptions that (sub-)brands in a brand portfolio share a common underlying logic of features reflected in design, personality, and status. The research differentiates it from other similar constructs such as brand fit, connection, positioning, trust, and loyalty and shows that perceived BPC improves loyalty regarding brands in the portfolio.	Brand identity theory.	Primary data via survey and experiment/236 U.S. consumers recruited by a marketing research firm.	Multiple research methods such as CFA, GLM, MANCOVA.	(1) Examine the effect of BPC cross-culturally. (2) Explore other components of the brand coherence such as technical skills. (3) Examine the link between BPC and firm performance.
Hsu, Fournier, & Srinivasan (2016)	Examining the impact of a five-part brand architecture strategy (branded house, sub-branding, hybrid branding, endorsed branding, and house of brands) on abnormal stock returns and risk, it shows that sub-branding leads to higher abnormal returns and risk relative to BH. Endorsed branding lowers risk relative to sub-branding. Hybrid architecture does not offer consistent performance improvements over the component HOB and BH strategies of which it is comprised.	Marketing-finance interface and prior literature on brand management.	Secondary data collected from multiple sources/302 firms listed on the NYSE between 1996–2006.	Carhart four-factor model estimation.	(1) Assess the firm value impact of discrete shifts in brand architectures resulting from M&A activity with methods such as event-study and calendar time portfolio approaches. (2) Examine the role of endogeneity in discrete shifts in architecture strategy driven by the firm's intangible value. (3) Measure the provided typology of brand-relevant drivers of idiosyncratic risk.

Authors (Year)	Key Findings	Theoretical Approaches	Data Source/ Research Context	Method	Future Research Directions
Talay, Townsend, & Yeniyurt (2015)	Brand multi-nationality can be better conceptualized as a hierarchical continuum and brands that are higher in global brand architecture perform better in the marketplace than their nonglobal counterparts. Cultural values provide boundary conditions such that all the Hofstede cultural dimensions amplify the impact of the brand multi-nationality (i.e., global, multi-regional, and regional) signal on market performance.	Signaling theory and national culture theory.	Secondary panel data collected from multiple sources/165 automotive brands operating in 65 countries between 2002–2008.	Random-effects econometric estimation.	(1) Examine the GBA framework in other industries such as complex and credence products. (2) Add consumer-based perceptual measures to the actual industry data and test for mediation effects. (3) Examine the interactions between cultural and macroeconomic conditions on the market performances of global brands.
Strebinger (2014)	Branding strategies are determined by the industry, company strategy, and product-level decisions. Service and consumer durables companies lean more towards corporate branding than consumer nondurables. On the company level, synergies in advertising, e-commerce, and e-CRM increase the usage of shared brands. On the product level, quality differences between products and differences in experiential product positioning favor individual brands.	Prior literature on brand management.	Primary multi-level data collected from an executive survey along with secondary data and observational data/75 largest B2C companies in Austria.	Multi-level regression.	(1) Investigate additional drivers, measures as well as small- and medium-sized enterprises (SMEs). (2) Examine other country markets, particularly non-Western cultures. (3) Examine different industries using longitudinal data.

Authors (Year)	Key Findings	Theoretical Approaches	Data Source/ Research Context	Method	Future Research Directions
Sood & Keller (2012)	Sub-branded extensions evoke a slower, more thoughtful subtyping processing strategy than family-branded extensions. Category similarity affects extension evaluations when the extension is family-branded but not when it is sub-branded. Hence, sub-branding offers two key benefits to marketers: (i) enhance extension evaluations; and (ii) protect the parent brand from any unwanted negative feedback.	Prior literature on brand management.	Primary data via experiment/ Undergraduate students in lab experiments.	ANOVA and ANCOVA.	(1) Investigate situations in which family branding should perform better than sub-branding. (2) Examine how individual differences affect the interpretation of experiences and affect brand dilution. (3) Configure guidelines to help design branding strategies based on consumer and competitor considerations.
Morgan & Rego (2009)	The five different brand portfolio characteristics (number of brands owned, number of segments in which they are marketed, degree to which the brands in the firm's portfolio compete with one another, and consumer perceptions of the quality and price of the brands in the firm's portfolio) significantly affect firms' marketing and financial performance.	Prior literature on brand management and brand portfolio strategy.	Secondary data collected from multiple sources (e.g., ACSI, COMPUSTAT)/72 large publicly traded B2C firms in the U.S., tracked by ACSI, between 1994–2003.	System of simultaneous regressions.	(1) Investigate the existence and impact of firm and industry boundary conditions on these relationships. (2) Examine interactions between brand portfolio strategy variables and their performance outcomes under various firm, market, and environmental conditions. (3) Study the changes in individual brand portfolio strategy decisions over time.

Authors (Year)	Key Findings	Theoretical Approaches	Data Source/ Research Context	Method	Future Research Directions
Aribarg & Arora (2008)	Across-tier interbrand variant overlap diminishes preference for an upper-tier brand and enhances preference for a lower-tier brand. Variant overlap within a tier is likely to increase preferences of a brand belonging to the tier. A multi-brand firm enhances its brand portfolio profits by pruning its variants to reduce overlap.	Prior literature on brand and product portfolio management.	Secondary panel data/Weekly sales data for Kraft and Schwan frozen pizza products across 171 retail stores in the Chicago, Detroit, and Minneapolis in 2000.	Nested logit demand model.	(1) Replicate the current study findings for durable goods and examine competing effects between within-tier variant overlap and uniqueness. (2) Re-examine the impact of variant overlap using SKU-level models that rely on panel data. (3) Examine moderating factors such as usage level and variety seeking.
Völckner and Sattler (2006)	Fit between the parent brand and an extension product is the most important driver of brand extension success, followed by marketing support, parent-brand conviction, retailer acceptance, and parent-brand experience. The interaction terms of fit with the quality of the parent brand and with parent-brand conviction are statistically significant, albeit of relatively low importance.	Prior literature on brand management.	Primary data collected via door-to-door interviews/6668 cases from 66 different extensions of brands from the German FMCG industry between 1998 and 2001.	Multi-level structural equation modeling with maximum likelihood estimation.	(1) Replicate the current study in a laboratory setting using hypothetical parent brands and extension products that enable explicit manipulation of success factors. (2) Examine consumer durables or services or multiple categories in FMCG for generalizability purposes.

Authors (Year)	Key Findings	Theoretical Approaches	Data Source/ Research Context	Method	Future Research Directions
Madden, Fehle, & Fournier (2006)	The portfolio of brands identified as strong according to Interbrand's valuation method displays statistically and economically significant performance advantages compared with the overall market.	Prior literature on the branding and financial performance of a firm.	Monthly stock returns for the WMVB portfolio created through Interbrand list and the reduced market and full market portfolio for the period 1994–2000.	Fama-French method.	(1) Revisit the active brand research using risk as a dependent variable and quantify the ways for brand management practices to decrease firm risk. (2) Examine the role of other factors (e.g., brand portfolio breadth, brand life cycle) that may be correlated to the brand asset value. (3) Examine whether the current results hold across different types of brands, industries, and brand equity operationalizations.

Authors (Year)	Key Findings	Theoretical Approaches	Data Source/ Research Context	Method	Future Research Directions
Rao, Agarwal, & Dahlhoff (2004)	There are significant relationships between the three types of branding strategies (corporate branding, house of brands, and mixed branding) and firm value. Corporate branding is associated with a higher and mixed branding is associated with a lower value of Tobin's Q.	Marketing–finance interface and prior literature on brand management.	Secondary data collected from multiple sources (e.g., Compustat and Competitive Media Reporting)/113 U.S. firms from S&P 500 index between 1996–2000.	OLS and Hierarchical Bayesian regression.	(1) Estimate aggregate-level effects of marketing variables at the individual unit level. (2) Examine the relationship between different branding strategies and customer assets. (3) Account for the direct effects of competition on branding strategies. (4) Examine the relationships with time-series data and the interdependence of the branding strategy and firm's intangible value.

Authors (Year)	Key Findings	Theoretical Approaches	Data Source/ Research Context	Method	Future Research Directions
Steenkamp, Batra, & Alden (2003)	Perceived Brand Globalness is positively related to both perceived brand quality and prestige and, through them, to purchase likelihood. The effect through perceived quality is strongest. PBG effects are weaker for more ethnocentric consumers.	Previous literature on branding, perceived quality, and international marketing.	Primary data via survey/ Household data (USA=247 and Korea=370) for B2C product categories from Korea and USA.	Structural equation modeling.	(1) Sample a larger number of countries and product categories as well as services. (2) Test specific hypotheses concerning the effects of national culture and other country-level drivers on the ways in which PBG creates brand value. (3) Study additional moderating variables such as the extent to which GCC is popular in the country and consumer segment of interest.
Desai & Keller (2002)	With slot-filler expansions, a co-branded ingredient facilitates initial expansion acceptance, but a self-branded ingredient leads to more favorable subsequent category extension evaluations. With more dissimilar new attribute expansions, however, a co-branded ingredient leads to more favorable evaluations of both the initial expansion and the subsequent category extension.	Brand management, product schema, and concept combinations; and schema incongruity models.	Primary data collected via lab experiment/ undergraduate students.	ANOVA, ANCOVA.	(1) Examine whether there are any other feedback effects of brand expansions and category extensions on the ingredient brand over and above those at the brand attitude level. (2) Explore the design and implementation of ingredient branding strategies to provide managerial guidelines on when and how to brand ingredients.

4 How does brand equity work? A review of theory and a research agenda

Salvador del Barrio-García, María Eugenia Rodríguez-López and Álvaro J. Rojas-Lamorena

1. Brand equity in the context of brand management

Market competition requires firms to focus their efforts on obtaining sources of competitive advantage. One of the principal means that firms can employ to achieve this is by building strong brands (Castañeda-García et al., 2020). The importance of brands as a key identifier is widely recognized, as they are considered primary assets for organizations. Indeed, the brand can be considered a firm's most valuable asset, par excellence, facilitating the consumer's choice by differentiating products associated with the different brands and encouraging the purchase process (Sasmita & Mohd Suki, 2015). In turn, brands also help the customer achieve a degree of long-term commitment and loyalty (Aaker & Joachimsthaler, 2000). But the power of brands resides in the minds of consumers. Therefore, marketers must endeavor to design marketing strategies that successfully generate positive perceptions, feelings, beliefs, and opinions among consumers toward the brand (Hoeffler & Keller, 2002). Veloutsou and Delgado-Ballester (2018) define the brand as "an evolving mental collection of actual (offer related) and emotional (human-like) characteristics and associations which convey benefits of an offer identified through a symbol, or a collection of symbols, and differentiates this offer from the rest of the marketplace". Based on this definition, firms logically aspire to establish strong brands among their target audiences, given the advantages they provide in terms of marketing communications effectiveness and customer loyalty, and an increased ability to deal with crisis situations—in short, market power (Poulis & Wisker, 2016).

Viewed from this perspective, business managers must plan brand management with caution, since either overextension or lack of investment in the brand can lead to failure. Hence, it is important to manage the brand correctly in all strategic aspects to build brand equity. The brand management literature proposes that the brand equity model developed by Aaker (1991) and Keller (1993) is a useful tool for marketing managers to measure and evaluate overall consumer perceptions of brands. Ultimately, brand equity plays an essential role in firms' achievement of competitive advantage, by supporting business performance and increasing business value (Ahmad & Thyagaraj, 2014).

This chapter offers the reader a theoretical and updated vision of how brand equity works and its importance within brand management. We address the conceptual delimitation of the construct, from the classic proposals of Aaker (1991) and Keller (1993) to more contemporary ones (Yoo & Donthu, 2001; Rojas-Lamorena et al., 2022). Particular attention is paid to the analysis of the measurement of brand equity, as well as their dimensions and the academic attempts to develop a measurement scale. Finally, we dedicate a relevant section of the chapter to pointing out the challenges that remain to be investigated in relation to the brand equity, from its measurement from the customer's perspective to their main antecedents.

2. Conceptual definition of brand equity

Since the 1980s, brand equity has been a research topic that has generated significant interest in both academic and professional circles (Buil et al., 2008). However, although recognized as an essential concept for brand management, there remains a lack of consensus over its conceptual definition, the dimensions it encompasses, and how best to measure it (Keller, 2014).

Three major perspectives or research approaches associated with brand equity can be distinguished in the scientific literature: (1) the financial perspective; (2) the customer perspective; and (3) the combined perspective.

The financial perspective: Research associated with this approach centers on the analysis of brand equity from the point of view of financial markets, cash flow, or value added, and emphasizes the value of the brand to the firm (Pappu et al., 2005). Although the financial approach can provide a more accurate view of the valuation of a brand, it is not entirely useful for firms in terms of generating and implementing marketing strategies (Keller, 1993), since it disregards the brand-related cognitive and behavioral aspects of the customer. In the early 1990s, this gap gave rise to an interest in analyzing brand equity from the consumer's point of view.

The customer perspective is concerned with the relationship between customers, in a broad sense, and the brand (expressed in terms of customer-based brand equity or CBBE). This perspective relates to the value of a brand for the customer (Pappu et al., 2005), on the premise that a brand will generate value for the firm only when it generates value for that customer (Yoo & Donthu, 2001). This approach consequently evaluates the response of consumers, employees, or stakeholders, in general, to a given brand, based on the idea that strong brands are those that remain at the forefront of individuals' minds (Christodoulides et al., 2015).

The combined financial–customer perspective arose in response to the potential weaknesses of using just one interpretation in isolation (Kim & Kim, 2005). Among the studies taking this more 'global' approach is that of Dyson, Farr, and Hollis (1996), which was based on the design of surveys to measure the financial value linked to brand images and brand associations, according to consumer perceptions; or that of Motameni and Shahrokhi (1998), who proposed overall brand valuations that combine both perspectives by means of a global measurement model.

Several different approaches to defining brand equity have emerged from these perspectives. Among the definitions of brand equity from a financial perspective, the one proposed by Kapferer (2004) is worth mentioning: "The net cash flow attributable to the brand after paying the cost of capital invested to produce and run the business and the cost of marketing". There are far more definitions in the literature of brand equity from a customer perspective. For Aaker (1991) brand equity "creates value for the customer by enhancing their understanding of the brand and increasing their information-processing in relation to it, building confidence in the decision-making process and heightening satisfaction". Keller (1993) understands brand equity as "the differential effect of brand knowledge on consumer response to the marketing activity for that brand". A few years later Yoo and Donthu (2001) defined this concept as "the difference in consumer preference between a branded product and an otherwise identical unbranded product". Also, Christodoulides and de Chernatony (2010) propose that brand equity is "a set of perceptions, attitudes, knowledge, and behaviors on the part of consumers that results in increased utility and allows a brand to earn greater volume or greater margins than it could without the brand name". In short, brand equity is the incremental value added by a brand name to a product.

3. Review of academic research on brand equity. A bibliometric perspective

Academic research on brand equity, as an essential marketing topic and a valuable asset for firms, has grown notably since its origins in the late 1980s. Given the importance of this construct and the many theoretical and methodological contributions related to its conceptual definition, its measurement, and its management in multiple areas of knowledge, it calls for a deeper analysis than those conducted in the past. A bibliometric perspective can offer this more detailed understanding, providing a better understanding of the state-of-the-art in the discipline in question.

In this section, we take this bibliometric perspective to analyzing the published scientific output on the brand equity construct for 1990–2021. In this period, 3,047 articles indexed in the Web of Science (WoS) and Scopus databases were published, which include those publications with the greatest impact. Figure 4.1 shows that, in the first 15 years, research on this topic grew slowly. However, from 2005 onward, there was sustained growth in the volume of publications, crossing the threshold of 100 articles per year in 2008, and tripling that figure just 10 years later. As for the citations received by these works, we can observe how the early contributions stand out, supported by the work of Keller (1993) as a precursor to this concept, taking into account the absence of Aaker (1991) because it was not indexed in either of these databases for being a book.

The *Journal of Product and Brand Management* (151) and *Journal of Business Research* (115) stand out in particular as they also account for the highest number of citations both in WoS and Scopus. Keller figures as one of the most predominant researchers on this topic, in terms of number of publications and citations, since his article 'Conceptualizing, Measuring, and Managing Customer-based Brand Equity' (*Journal of Marketing*, 1993) has served as the basis for the vast majority of subsequent research, thanks to its proposal for the conceptualization and measurement of brand equity, as discussed above. Gil-Saura is the author with the most published works on the topic, although her research is more applied than theory-developing. Also, among the primary articles in terms of the most-cited in the scientific literature, we find the contributions of Yoo et al. (2000) and Yoo and Donthu (2001), with their analysis of the effect of the marketing mix on brand equity and their proposal for a multidimensional and a unidimensional measurement scale.

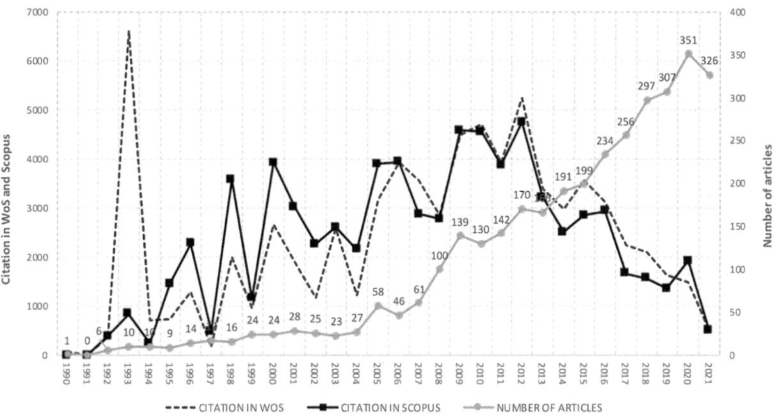

Figure 4.1 Evolution in the number of scientific articles about brand equity and citation (1990-2021)

The analysis of academic research around the concept of brand equity reveals its generalization in recent years and its application in different realms, especially in the tourism and hospitality fields, both of which represent major themes for academic research in the near future. This trend is verified by the results of a bibliographic coupling analysis, which reveals four clusters of publications. Cluster 1 comprises works that continue to focus on the conceptualization and measurement of the brand equity construct in different contexts, corroborating the lack of consensus on this topic despite its growing importance. Clusters 2 and 3 stand out, encompassing works on the tourism and hospitality contexts. Finally, Cluster 4 includes articles dealing with corporate variables and how they affect brand equity, its dimensions, and the consumer experience. The authors themselves in a paper recently published in the *Journal of Business Research* provide more details about how the clusters were created, how large are the clusters, and examples of articles in each cluster (Rojas-Lamorena et al., 2022).

4. Measuring customer-based brand equity

Identifying those dimensions that make up brand equity is a primary task for academics and marketing professionals alike (Buil et al., 2008). There is no absolute consensus on the best way to measure the concept of brand equity, with both one-dimensional and multidimensional models being applied. That said, most of the literature concurs on the multidimensional nature of the concept (Christodoulides et al., 2015), with the seminal works of Aaker (1991) and Keller (1993) being the most widely referenced contributions on this topic. However, there have also been studies that seek to approach the measurement of the brand equity concept from a one-dimensional and global perspective (Yoo & Donthu, 2001).

4.1 Aaker's model

In his book *Managing Brand Equity: Capitalizing on the Value of a Brand Name*, Aaker (1991) states that, while the assets and liabilities that constitute the foundation of brand equity can differ depending on the context, they can be grouped into five broad dimensions: (1) brand loyalty; (2) perceived quality; (3) brand associations; (4) brand awareness; and (5) market behavior measures. However, from a purely customer-based perspective, it comprises the first four elements only, with the fifth being related to financial aspects such as market share or price indices.

Brand loyalty is a core marketing concept and is defined as the special attachment that a customer has to a particular brand. Brand loyalty is a foundational dimension of brand equity that, unlike the other dimensions, requires prior purchase experience and use on the part of the consumer.

Perceived quality is defined as the consumer's judgment about a product's excellence or superiority regarding the function or purpose to be fulfilled, compared to possible substitutes. It is based, therefore, on customers' perceptions of the brand in relation to what matters to them. Consequently, perceived quality is not the objective quality of the product in terms of the absence of errors but, rather, a subjective assessment made by consumers (Su, 2016).

Brand associations refer to the knowledge about a given brand that is stored in the minds of consumers and can thus be both positive and negative. Such associations can deliver value to consumers that prompts them to purchase a given brand over its rivals due to the positive feelings it generates in them (Su, 2016).

Brand awareness refers to how potential consumers associate a certain brand—linking the logo, symbols, and other characteristics—with a specific product category. This dimension can affect consumers' perceptions and attitudes and is capable of motivating the choice of brand and, in turn, generating loyalty (Aaker, 1996).

4.2 Keller's model

Keller approached the study of brand equity from a cognitive psychology perspective (Christodoulides et al., 2015), defining it as the differential effect of brand knowledge on consumer responses to brand marketing actions (Keller, 1993). From this perspective, a brand's CBBE will be positive when customers react more favorably to the elements of the marketing mix for the brand in question than to the same marketing-mix elements attributed to a fictitiously named or unbranded version of the product or service (Keller, 1993).

As Keller (2014) notes, the brand knowledge that marketers create over time will set the brand's future direction, as it is on the basis of that knowledge that consumers will decide its future trajectory. Therefore, Keller's model considers brand knowledge to be the key to building brand equity, with brand awareness and brand image being the sources of that knowledge. Brand awareness is related to the strength of the brand in the consumer's memory, which enables them to identify it in different contexts. On the other hand, brand image is defined as the perceptions of a brand that are reflected in the brand associations held in consumer memory.

In more recent works, Keller (2014) proposes that the construction of CBBE occurs over time through four sequential, incremental stages: (1) Who are you? (brand identity); (2) What are you? (brand meaning); (3) What about you? (brand response); and (4) What about you and me? (brand relationships). These four stages are, in turn, reflected in what Keller terms the Brand Resonance Pyramid, which comprises six building blocks that contribute to brand-building, starting with identity (salience) at the base. Only those brands that reach the top of the pyramid achieve significant brand equity.

4.3 The Yoo and Donthu model

Yoo and Donthu (2001) define brand equity from a perspective similar to that of Aaker (1991) and Keller (1993): the difference in consumer preference between a branded product and an otherwise identical unbranded product when both have the same level of marketing stimuli and product attributes. These authors developed a multidimensional measure of CBBE that is easy to implement among consumers, aiming to provide a means of testing the brand equity models proposed by Aaker and Keller and to link a firm's brand equity to its brand performance. To do this, they took an etic approach to developing the scale—one that can be applied in all cultures simultaneously so that comparisons can be made between diverse contexts. This is in contrast to the more traditional (emic) approach, which is based on developing scales for one culture and subsequently validating them in others. To generate the scale, Yoo and Donthu (2001) drew on the component dimensions proposed by Aaker (1991) and Keller (1993): brand loyalty, perceived quality, brand awareness, and brand associations. Following the results of a field study among consumers from three cultures, however, they opted to merge the 'awareness' and 'associations' dimensions, ultimately proposing a rather parsimonious three-dimensional CBBE measurement model:

- Brand loyalty measurement: (1) I consider myself to be loyal to X; (2) X would be my first choice; and (3) I will not buy other brands if X is available at the store.
- Perceived quality measurement: (1) The likely quality of X is extremely high; and (2) the likelihood that X would be functional is very high.
- Brand awareness/associations measurement: (1) I can recognize X among other competing brands; (2) I am aware of X; (3) some characteristics of X come to my mind quickly; (4) I can quickly recall the symbol or logo of X; and (5) I have difficulty in imagining X in my mind.

Another interesting contribution of these authors to the academic literature on CBBE measurement is the unidimensional measure of overall brand equity that they developed, which comprises four items: (1) it makes sense to buy X instead of any other brand, even if they are the same; (2) even if another brand has the same features as X, I would prefer to buy X; (3) if there is another brand as good as X, I prefer to buy X; and (4) if another brand is not different from X in any way, it seems smarter to purchase X. This measure was subsequently examined by Frías-Jamilena et al. (2017), who verified that it had psychometric properties equivalent to the multidimensional measure. Due to its great parsimony, this overall measure has been used by various authors in recent years (Rodríguez-López et al., 2020; Zollo et al., 2020).

Table 4.1 summarizes the main studies from the brand equity literature that deal with the measurement of CBBE, detailing the dimensions they address, the nature of the measurement used, and the scope of each study.

Table 4.1 Summary of main studies dealing with brand equity conceptualization and measurement

Article	Dimensions	Measurement	Research field
Aaker (1991)	Brand awareness, perceived quality, brand associations, and brand loyalty	Conceptual paper	Brands in general
Keller (1993)	Brand awareness (recall and recognition), brand image (attributes, benefits, attitudes)	Conceptual paper	Brands in general
Kamakura & Russell (1993)	Perceived value, brand dominance, intangible value	Scanner data	Hotels
Park & Srinivasan (1994)	Attribute-based and non-attribute-based components	Conjoint analysis	Toothpaste and mouthwash
Yoo & Donthu (2001)	Brand loyalty, perceived quality, awareness/ associations	10-item scale + 4 items, Overall brand equity	Athletic shoes, camera film, and color TV sets
Ailawadi et al. (2003)	Revenue premium measure	Revenue premium measure over a private label product	Consumer packaged goods industry
Netemeyer et al. (2004)	Perceived quality, perceived value for the cost, uniqueness, and the willingness to pay a price premium	16 items	Fast-food restaurant, colas, pastes, jeans, shoes
Pappu et al. (2005)	Brand awareness, associations, perceived quality, and loyalty	13 items	Car and TV brands
Konecnik & Gartner (2007)	Awareness, image, quality, and loyalty	37 items	Destination: Slovenia

Article	Dimensions	Measurement	Research field
Buil et al. (2008)	Brand awareness, perceived quality, brand loyalty, brand associations (perceived value, brand personality, and organization)	21 items	Soft drinks, sportswear, cars, and consumer electronics
Nam et al. (2011)	Physical quality, staff behavior, ideal self-congruence, brand identification, and lifestyle-congruence	16 items	Hotel and restaurant industry
Spry et al. (2011)	Brand awareness, associations, loyalty, and perceived quality	Field experiment + questionnaire	Plasma TV and USB
Frías-Jamilena et al. (2017)	Destination brand awareness, brand quality, brand image, brand loyalty, brand value, and overall destination brand equity (ODBE)	19 items + 4 items ODBE	Destination
Sürücü et al. (2019)	Brand awareness, physical quality, staff behavior, brand image	15 items	Hotels

Source: The authors, adapted from Rojas-Lamorena et al. (2022).

5. A research agenda for customer-based brand equity

Having surveyed the conceptual definition and measurement of this essential indicator of business success (Tasci, 2021), together with its impact on academic research, in this section, we turn to the research topics that are currently being studied on the topic of brand equity and the possible research directions that can be developed in the coming years.

In light of the literature review, it can be concluded that the main concern of researchers dealing with brand equity has been how to measure this concept and its main dimensions. This interest reflects the lack of consensus regarding its conceptualization, dimensionality, and measurement.

As we saw earlier in the chapter, one of the most interesting proposals on how to develop and validate a multidimensional consumer-based brand equity scale was that of Yoo and Donthu (2001). Starting out from the conceptualizations of Aaker (1991) and Keller (1993), and taking an emic approach, the authors developed a dual measure of CBBE, comprising: (1) a multidimensional 10-item scale capturing the dimensions of brand loyalty, perceived quality, and brand awareness/associations; and (2) a one-dimensional four-item overall brand equity (OBE) scale, which is highly correlated with the previous one. Their work paved the way toward approaching the measurement of brand equity from the customer's perspective, above and beyond the various ad-hoc measures previously used by the literature, such as a scanner data-based measure (Kamakura & Russell, 1993), composite multi-attribute weighted scores of the brand name (Park & Srinivasan, 1994), or equalization price (Swait et al., 1993). It is important to highlight the important contribution to the scientific literature on marketing made by the unidimensional OBE scale, which was designed to be used by researchers working with complex models to analyze the antecedents and consequences of CBBE. Yet, despite this significant contribution, there remain certain questions about CBBE measurement that future research should address.

The first question is concerned with the dimensions that CBBE comprises. While later authors added new dimensions such as perceived brand value (Boo et al., 2009; Pike & Bianchi, 2016), future studies should investigate which is the best option for measuring CBBE in terms of parsimony and content validity. This issue should be brought to the attention of top marketing journals.

The second question that requires greater attention from the scholarship relates to the true validity of the OBE scale for capturing the different facets of a concept as complex as brand equity. Although Yoo and Donthu (2001) obtained good psychometric properties, and later authors such as Im et al. (2012) and Frías-Jamilena et al. (2017) have corroborated those results, further research should validate the measure using different types of products, such as services and industrial goods. Similarly, these studies should be extended to other areas and sectors and to other cultures and languages, in order to verify the universal validity of this proposed CBBE measure.

In addition to the conceptual definition of brand equity and its measurement, future research should direct its efforts toward examining the main drivers of this concept. While the academic literature has certainly made great strides in this direction, many issues still call for further clarity. Increasingly, studies endeavor to identify the antecedent variables that contribute to promoting CBBE-formation, albeit most of these works have been limited to variables based on the consumer's personal evaluations (e.g., self-congruity, satisfaction, value co-creation, credibility, behavioral intention, experience, motivations, and so on) and have centered on the tourism sector (e.g., Castañeda-García et al., 2020; Ferns & Walls, 2012; Frías-Jamilena et al., 2017; Frías et al., 2020; Prados-Peña & del Barrio-García, 2021; Rodríguez-López et al., 2020). In any study that deals with consumer behavior, it is important to bear in mind that such behavior is influenced not only by antecedent variables related to the subjective evaluations of the consumer but also by other external and contextual factors. These, too, must be taken into account. From the Service-Dominant Logic (SDL) perspective (Vargo & Lusch, 2011), the context of the consumer plays a fundamental role in studies dealing with marketing and consumer behavior. In this regard, looking to the future, researchers should pay more attention to those contextual factors that contribute to CBBE-formation. We will briefly mention a few of the factors that hold the greatest research potential.

First of all, the geographical factor—as highlighted by Vargo and Lusch (2016)—is a key element in promoting value co-creation. Furthermore, it is very useful in marketing as it helps to define segments of consumers presenting similar behaviors (Berry et al., 1991) and can encourage regular interaction between certain members of those segments (Shaw & Williams, 2009). Geographical proximity allows people to interact on a daily basis and share their brand experiences. For this reason, it may be of significant interest for future research to analyze the effect of the consumer's geographical environment on brand equity formation. The aim here would be to study the degree to which other consumers in the same geographical environment influence CBBE-formation. This type of study would require a spatial econometric model to be designed on the basis of a set of explanatory variables derived from the consumer's personal experience (self-congruity, motivations, credibility, and so on), thereby measuring the impact on the dependent variable (CBBE) in neighboring locations due to a change in the explanatory variable in location.

On the other hand, the marketing investment made by a brand is also another factor external to the consumer that can ultimately exert a major influence on the brand equity achieved—a factor that remains under-studied in the literature. It is known that an increase in communications spend (advertising, promotions, events, digital marketing and so on) delivers positive results in terms of brand performance. As early as 1993, Keller observed, from a theoretical perspective, that brand equity can be enhanced if a company is able to create a favorable consumer response to pricing, distribution, advertising, and promotional activity for a given brand. Therefore, we encourage future research to further study the effect that companies' implementation of pricing, distribution, and communication programs, especially those related to digital marketing, will have on customer brand equity formation. It is also necessary in our view to call for research on social media influencers and their role in brand equity formation. Such an investigation will provide a comprehensive understanding of how influencers' brand equity can be enhanced.

Meanwhile, the effect of the corporate reputation of the brand on CBBE-formation is not well addressed in the extant literature (Davcik, 2013). The fact that a brand enjoys a good reputation could be interpreted by the consumer as a signal that increases its perceived quality, its perceived value, and, by extension, the brand equity. At the same time, other authors have postulated that one of the main benefits delivered by brand equity is the superior corporate reputation it can lend to the firm. We encourage scholars to undertake research to clarify under what circumstances corporate reputation influences brand equity and under what conditions the reciprocal relationship occurs, to help achieve a better understanding of this reciprocal relationship.

Among the factors external to the consumer that have acquired special relevance for marketing in recent times, it is worth highlighting authenticity, be it of the product or the service offered to the consumer (Kovács et al., 2017). The stronger the authenticity of a product/service, the more consumers are likely to defend it and the higher the level of equity it will generate, compared to rival brands (Beverland, 2009). The mechanism by which authenticity influences CBBE can be explained using the extended stimulus–organism–response (SOR) model, that comprises a stimulus (authentic experience), process (cognitive and affective response), and output (brand equity). Previous studies have examined the antecedent role of authenticity in certain component dimensions of CBBE (brand image, brand loyalty, and brand quality) but further research is needed to help better understand the mechanism by which CBBE is formed according to different levels of authenticity, in different types of products and services, and in different fields of study.

Finally, future research should examine how the current social environment as a result of COVID-19, supply chain disruptions, and inflation have affected customer-based brand equity formation, particularly in the services sector.

References

Aaker, D. A. (1991). *Managing Brand Equity: Capitalizing on the Value of a Brand Name*. New York: The Free Press.

Aaker, D. A. (1996). Measuring brand equity across products and markets. *California Management Review, 38*(3), 102–120.

Aaker, D. A., & Joachimsthaler, E. (2000). The brand relationship spectrum: The key to the brand architecture challenge. *California Management Review, 42*(4), 8–23.

Ahmad, A., & Thyagaraj, K. S. (2014). Brand personality and brand equity research: Past developments and future directions. *The IUP Journal of Brand Management, 11*(3), 19–56.

Ailawadi, K. L., Lehmann, D. R., & Neslin, S. A. (2003). Revenue premium as an outcome measure of brand equity. *Journal of Marketing, 67*(4), 1–17.

Berry, L. L., Parasuraman, A., & Zeithaml, V. A. (1991). *Quality Service*. New York: The Free Press.

Beverland, M. B. (2009). *Building Brand Authenticity: 7 Habits of Iconic Brands*. Basingstoke: Palgrave Macmillan.

Boo, S., Busser, J., & Baloglu, S. (2009). A model of customer-based brand equity and its application to multiple destinations. *Tourism Management, 30*(2), 219–231.

Buil, I., de Chernatony, L., & Martínez, E. (2008). A cross-national validation of the consumer-based brand equity scale. *Journal of Product & Brand Management, 17*(6), 384–392.

Castañeda-García, J. A., Frías-Jamilena, D. M., del Barrio-García, S., & Rodríguez-Molina, M. A. (2020). The effect of message consistency and destination-positioning brand strategy type on consumer-based destination brand equity. *Journal of Travel Research, 59*(8), 1447–1463.

Christodoulides, D., Cadogan, J. W., & Veloutsou, C. (2015). Consumer-based brand equity measurement: Lessons learned from an international study. *International Marketing Review, 32*(3/4), 307–328.

Christodoulides, G., & de Chernatony, L. (2010). Consumer-based brand equity conceptualisation and measurement. *International Journal of Market Research, 52*(1), 43–66.

Davcik, N. (2013). An empirical investigation of brand equity: Drivers and their consequences. *British Food Journal, 115*(9), 1342–1360.

Dyson, P., Farr, A., & Hollis, N. (1996). Understanding, measuring, and using brand equity. *Journal of Advertising Research, 36*(6), 9–21.

Ferns, B. H., & Walls, W. (2012). Enduring travel involvement, destination brand equity, and travelers' visit intentions: A structural model analysis. *Journal of Destination Marketing and Management, 1*, 27–35.

Frías, D. M., Castaneda, J. A., del Barrio-García, S., & Lopez-Moreno, L. (2020). The effect of self-congruity and motivation on consumer-based destination brand equity. *Journal of Vacation Marketing, 26*(3), 287–304.

Frías-Jamilena, D. M., Polo-Peña, A. I., & Rodríguez-Molina, M. Á. (2017). The effect of value-creation on consumer-based destination brand equity. *Journal of Travel Research, 56*(8), 1011–1031.

Hoeffler, S., & Keller, K. L. (2002). Building brand equity through corporate societal marketing. *Journal of Public Policy & Marketing, 21*(1), 78–89.

Im, H. H., Kim, S. S., Elliot, S., & Han, H. (2012). Conceptualizing destination brand equity dimensions from a consumer-based brand equity perspective. *Journal of Travel & Tourism Marketing, 29*(4), 385–403.
Kamakura, W. A., & Russell, G. J. (1993). Measuring brand value with scanner data. *International Journal of Research in Marketing, 10*(1), 9–22.
Kapferer, J. N. (2004). *The New Strategic Brand Management: Creating and Sustaining Brand Equity Long Term.* London: Kogan Page.
Keller, K. L. (1993). Conceptualizing, measuring, and managing customer-based brand equity. *Journal of Marketing, 57*(1), 1–22.
Keller, K. L. (2014). *Strategic Brand Management: Building, Measuring, and Managing Brand Equity* (4th edn). Upper Saddle River, NJ: Prentice Hall.
Kim, H. B., & Kim, W. G. (2005). The relationship between brand equity and firms' performance in luxury hotels and chain restaurants. *Tourism Management, 26*(4), 549–560.
Konecnik, M., & Gartner, W. C. (2007). Customer-based brand equity for a destination. *Annals of Tourism Research, 34*(2), 400–421.
Kovács, B., Carroll, G. R., & Lehman, D. W. (2017). The perils of proclaiming an authentic organizational identity. *Sociological Science, 4*(3), 80–106.
Motameni, R., & Shahrokhi, M. (1998). Brand equity valuation: A global perspective. *Journal of Product & Brand Management, 7*(4), 275–290.
Nam, J., Ekinci, Y., & Whyatt, G. (2011). Brand equity, brand loyalty and consumer satisfaction. *Annals of Tourism Research, 38*(3), 1009–1030.
Netemeyer, R. G., Krishnan, B., Pullig, C., Wang, G., Yagci, M., Dean, D., ... and Wirth, F. (2004). Developing and validating measures of facets of customer-based brand equity. *Journal of Business Research, 57*(2), 209–224.
Pappu, R., Quester, P., & Cooksey, R. (2005). Consumer-based brand equity: Improving the measurement – empirical evidence. *Journal of Product & Brand Management, 14*(3), 143–154.
Park, C. S., & Srinivasan, V. (1994). A survey-based method for measuring and understanding brand equity and its extendibility. *Journal of Marketing Research, 31*(2), 271–288.
Pike, S., & Bianchi, C. (2016). Destination brand equity for Australia: Testing a model of CBBE in short-haul and long-haul markets. *Journal of Hospitality & Tourism Research, 40*(1), 114–134.
Poulis, A., & Wisker, Z. (2016). Modeling employee-based brand equity (EBBE) and perceived environmental uncertainty (PEU) on a firm's performance. *Journal of Product and Brand Management, 25*(5), 490–503.
Prados-Peña, M. B., & del Barrio-García, S. (2021). Key antecedents of brand equity in heritage brand extensions: The moderating role of tourist heritage experience. *European Research on Management and Business Economics, 27*(3), 100153.
Rodríguez-López, M. E., del Barrio-García, S., & Alcántara-Pilar, J. M. (2020) Formation of customer-based brand equity via authenticity. *International Journal of Contemporary Hospitality Management, 32*(2), 815–834.
Rojas-Lamorena, Á. J., del Barrio-García, S., & Alcántara-Pilar, J. M. (2022). A review of three decades of academic research on brand equity: A bibliometric approach using co-word analysis and bibliographic coupling. *Journal of Business Research, 139*, 1067–1083.
Sasmita, J., & Mohd Suki, N. (2015). Young consumers' insights on brand equity. *International Journal of Retail & Distribution Management, 43*(3), 276–292.

Shaw, G., & Williams, A. M. (2009). Knowledge transfer and management in tourism organisations: An emerging research agenda. *Tourism Management, 30*(3), 325–335.

Spry, A., Pappu, R., & Cornwell, T. B. (2011). Celebrity endorsement, brand credibility and brand equity. *European Journal of Marketing, 45*(6), 882–909.

Su, J. (2016). Examining the relationships among the brand equity dimensions: Empirical evidence from fast fashion. *Asia Pacific Journal of Marketing and Logistics, 28*(3), 464–480.

Sürücü, Ö., Öztürk, Y., Okumus, F., & Bilgihan, A. (2019). Brand awareness, image, physical quality and employee behavior as building blocks of customer-based brand equity: Consequences in the hotel context. *Journal of Hospitality and Tourism Management, 40*, 114–124.

Swait, J., Erdem, T., Louviere, J., & Dubelaar, C. (1993). The equalization price: A measure of consumer-perceived brand equity. *International Journal of Research in Marketing, 10*(1), 23–45.

Tasci, A. D. (2021). A critical review and reconstruction of perceptual brand equity. *International Journal of Contemporary Hospitality Management, 33*(1), 166–198.

Vargo, S. L., & Lusch, R. F. (2011). It's all B2B … and beyond: Toward a systems perspective of the market. *Industrial Marketing Management, 40*(2), 181–187.

Vargo, S. L., & Lusch, R. F. (2016). Institutions and axioms: An extension and update of service-dominant logic. *Journal of the Academy of Marketing Science, 44*(1), 5–23.

Veloutsou, C., & Delgado-Ballester, E. (2018). New challenges in brand management. *Spanish Journal of Marketing-ESIC, 22*(3), 254–271.

Yoo, B., & Donthu, N. (2001). Developing and validating a multidimensional consumer-based brand equity scale. *Journal of Business Research, 52*(1), 1–14.

Yoo, B., Donthu, N., & Lee, S. (2000). An examination of selected marketing mix elements and brand equity. *Journal of the Academy of Marketing Science, 28*(2), 195–211.

Zollo, L., Filieri, R., Rialti, R., & Yoon, S. (2020). Unpacking the relationship between social media marketing and brand equity: The mediating role of consumers' benefits and experience. *Journal of Business Research, 117*, 256–267.

5 Brand value co-creation: field emergence, applications, measurement and future research directions

Michela Mingione and Samuel Kristal

1. Scope and purpose

At the beginning of the third millennium the brand domain has dealt with an important new phenomenon that shifts brand management and branding from a unilateral and managerially controlled creation of value towards a new brand logic, where brands co-create value with their customers (Prahalad & Ramaswamy, 2000; Vargo & Lusch, 2004).

The scope of this chapter is to provide an overview of what brand value co-creation is, what are its fields of applications, how it can be measured, what are the outcomes that can be achieved when brands apply value co-creation strategies and actions, and what are the potential avenues for future research. In particular, the chapter begins by outlining how and when the field of brand value co-creation has emerged, followed by a narrative that defines the construct, along with the fundamentals related to how co-created brand value is built and managed. Then, the main fields of brand co-creation research and practice are outlined. Specifically, this chapter presents traditional fields of application (i.e., business-to-consumer and business-to-business contexts), which represent the status quo of research. Then, it continues by pointing to new fields of application (i.e., emotional brand value; brand alignment; non-collaborative behaviour of co-creators), which provide a valuable starting point for further work. Afterwards, measurement and outcomes are discussed with the purpose to present validated constructs and established results. Finally, directions for future research are suggested. New leadership styles, new managerial models, performance indicators (qualitative and quantitative) and brand value co-creation facilitators (artificial and non-artificial, digital and face-to-face) constitute, amongst the others, worthwhile directions for further research.

2. Field emergence and definition

The new paradigm of brand value co-creation finds its roots in Service-Dominant (S-D) logic. By combining the views of various authors, Mingione and Leoni (2020, p. 74) define the process of value co-creation as "the interactions between the firm and customers, which involve dialogue and integration of resources and capabilities, resulting in mutual beneficial outcomes".

In the context of the branding stream of research, the brand interacts daily with customers (Hatch & Schultz, 2010) and a vast plethora of stakeholders (e.g., employees, suppliers, distributors, governments, NGOs) continuously contributing to its overall value (Kristal et al., 2018, 2020; Ramaswamy, 2022). This approach is reflected in the Organic View of the Brand, which conceives the brand as an organic entity whose value is co-created with its stakeholders in a fluid space, where diverse actors meet, interact and influence the meaning of the brand (Iglesias et al., 2013). Brand managers are no longer in a position to control stakeholders' sense-giving and sense-making of the brand, thus challenging traditional perspectives on brand management (Vallaster & von Wallpach, 2013). It is important to highlight that these considerations do not impede management's contribution to the brand value co-creation process (Mingione et al., 2020a). Instead, managers are called to carefully create, manage and maintain dialogue and connections over time by designing encounters to leverage interactions between the brand and its stakeholders (Merz et al., 2018; Payne et al., 2009). Specifically, in order to successfully co-create, interactions should be participatory and engaging (Hatch & Schultz, 2010; Ind, 2014; Mingione & Leoni, 2020; Nardi et al., 2020). To summarise, it is not a matter of managerial control, but managerial persuasion (Vallaster & von Wallpach, 2013) supported by a high degree of openness and transparency (Hatch & Schultz, 2010), along with a more participatory leadership style (Ind et al., 2013).

In this framework, adopting a corporate marketing perspective fits perfectly with the essence inherent to the new brand paradigm (Iglesias et al., 2022), because it typically refers to the interplay between multiple and interconnected actors (Balmer, 2012; Iglesias et al., 2013). In fact, the corporate brand typically deals with multiple stakeholders, which represents one of the main characteristics differentiating corporate brands from product brands (Greyser & Urde, 2019).

3. Traditional fields of applications

3.1 Brand value co-creation with consumers with a specific focus on brand communities

Consumers appear strongly empowered by the recent rise of new technologies and web-based platforms such as social media (Le et al., 2022). In particular, consumers can take polarised stands and co-create value by acting, for instance, as brand ambassadors (Hatch & Schultz, 2010; Mingione & Abratt, 2020), but also co-destroying brand value, for example by altering the managerial-desired meaning of the brand (Kristal et al., 2018).

In this context, brand communities and their members play an active role in the value co-creation process (Cova & Pace, 2006; Veloutsou & Black, 2020). Within a 'brand community' (Muniz & O'Guinn, 2001) consumers autonomously co-create meaning for the brand. Specifically, symbolic interpretations of brand-related information plus personal narratives based on both personal and impersonal experiences with a brand make a key contribution to co-created branding (Muniz & O'Guinn, 2001). Through digitalisation consumers have not only become increasingly empowered to interrelate with other consumers and with brands, but also to generate and share their own content, which has in turn led to a more participative approach to branding. In particular, online brand communities have recently gained major importance given the endless opportunities of social interactions offered by web-based technologies and platforms (Hajli et al., 2017). Successfully co-creating value with online brand communities can lead to a number of outcomes, such as brand loyalty (Hajli et al., 2017), quality of the relationship (Hajli et al., 2017; Haverila et al., 2022), brand engagement (Chapman & Dilmperi, 2022; Haverila et al., 2022) and innovation (Ind et al., 2012). Referring to the latter, community members can also co-design products, such as in the case of the LEGO community (Hatch & Schultz, 2010).

3.2 Brand value co-creation in business-to-business

The existing base of research on brand value co-creation is dominated by a strong focus on B2C (business-to-consumer) settings, whereas the B2B (business-to-business) field is comparatively underexplored. This lack of attention seems surprising when considering three factors. First, the field of industrial branding is distinctly richer in interactions between a variety of stakeholders and, thereby, exceeds the company–customer duality that is prevalent in B2C (Kotler & Pfoertsch, 2007). Second, one essential factor in brand co-creation is the 'organisation' of co-creators into networks or ecosystems in which the ongoing negotiations take place (Kornum et al., 2017; Vallaster & von Wallpach, 2013), discussion of which is dominant in B2B and lies in its nature. Lastly, a consequence of the focus on B2C is that the bulk of research on co-creation is concerned with product brands. However, there is also the notion that involving many different stakeholders in branding seems especially relevant to corporate branding (e.g., Balmer, 2012), which is often of the utmost importance in B2B marketing. Preliminary deliberations in B2B brand value co-creation indicate that a (corporate) brand identity stems from the company's founders or top management, but ultimately has to be seen as a temporary outcome of a dynamic multistakeholder co-creation process (Iglesias et al., 2020; Kristal et al., 2020; Törmälä & Gyrd-Jones, 2017). Once the brand is exposed to stakeholders, it is in constant flux and stakeholders continuously reinterpret the brand's meaning. However, before brand meaning can be co-created, (1) its management needs to be professionalised, (2) brand values need to be internalised into the minds of all employees and (3) brand managers might need to change their leadership style of deciding and commanding into listening and participating. Hence, essential prerequisites of readiness for brand co-creation are a stabilisation of brand management and (corporate) brand orientation (Kristal et al., 2020).

4. New fields of application

4.1 Emotional brand value

Beyond cognitive-related factors, emotions represent an important dimension to be considered in the co-creation paradigm, as positive and negative emotions can act as key drivers for successful or failed brand value co-creation, respectively (Mingione et al., 2020b). In particular, positive emotions stem from: emotional bonding and ties with the brand (Asmussen et al., 2013), emotional engagement (Merrilees, 2016; Payne et al., 2009), passion for the brand (Essamri et al., 2019; Merz et al., 2018), and authentic empowerment (Cova & Pace, 2006). It is, thus, remarkable to note the paucity of consideration of the experiential side of brand communities (Muniz & O'Guinn, 2001) and online brand communities (Chapman & Dilmperi, 2022), given members' participation is strongly motivated by the positive emotions they feel when joining a community (Mingione & Abratt, 2020; Mingione et al., 2020b). Despite the evident role of emotions in the brand value co-creation paradigm, authors have cited emotions only in passing, without giving them prominence. For instance, France et al. (2020) found that two specific typologies of co-creation (i.e., co-creation development and co-creation advocacy) positively influence the perceived emotional value of the brand. To the best of the authors' knowledge, the work of Mingione et al. (2020b, p. 311) is pioneering in defining and measuring the co-created emotional value of the brand, which can be conceived as an "experiential (emotional-based) source of the brand value generated during brand–consumer interactions".

4.2 Corporate brand alignment

By taking a meta-paradigmatic approach, which merges opposite philosophical views (i.e., functionalist vs. interpretivist), corporate brand alignment has been defined as a "strategic enabler to develop a more coherent and elucidated representation of multiple corporate brand symbolisms" (Mingione & Abratt, 2022, p. 157). In particular, corporate brand alignment represents a strategic driver to successfully co-create brand value across a multiplicity of stakeholders, such as in the case of the business-to-business-to-consumer (B2B2C) marketplace (Mingione & Leoni, 2020). When stakeholders converge towards an aligned aim, they can co-create a value that goes beyond the singular interest of each stakeholder (Mingione & Abratt, 2022; Mingione & Leoni, 2020). Hence, the creation and management of a symbolic common ground is key to achieve a fruitful collaboration amongst internal and external stakeholders. Remarkably, the presence of an aligned strategic vision can also lead to cooperation between competitors, who collaborate to achieve a "higher" aim (Mingione & Leoni, 2020, p. 87). For instance, to accomplish relevant goals such as integrity and transparency, competitors of the global financial industry collaborate by joining projects and initiatives driven by the same specific purpose, namely the "fight against cash" (Mingione & Leoni, 2020, p. 87). In doing so, stakeholders actively work together to "achieve mutual outcomes and to co-create long-term value" (Mingione & Abratt, 2022, p. 163). Hence, alignment also plays a critical role in the building and management of conscientious corporate brands (Mingione & Abratt, 2022; Rindell et al., 2011). In fact, these are driven by purpose-led objectives calling for broader responsibilities within a long-term view (Iglesias & Ind, 2020; Ind & Horlings, 2016) and which aim at creating shared value amongst stakeholders (Edmans, 2020). In this context, the Earth emerges as an additional and relevant stakeholder to be served and preserved (Iglesias & Ind, 2020).

4.3 Non-collaborative brand value co-creation

The involvement of consumers in co-creation processes around branding entails the risk of negative forms of engagement (Greer, 2015). It has, in fact, been argued that such negative relationships with brands are even more common than the positive alternative, and that value co-creation is strongly driven by risk (Fournier & Alvarez, 2013). As shown by research, brand value co-creation can mean that companies lose control over the brand's meaning (Kristal et al., 2018). Commercial interests of the organisation can come into conflict with the intrinsic motivations of consumers and other stakeholders who may push the brand in unwanted directions (Ind, 2014). Instead of acting as valuable contributors, co-creators could misuse their empowerment by behaving in a non-collaborative way (Kristal et al., 2018). Existing literature and real-life cases suggest that non-collaborative co-creators may either playfully parody brands or express negative emotions they feel towards the brand (Hegner et al., 2017; Zarantonello et al., 2016), with the danger that altered brand meanings can start to compete with those initially created by brand managers (Cova & D'Antone, 2016). An inconsistency could, thus, emerge between initial brand beliefs and the distorted brand and consumers might revise their initial brand value evaluation towards the non-collaborative co-creation. In such a situation, brand value is collaboratively co-destroyed, which presents a serious threat to a brand and its equity (Kristal et al., 2018).

5. Measurement and outcomes

The field of research on brand value co-creation cannot yet be considered mature, but certainly it can be conceived as an established paradigm (please see the following reviews on value co-creation and brand value co-creation, Ranjan & Read, 2016, Sarasvuo et al., 2022, respectively). It can be considered thereafter as shifting from a nascent state to an intermediate state of research that also makes use of quantitative methodologies, aside from qualitative ones and conceptual studies (Edmondson & McManus, 2007). Accordingly, scholars only recently provided scales to measure brand value co-creation, specifically by considering the customer perspective (France et al., 2018, 2020; Merz et al., 2018). Moreover, by focusing on the impact brand value co-creation may have on consumers' and employees' engagement, Seifert and Kwon (2020) and Hsieh and Chang (2016) provided additional scales. Tables 5.1 and 5.2 report the highlighted measurements.

Table 5.1 Customer-based brand co-creation scales

Customer brand co-creation behaviour (CBCB) (France et al., 2018, 2020)	
Development	I take photos of myself with the brand and share them with the brand and others
	I create advertising for the brand and share it with the brand and others
	I develop new products or services for the brand
	I create online content about the brand
	I develop ideas for the brand (e.g., when participating in competitions)
Feedback	When I have a positive brand experience, I provide them feedback
	I provide useful ideas on how to improve the brand
	If I notice a problem with the brand, I tell an employee, even if it doesn't affect me
	I tell the brand my ideas for improvement
Advocacy	I recommend the brand to others
	I say positive things about the brand to others
	I spread the good word about the brand
	I encourage my friends and relatives to use the brand
Helping	I help other customers of the brand if they seem to have problems
	I give advice to other customers about the brand
	I tell others about new things with the brand
Customer co-creation value (CCCV) scale (Merz et al., 2018)	
Customer-owned resources	
Knowledge	I am informed about what this brand has to offer
	I am knowledgeable about this brand
	I am an expert of this brand
Skills	I think analytically when I deal with this brand
	I think logically when I deal with this brand
	I think critically when I deal with this brand

Creativity	I become imaginative when I interact with this brand
	I become creative when I interact with this brand
	I become curious when I interact with this brand
Connectedness	I am networked with other consumers of this brand
	I am connected to other consumers of this brand
	I belong to one or more brand communities related to this brand
	I socialise with other consumers of this brand
Customer motivation	
Passion	I am addicted to this brand
	I am a fan of this brand
	I love this brand
	I admire this brand
Trustworthiness	I trust this brand
	This brand addresses my concerns honestly
	I rely on this brand when I have a problem
	I depend on this brand to satisfy my needs
Commitment	My goal is to make this brand a success
	I am driven to make this brand a success
	I am committed to making this brand a success
	I am enthusiastic about making this brand a success

Table 5.2 Brand value co-creation engagement scales

Value co-creation engagement (Seifert & Kwon, 2020)	
Value co-creation engagement behaviour	I have recommended the brand to others on SNSs (Social Network Sites)
	Through SNSs, I have encouraged friends and family to use this brand
	When I had a useful idea to improve the brand, I have let the brand know through SNSs
	When I had a good experience with the brand, I have commented about it on SNSs
	When I experienced a problem, I have let the brand know about it, through SNSs
	On SNSs, I have assisted other people if they need my help about the brand
	On SNSs, I have helped other people if they seem to have problems with the brand
	On SNSs, I have taught other people to use the brand correctly
	On SNSs, I have given advice to other people about the brand
	Through SNSs, I have asked others for information on what the brand offers
	Through SNSs, I have said what I wanted the brand to do
	Through SNSs, I have given the brand my information
	Through SNSs, I have provided necessary information so that the brand could perform its duties
	Through SNSs, I have answered the brand's product- or service-related questions
Value co-creation engagement attitude	I have been friendly to the brand on SNSs
	I have been kind to the brand on SNSs
	I have been polite to the brand on SNSs
	I have been courteous to the brand on SNSs

Brand co-creation engagement (Hsieh & Chang, 2016)	
Vigour	When I work on the task for the brand contest, I feel bursting with energy
	At my work I always persevere, even when things do not go well
	I can continue working on the task for the brand contest for very long periods of time
	I am very resilient mentally when working on the task for the brand contest
Dedication	To me, my task in the brand contest is challenging
	My task in the brand contest inspires me
	I am proud of the things that I do in the brand contest
	I find the task that I do in the brand contest is full of meaning and purpose
Absorption	When I am working on the task for the brand contest, I forget everything else around me
	Time flies when I am working on the task for the brand contest
	I get carried away when I am working on the task
	I feel happy when I am working intensely on the task for the brand contest

Two main considerations stem from observing the scales. First, brand value co-creation is always measured as a higher-order multidimensional construct, which is delineated in different ways depending on the authors' perspective. For instance, whilst France et al. (2018, 2020) include the themes of development, feedback, advocacy and help, Merz et al. (2018) divide the customer co-creation value scale into customer-owned resources, which considers knowledge, creativity, skills and connectedness and also customer motivation, which reflects customers' passion, trustworthiness and commitment. Similarly, scholars concentrating on brand value co-creation engagement examined behavioural and attitudinal themes (Seifert & Kwon, 2020), as well as scrutinised brand co-creation engagement as a secondary-order construct stemming from consumers' vigour, dedication and absorption (Hsieh & Chang, 2016). Second, all measurements shed light on the active and participative role of stakeholders in the creation of the brand value (Hatch & Schultz, 2010; Iglesias et al., 2013; Ind, 2014; Mingione & Leoni, 2020). This is reflected by functional-related (i.e., cognitive) themes, such as knowledge, skills and feedback, and by emotional-based themes, examining, for instance, stakeholders' connectedness, passion and vigour, further remarking on the key role of emotions in the brand value co-creation process (please see Section 3.1). For instance, positive and negative sentiments have been found to predict brand value co-creation engagement behaviour and value co-creation engagement attitude (Seifert & Kwon, 2020). Moreover, Mingione et al. (2020b) provided a specific measurement (i.e., the Emotional Co-Creation Score) of the co-created emotional value of the brand based on a netnographic sentiment analysis of 7,605 brand-users' interactions retrieved from 18 brand-owned profiles on Twitter.

In general, brand value co-creation finds its main outcomes in creating, managing and maintaining a strong, authentic and possibly unique relationship between the brand and its stakeholders (Hatch & Schultz, 2010; Iglesias et al., 2013). In particular, scholars have highlighted a number of potential outcomes: customer purchase intention (Choi et al., 2016; Merz et al., 2018; Seifert & Kwon, 2020); increased perceived value of the brand (France et al., 2018); customer enjoyment (Ind et al., 2020); brand engagement (Hsieh & Chang, 2016); customers' feedback and help intention (Merz et al., 2018); willingness to pay a premium price (Merz et al., 2018); and word of mouth (Merz et al., 2018). The work by France et al. (2020) observed that brand value co-creation has positive consequences on four specific typologies of customer-based brand value. Specifically, it positively affects quality value, financial value (i.e., functional-based value related to the value ascribed by customers to quality excellence and to money, respectively), emotional value, and social value (i.e., feeling-based and relational-based value).

Finally, it is important to highlight the construct of observer-based brand equity (OBBE), which was developed in the context of investigating the effect of co-creation on the perceptions of brand equity held by consumers who are observers rather than participants in the process of brand value co-creation (Kristal et al., 2016). The scales to be applied to the measurement of OBBE (Table 5.3) combine three of Aaker's (1996) dimensions (brand awareness, brand associations, perceived quality) with three others (innovation, differentiation, relevance) of Lehmann et al. (2008). The total set of measures incorporates 11 different items derived from well-established scales previously used to measure consumer-based brand equity (Atilgan et al., 2005; Bravo Gil et al., 2007; Lehmann et al., 2008; Yoo & Donthu, 2001).

Table 5.3 Scales for the measurement of observer-based brand equity (OBBE)

Theme	Item(s)	Source(s)
Brand awareness	I can recognise brand X among other competing brands.	Yoo and Donthu (2001)
		Atilgan et al. (2005)
		Bravo Gil et al. (2007)
Brand associations	Some characteristics of brand X come to my mind quickly.	Yoo and Donthu (2001)
		Atilgan et al. (2005)
	I can quickly recall the symbol or logo of brand X.	Bravo Gil et al. (2007)
Perceived quality	Brand X is good quality.	Atilgan et al. (2005)
	Brand X performs well.	Lehmann et al. (2008)
Innovation	Brand X is innovative.	Lehmann et al. (2008)
	Brand X constantly improves its products.	
Differentiation	Brand X stands out from its competitors.	Lehmann et al. (2008)
	Brand X is in a class by itself.	
Relevance	Brand X is relevant to me.	Lehmann et al. (2008)
	Brand X fits my lifestyle.	

Kristal et al. (2016) found that in contrast to the typically positive tenor in studies of brand co-creation that mostly relate to participating consumers, co-creation does not confer any noticeable benefit on the OBBE. The temptation to blindly transfer the positive influence of co-creation on participants' brand equity to that of observers has to be challenged. Instead of focusing on the communication of the user-designed product that is the result of co-creation, managers should plan to increase the number of participants in co-creation, so as to improve the overall level of consumer-based brand equity.

6. Challenges and future research directions

Managers nowadays face diverse challenges in order to transform brand value co-creation into a strategic and day-to-day practice and not a rhetorically based one (Biraghi & Gambetti, 2017; Ind et al., 2017). This relevant shift requires diverse lines of additional research.

First, managers would be well advised to adapt their management and leadership styles. One based on deciding and commanding would oppose the idea of value co-creation, which requires managers to become humbler, to listen and to participate (Iglesias et al., 2013). There is, therefore, a further need for research to foster understanding of the 'new' role and skillset of brand managers to embrace co-creation. Also, the question arises: how can brand managers control brand co-creation and measure its effectiveness? Despite the inevitability of some loss of control over brand meaning when co-creation takes place, managers are not consequently absolved from the need to apply key performance indicators. Future research could usefully make a contribution to that end by developing a control tool plus concrete performance indicators exclusively relating to brand co-creation.

Second, future research could provide more details on brand value co-creation facilitators. For instance, scholars are called to further investigate the role of emotional drivers, along with the understanding of how to activate positive emotions that stimulate a participatory relationship. Moreover, given the presence of machine learning and artificial intelligence-based tools, there is the need to understand their role in the value co-creation process. Is it possible to co-create functional and/or emotional brand value by using AI tools? How can they facilitate co-creation?

Third, given the potential mismatch between rhetoric and day-to-day practice (Biraghi & Gambetti, 2017), and the risks associated with decoupling and the consequential negative effects it may have on stakeholders' perceptions (Maon et al., 2021; Vredenburg et al., 2020), important further insights could be derived from additional research into how brand value co-creation could be developed in an authentic manner. In particular, scholars are called to thoroughly investigate if corporations really understand the importance of strategic alignment, which views all the stakeholders as belonging to the corporate ecosystem, including competitors, and collaborating towards an aligned vision (Mingione & Leoni, 2020). Accordingly, do managers authentically understand the mutuality of a higher and purpose-led aim? How do they transform their strategies into day-to-day practice?

Fourth, the study of Kristal et al. (2020) on B2B brand co-creation suggests that before the host company was prepared to open its brand to co-creation, two stages of brand development had been necessary: to achieve the professionalisation of brand management; and a brand orientation. However, it remains unclear whether those two preliminary stages are a general 'must-have' or even a formula for success, when brands aim to interconnect with stakeholders. Future research might usefully follow up on that lack of clarity by investigating more brands in a wider range of settings and contexts. If such studies were to find that the brand was strengthened by, first, a solid basis achieved by professionalising brand management and, second, the integration of brands and branding into the daily mindsets of all employees (that is, 'brand orientation') and third, the elasticity necessary for co-creation, the following implication would arise: though the brand co-creation paradigm challenges other dominant concepts in brand management, such as identity-based approaches or brand orientation, they are not necessarily contradictory to it. Hence, the question would not be 'either/or' but rather how to connect the paradigms with one another in order to have a clear internal approach to brand building, while at the same time allowing for external inputs to be integrated and co-created.

Finally, and linked to the above, one additional key challenge in brand value co-creation is concerned with the integration of all participants into a new model of brand management. There is, to date, no universal framework capturing the brand co-creation paradigm that respects the network-like structure, the heterogeneity of the participants in brand creation and the low controllability of the process. Future research effort by scholars and practitioners is called for towards the development of an appropriate framework. It will need to provide clear management-oriented guidelines, a set of steps aimed at showing how to institutionalise and maintain co-creator networks and concrete performance indicators exclusively relating to brand value co-creation. Accordingly, scholars are further called to provide quantitative measures considering the vast number of stakeholders participating in the co-creation of brand value. Hence, beyond customers (France et al., 2018, 2020; Merz et al., 2018; Seifert & Kwon, 2020) and employees (Hsieh & Chang, 2016), it would be timely and salient for researchers to include more criteria in their brand value co-creation scales, such as additional stakeholders, namely suppliers, distributors, NGOs and the media, amongst others. In fact, despite the recent advancements of Sarkar and Banerjee (2021) in measuring brand co-creation processes from a triadic perspective (i.e., brand, consumers, suppliers), a quantitative multistakeholder-based perspective on brand value co-creation constitutes a worthwhile direction for future research. For instance, scholars are encouraged to investigate what is the overall brand value when stakeholders attach to the brand diverse meanings, display diverse attitudes, or when they feel diverse emotions. Accordingly, scholars may provide insights on if and how companies measure the value co-created with the plethora of stakeholders their brand interacts with daily. Relatedly, further studies could investigate the net effect on brand value stemming from stakeholders who successfully contribute to value co-creation, and those who destroy it (i.e., value co-destruction, please see Section 4.3). Accordingly, do companies categorise and prioritise stakeholders on the basis of their contribution to the brand value? The answers to these suggested lines of research may have a relevant impact from a practical standpoint, by helping marketing managers comprehend how different stakeholders may contribute to the creation of the brand value and how to plan and manage interactions and relationships with them accordingly.

References

Aaker, D. A. (1996). Measuring brand equity across products and markets. *California Management Review*, *38*(3), 102–120.

Asmussen, B., Harridge-March, S., Occhiocupo, N., & Farquhar, J. (2013). The multi-layered nature of the internet-based democratization of brand management. *Journal of Business Research*, *66*(9), 1473–1483.

Atilgan, E., Aksoy, Ş., & Akinci, S. (2005). Determinants of the brand equity: A verification approach in the beverage industry in Turkey. *Marketing Intelligence and Planning*, *23*(3), 237–248.

Balmer, J. M. T. (2012). Strategic corporate brand alignment: Perspectives from identity based views of corporate brands. *European Journal of Marketing*, *46*(7/8), 1064–1092.

Biraghi, S., & Gambetti, R. C. (2017). Is brand value co-creation actionable? A facilitation perspective. *Management Decision*, *55*(7), 1476–1488.

Bravo Gil, R., Fraj Andrés, E., & Martínez Salinas, E. (2007). Family as a source of consumer-based brand equity. *Journal of Product & Brand Management*, *16*(3), 188–199.

Chapman, A., & Dilmperi, A. (2022). Luxury brand value co-creation with online brand communities in the service encounter. *Journal of Business Research*, *144*, 902–921.

Choi, E., Ko, E., & Kim, A. J. (2016). Explaining and predicting purchase intentions following luxury-fashion brand value co-creation encounters. *Journal of Business Research*, *69*(12), 5827–5832.

Cova, B., & D'Antone, S. (2016). Brand iconicity vs. anti-consumption well-being concerns: The Nutella palm oil conflict. *Journal of Consumer Affairs*, *50*(1), 166–192.

Cova, B., & Pace, S. (2006). Brand community of convenience products: New forms of customer empowerment: The case 'my Nutella the Community'. *European Journal of Marketing*, *40*(9/10), 1087–1105.

Edmans, A. (2020). Company purpose and profit need not be in conflict if we 'grow the pie'. *Economic Affairs*, *40*(2), 287–294.

Edmondson, A. C., & McManus, S. E. (2007). Methodological fit in management field research. *Academy of Management Review*, *32*(4), 1246–1264.

Essamri, A., McKechnie, S., & Winklhofer, H. (2019). Co-creating corporate brand identity with online brand communities: A managerial perspective. *Journal of Business Research*, *96*, 366–375.

Fournier, S., & Alvarez, C. (2013). Relating badly to brands. *Journal of Consumer Psychology*, *23*(2), 253–264.

France, C., Grace, D., Lo Iacono, J., & Carlini, J. (2020). Exploring the interplay between customer perceived brand value and customer brand co-creation behaviour dimensions. *Journal of Brand Management*, *27*(4), 466–480.

France, C., Grace, D., Merrilees, B., & Miller, D. (2018). Customer brand co-creation behavior: Conceptualization and empirical validation. *Marketing Intelligence & Planning*, *36*(3), 334–348.

Greer, D. A. (2015). Defective co-creation: Developing a typology of consumer dysfunction in professional services. *European Journal of Marketing*, *49*(1/2), 238–261.

Greyser, S. A., & Urde, M. (2019). What does your corporate brand stand for? *Harvard Business Review*, *97*(January–February), 82–89.

Hajli, N., Shanmugam, M., Papagiannidis, S., Zahay, D., & Richard, M. O. (2017). Branding co-creation with members of online brand communities. *Journal of Business Research*, *70*, 136–144.

Hatch, M. J., & Schultz, M. (2010). Toward a theory of brand co-creation with implications for brand governance. *Journal of Brand Management*, *17*(8), 590–604.

Haverila, K., Haverila, M., & McLaughlin, C. (2022). Development of a brand community engagement model: A service-dominant logic perspective. *Journal of Consumer Marketing*, *39*(2), 166–179.

Hegner, S., Fetscherin, M., & van Delzen, M. (2017). Determinants and outcomes of brand hate. *Journal of Product & Brand Management*, *26*(1), 13–25.

Hsieh, S. H., & Chang, A. (2016). The psychological mechanism of brand co-creation engagement. *Journal of Interactive Marketing*, *33*, 13–26.

Iglesias, O., & Ind, N. (2020). Towards a theory of conscientious corporate brand co-creation: The next key challenge in brand management. *Journal of Brand Management*, *27*(6), 710–720.

Iglesias, O., Ind, N., & Alfaro, M. (2013). The organic view of the brand: A brand value co-creation model. *Journal of Brand Management*, *20*(8), 670–688.

Iglesias, O., Ind, N., & Schultz, M. (Eds.). (2022). *The Routledge companion to corporate branding*. Routledge.

Iglesias, O., Landgraf, P., Ind, N., Markovic, S., & Koporcic, N. (2020). Corporate brand identity co-creation in business-to-business contexts. *Industrial Marketing Management*, *85*, 32–43.

Ind, N. (2014). How participation is changing the practice of managing brands. *Journal of Brand Management*, *21*(9), 734–742.

Ind, N., & Horlings, S. (2016). *Brands with a conscience: How to build a successful and responsible brand*. Kogan Page.

Ind, N., Coates, N., & Lerman, K. (2020). The gift of co-creation: What motivates customers to participate. *Journal of Brand Management*, *27*(2), 181–194.

Ind, N., Fuller, C., & Trevail, C. (2012). *Brand together: How co-creation generates innovation and re-energizes brands*. Kogan Page.

Ind, N., Iglesias, O., & Markovic, S. (2017). The co-creation continuum: From tactical market research tool to strategic collaborative innovation method. *Journal of Brand Management*, *24*(4), 310–321.

Ind, N., Iglesias, O., & Schultz, M. (2013). Building brands together: Emergence and outcomes of co-creation. *California Management Review*, *55*(3), 5–26.

Kornum, N., Gyrd-Jones, R., Al Zagir, N., & Brandis, K. A. (2017). Interplay between intended brand identity and identities in a Nike-related brand community: Co-existing synergies and tensions in a nested system. *Journal of Business Research, 70*, 432–440.

Kotler, P., & Pfoertsch, W. (2007). Being known or being one of many: The need for brand management for business-to-business (B2B) companies. *Journal of Business and Industrial Marketing, 22*(6), 357–362.

Kristal, S., Baumgarth, C., & Henseler, J. (2018). 'Brand play' versus 'Brand attack': The subversion of brand meaning in non-collaborative co-creation by professional artists and consumer activists. *Journal of Product & Brand Management, 27*(3), 334–347.

Kristal, S., Baumgarth, C., & Henseler, J. (2020). Performative corporate brand identity in industrial markets: The case of German prosthetics manufacturer Ottobock. *Journal of Business Research, 114*, 240–253.

Kristal, S., Baumgarth, C., Behnke, C., & Henseler, J. (2016). Is co-creation really a booster for brand equity? The role of co-creation in observer-based brand equity. *Journal of Product & Brand Management, 25*(3), 247–261.

Le, Q. H., Phan Tan, L., & Hoang, T. H. (2022). Customer brand co-creation on social media: A systematic review. *Marketing Intelligence & Planning*. https://doi.org/10.1108/MIP-04-2022-0161

Lehmann, D., Keller, K., & Farley, J. (2008). The structure of survey-based brand metrics. *Journal of International Marketing, 16*(4), 29–56.

Maon, F., Swaen, V., & De Roeck, K. (2021). Corporate branding and corporate social responsibility: Toward a multi-stakeholder interpretive perspective. *Journal of Business Research, 126*, 64–77.

Merrilees, B. (2016). Interactive brand experience pathways to customer-brand engagement and value co-creation. *Journal of Product & Brand Management, 25*(5), 402–408.

Merz, M. A., Zarantonello, L., & Grappi, S. (2018). How valuable are your customers in the brand value co-creation process? The development of a Customer Co-Creation Value (CCCV) scale. *Journal of Business Research, 82*, 79–89.

Mingione, M., & Abratt, R. (2020). Building a corporate brand in the digital age: Imperatives for transforming born-digital startups into successful corporate brands. *Journal of Marketing Management, 36*(11/12), 981–1008.

Mingione, M., & Abratt, R. (2022). In search of corporate brand alignment: Philosophical foundations and emerging trends. In Iglesias, O., Ind, N., & Schultz, M. (Eds.), *The Routledge companion to corporate branding*. Routledge, pp. 148-168.

Mingione, M., & Leoni, L. (2020). Blurring B2C and B2B boundaries: Corporate brand value co-creation in B2B2C markets. *Journal of Marketing Management, 36*(1/2), 72–99.

Mingione, M., Cristofaro, M., & Mondi, D. (2020b). 'If I give you my emotion, what do I get?' Conceptualizing and measuring the co-created emotional value of the brand. *Journal of Business Research, 109*, 310–320.

Mingione, M., Kashif, M., & Petrescu, M. (2020a). Brand power relationships: A co-evolutionary conceptual framework. *Journal of Relationship Marketing, 19*(1), 1–28.

Muniz, A. M., & O'Guinn, T. C. (2001). Brand community. *Journal of Consumer Research, 27*(4), 412–432.

Nardi, V. A. M., Jardim, W. C., Ladeira, W. J., & Santini, F. (2020). A meta-analysis of the relationship between customer participation and brand outcomes. *Journal of Business Research, 117*, 450–460.

Payne, A., Storbacka, K., Frow, P., & Knox, S. (2009). Co-creating brands: Diagnosing and designing the relationship experience. *Journal of Business Research, 62*(3), 379–389.

Prahalad, C. K., & Ramaswamy, V. (2000). Co-opting customer competence. *Harvard Business Review, 78*(1), 79–90.

Ramaswamy, V. (2022). Embracing a co-creation paradigm of lived-experience ecosystem value creation. In Iglesias, O., Ind, N., & Schultz, M. (Eds.), *The Routledge companion to corporate branding*. Routledge, pp. 95-110.

Ranjan, K. R., & Read, S. (2016). Value co-creation: Concept and measurement. *Journal of the Academy of Marketing Science, 44*(3), 290–315.

Rindell, A., Svensson, G., Mysen, T., Billström, A., & Wilén, K. (2011). Towards a conceptual foundation of 'conscientious corporate brands'. *Journal of Brand Management, 18*(9), 709–719.

Sarasvuo, S., Rindell, A., & Kovalchuk, M. (2022). Toward a conceptual understanding of co-creation in branding. *Journal of Business Research, 139*, 543–563.

Sarkar, S., & Banerjee, S. (2021). Brand co-creation through participation of organization, consumers, and suppliers: An empirical validation. *Journal of Product & Brand Management, 30*(8), 1094–1114.

Seifert, C., & Kwon, W. S. (2020). SNS eWOM sentiment: Impacts on brand value co-creation and trust. *Marketing Intelligence & Planning, 38*(1), 89–102.

Törmälä, M., & Gyrd-Jones, R. (2017). Development of new B2B venture corporate brand identity: A narrative performance approach. *Industrial Marketing Management, 65*, 76–85.

Vallaster, C., & von Wallpach, S. (2013). An online discursive inquiry into the social dynamics of multi-stakeholder brand meaning co-creation. *Journal of Business Research, 66*(9), 1505–1515.

Vargo, S. L., & Lusch, R. F. (2004). Evolving to a new dominant logic for marketing. *Journal of Marketing, 68*(1), 1–17.

Veloutsou, C., & Black, I. (2020). Creating and managing participative brand communities: The roles members perform. *Journal of Business Research, 117*, 873–885.

Vredenburg, J., Kapitan, S., Spry, A., & Kemper, J. A. (2020). Brands taking a stand: Authentic brand activism or woke washing? *Journal of Public Policy & Marketing, 39*(4), 444–460.

Yoo, B., & Donthu, N. (2001). Developing and validating a multidimensional consumer-based brand equity scale. *Journal of Business Research, 52*(1), 1–14.

Zarantonello, L., Romani, S., Grappi, S., & Bagozzi, R. (2016). Brand hate. *Journal of Product and Brand Management, 25*(1), 11–25.

6 Consumer responses to branding

Kevin Kam Fung So, Jing Li and Hyunsu Kim

1. Introduction

For many years, branding strategies have been considered a top management priority. Brands are one of firms' most valuable intangible assets (Keller, 2020; Keller & Lehmann, 2006): they constitute a strategic weapon with which firms can gain a competitive edge in the global marketplace (So, King, & Sparks, 2014). Branding refers to the process of ascribing distinctive features to an organization to prompt customers to associate brands with certain products or services; this framing sets a firm's offerings apart from those of their competitors (Choi & Chu, 2001). A brand contains both functional and non-functional elements. Functional elements are meant to fulfill customers' functional needs or values while non-functional elements seek to differentiate a brand from others. Statistics show that 71% of consumers prefer purchasing products and services from brands they know (Global Banking & Finance Review, 2022).

Brands have served for centuries as carriers of functional and symbolic information about goods, services, and experiences. Such details enable customers to imbue a company's products with personal meaning (Oh et al., 2020). From a consumer perspective, brands can create a sense of status and recognition among users (Sarwar, Aftab, & Iqbal, 2014), simplify choice (Aaker, 1991; Keller & Lehmann, 2006), signify quality (Keller, 1998), and reduce customer risk (Tepeci, 1999). A survey conducted in the United States by Salsify (2022) revealed that 46% of consumers would pay a premium price for trusted brands, and 59% would prefer to buy new products from brands they trust. From a firm standpoint, an established brand can generate greater sales volume and profit margins (Cobb-Walgren, Ruble, & Donthu, 1995). Strong branding also acts as a natural barrier to new market entrants (Dev, Morgan, & Shoemaker, 1995) and can hence lead to larger market share (Chaudhuri & Holbrook, 2001) and premium revenue (Ailawadi, Lehmann, & Neslin, 2003). Brands are similarly critical in attracting, retaining, and motivating talent. For example, employer branding reflects a company's efforts to maintain and enhance the perceptions of potential workers, current employees, and other stakeholders towards a given firm (Backhaus & Tikoo, 2004). Brands additionally help investors lower financing costs and create economic value by producing higher profit returns and mitigating risk. Approximately 82% of investors view name recognition as a key factor in their investment decisions (Global Banking & Finance Review, 2022).

The benefits of branding are clear as evidenced by consistent academic and practical attention to the matter. However, a rapidly changing consumer environment and technological advances have spawned a hyperconnected world. This setting calls for a reassessment of branding research from the viewpoints of firms, consumers, and society (Swaminathan et al., 2020). This chapter reviews relevant literature with an emphasis on constructs representing widely studied consumer responses to branding. Outcomes include relationship quality, emotional brand attachment, customer brand identification, brand equity, brand switching, and brand loyalty. A number of open questions on certain facets (brand coolness, customer engagement, psychological brand ownership) are also posed. Ultimately, this chapter is intended to inspire the next generation of empirical and conceptual efforts around branding.

2. Evolution of branding

Branding has developed into a vital aspect of business success. Brands originated in the 1860s with the aim of creating marks to convey ownership and distinction (Cantor, 2020). These marks provided information about handcrafted merchandise (Keller, 2013). From the 1750s to the 1870s, much of the world—especially Europe and the United States—experienced the Industrial Revolution and entered the manufacturing era (Cantor, 2020). Mechanization and improved workforce efficiency caused various industries to begin mass production. This phenomenon made an array of product options available to consumers. At the same time, companies and organizations started to pay closer attention to the competition, sparking the need to highlight ownership. Trademarks, consisting of words, symbols, designs, and colors, were hence designed to characterize companies or products.

In the early 20th century, technology began to permeate into consumers' lives. Brands turned to newspapers and magazines to describe their products via logos and illustrations in an attempt to differentiate themselves from one another. By the 1920s, firms had begun to use radio to make brands more audible, memorable, and relatable. Later, with the rise of television, brands were able to connect with consumers more intensively through sound, music, and visuals by sponsoring shows or designing commercials. Some firms took the lead in conducting brand management and crafting unique identities for their products after World War II. Advertisements focused on cultivating emotional resonance with consumers. Branding thus evolved from being informational to being more intimate (Gensler et al., 2013).

Over time, technology has continued to help brands stand out—particularly as social media platforms now facilitate customer–brand interaction. Consumers today have great access to product information as well as reviews from other consumers. Individuals' purchase decisions are based on not only products' functions but also product reviews and ratings, pushing firms to innovate and place more emphasis on post-purchase community involvement and customer engagement (So et al., 2014, 2016; So, Kim, & King, 2021).

2.1 Relationship quality

Relationship quality is a major factor in consumer responses to branding. This construct embodies a customer's perceptions of how well a relationship fulfills associated expectations, predictions, goals, and desires (Jarvelin & Lehtinen, 1996). Relationship quality includes constructs such as trust, commitment, customer satisfaction, conflict, and cooperation (Athanasopoulou, 2009). Crosby, Evans, and Cowles' (1990) popular approach more simply depicts relationship quality as a higher-order construct composed of two dimensions: trust and satisfaction. This conceptualization has been extensively adopted in marketing, business, hospitality, and tourism studies (e.g., Fernandes & Pinto, 2019).

Trust is defined as "a willingness to rely on an exchange partner in whom one has confidence" (Moorman, Zaltman, & Deshpande, 1992, p. 315). In the brand management literature, trust implies that a brand operates in the customer's best interests based on shared values, thereby encouraging exchange partners to maintain a committed relationship (e.g., Chaudhuri & Holbrook, 2001). In addition, satisfaction is an important dimension of relationship quality; it captures the degree to which a consumer believes that possession or use of a service evokes positive feelings (Rust & Oliver, 1994). The satisfaction a customer obtains signals the health of the exchange relationship (Fernandes & Pinto, 2019). One way to develop strong relationships with brands is to nurture trust and satisfaction.

Relationship quality lies at the heart of relationship marketing and indicates the health and potential prosperity of long-term partnerships (de Kerviler &

Rodriguez, 2019). A strong relationship is an intangible asset that is difficult for competitors to replicate. Customers who have strong relationships with brands tend to shop more frequently and are willing to pay a premium for products or services (e.g., Akrout & Nagy, 2018).

2.2 Emotional brand attachment

Another consumer response to branding is emotional brand attachment, which marks the strength of the customer–brand relationship. The field of psychology defines attachment as a fundamental human need, referring to emotion-laden relationships between people and specific objects (Bowlby, 1979). In the marketing context, consumers can build emotional bonds with brands (Belk, 1988; Malär et al., 2011). These bonds encompass consumers' thoughts and feelings towards a brand as well as the brand's relationship to the consumer (Mikulincer & Shaver, 2007). Building on Bowlby's (1979) work, Thomson, MacInnis, and Park (2005) suggested that the essence of attachment is emotional. Emotional brand attachment therefore embodies a bond between consumers and a specific brand, which can be measured based on three components: connection, affection, and passion.

Emotional brand attachment is also a marketing strategy through which brands can maintain long-term customer connections (Park et al., 2010) and improve business performance (Bian & Haque, 2020). According to Thomson et al. (2005), the strength of emotional brand attachment varies and may influence consumers' behavior. This form of attachment has accordingly drawn extensive interest in the marketing domain. For instance, understanding emotional brand attachment may help marketers predict consumers' brand commitment or loyalty (Charton-Vachet & Lombart, 2018) along with their willingness to pay a price premium (Thomson et al., 2005). Furthermore, the emotional bond that consumers build with a brand distinguishes this brand from its competitors (Park et al., 2010). Scholars have relatedly investigated linkages between emotional brand attachment and other behavior-related constructs, such as brand involvement (Bian & Haque, 2020) and positive word of mouth (Magnoni, Valette-Florence, & De Barnier, 2021).

2.3 Customer brand identification

Customer brand identification is a principal consequence of branding. Different from other mainstream constructs such as brand loyalty, customer brand identification offers a deeper understanding of the effects of brand management (Kuenzel & Halliday, 2008) thanks to its capacity to signal a stronger customer–brand relationship. Customer brand identification is derived from social identity theory, which holds that one's self-concept consists of two parts: a personal identity, including idiosyncratic characteristics such as abilities and interests; and a social identity, which covers salient group classifications (Ashforth & Mael, 1989). Identification is a perceptual construct that involves an identity fit; people create a social identity by classifying themselves and others into social categories (e.g., member of a brand community, organizational membership) (Mael & Ashforth, 1992). From a branding perspective, identification is likely to occur when a person feels psychologically aligned with a brand's attributes.

Social identity plays an important part in shaping consumer behavior in social settings, such as assimilating to group preferences when choosing products (Chan, Berger, & Van Boven, 2012) and adhering to group behavioral norms (Griskevicius, Cialdini, & Goldstein, 2008). Belk's (1988) work on extended self supports the premise that possessions are major contributors to, and reflections of, consumers' identities. Strong consumer–firm relationships are rooted in consumers' identification with companies or brands that help them satisfy self-definitional needs (Bhattacharya & Sen, 2003). Scholars have explored the impacts of customer brand identification and demonstrated its roles in consumers' evaluations of service quality, perceived value, and brand trust (So et al., 2013) as well as positive word of mouth and resistance to negative brand-related information (So et al., 2018).

2.4 Brand equity

Brand equity has long been seen as a driving force behind branding strategies. No consensus exists concerning the term's definition, dimensions, and measurement. The concept has instead been regarded as the added value endowed by a brand name (Farquhar, 1989), the differential effect that brand knowledge has on consumer responses to brand marketing (Keller, 1993), incremental cash flows (Ailawadi et al., 2003), and incremental preferences (Park & Srinivasan, 1994). Aaker (1991) described brand equity as "a set of brand asset[s] and liabilities linked to a brand, its name and symbol, that add to or subtract from the value provided by a product or service to a firm and/or to that firm's customers" (p. 15).

Marketing researchers and practitioners have traditionally considered brand equity through two lenses: financial and consumer-based. From a financial perspective, Simon and Sullivan (1993) defined brand equity as "the incremental cash flows that accrue to branded products over and above the cash flows which would result from the sale of unbranded products" (p. 29). More recent work has investigated various brand actions and financial impacts

(Swaminathan et al., 2022). Conversely, customer-based brand equity manifests when a consumer responds more favorably to a marketing activity for one brand than they do to the same activity for an unbranded product or service in the same category (Keller, 2016). A relatively new, third perspective is employee-based brand equity: King and Grace (2009) operationalized it as the differential effect of brand knowledge on an employee's response to their work environment.

2.5 Brand switching

Brand switching, referring simply to changing to another brand (Deighton, Henderson, & Neslin, 1994), has been widely acknowledged as essential to consumer responses to branding. Most often, brand switching has been related to customers' overall assessment of a brand's utility based on what is received and given from a functional utility maximization perspective (Zeithaml, 1988). A typical practice among marketing researchers is to model consumer brand switching as choices based on product attributes and the marketing mix (Deighton et al., 1994). However, according to multi-attribute utility theory (Lancaster, 1966), consumer utility includes a brand's functional and socio-psychological features. Lam et al. (2010) contended that brand switching can also be a display of social mobility between brand identities. In line with developments in choice modeling, social identity theory posits that brand switching serves socio-psychological purposes besides functional utility maximization (Lam et al., 2010). This theory asserts that people construct identities from their affiliations with social groups. Accordingly, customers may switch to a new brand for self-enhancement purposes to maximize socio-psychological utility (e.g., symbolic benefits).

It is generally agreed that brand switching accompanies a lack of service quality and customer satisfaction. Brand switching also reflects consumer behavior on the basis of one's satisfaction with a provider or firm (Appiah et al., 2019). A stream of research has underscored how employee–customer interaction influences service quality and customer satisfaction (Zolfagharian, Hasan, & Iyer, 2017). In one of the earlier conceptualizations of brand switching, Keaveney (1995) identified service quality-related factors (e.g., core service failure and inconvenience, response to failed service encounters, and failed service encounters) as triggers of brand switching.

2.6 Brand loyalty

Brand loyalty is arguably one of the best-known indicators of branding effectiveness. It is also seen as the ultimate goal of marketing activities for many organizations. Marketers therefore devote substantial effort to retaining or increasing brand loyalty (Casteran, Chrysochou, & Meyer-Waarden, 2019). This form of loyalty can be attitudinal, behavioral, or composite. Attitudinal aspects of loyalty include customers' stated preferences and commitment (Bennett & Rundle-Thiele, 2002). Behavioral loyalty suggests that repeat transactions signal a customer's loyalty to a brand or company (Dunn & Wrigley, 1984). Composite loyalty refers to biased behavioral purchases that occur as a result of a psychological process (Jacoby, 1971), insinuating that measures of customer loyalty should include attitudinal and behavioral components (Dick & Basu, 1994). Composite loyalty provides a holistic view and has hence appeared in multiple studies of customer or brand loyalty (Evanschitzky et al., 2006; Li & Petrick, 2008).

Brand loyalty has been researched extensively. Initial efforts focused on key marketing concepts that act as loyalty antecedents, such as service quality (e.g., Kandampully, Juwaheer, & Hu, 2011), perceived value (e.g., Sirdeshmukh, Singh, & Sabol, 2002), customer satisfaction (e.g., Li & Petrick, 2008), and brand trust (e.g., Han & Jeong, 2013). Later work expanded the determinants of loyalty formation to include more novel constructs such as customer engagement (Harrigan et al., 2017; So et al., 2016), corporate social responsibility (Cha, Yi, & Bagozzi, 2016), and memorable tourism experiences (Kim, 2018). Others have contemplated how digital content marketing augments brand loyalty (Lou & Xie, 2021). Khamitov, Wang, and Thomson (2019) performed a meta-analysis on how well customer–brand relationships boost loyalty and discovered that characteristics related to brands, loyalty, time, and consumers affect brand relationship elasticity.

3. Future research directions

The preceding discussion makes clear that key constructs of consumer responses to branding have drawn careful attention from brand management scholars. Meanwhile, recent conceptual and empirical studies have laid a foundation for new initiatives in this area. Three novel theoretical constructs are profiled below along with research opportunities.

3.1 Brand coolness

Brand coolness is an emerging but important aspect of consumer responses to branding. Many companies have lately striven to establish "cool" brands. Although a uniform definition of coolness remains elusive, four defining characteristics apply: (1) coolness is socially constructed; (2) coolness is subjective and dynamic; (3) coolness is perceived to be a positive quality; and (4) although coolness is a positive trait, it is more than the mere perception that something is positive or desirable (e.g., Warren & Campbell, 2014; Warren et al., 2019). Warren and Campbell (2014) explained coolness as "a subjective and dynamic, socially constructed positive trait attributed to cultural objects inferred to be appropriately autonomous" (p. 544). This concept presents several lines of inquiry: How do customers evaluate the coolness of a brand in various service settings (e.g., automobiles, banks, financials, food and beverage, accommodation, retailing, transportation, hotels, and insurance)? How differently do customers respond in hedonic (e.g., entertainment, food and beverage) versus utilitarian (e.g., insurance and financials) settings?

Prior studies have investigated what makes a brand seem cool. Brands may be said to be cool if they emulate the behavior of other cool brands or if they follow the rules, standards, and goals of a certain subculture (e.g., O'Donnell & Wardlow, 2000). It has been suggested that a rebellious, individualistic, or non-conformist mindset might contribute to coolness impressions (e.g., Dar-Nimrod et al., 2012). Warren and Campbell (2014) argued that all these factors are related to autonomy—namely one's willingness to pursue a course of action irrespective of others' norms, beliefs, and expectations (Ryan & Deci, 2000). Brand coolness is underpinned by a desire to adhere to one's own brand regardless of what is typical (Warren & Campbell, 2014). Warren et al. (2019) further identified 10 brand coolness traits, including useful/extraordinary, aesthetically appealing, energetic, high status, original, authentic, rebellious, subcultural, iconic, and popular. A few authors have investigated brand coolness in luxury contexts, including fashion (e.g., Loureiro, Jiménez-Barreto, & Romero, 2020) and hotels (e.g., Khoi & Le, 2022). Building on this literature, the following questions could extend the understanding of brand coolness: What are the key antecedents, outcomes, mediators, and moderators of brand coolness? How may these factors differ between online and offline customer–brand interactions?

Consumers of luxury brands have been described as seekers of products that signal virtue to others while enriching the user's self-concept via an existentialist spirit, potentially linked to being cool or not (Khoi & Le, 2022). Loureiro et al. (2020) showed that luxury values (i.e., individual, social, financial, and functional) positively influence brand coolness, which in turn affects passionate desire. This evolving understanding of brand coolness reveals a number of promising areas for future research. For instance, what are the impacts of brand coolness, including return on investment, sales growth, and profit growth, from an organizational perspective? Can brand coolness be measured using different analytical techniques (e.g., social media monitoring, natural language processing, electroencephalography, and experience sampling)? What are the key advantages and disadvantages of such measures?

3.2 Customer engagement

Over the past 15 years, customer engagement has gained scholarly and practical traction in broad service industries (Brodie et al., 2011; Kumar et al., 2019) and in sector-specific domains such as hospitality and tourism (So et al., 2021). The construct sheds light on dynamic and interactive consumer/brand communication. Brodie et al. (2011) offered one of the most precise definitions of customer engagement: "a psychological state that occurs by virtue of interactive, cocreative customer experiences with a focal agent/object (e.g., a brand) in focal service relationships. It occurs under a specific set of context-dependent conditions generating differing customer engagement levels; and exists as a dynamic, iterative process within service relationships that cocreate value" (p. 260). Several avenues of investigation follow from this conceptualization: How does customer engagement stability differ across product/service categories, and how does such stability compare to that of other consumer response constructs? How does customer engagement change over time?

Customer engagement "plays a central role in a nomological network governing service relationships in which other relational concepts (e.g., involvement and loyalty) are antecedents and/or consequences in the iterative customer engagement processes. It is a multidimensional concept subject to context- and/or stakeholder-specific expression of relevant cognitive, emotional and/or behavioral dimensions" (Brodie at al., 2011, p. 260). So et al. (2014, 2016) defined this type of engagement as "a customer's personal connection to a brand as manifested in cognitive, affective, and behavioral responses outside of the purchase situation" (2014, p. 310; 2016, p. 65). This understanding has been widely adopted (e.g., Xi & Hamari, 2020). Several questions are worthy of consideration through this lens: How should customer engagement be managed in the wider service ecosystem to maximize its desirable benefits for both consumers and organizations? How can customer engagement research be extended from traditional dyadic relationships to multi-actor (e.g., stakeholder, peers) engagement to illustrate the evolving nature of actors' roles within the service ecosystem?

Customer engagement affects customers' brand evaluations (So et al., 2016) and purchase intentions (Hollebeek, Glynn, & Brodie, 2014). It is a metric of firms' success as well—engaged customers are reluctant to switch to other brands, frequently participate in product and service development, advocate for organizations, and are less price-sensitive than non-engaged customers (Hollebeek, Conduit, & Brodie, 2016). A number of fruitful areas for research hence exist: What factors may trigger or accelerate an increase or decrease in customer engagement? What is the financial value of customer engagement? Are certain underlying dimensions of customer engagement more prominent in driving consumers' preferences and behavior?

3.3 Psychological brand ownership

Psychological brand ownership has come to the fore as a favorable consumer response to branding. Brands are pursuing ways to establish enduring connections with consumers. Psychological ownership, referring to a cognitive-affective state that describes people's sense of ownership towards tangible and intangible assets (Pierce, Kostova, & Dirks, 2003), contributes to these connections. Pierce et al. (2003) helpfully distinguished psychological ownership from legal ownership: the former concerns legal ownership of target assets recognized by society (Kumar & Kaushal, 2021), whereas the latter involves a personal feeling of possession (e.g., "This object is mine"). Building on psychological ownership theory, psychological brand ownership is "the psychological state in which people feel possessive of a brand and as if they have control over the brand" (Chang et al., 2015, p. 595). Pierce et al. (2001, 2003) suggested two subsets of psychological ownership antecedents, specifically "roots" and "routes". Roots, which include efficacy and effectance, self-identity, and having a place, motivate consumers' sense of ownership. Routes entail interactions between individuals and objects: controlling the "owned" object, coming to know the object intimately, or investing oneself in the object. Despite swift growth in the knowledge of psychological brand ownership, several intriguing topics lend themselves to research. For example, what are the possible antecedents, outcomes, and moderators of psychological brand ownership? Under what conditions/consumer environments is psychological brand ownership likely to occur? Does psychological brand ownership perform differently across product brand categories, service categories, or cultures?

Psychological brand ownership, as part of one's psychological experience, produces clear brand cognitions and positive brand attitudes (Pierce et al., 2001). This form of ownership can also help consumers identify with a brand and believe they can effectively partake in brand-related activities (Kumar & Kaushal, 2021). The following topics may enlarge this stream of literature by drawing on earlier work: In addition to psychological ownership theory, what other theories from psychology/social psychology can be used or developed to explain psychological brand ownership and related consumer responses (e.g., psychological and behavioral)? What types of advanced analytic techniques (e.g., machine learning and natural language processing) will allow for a richer analysis and understanding of psychological brand ownership?

4. Conclusion

Branding and consumers' responses to it are prime managerial and strategic priorities for firms in all industries. Our discussion of academic research on branding has highlighted numerous constructs that have garnered intrigue among scholars and practitioners. The studies reviewed in this chapter, which cover topics in diverse settings, have advanced the understanding of branding as a marketing strategy and overall consumer responses to this tactic. Branding can evoke competitive advantages for firms. Yet market conditions are constantly evolving, leading to research questions that could help businesses overcome managerial challenges and elevate brand management to new heights. Scholars have made noteworthy contributions to this knowledge base; however, more progress can be realized. This chapter outlines select foci associated with consumer response factors. These fertile areas will hopefully resonate with researchers and graduate students who wish to push the boundaries of brand management studies.

References

2022 Salsify Shopping Research Reveals Critical Global Consumer Insights. (2022, February 22). Salsify. Retrieved June 22, 2022 from https://www.salsify.com/blog/2022-shopping-research-reveals-consumer-insights

Aaker, D. A. (1991). *Managing Brand Equity.* New York, NY: The Free Press.

Ailawadi, K. L., Lehmann, D. R., & Neslin, S. A. (2003). Revenue premium as an outcome measure of brand equity. *Journal of Marketing, 67*(4), 1–17.

Akrout, H., & Nagy, G. (2018). Trust and commitment within a virtual brand community: The mediating role of brand relationship quality. *Information & Management, 55*(8), 939–955.

Appiah, D., Howell, K. E., Ozuem, W., & Lancaster, G. (2019). Building resistance to brand switching during disruptions in a competitive market. *Journal of Retailing and Consumer Services, 50*, 249–257.

Ashforth, B. E., & Mael, F. (1989). Social identity theory and the organization. *Academy of Management Review, 14*(1), 20–39.

Athanasopoulou, P. (2009). Relationship quality: A critical literature review and research agenda. *European Journal of Marketing, 43*(5–6), 583–610.

Backhaus, K., & Tikoo, S. (2004). Conceptualizing and researching employer branding. *Career Development International, 9*(5), 501–517.

Belk, R. W. (1988). Possessions and the extended self. *Journal of Consumer Research, 15*(2), 139–168.

Bennett, R., & Rundle-Thiele, S. (2002). A comparison of attitudinal loyalty measurement approaches. *Journal of Brand Management, 9*(3), 193–209.

Bhattacharya, C. B., & Sen, S. (2003). Consumer–company identification: A framework for understanding consumers' relationships with companies. *Journal of Marketing, 67*(2), 76–88.

Bian, X., & Haque, S. (2020). Counterfeit versus original patronage: Do emotional brand attachment, brand involvement, and past experience matter? *Journal of Brand Management, 27*(4), 438–451.

Bowlby, J. (1979). *The Making and Breaking of Affectional Bonds*. London: Tavistock.

Brodie, R. J., Hollebeek, L. D., Jurić, B., & Ilić, A. (2011). Customer engagement: Conceptual domain, fundamental propositions, and implications for research. *Journal of Service Research, 14*(3), 252–271.

Cantor, A. (2020). A brief history of branding. Retrieved from https://99designs.com/blog/design-history-movements/history-of branding/

Casteran, G., Chrysochou, P., & Meyer-Waarden, L. (2019). Brand loyalty evolution and the impact of category characteristics. *Marketing Letters, 30*(1), 57–73.

Cha, M. K., Yi, Y., & Bagozzi, R. P. (2016). Effects of customer participation in corporate social responsibility (CSR) programs on the CSR–brand fit and brand loyalty. *Cornell Hospitality Quarterly, 57*(3), 235–249.

Chan, C., Berger, J., & Van Boven, L. (2012). Identifiable but not identical: Combining social identity and uniqueness motives in choice. *Journal of Consumer Research, 39*(3), 561–573.

Chang, H., Kwak, H., Puzakova, M., Park, J., & Smit, E. G. (2015). It's no longer mine: The role of brand ownership and advertising in cross-border brand acquisitions. *International Journal of Advertising, 34*(4), 593–620.

Charton-Vachet, F., & Lombart, C. (2018). Impact of the link between individuals and their region on the customer–regional brand relationship. *Journal of Retailing and Consumer Services, 43*, 170–187.

Chaudhuri, A., & Holbrook, M. B. (2001). The chain of effects from brand trust and brand affect to brand performance: The role of brand loyalty. *Journal of Marketing, 65*(2), 81–93.

Choi, T. Y., & Chu, R. (2001). Determinants of hotel guests' satisfaction and repeat patronage in the Hong Kong hotel industry. *International Journal of Hospitality Management, 20*(3), 277–297.

Cobb-Walgren, C. J., Ruble, C. A., & Donthu, N. (1995). Brand equity, brand preference, and purchase intent. *Journal of Advertising, 24*(3), 25–40.

Crosby, L. A., Evans, K. R., & Cowles, D. (1990). Relationship quality in services selling: An interpersonal influence perspective. *Journal of Marketing, 54*(3), 68–81.

Dar-Nimrod, I., Hansen, I. G., Proulx, T., Lehman, D. R., Chapman, B. P., & Duberstein, P. R. (2012). Coolness: An empirical investigation. *Journal of Individual Differences, 33*(3), 175–185.

de Kerviler, G., & Rodriguez, C. M. (2019). Luxury brand experiences and relationship quality for Millennials: The role of self-expansion. *Journal of Business Research, 102*, 250–262.

Deighton, J., Henderson, C. M., & Neslin, S. A. (1994). The effects of advertising on brand switching and repeat purchasing. *Journal of Marketing Research, 31*(1), 28–43.

Dev, C. S., Morgan, M. S., & Shoemaker, S. (1995). A positioning analysis of hotel brands: Based on travel-manager perceptions. *Cornell Hotel and Restaurant Administration Quarterly*, *36*(6), 48–55.

Dick, A. S., & Basu, K. (1994). Customer loyalty: Toward an integrated conceptual framework. *Journal of the Academy of Marketing Science*, *22*(2), 99–113.

Dunn, R., & Wrigley, N. (1984). Store loyalty for grocery products: An empirical study. *Area*, *16*(4), 307–314.

Evanschitzky, H., Iyer, G. R., Plassmann, H., Niessing, J., & Meffert, H. (2006). The relative strength of affective commitment in securing loyalty in service relationships. *Journal of Business Research*, *59*(12), 1207–1213.

Farquhar, P. H. (1989). Managing brand equity. *Marketing Research*, *1*(3), 24–33.

Fernandes, T., & Pinto, T. (2019). Relationship quality determinants and outcomes in retail banking services: The role of customer experience. *Journal of Retailing and Consumer Services*, *50*, 30–41.

Gensler, S., Völckner, F., Liu-Thompkins, Y., & Wiertz, C. (2013). Managing brands in the social media environment. *Journal of Interactive Marketing*, *27*(4), 242–256.

Global Banking & Finance Review. (2022). 71% of consumers more likely to buy a product or service from a name they recognize. Retrieved June 22, 2022 from https://www.globalbankingandfinance.com/71-of-consumers-more-likely-to-buy-a-product-or-service-from-a-name-they-recognise/

Griskevicius, V., Cialdini, R. B., & Goldstein, N. J. (2008). Social norms: An underestimated and underemployed lever for managing climate change. *International Journal of Sustainability Communication*, *3*, 5–13.

Han, H., & Jeong, C. (2013). Multi-dimensions of patrons' emotional experiences in upscale restaurants and their role in loyalty formation: Emotion scale improvement. *International Journal of Hospitality Management*, *32*, 59–70.

Harrigan, P., Evers, U., Miles, M., & Daly, T. (2017). Customer engagement with tourism social media brands. *Tourism Management*, *59*, 597–609.

Hollebeek, L. D., Conduit, J., & Brodie, R. J. (2016). Strategic drivers, anticipated and unanticipated outcomes of customer engagement. *Journal of Marketing Management*, *32*(5–6), 393–398.

Hollebeek, L. D., Glynn, M. S., & Brodie, R. J. (2014). Consumer brand engagement in social media: Conceptualization, scale development and validation. *Journal of Interactive Marketing*, *28*(2), 149–165.

Jacoby, J. (1971). Brand loyalty: A conceptual definition. In *Proceedings of the Annual Convention of the American Psychological Association* (pp. 655–656). Washington, DC: American Psychological Association.

Jarvelin, A., & Lehtinen, U. (1996). Relationship quality in business-to-business service context. In B. B. Edvardsson, S. W. Johnston, & E. E. Scheuing (Eds.), *QUIS 5 Advancing Service Quality: A Global Perspective* (pp. 243–254). Lethbridge, Canada: Warwick Printing.

Kandampully, J., Juwaheer, T. D., & Hu, H. H. (2011). The influence of a hotel firm's quality of service and image and its effect on tourism customer loyalty. *International Journal of Hospitality & Tourism Administration, 12*(1), 21–42.

Keaveney, S. M. (1995). Customer switching behavior in service industries: An exploratory study. *Journal of Marketing*, *59*(2), 71–82.

Keller, K. L. (1993). Conceptualizing, measuring, and managing customer-based brand equity. *Journal of Marketing*, *57*(1), 1–22.

Keller, K. L. (1998). Branding perspectives on social marketing. In J. W. Alba & J. W. Hutchinson (Eds.), *ACR North American Advances* (Vol. 25, pp. 299–302). Provo, UT: Association for Consumer Research.

Keller, K. L. (2013). Building strong brands in a modern marketing communications environment. In D. Schultz, C. Patti, & P. Kitchen (Eds.), *The Evolution of Integrated Marketing Communications* (pp. 73–90). Abingdon: Routledge.

Keller, K. L. (2016). Unlocking the power of integrated marketing communications: How integrated is your IMC program? *Journal of Advertising, 45*(3), 286–301.

Keller, K. L. (2020). Consumer research insights on brands and branding: A JCR curation. *Journal of Consumer Research, 46*(5), 995–1001.

Keller, K. L., & Lehmann, D. R. (2006). Brands and branding: Research findings and future priorities. *Marketing Science, 25*(6), 740–759.

Khamitov, M., Wang, X., & Thomson, M. (2019). How well do consumer–brand relationships drive customer brand loyalty? Generalizations from a meta-analysis of brand relationship elasticities. *Journal of Consumer Research, 46*(3), 435–459.

Khoi, N. H., & Le, A. N. H. (2022). Is coolness important to luxury hotel brand management? The linking and moderating mechanisms between coolness and customer brand engagement. *International Journal of Contemporary Hospitality Management, 34*(7), 2425–2449.

Kim, J. H. (2018). The impact of memorable tourism experiences on loyalty behaviors: The mediating effects of destination image and satisfaction. *Journal of Travel Research, 57*(7), 856-870.

King, C., & Grace, D. (2009). Employee-based brand equity: A third perspective. *Services Marketing Quarterly, 30*(2), 122–147.

Kuenzel, S., & Halliday, S. V. (2008). Investigating antecedents and consequences of brand identification. *Journal of Product & Brand Management, 17*(5), 293–304.

Kumar, V., & Kaushal, V. (2021). Perceived brand authenticity and social exclusion as drivers of psychological brand ownership. *Journal of Retailing and Consumer Services, 61*, 102579.

Kumar, V., Rajan, B., Gupta, S., & Pozza, I. D. (2019). Customer engagement in service. *Journal of the Academy of Marketing Science, 47*(1), 138–160.

Lam, S. K., Ahearne, M., Hu, Y., & Schillewaert, N. (2010). Resistance to brand switching when a radically new brand is introduced: A social identity theory perspective. *Journal of Marketing, 74*(6), 128–146.

Lancaster, K. J. (1966). A new approach to consumer theory. *Journal of Political Economy, 74*(2), 132–157.

Li, X., & Petrick, J. F. (2008). Reexamining the dimensionality of brand loyalty: A case of the cruise industry. *Journal of Travel & Tourism Marketing, 25*(1), 68–85.

Lou, C., & Xie, Q. (2021). Something social, something entertaining? How digital content marketing augments consumer experience and brand loyalty. *International Journal of Advertising, 40*(3), 376–402.

Loureiro, S. M. C., Jiménez-Barreto, J., & Romero, J. (2020). Enhancing brand coolness through perceived luxury values: Insight from luxury fashion brands. *Journal of Retailing and Consumer Services, 57*, 102211.

Mael, F., & Ashforth, B. E. (1992). Alumni and their alma mater: A partial test of the reformulated model of organizational identification. *Journal of Organizational Behavior, 13*(2), 103–123.

Magnoni, F., Valette-Florence, P., & De Barnier, V. (2021). Modeling the effects of place heritage and place experience on residents' behavioral intentions toward a city: A mediation analysis. *Journal of Business Research, 134*, 428–442.

Malär, L., Krohmer, H., Hoyer, W. D., & Nyffenegger, B. (2011). Emotional brand attachment and brand personality: The relative importance of the actual and the ideal self. *Journal of Marketing, 75*(4), 35–52.

Mikulincer, M., & Shaver, P. R. (2007). Boosting attachment security to promote mental health, prosocial values, and inter-group tolerance. *Psychological Inquiry, 18*(3), 139–156.

Moorman, C., Zaltman, G., & Deshpande, R. (1992). Relationships between providers and users of market research: The dynamics of trust within and between organizations. *Journal of Marketing Research, 29*(3), 314–328.

O'Donnell, K. A., & Wardlow, D. L. (2000). A theory on the origins of coolness. *Advances in Consumer Research, 27*, 13–18.

Oh, T. T., Keller, K. L., Neslin, S. A., Reibstein, D. J., & Lehmann, D. R. (2020). The past, present, and future of brand research. *Marketing Letters, 31*(2), 151–162.

Park, C. S., & Srinivasan, V. (1994). A survey-based method for measuring and understanding brand equity and its extendibility. *Journal of Marketing Research, 31*(2), 271–288.

Park, C. W., MacInnis, D. J., Priester, J., Eisingerich, A. B., & Iacobucci, D. (2010). Brand attachment and brand attitude strength: Conceptual and empirical differentiation of two critical brand equity drivers. *Journal of Marketing, 74*(6), 1–17.

Pierce, J. L., Kostova, T., & Dirks, K. T. (2001). Toward a theory of psychological ownership in organizations. *Academy of Management Review, 26*(2), 298–310.

Pierce, J. L., Kostova, T., & Dirks, K. T. (2003). The state of psychological ownership: Integrating and extending a century of research. *Review of General Psychology, 7*(1), 84–107.

Rust, R. T., & Oliver, R. L. (1994). Service quality: Insights and managerial implications from the frontier. *Service Quality: New Directions in Theory and Practice, 7*(12), 1–19.

Ryan, R. M., & Deci, E. L. (2000). Self-determination theory and the facilitation of intrinsic motivation, social development, and well-being. *American Psychologist, 55*(1), 68–78.

Sarwar, F., Aftab, M., & Iqbal, M. T. (2014). The impact of branding on consumer buying behavior. *International Journal of Technology and Research, 2*(2), 54–64.

Simon, C. J., & Sullivan, M. W. (1993). The measurement and determinants of brand equity: A financial approach. *Marketing Science, 12*(1), 28–52.

Sirdeshmukh, D., Singh, J., & Sabol, B. (2002). Consumer trust, value, and loyalty in relational exchanges. *Journal of Marketing, 66*(1), 15–37.

So, K. K. F., Kim, H., & King, C. (2021). The thematic evolution of customer engagement research: A comparative systematic review and bibliometric analysis. *International Journal of Contemporary Hospitality Management, 33*(10), 3585–3609.

So, K. K. F., King, C., & Sparks, B. (2014). Customer engagement with tourism brands: Scale development and validation. *Journal of Hospitality & Tourism Research, 38*(3), 304–329.

So, K. K. F., King, C., Sparks, B. A., & Wang, Y. (2013). The influence of customer brand identification on hotel brand evaluation and loyalty development. *International Journal of Hospitality Management, 34*, 31–41.

So, K. K. F., King, C., Sparks, B. A., & Wang, Y. (2016). The role of customer engagement in building consumer loyalty to tourism brands. *Journal of Travel Research, 55*(1), 64–78.

So, K. K. F., Wu, L., Xiong, L., & King, C. (2018). Brand management in the era of social media: Social visibility of consumption and customer brand identification. *Journal of Travel Research, 57*(6), 727–742.

Swaminathan, V., Gupta, S., Keller, K. L., & Lehmann, D. (2022). Brand actions and financial consequences: A review of key findings and directions for future research. *Journal of the Academy of Marketing Science*, 1–26.

Swaminathan, V., Sorescu, A., Steenkamp, J. B. E., O'Guinn, T. C. G., & Schmitt, B. (2020). Branding in a hyperconnected world: Refocusing theories and rethinking boundaries. *Journal of Marketing, 84*(2), 24–46.

Tepeci, M. (1999). Increasing brand loyalty in the hospitality industry. *International Journal of Contemporary Hospitality Management, 11*(5), 223–229.

Thomson, M., MacInnis, D. J., & Park, C. W. (2005). The ties that bind: Measuring the strength of consumers' emotional attachments to brands. *Journal of Consumer Psychology, 15*(1), 77–91.

Warren, C., & Campbell, M. C. (2014). What makes things cool? How autonomy influences perceived coolness. *Journal of Consumer Research, 41*(2), 543–563.

Warren, C., Batra, R., Loureiro, S. M. C., & Bagozzi, R. P. (2019). Brand coolness. *Journal of Marketing, 83*(5), 36–56.

Xi, N., & Hamari, J. (2020). Does gamification affect brand engagement and equity? A study in online brand communities. *Journal of Business Research, 109*, 449–460.

Zeithaml, V. A. (1988). Consumer perceptions of price, quality, and value: A means–end model and synthesis of evidence. *Journal of Marketing, 52*(3), 2–22.

Zolfagharian, M., Hasan, F., & Iyer, P. (2017). Employee, branch, and brand switching: The role of linguistic choice, use and adaptation. *Journal of Services Marketing, 31*(4–5), 452–470.

7 A roadmap of brand experience

Lia Zarantonello and Daniela Andreini

> Brands are not what they say they are. They are what the customer experiences.
> (Ogilvy and Mather, 360 Degree Brand Stewardship)

1. Introduction

This chapter focuses on the concept of brand experience – one of the key concepts present in the branding literature in the past 30 years. As of March 2022, *Business Source Premier* identified 328 publications with "brand experience" in their title, whereas Google Scholar retrieved 2,020 of such items. To further support the popularity and importance of the concept not only for academic research but also for managerial practice, several brand experience agencies operate around the world – from the global Jack Morton (https://www.jackmorton.com/) and FIRST (https://firstagency.com/) to more local ones – as well as brand experience management roles in various reputable companies. This decades-long attention of both academic scholars and professionals to brand experience reflects the broader customer-centric orientation in marketing, which emphasizes the role of consumers in relation to the other stakeholders in the company (Latinovic & Chatterjee, 2019; Shah et al., 2006).

The objective of this chapter is therefore to review the prominent concept of brand experience by describing its origin, examining its conceptualization and measurement, and then suggesting directions for future research. Similar studies have been carried out in the past, including those by Pauwels-Delassus and Zarantonello (2015), who focused on the measurement of brand experience, and by Schmitt, Brakus, and Zarantonello (2014) and Schmitt and Zarantonello (2013), who reviewed the theoretical framework of brand experience. Compared to these past works, the current chapter intends to provide an updated, concise overview of the brand experience concept by paying attention to both conceptual and operational aspects, and by suggesting directions for future research.

2. Origins of brand experience

The concept of brand experience has been developed within the framework of experiential marketing (Schmitt, 1999). The rise of experiential marketing in the 1990s was possible because of changes in economic, socio-cultural, and consumption levels. At the economic level, the end of the 1990s saw the birth of what was called the "experience economy" (Pine & Gilmore, 1998). This economy followed the service-based economy, the goods-based economy, and the agrarian economy, and it was characterized by the emergence of a new economic offer called "experience", which was described as personal and memorable (contrary to services which are customized and intangible, goods that are standardized and tangible, and commodities which are natural and fungible) (Pine & Gilmore, 1998). At the socio-cultural level, societies moving from a modern to a postmodern status exhibited a significant shift in values: from traditional and survival values to self-expression and secular ones (Inglehart, 1997). At the consumption level, new trends emerged (Firat & Venkatesh, 1995), with scholars urging consideration of experiential aspects of consumption in addition to established rational ones (Holbrook & Hirschman, 1982).

Within this context, several new marketing approaches emerged, including experiential marketing, which differs from the traditional approach in terms of its focus, definition of competition, view of consumers, and methods of research (Batat, 2019; Schmitt, 1999). Whereas traditional marketing focuses on product features and benefits, experiential marketing is centered on the experience lived by consumers in their interaction with the company and its products. Whereas traditional marketing defined product category and competition narrowly, experiential marketing views consumption as a holistic experience. Whereas traditional marketing considered consumers as mainly rational, experiential marketing views them as both rational and emotional decision-makers. Whereas traditional marketing mainly used methods and tools that were analytical, quantitative, and verbal, experiential marketing is based on a combination of different quantitative and qualitative tools with which to capture the various aspects of consumer experience. In this new framework, the brand is also given an expanded role. Far from being considered a mere identifier of products, the brand is seen as a provider of an experience. The focus, therefore, is less on traditional branding concepts, such as awareness and image, and more on the holistic stimulation that brands are able to provide to consumers. The idea of "brand experience" becomes central in this framework (Brakus et al., 2009).

3. Conceptualization and measurement of brand experience

Brand experience is defined as "subjective, internal consumer responses (sensations, feelings, and cognitions) and behavioral responses evoked by brand-related stimuli that are part of a brand's design and identity, packaging, communications, and environments" (Brakus et al., 2009, p. 53). Brand experience is conceptualized by Brakus et al. (2009) as a multidimensional phenomenon which comprises four dimensions: (1) a sensory dimension, which refers to the visual, auditory, olfactory, gustatory, and tactile stimulation provided by the brand; (2) an affective dimension, which refers to the feelings and emotions triggered by the brand; (3) an intellectual dimension, which refers to the cognitive stimulation provided by the brand; and (4) a behavioral dimension, which refers to the actions and behaviors stimulated by the brand.

These four brand experience dimensions derived by Brakus et al. (2009) from the literature review have been corroborated by a qualitative study investigating consumers' experiences with brands, and they have been operationalized in a series of quantitative studies by the same scholars. The latter made it possible to generate and select the brand experience scale items; reduce the set of items and confirm the dimensionality of the scale; further establish the reliability and validity of the scale; and use the brand experience scale to predict key consumer behavior outcomes such as consumer satisfaction and brand loyalty.

Brand experience is conceptually and empirically different from other brand-related constructs. Brand experiences differ from brand attitudes because they are not general evaluations of a brand, but the actual sensations, feelings, cognitions, and behavioral responses that are triggered by a brand. Brand experiences also differ from brand involvement and attachment because they do not presume a motivational state or they are not an emotional relationship construct; instead, they can occur when consumers do not show interest in, or have a personal connection with, the brand. Finally, brand experiences differ from brand personality because they are not brand associations and derived through an inferential process; rather, they are dynamic sensations, feelings, cognitions, and behavioral responses to a brand.

The brand experience scale is presented in Table 7.1. Overall, the scale-development process involved more than 1,000 respondents and 70 brands from different product categories including consumer electronics (e.g., Apple), food and beverages (e.g., Tropicana, Dannon), apparel and fashion (e.g., Adidas).

Table 7.1 The brand experience scale

Scale dimensions and items
Sensory dimension
• This brand makes a strong impression on my visual sense or other senses
• I find this brand interesting in a sensory way
• This brand does not appeal to my senses*
Affective dimension
• This brand induces feelings and sentiments
• I do not have strong emotions for this brand*
• This brand is an emotional brand
Intellectual dimension
• I engage in physical actions and behaviors when I use this brand
• This brand results in bodily experiences
• This brand is not action oriented*
Behavioral dimension
• I engage in a lot of thinking when I encounter this brand
• This brand does not make me think*
• This brand stimulates my curiosity and problem solving

Note: * indicates that the item is negatively phrased and reverse-coded.

4. Further conceptualizations and measurements of brand experience

The original conceptualization provided by Brakus et al. (2009) was subsequently expanded by the same authors (Schmitt et al., 2014), incorporating a fifth dimension of brand experience which referred to social/relational stimulation. This dimension, especially in some contexts, constitutes an important part of how consumers experience brands.

Differently from other brand conceptualizations, most of the brand experience literature focuses on a single operationalization of the construct (Brakus et al., 2009; Schmitt et al., 2014), and a monolithic theoretical perspective through which the phenomenon of brand experience is approached. Some scholars, however, have proposed a modified version of the original conceptualization and measurement related to one specific dimension of the brand experience construct – such as *sensory brand experience* (Hepola et al., 2017; Hultén, 2011), or a specific industry – such as *brand experience in service organizations* (Nysveen et al., 2013), *retail brand experience* (Khan & Rahman, 2015; 2016), and *omnichannel brand experience* (Frasquet-Deltoro et al., 2021). More limited are the studies that advance the conceptualization of brand experience, such as the *multidimensional socially constructed brand experience* notion (Andreini et al., 2018).

4.1 Sensory brand experience

The sensory brand experience is defined as "how individuals react when a firm interacts and supports their purchase and consumption processes through the involvement of the five human senses in generating customer value, experiences, and brand as image" (Hultén, 2011, p. 257). The operationalization of this sensory brand experience has been limited to the use of the sensory dimension of the scale developed by Brakus et al. (2009) – see for instance Iglesias et al. (2011) – composed of three items devoted to measuring consumers' sensory stimulation activated during a brand experience.

4.2 Brand experience in service organizations

With the focus on service brands, a conceptualization and operationalization of brand experience in service organization is proposed by Nysveen et al. (2013). Brand experiences in service organizations consist of sensory, affective, intellectual, and behavioral dimensions; in addition, they comprise a social or relational dimension which considers the relational nature of services compared to products. The brand experience in service organizations scale uses the same items as the original scale by Brakus et al. (2009), plus three additional ones for the relational dimension (i.e., "As a customer of 'brand' I feel that I am part of a community"; "I feel that I am part of the 'brand' family"; "When I use 'brand' I do not feel left alone").

4.3 Retail brand experience

The retail brand experience is conceptualized as "the sum total of sensations, feelings, cognitions, and behavioral responses evoked by retail brand-related stimuli during the complete buying process, involving an integrated series of interactions with retail store design, service interface, packaging of own private labels, communications, and environments" (Khan & Rahman, 2015, p. 62). In

2016, the same authors operationalized and developed a retail brand experience scale composed of 22 items and seven dimensions.

The seven dimensions of retail brand experience can be described as consumers' reactions (sensations, feelings, cognitions, and behavioral responses) related to: (1) "retail brand name influence", which measures the appeal for consumers of the name of the retail brand; (2) "customer billing, order and application forms", that is, customers' requirement for transparency and useful information in bills, orders, and application forms; (3) "mass media impression", which is related to customers' emotional reactions to the retailers' mass media branded stimuli; (4) "recommendation by a salesperson", which is connected to the interactions and relationships with salespersons; (5) "point-of-sales assistance", which is related to the arrangement of shelf talkers and product displays at a retail store; (6) "emotional event experience", which refers to consumers' feeling of affection for events organized by the retail brand; and (7) "brand stories connectedness", which is the extent to which a customer finds the retailers' brand stories resonant with his/her life.

This scale broadens the domain of the construct of brand experience suggested by Brakus et al. (2009) by adding the dimensions related to the specific experiences lived in retail stores.

4.4 Omnichannel retailer brand experience (ORBE)

Omnichannel retailer brand experience (ORBE) has been conceptualized by Frasquet-Deltoro et al. (2021) as the single-brand experience of consumers in a multifaceted omnichannel environment composed of multiple touch points and relationship opportunities. Defining ORBE as the brand experience affected by the multifaceted omnichannel environment, Frasquet-Deltoro et al. (2021) developed a multidimensional scale comprising 19 items and eight dimensions: (1) the sensory dimension measured consumers' senses activated by aesthetic and visual identity of the omnichannel retailer; (2) the affective dimension rated consumers' emotions and feelings induced by omnichannel retailers; (3) the intellectual dimension referred to the consumer's curiosity, creativity, and thoughts activated by omnichannel retailers; (4) the behavioral dimension computed consumers' impulsive behaviors and physical actions provoked by omnichannel retailers; (5) the relational dimension assessed the sharing and interacting experience of consumers inside physical outlets as well as in virtual social environments; (6) the lifestyle dimension considered consumers' identification with the system of values and beliefs of the omnichannel retailer brands; (7) the pragmatic dimension was utilized when omnichannel retailer brands included usability and convenience; and (8) the social dimension measured consumers' sense of being part of a social group facilitated by the omnichannel retailer brands.

This scale broadened the domain of the construct of brand experience suggested by Brakus et al. (2009) by adding the dimensions of lifestyle – pragmatic, relational, and social – that reflect the omnichannel retail environment.

4.5 Multidimensional socially constructed brand experience

By focusing on influential marketing streams relying on non-positivist epistemologies (i.e., relationship theory, consumer culture theory, and service-dominant logic), Andreini et al. (2018) identified a dynamic and multi-level model of brand experience. The multidimensional socially constructed brand experience is articulated on three levels – namely micro, meso, and macro – corresponding to as many layers of embeddedness of subjective experience in wider social contexts. Each of these levels can be defined as a distinct yet interconnected constituent of social reality, each with its own emergent properties, ranging from dyadic interactions and encounters (the micro level), through structured patterns of action and interaction in collectives (the meso level) such as communities, social groups, sub-cultural or counter-cultural aggregates, and even firms, to broader social categories in which both the micro and macro level are embedded (the macro level), such as institutions, class systems, society, and inter-societal systems. Although this conceptualization has not yet been operationalized, it is a first attempt to show how more interpretative theoretical streams (i.e., relationship theory, consumer culture theory, and service-dominant logic) have advanced the brand experience conceptualization, even if it is not explicitly mentioned.

5. The nomological network of brand experience

Brand experience arises from the exposure of consumers to a series of brand-related stimuli (Brakus et al., 2009). To understand the nomological network of brand experience, it is important to start from brand stimuli as part of a brand's design and identity, brand communications and events, new technologies, packaging, service, and the service environments where the brand is marketed or sold. Khan (2014) suggests that brand stimuli are all forms of the interactions that consumers have with either the specific company or its products or services. Table 7.2 summarizes the main sources of brand experience.

Table 7.2 Sources of brand experience in the extant literature

Sources of brand experience	References
Brand's design and identity (name, logo, signage, character, etc.)	Brakus et al. (2009); Hamzah et al. (2014)
Brand communication and storytelling	Brakus et al. (2009); Chattopadhyay & Laborie (2005); Khan & Rahman (2015)
Events	Brakus et al. (2009); Fransen et al. (2013); Khan & Rahman (2015); Whelan & Wohlfeil (2006); Zarantonello & Schmitt (2013)
New technologies (AI, AR/VR, social media, etc.)	Batat & Hammedi (2023); Puntoni et al. (2021); Yu & Yuan (2019); Zarantonello & Schmitt (2023);
Packaging (colors, shapes, etc.)	Brakus et al. (2009); Shukla et al. (2023); Underwood (2003)
Service and service environment (stores, staff, self-service, etc.)	Brakus et al. (2009); Khan (2014); Tafesse (2016); Shahid et al. (2022)

In addition to brand stimuli, there are studies that have helped to understand some other brand experience antecedents. Chen et al. (2014) examined brand love as an antecedent of brand experience and supported the concept of intrinsic motivation as fostering brand experience. In the same years, Morgan-Thomas and Veloutsou (2013), and again Chen together with some colleagues (2014), viewed trust and perceived usefulness as an input of brand experience. One year later, Khan and Rahman (2015) focused on event marketing and storytelling as brand experience predecessors.

Studies focusing on the outcomes of brand experience have detected cognitive outcomes such as brand satisfaction (Chinomona, 2013; Hwang et al., 2021; Khan & Fatma, 2017; Nysveen et al., 2013), brand attitude (Hwang et al., 2021; Nayeem et al., 2019; Roswinanto & Strutton, 2014), brand credibility (Khan & Fatma, 2017; Shamim & Butt, 2013), brand distinctiveness (Roswinanto & Strutton, 2014), and brand image (Kim & Chao, 2019; Semadi & Ariyanti, 2018). Emotional outcomes have been identified as brand attachment (Huaman-Ramirez & Merunka, 2019), brand commitment (Jung & Soo, 2012; Şahin et al., 2013), brand trust (Chinomona, 2013; Jung & Soo, 2012; Kim et al., 2015; Şahin et al., 2013), brand personality (Ishida & Taylor, 2012; Japutra & Molinillo, 2019; Nysveen et al., 2013), and brand relationship quality (Francisco-Maffezzolli et al., 2014). Behavioral results such as brand loyalty (Chen et al., 2014; Iglesias et al., 2011; Kim et al., 2015) and other behavioral intentions (Morgan-Thomas & Veloutsou, 2013; Şahin et al., 2013) have also been distinguished. Furthermore, other studies have examined brand experience in relation to brand performances, such as brand equity (Hultén, 2011; Lin, 2015; Shamim & Butt, 2013) and premium price (Dwivedi et al., 2018; Şahin et al., 2013).

A summary of the main consequences of brand experience, including emotional/cognitive, behavioral, and performance, is presented in Table 7.3.

Table 7.3 Consequences of brand experience in extant literature

Consequences	**References**
Behavioral	
Behavioral intentions	Morgan-Thomas & Veloutsou (2013)
Repurchase intention	Şahin et al. (2013)
WOM	Chen et al. (2014); Şahin et al. (2013); Khan & Fatma (2017)
Consumer loyalty	Brakus et al. (2009); Hwang et al. (2021); Khan & Fatma (2017)
Relational	
Brand attachment	Huaman-Ramirez & Merunka (2019); Kim & Chao (2019); Hwang et al. (2021)
Brand loyalty	Ding & Tseng (2015); Francisco-Maffezzolli et al. (2014); Iglesias et al. (2011); Ishida & Taylor (2012); Kim & Ah Yu (2016); Nysveen et al. (2013); Ramaseshan & Stein (2014); van der Westhuizen (2018)
Brand commitment	Jung & Soo (2012); Şahin et al. (2013)
Brand relationship quality	Francisco-Maffezzolli et al. (2014); Jung & Soo (2012)
Brand trust	Chinomona (2013); Jung & Soo (2012); Kim et al. (2015); Kim & Chao (2019); Khan & Fatma (2017); Şahin et al. (2013)
Customer experiential value	Keng et al. (2013)
Cognitive/Emotional	
Brand attitude	Hwang et al. (2021); Nayeem et al. (2019); Roswinanto & Strutton (2014); Shamim & Butt (2013)

Consequences	References
Brand credibility	Dwivedi et al. (2018); Jiménez-Barreto et al. (2020); Khan & Fatma (2017); Nayeem et al. (2019); Shamim & Butt (2013)
Brand distinctiveness	Roswinanto & Strutton (2014)
Brand personality	Brakus et al. (2009); Japutra & Molinillo (2019); Keng et al. (2013); Nysveen et al. (2013); Ishida & Taylor (2012)
Brand image	Kim & Chao (2019); Semadi & Ariyanti (2018)
Brand satisfaction	Chinomona (2013); Hwang et al. (2021); Ishida & Taylor (2012); Khan & Fatma (2017); Nysveen et al. (2013); Şahin et al. (2013)
Consumer satisfaction	Brakus et al. (2009); Khan & Rahman (2015); Lin (2015); Kim et al. (2015); Morgan-Thomas & Veloutsou (2013); Şahin et al. (2013)
Performance	
Brand equity	Chen (2012); Hepola et al. (2017); Lin (2015); Shamim & Butt (2013)
Premium price	Dwivedi et al. (2018); Şahin et al. (2013)

6. Emerging areas in brand experience research

Two main areas of research on brand experience are currently emerging. The first one considers brand experience in relation to new technologies such as the Internet of Things (IoT), augmented reality (AR)/virtual reality (VR)/mixed reality (MR), as well as virtual assistants, chatbots, and robots empowered by artificial intelligence (AI). The second research area considers brand experience in relation to society at large and establishes a connection with broader societal goals, including individual and social well-being.

Regarding brand experience and new technologies, scholars are examining how these technologies are changing the way in which consumers experience brands at different stages of the consumer journey (Hoyer et al., 2020). In the case of AR/VR, for example, it has been shown that these new technologies can enhance the experience of consumers with brands and increase the overall value that they provide to consumers (Zarantonello & Schmitt, 2023). They can enrich brand experiences by providing additional informative contents, sensorial stimulation, imagination, and opportunities for closer interaction with peers and the brand or company in a variety of settings such as stores (Cuomo et al., 2020) and advertisements (Song et al., 2021).

While some scholars have examined how new technologies can enhance consumers' stimulation and interaction with a brand, other scholars have examined how new technologies can replace the interactions between consumers and brands or companies. Specifically in service industries, AI-empowered technologies – such as digital assistants, robots, and augmented reality – are jointly involved in the process of creating brand experiences. In tourism, for instance, some researchers have explored how service robots change the consumer brand experience in the hotels and hospitality industry (e.g., Chan & Tung, 2019; Hwang et al., 2021; Rosete et al., 2020). These new technologies, contrasting with others like online communities and social media, are not just contexts of interaction; they are both contexts and actors because they deploy agency in interactive dynamics (Kaartemo & Helkkula, 2018). AI can prove to be a pivotal operant resource (Ramaswamy & Ozcan, 2018; Purvis & Long, 2011) assuming the role traditionally attributed to human agents. This new theoretical understanding of AI-powered, brand experience co-creation processes and networks opens up entirely new landscapes for both the scholars and practitioners of brand management (Mangiò et al., 2022).

The second main research area links brand experience to broader societal goals including individual and social well-being. Individual happiness and psychological well-being are concepts that derive from "positive psychology" (Gable & Haidt, 2005), which deals with positive influences in people's lives, contrary to other, more traditional branches of psychology which study dysfunctional and abnormal behavior. Because consumers establish meaningful relationships with brands (Fetscherin et al., 2019), develop attachment to them (Park et al., 2008), and use them to build their self (Escalas & Bettman, 2005), brands are seen as means to boost consumers' happiness and psychological well-being (Schnebelen & Bruhn, 2018). Put otherwise, brands can foster consumer happiness and psychological well-being by evoking different types of experience (Schmitt et al., 2014). The specific relationship between brand experience and happiness (Karam, 2017), the role of self-related variables (e.g., self-congruence; Sheeraz et al., 2020), and food contexts (Batat, 2021; Zarantonello et al., 2021) are examples of matters currently subject to investigation. Moreover, the social structural characterization of brand experience allows consumers to address social concerns by activating meaningful relationship with brands, peers, and organizations (Schmitt et al., 2014). In this stance, an example is the continuous consumers' request toward brands to make a stand for socio-political issues, forcing brands to demonstrate their activism toward critical matters such as racism, sexism, and wars ("woke brands"), and going beyond the individual level of brand experience toward a more social dimension of it (Andreini et al., 2018; Mirzaei et al., 2022).

7. Future research directions

Considering the brand experience research conducted to date, and its currently emerging areas of inquiry, future research could focus on (i) further advancing the conceptualization and measurement of the construct of brand experience, (ii) examining brand experience through a longitudinal perspective, and (iii) expanding the set of antecedents and outcomes considered in relation to brand experience.

In relation to point (i) above, several conceptualizations and measurements have been proposed over the years and more are currently being developed in relation to new technologies (Hoyer et al., 2020; Zarantonello & Schmitt, 2023). This highlights the complexity of the brand experience phenomenon and the different meanings that brand experience can have in specific contexts, but also the need for advancing the conceptualization of brand experience especially in the light of the changes deriving from new technologies. The enhanced interaction between consumers and brands, the increased levels of sensorial, cognitive, and affective stimulation of consumers, as well as the possibility that consumers have to share their own brand experiences with other consumers or to participate in others' brand experiences in real time, are examples of aspects that are affecting how brand experiences are formed, lived, and shared by consumers today. Hence, examples of questions that could be addressed by future research are the following:

- How is brand experience evolving because of digital technologies such as the IoT and AR/VR/MR, as well as virtual assistants, chatbots, and robots empowered by AI?
- How can these new, enhanced brand experiences be conceptualized and operationalized?
- What dimensions do these new, enhanced brand experiences have? And how do these dimensions relate to brand experience dimensionality as found in previous conceptualizations?
- Are new measurement scales needed in order to capture the specificities of these new, enhanced brand experiences?
- How and to what extent is the overall brand experience affected by the specific new technology used? Do different new technologies enhance

different, specific, aspects of brand experience? Do they trigger different underlying psychological mechanisms?

Moreover, if most studies to date have focused on brand experience in one point in time, understanding its evolution over an extended period represents another important area of research for the future, as per point (ii) above. Longitudinal studies on brand experiences might reveal important aspects of how these change over time, in the light of consumers' relationships with brands, personal experiences, and the influence (whether positive or negative) of other consumers. Brand experiences might acquire specific, distinct meanings and roles in each phase of the consumer experience (i.e., anticipated consumption, purchase experience, core consumption experience, and remembered consumption; see Arnould et al., 2002) or the consumer journey (i.e., pre-purchase, purchase, post-purchase; see Lemon and Verhoef, 2016). Similarly, brand experiences could be considered in the context of consumer–brand relationships (Fetscherin et al., 2019). Different consumer–brand relationships could be examined, including relationships varying in valence (positive vs. negative), duration (short vs. long term), and intensity (highly emotional vs. mild). Understanding how brand experiences affect and are affected by the type and nature of relationships that consumers have with brands might shed additional light on the role of brand experiences in shaping consumers' attitudes and preferences. Examples of research questions to consider include the following:

- How are brand experiences formed, lived, and shared with other consumers in the different phases of the consumer experience/consumer journey? What role do brand experiences have in each of these phases? How do they evolve?
- What role do brand experiences have in short-term, highly affective consumer–brand relationships versus long-term, more established relationships?
- How do brand experiences relate to different types of consumer–brand relationships incidents? What role do positive (negative) brand experiences have in the context of negative (positive) consumer–brand relationships? How can brand experience help recover from consumer–brand relationship incidents?

Based on point (iii) above, future research could also go beyond the study of traditional variables such as satisfaction and loyalty, whose relationship with brand experience has been already demonstrated in the literature. Future research could expand the set of possible antecedents and outcomes of brand experience, and examine constructs related to individual and social well-being.

Psychological constructs that could be further examined in association with brand experience include consumers' overall happiness and its three components of pleasure, meaning, and engagement (Peterson et al., 2005), as well as consumers' personalities, values, and identities. Brand experience could also be analyzed in relation to different forms of brand activism (e.g., multicultural) and woke citizenship. Examples of research questions that could be addressed are the following:

- How do brand experiences relate to overall happiness and its dimensions of pleasure, meaning, and engagement?
- To what extent do traditional versus new, enhanced brand experiences differ in their relationship with consumers' happiness and well-being?
- To what extent do consumers' personal traits impact on the relationship between brand experiences and happiness/well-being?
- To what extent do consumers' values and identity impact on the relationship between brand experiences and happiness/well-being?
- How do brand experiences change when brands take a stand on socio-political issues?
- Under what circumstances and for what types or categories of consumers do brand experiences improve when brands support socio-political issues?

In sum, future research could further advance the construct of brand experience considering its evolution over an extended period and considering a new, technology-driven context that characterizes today's societies and includes variables related to the psychological well-being of society at large.

References

Andreini, D., Pedeliento, G., Zarantonello, L., & Solerio, C. (2018). A renaissance of brand experience: Advancing the concept through a multi-perspective analysis. *Journal of Business Research, 91*, 123–133.

Arnould, E.J., Price, L., & Zinkhan, G.M. (2002). *Consumers.* New York: McGraw-Hill.

Batat, W. (2019). *Experiential marketing: Consumer behavior, customer experience and the 7Es.* Abingdon: Routledge.

Batat, W. (2021). How augmented reality (AR) is transforming the restaurant sector: Investigating the impact of "Le Petit Chef" on customers' dining experiences. *Technological Forecasting and Social Change, 172*(November), 121013.

Batat, W., & Hammedi, W. (2023). The extended reality technology (ERT) framework for designing customer and service experiences in phygital settings: A service research agenda. *Journal of Service Management, 34*(1), 10–33.

Brakus, J.J., Schmitt, B.H., & Zarantonello, L. (2009). Brand experience: What is it? How is it measured? Does it affect loyalty? *Journal of Marketing, 73*(3), 52–68.

Chan, A.P.H., & Tung, V.W.S. (2019). Examining the effects of robotic service on brand experience: The moderating role of hotel segment. *Journal of Travel & Tourism Marketing, 36*(4), 458–468.

Chattopadhyay, A., & Laborie, J.L. (2005). Managing brand experience: The market contact audit. *Journal of Advertising Research, 45*(1), 9–16.

Chen, H., Papazafeiropoulou, A., Chen, T.K., Duan, Y., & Liu, H.W. (2014). Exploring the commercial value of social networks: Enhancing consumers' brand experience through Facebook pages. *Journal of Enterprise Information Management, 27*(5), 576–598.

Chen, L.S.L. (2012). What drives cyber shop brand equity? An empirical evaluation of online shopping system benefit with brand experience. *International Journal of Business and Information, 7*(1), 81–104.

Chinomona, R. (2013). The influence of brand experience on brand satisfaction, trust and attachment in South Africa. *International Business & Economics Research Journal (IBER), 12*(10), 1303–1316.

Cuomo, M.T., Tortora, D., Festa, G., Ceruti, F., & Metallo, G. (2020). Managing omni-customer brand experience via augmented reality: A qualitative investigation in the Italian fashion retailing system. *Qualitative Market Research, 23*(3), 427–445.

Ding, C.G., & Tseng, T.H. (2015). On the relationships among brand experience, hedonic emotions, and brand equity. *European Journal of Marketing, 49*(7/8), 994–1015.

Dwivedi, A., Nayeem, T., & Murshed, F. (2018). Brand experience and consumers' willingness-to-pay (WTP) a price premium: Mediating role of brand credibility and perceived uniqueness. *Journal of Retailing and Consumer Services, 44*, 100–107.

Escalas, J.E., & Bettman, J.R. (2005). Self-construal, reference groups, and brand meaning. *Journal of Consumer Research, 32*(3), 378–389.

Fetscherin, M., Guzman, F., Veloutsou, C., & Cayolla, R.R. (2019). Latest research on brand relationships: Introduction to the special issue. *Journal of Product and Brand Management, 28*(2), 133–139.

Firat, A.F., & Venkatesh, A. (1995). Liberatory postmodernism and the reenchantment of consumption. *Journal of Consumer Research, 22*(3), 239–267.

Francisco-Maffezzolli, E.C., Semprebon, E., & Muller Prado, P.H. (2014). Construing loyalty through brand experience: The mediating role of brand relationship quality. *Journal of Brand Management, 21*(5), 446–458.

Fransen, M.L., van Rompay, T.J., & Muntinga, D.G. (2013). Increasing sponsorship effectiveness through brand experience. *International Journal of Sports Marketing and Sponsorship, 14*(2), 37–50.

Frasquet-Deltoro, M., Molla-Descals, A., & Miquel-Romero, M.J. (2021). Omnichannel retailer brand experience: Conceptualisation and proposal of a comprehensive scale. *Journal of Brand Management, 28*(4), 388–401.

Gable, S.L., & Haidt, J. (2005). What (and why) is positive psychology? *Review of General Psychology, 9*(2), 103–110.

Hamzah, Z.L., Alwi, S.F.S., & Othman, M.N. (2014). Designing corporate brand experience in an online context: A qualitative insight. *Journal of Business Research, 67*(11), 2299–2310.

Hepola, J., Karjaluoto, H., & Hintikka, A. (2017). The effect of sensory brand experience and involvement on brand equity directly and indirectly through consumer brand engagement. *Journal of Product & Brand Management, 26*(3), 282–293.

Holbrook, M.B., & Hirschman, E.C. (1982). The experiential aspects of consumption: Consumer fantasies, feelings, and fun. *Journal of Consumer Research, 9*(2), 132–140.

Hoyer, W.D., Kroschke, M., Schmitt, B., Kraume, K., & Shankar, V. (2020). Transforming the customer experience through new technologies. *Journal of Interactive Marketing, 51*(August), 57–71.

Huaman-Ramirez, R., & Merunka, D. (2019). Brand experience effects on brand attachment: The role of brand trust, age, and income. *European Business Review, 31*(5), 610–645.

Hultén, B. (2011). Sensory marketing: The multi-sensory brand-experience concept. *European Business Review, 23*(3), 256–273.

Hwang, J., Choe, J.Y.J., Kim, H.M., & Kim, J.J. (2021). Human baristas and robot baristas: How does brand experience affect brand satisfaction, brand attitude, brand attachment, and brand loyalty? *International Journal of Hospitality Management, 99*, 103050.

Iglesias, O., Singh, J.J., & Batista-Foguet, J.M. (2011). The role of brand experience and affective commitment in determining brand loyalty. *Journal of Brand Management, 18*(8), 570–582.

Inglehart, R. (1997). *Modernization and postmodernization: Cultural, economic, and political change in 43 societies*. Princeton, NJ: Princeton University Press.

Ishida, C., & Taylor, S.A. (2012). Retailer brand experience, brand experience congruence, and consumer satisfaction. *Journal of Consumer Satisfaction, Dissatisfaction and Complaining Behavior, 25*, 63–79.

Japutra, A., & Molinillo, S. (2019). Responsible and active brand personality: On the relationships with brand experience and key relationship constructs. *Journal of Business Research, 99*, 464–471.

Jiménez-Barreto, J., Rubio, N., Campo, S., & Molinillo, S. (2020). Linking the online destination brand experience and brand credibility with tourists' behavioral intentions toward a destination. *Tourism Management, 79*, 104101.

Jung, L.H., & Soo, K.M. (2012). The effect of brand experience on brand relationship quality. *Academy of Marketing Studies Journal, 16*(1), 87–98.

Kaartemo, V., & Helkkula, A. (2018). A systematic review of artificial intelligence and robots in value co-creation: Current status and future research avenues. *Journal of Creating Value, 4*(2), 211–228.

Karam, Al Mandil (2017). From brand experience to happiness: Exploring the impacts on brand loyalty and price premium. In: 12th Global Brand Conference of the Academy of Marketing's SIG in Brand, Identity and Corporate Reputation, April 26-28, 2017, Linnaeus University, Kalmar, Sweden.

Keng, C.J., Tran, V.D., & Le Thi, T.M. (2013). Relationships among brand experience, brand personality, and customer experiential value. *Contemporary Management Research, 9*(3), 247–262.

Khan, G. (2014). The mediating role of employee engagement in relationship of internal branding and brand experience: Case of service organizations of Dera Ghazi Khan. *International Journal of Information, Business and Management, 6*(4), 26–41.

Khan, I., & Fatma, M. (2017). Antecedents and outcomes of brand experience: An empirical study. *Journal of Brand Management, 24*(5), 439–452.

Khan, I., & Rahman, Z. (2015). Brand experience anatomy in retailing: An interpretive structural modeling approach. *Journal of Retailing and Consumer Services, 24*, 60–69.

Khan, I., & Rahman, Z. (2016). Retail brand experience: Scale development and validation. *Journal of Product & Brand Management, 25*(5), 435–451.

Kim, J., & Ah Yu, E. (2016). The holistic brand experience of branded mobile applications affects brand loyalty. *Social Behavior and Personality: An International Journal, 44*(1), 77-87.

Kim, R.B., & Chao, Y. (2019). Effects of brand experience, brand image and brand trust on brand building process: The case of Chinese millennial generation consumers. *Journal of International Studies*, *12*(3), 9–21.

Kim, R.B., Yoon, D.H., & Yan, C. (2015). Effects of brand experience on brand trust, brand satisfaction & brand loyalty: Building SPA brands in South Korea. *Actual Problems of Economics*, *168*(6), 182–189.

Latinovic, Z., & Chatterjee, S.C. (2019). Customer centricity in the digital age. *MIT Sloan Management Review*, *60*(4), 01–02.

Lemon, K.N., & Verhoef, P.C. (2016). Understanding customer experience throughout the customer journey. *Journal of Marketing*, *80*(6), 69–96.

Lin, Y.H. (2015). Innovative brand experience's influence on brand equity and brand satisfaction. *Journal of Business Research*, *68*(11), 2254–2259.

Mangiò, F., Pedeliento, G., & Andreini, D. (2022). Brand experience co-creation at the time of artificial intelligence. In O. Iglesias, N. Ind, & M. Schultz (eds.), *The Routledge companion to corporate branding* (pp. 195–210). Abingdon: Routledge.

Mirzaei, A., Wilkie, D.C., & Siuki, H. (2022). Woke brand activism authenticity or the lack of it. *Journal of Business Research*, *139*, 1–12.

Morgan-Thomas, A., & Veloutsou, C. (2013). Beyond technology acceptance: Brand relationships and online brand experience. *Journal of Business Research*, *66*(1), 21–27.

Nayeem, T., Murshed, F., & Dwivedi, A. (2019). Brand experience and brand attitude: Examining a credibility-based mechanism. *Marketing Intelligence & Planning*, *37*(7), 821–836.

Nysveen, H., Pedersen, P.E., & Skard, S. (2013). Brand experiences in service organizations: Exploring the individual effects of brand experience dimensions. *Journal of Brand Management*, *20*, 404–423.

Park, W.C., Macinnis, D.J., & Priester, J. (2008). *Brand attachment: Construct, consequences and causes*. Norwell, MA: Now Publishers Inc.

Pauwels-Delassus, V., & Zarantonello, L. (2015). *Handbook of brand management scales*. Abingdon: Routledge.

Peterson, C., Park, N., & Seligman, M. (2005). Orientations to happiness and life satisfaction: The full life versus the empty life. *Journal of Happiness Studies*, *6*(1), 25–41.

Pine, B.J., & Gilmore, J.H. (1998). Welcome to the experience economy. *Harvard Business Review*, *76*, 97–105.

Puntoni, S., Reczek, R.W., Giesler, M., & Botti, S. (2021). Consumers and artificial intelligence: An experiential perspective. *Journal of Marketing*, *85*(1), 131–151.

Purvis, M., & Long, A. (2011). Affinities between multi-agent systems and service-dominant logic: Interactionist implications for business marketing practice. *Industrial Marketing Management*, *40*(2), 248–254.

Ramaseshan, B., & Stein, A. (2014). Connecting the dots between brand experience and brand loyalty: The mediating role of brand personality and brand relationships. *Journal of Brand Management*, *21*(7), 664–683.

Ramaswamy, V., & Ozcan, K. (2018). What is co-creation? An interactional creation framework and its implications for value creation. *Journal of Business Research*, *84*, 196–205.

Rosete, A., Soares, B., Salvadorinho, J., Reis, J., & Amorim, M. (2020). Service robots in the hospitality industry: An exploratory literature review. In H. Nóvoa, M. Drăgoicea, & N. Kühl (eds.), *International Conference on Exploring Services Science* (pp. 174–186). Cham: Springer.

Roswinanto, W., & Strutton, D. (2014). Investigating the advertising antecedents to and consequences of brand experience. *Journal of Promotion Management, 20*(5), 607–627.

Şahin, A., Turhan, L., & Zehir, A. (2013). Building behavioral intentions in automotive industry: Brand experience, satisfaction, trust, direct mail communication and attitudes toward advertising. *Business Management Dynamics, 3*(4), 45–61.

Schmitt, B. (1999). Experiential marketing. *Journal of Marketing Management, 15*(1–2), 53–67.

Schmitt, B.H., Brakus, J., & Zarantonello, L. (2014). The current state and future of brand experience. *Journal of Brand Management, 21*(9), 727–733.

Schmitt, B.H., & Zarantonello, L. (2013). Consumer experience and experiential marketing: A critical review. *Review of Marketing Research, 10*, 25–61.

Schnebelen, S., & Bruhn, M. (2018). An appraisal framework of the determinants and consequences of brand happiness. *Psychology and Marketing, 35*(2), 101–119.

Semadi, I.P., & Ariyanti, M. (2018). The influence of brand experience, brand image, and brand trust on brand loyalty of ABC-Cash. *Asian Journal of Management Sciences and Education, 7*(3), 12–23.

Shah, D., Rust, R.T., Parasuraman, A., Staelin, R., & Day, G.S. (2006). The path to customer centricity. *Journal of Service Research, 9*(2), 113–124.

Shahid, S., Paul, J., Gilal, F.G., & Ansari, S. (2022). The role of sensory marketing and brand experience in building emotional attachment and brand loyalty in luxury retail stores. *Psychology & Marketing, 39*, 1398–1412.

Shamim, A., & Butt, M.M. (2013). A critical model of brand experience consequences. *Asia Pacific Journal of Marketing and Logistics, 25*(1), 102–117.

Sheeraz, M., Qadeer, F., Khan, K.I., & Mahmood, S. (2020). What I am, what I want to be: The role of brand experience in the relationship of self-congruence facets and orientation toward happiness. *Journal of Business & Economics, 12*(1), 43–61.

Shukla, M., Misra, R., & Singh, D. (2023). Exploring relationship among semiotic product packaging, brand experience dimensions, brand trust and purchase intentions in an Asian emerging market. *Asia Pacific Journal of Marketing and Logistics, 35*(2), 249–265.

Song, H., Kim, J., Nguyen, T.P.H., Lee, K.M., & Park, N. (2021). Virtual reality advertising with brand experiences: The effects of media devices, virtual representation of the self, and self-presence. *International Journal of Advertising, 40*(7), 1096–1114.

Tafesse, W. (2016). Conceptualization of brand experience in an event marketing context. *Journal of Promotion Management, 22*(1), 34–48.

Underwood, R.L. (2003). The communicative power of product packaging: Creating brand identity via lived and mediated experience. *Journal of Marketing Theory and Practice, 11*(1), 62–76.

van der Westhuizen, L.M. (2018). Brand loyalty: Exploring self-brand connection and brand experience. *Journal of Product & Brand Management, 27*(2), 172–184.

Whelan, S., & Wohlfeil, M. (2006). Communicating brands through engagement with "lived" experiences. *Journal of Brand Management, 13*(4), 313–329.

Yu, X., & Yuan, C. (2019). How consumers' brand experience in social media can improve brand perception and customer equity. *Asia Pacific Journal of Marketing and Logistics, 31*(5), 1233–1251.

Zarantonello, L., & Schmitt, B.H. (2013). The impact of event marketing on brand equity. *International Journal of Advertising, 32*(2), 255–280.

Zarantonello, L., & Schmitt, B.H. (2023). Experiential AR/VR: A consumer and service framework and research agenda. *Journal of Service Management, 34*(1), 34–55.

Zarantonello, L., Grappi, S., Formisano, M., & Schmitt, B.H. (2021). A "crescendo" model: Designing food experiences for psychological well-being. *European Journal of Marketing*, *55*(9), 2414–2438.

8 Reflections on brand communities academic research[1]

Cleopatra Veloutsou

1. Introduction and aim

In the last two decades it has been documented that consumers who are passionate about a brand develop brand-centric relationships with the brand itself and/or other individual consumers or consumer groups (Veloutsou, 2009; Veloutsou & Ruiz-Mafe, 2020). Research into brand-centric groups was introduced in the early 2000s with work by Muñiz and O'Guinn (2001) and McAlexander, Schouten and Koenig (2002), and, since then, it has been on the rise (Roy Bhattacharjee et al., 2022). Given the state of research, it is not surprising that brand-centric groups have become appreciated as a key brand management evolutionary element in the last 30 years (Veloutsou & Guzmán, 2017). Although different terms are used to describe brand-centric groups, the dominant stream of research in this area uses the term brand communities, defined as "enduring, self-selected groups of consumers, who accept and recognize bonds of membership with each other and the brand" (Veloutsou & Moutinho, 2009, p. 316). Consumers' main motive to join brand communities is the desire to find like-minded individuals with similar brand-related feelings, share these feelings, and connect (Muñiz & O'Guinn, 2001; Veloutsou & Moutinho, 2009) to satisfy personal expression needs and gain access to brand-related information (Dessart & Veloutsou, 2021).

The constant increase of brand communities' academic work is evident. The Scopus database, accessed on April 1, 2022, searched the period 2001–2021 for journal articles only, using the search term "brand communit*" in the keywords, title or abstract. The year 2001 was selected because the first paper defining brand communities was published that year and, therefore, was a relevant starting point, while the year 2021 was chosen to allow replicability of the paper allocation procedure (Torgerson, 2003). The search returned 773 papers, contributed by several authors, and published in a wide variety of outlets (Figure 8.1). From the 280 Scopus listed journals, 15 have published more than 10 brand-community-related manuscripts each, with the *Journal of Business Research* and the *Journal of Product and Brand Management* being on the top, contributing 39 and 38 outputs respectively. Of the 1509 researchers with published work on brand communities, only 15 have produced more than five outputs in the area with Veloutsou and Cova producing the highest with 14 and 15 publications respectively.

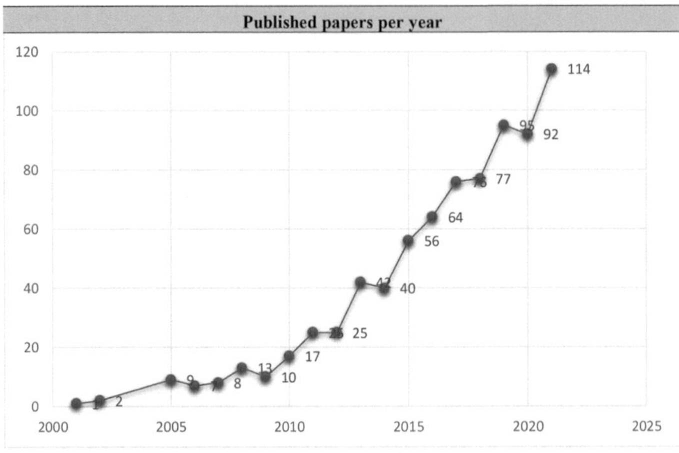

Journals with more than 10 papers	No.	Authors with more than 5 papers	No.
Journal of Business Research	39	Veloutsou, C.	14
Journal of Product and Brand Management	38	Cova, B.	13
European Journal of Marketing	21	Liao, J.	9
Journal of Brand Management	20	Kumar, J.	8
Journal of Marketing Management	16	Rahman, Z.	8
Journal of Retailing and Consumer Services	16	Heere, B.	7
Internet Research	15	Kamboj, S.	7
Journal of Research in Interactive Marketing	14	Loureiro, S.M.C.	7
Marketing Intelligence and Planning	13	Richard, M.O.	7
Computers in Human Behavior	12	Zhou, Z.	7
Electronic Commerce Research and Applications	12	Dessart, L.	6
Online Information Review	12	Flavián, C.	6
Sustainability Switzerland	12	Laroche, M.	6
Journal of Consumer Marketing	11	Thompson, S.A.	6
Marketing Theory	11	Wang, Y.	6

Source: Scopus database, accessed April 1, 2022

Figure 8.1 Production of academic work in the area of brand communities in the period 2001-2021

Although there has been ample work in this area, and recently researchers employed bibliometric analysis to examine online brand-centric relationships (Veloutsou & Ruiz-Mafe, 2020) and brand communities (Roy Bhattacharjee et al., 2022), much remains to be learned about brand communities' theoretical and methodological roadmap, and many potential future research routes to suggest. This chapter is a narrative review (Snyder, 2019) aiming to present the research development of communities, synthetize the existing knowledge, identify gaps and omissions of the published work, and suggest some relevant directions for future brand community-focused research. It starts by providing information on the progression of research, continues with highlighting key characteristics of the extant brand communities' research with shortcomings, suggesting research avenues for each characteristic and closes with concluding remarks.

2. Progression of research on brand communities

Both the data downloaded from Scopus (Figure 8.1) and existing bibliometric work on online brand-centric relationships (Veloutsou & Ruiz-Mafe, 2020) and brand communities (Roy Bhattacharjee et al., 2022) report a sharp and constant increase in relevant publications, indicating strong academic interest in the topic. A systematic literature review on brand-centric relationships (Veloutsou & Ruiz-Mafe, 2020) notes that some of the most recent brand community research papers feature in the top of the relevant outputs over time in terms of overall citations and citations per year (i.e. Brodie et al., 2013; Baldus et al., 2015; Dessart et al., 2015), indicating that influential work is still being produced. Based on this evidence, some researchers suggest that brand community research is in its late introductory phase or is entering its early development phase (Veloutsou & Ruiz-Mafe, 2020).

Other researchers, assessing the progression of brand community research propose that it has gone through four development stages (Roy Bhattacharjee et al., 2022). These researchers organize the work in the 20-year period 2001–2020 into five-year stages (2001–2004, 2005–2010, 2011–2015 and 2016–2020), labeling Stage I "Conceptualization and theoretical notion of brand communities", Stage II "Behavioural mechanism and exploration of brand communities' usefulness", Stage III "Development and expansion" and Stage IV "Brand communities in the new age technology". Each stage consists of a hugely different number of papers, 3, 42, 100 and 140 respectively. Although this work argues that these stages are proposed using a bibliometric software (VOSviewer) that identified common and dominant research themes

(Roy Bhattacharjee et al., 2022), it is very difficult to support that a stage may have as few as three outputs, as in Stage I, or that brand communities research in Stage IV concentrates on reporting findings from the online/new technology context rather than theoretical brand community-related aspects that can push the understanding of structural, functional and behavioral brand community issues.

3. Characteristics of brand communities' research output and research opportunities

This work identified research opportunities related to characteristics organized in definitional, context, and method and focus categories of the existing output. This section summarizes several key characteristics of this body of knowledge, acknowledges issues and shortcomings associated with each of these characteristics and suggests questions and directions that future research should address.

3.1 Definitional characteristics

The three identified, unclear, definitional characteristics of academic research on brand communities that can lead to new research projects are: (1) unclear brand communities' definition; (2) unclear understanding of the brand communities' function; and (3) emphasis on members' active behaviors.

Unclear brand communities' definition

The existing research struggles with the classification of brand-centric groups. The literature uses different terms to refer to brand-centered groups, including brand communities, brand tribes and brand fan pages (Ruiz-Mafe et al., 2014; Veloutsou & Moutinho, 2009), with attempts to define them not necessarily securing the needed clarity. For example, some researchers see differences between brand communities and brand tribes and identify the closeness of ties between the members of these brand-centric groups as the main difference, suggesting that groups where members feel part of and develop a moral responsibility towards other members are typically named brand communities while less coherent brand-centric groupings are brand tribes (Veloutsou & Moutinho, 2009). This view is consistent with a lot of the literature arguing that brand communities' members are expected to develop a shared consciousness, rituals and traditions that strengthen the relationships between them (Algesheimer et al., 2005; Muñiz & O'Guinn, 2001). However, the difference between brand communities and brand tribes is not always appreciated and there is work that uses these terms interchangeably (Miliopoulou, 2021), and other work approaching brand tribes as a brand community type (Fournier & Lee, 2009).

Researchers also question the degree to which existing work reports findings from brand communities. Recent research (Dessart & Veloutsou, 2021) highlights that some valuable studies do not recruit participants from contexts securing brand community membership but people who self-identify as brand community members, including students (Kumar, 2019; Kumar & Nayak, 2019b) or panel members (Mousavi et al., 2017). In a similar line of argument, one may question whether brand fan pages can be classified as brand communities or not, since the extent that the brand page followers exhibit attitudes and behaviors necessary for a brand-centric group to be characterized as such is typically not considered, or at least not reported. The confusion is further supported by the use of brand community measures to examine the behavior of brand page followers but without portraying these pages as brand communities by some researchers (i.e. Halaszovich & Nel, 2017), while other researchers also collect data from brand fan pages but suggest that this is brand community data (i.e. Dessart et al., 2016).

There is evidence to support that existing research output does not clearly classify the different brand-centric group types and does not use a consistent terminology to describe these groups. There is a need to provide clear guidelines on what brand communities and other brand-centric groups really are and how researchers can secure that the collected data report issues related to brand communities. A clear mapping of different stages of brand communities' development and clear classification of types of brand communities would also be helpful.

Unclear understanding of the brand communities' function

Existing research repeatedly approaches brand communities as a management tool. Recent systematic engagement with brand community research (Roy Bhattacharjee et al., 2022) posed key research questions such as the firm's benefits and value creation, and the enhancement of understanding the ways that marketers can foster brand community members' interactions and increase their purchase intentions. Even when anti-brand communities are mentioned, the focus of suggested future research engagement remains primarily on controlling the spread of negative word of mouth (Roy Bhattacharjee et al., 2022). This company benefit research focus almost ignores the real brand communities' nature. The relatively early fundamental conceptual brand communities work (Fournier & Lee, 2009) established that brand communities exist to serve their members (and not the brands or the firms). The same research highlighted that smart marketers should embrace the conflicts that make communities thrive (and not expect all community members to love the brand and be supportive) and adds that successful brand communities allow their members to express, while marketers should not try to tightly manage and control, engagement. The focus on brand-related benefits, and often actions, also totally sidelines the fact that not all brand communities are firm managed. Many brand, and all anti-brand communities, are initiated and managed by their members (Dessart et al., 2020; Dholakia & Vianello, 2011; Pedeliento et al., 2020) and, for these kinds of communities, firms' influence and involvement are unknown and often unwanted.

Given that brand communities develop because their members want to satisfy their needs and desires, research should spotlight underlying mechanisms and approaches that will bring this research closer to consumer behavior rather than marketing strategy, tactics or control. Researchers need to appreciate that brand communities are either totally uncontrollable or, in the best case, semi-controllable entities and try to develop a knowledge base that can help companies and brands operate with this notion and benefit from the brand community members' interactions. Future studies should also focus on the development of strategies that help brand community members to increase the value received in brand communities, rather than identifying ways to manage such communities.

Emphasis on members' active behaviors

Although existing work appreciates that not all brand-centered group members are behaviorally active (Dessart et al., 2019; Dessart & Veloutsou, 2021; Kumar & Nayak, 2019b; Mousavi et al., 2017), most brand community research output concentrates on active members' engagement (Hook et al., 2018), especially in the online context (Roy Bhattacharjee et al., 2022). Indeed, brand community members interact around a brand's multiple entities, mainly with other community members and the brand (Brodie et al., 2013; Dessart et al., 2015; Gummerus et al., 2012), in a variety of online and offline settings (Algesheimer et al., 2005; Carlson et al., 2019; Sanz-Blas et al., 2019), playing active roles (Fournier & Lee, 2009) to support the community as an entity, their personal status in it, or the focal brand (Veloutsou & Black, 2020). The active engagement research is acknowledged as a stream of brand community research (Veloutsou & Ruiz-Mafe, 2020), and reports social interaction and drivers to participation (Snyder & Newman, 2019), active brand community members' roles (Özbölük & Dursun, 2017; Veloutsou & Black, 2020), and practices leading to the increase of community participation and trust (Casaló et al., 2008; Kang et al., 2014). The perceived importance of active participation is also highlighted by the brand community engagement measures. Specifically, unidimensional measures primarily rely on behavioral statements (i.e. Algesheimer et al., 2005; Dessart et al., 2020; Kumar and Kumar, 2020; Rabbanee et al., 2020), multi-dimensional measures tend to have a behavioral component (Baldus et al., 2015; Dessart et al., 2016), while other research captures engagement through actual behaviors, such as brand pages' "likes" or the number or content of comments (i.e. Thompson et al., 2019).

Given that most brand community members are lurkers, or engage through non-visible behaviors such as reading online content (Dessart & Veloutsou, 2021), and research highlights community engagement and identification of non-visibly active members (Dessart & Veloutsou, 2021), more research is needed to better understand non-active or non-visible behaviors, and the community members adopting them. Research should also further examine if visible behavioral engagement is a required brand-related behavior driver, or if passive community engagement behavior is enough to generate brand-related behaviors, as some recent research suggests (Dessart et al., 2019).

3.2 Context characteristics

Five context-specific characteristics introduce room for additional research; in particular: (1) emphasis on online contexts; (2) most research in company-initiated and -managed communities; (3) emphasis on supportive brand communities; (4) most research on consumer brands; and (5) the geography of the research output.

Emphasis on online contexts

Given the opportunities that the online environment provides to consumer interaction (Veloutsou & Guzmán, 2017) and its accessibility to researchers, it is not surprising that a lot of the brand community research produced in the last 15 years focuses on online social media-based brand communities and technology-driven marketing (Roy Bhattacharjee et al., 2022). Brand community members interact and develop bonds online even with brands that are not sold online (Dessart et al., 2015; 2016; Popp et al., 2016; Halaszovich & Nel, 2017). Although most of the social media brand community research is contacted on Facebook (Veloutsou & Ruiz-Mafe, 2020), there are research outputs with data collected from other social media platforms, including Twitter, Pinterest, Google+ (i.e. Habibi et al., 2014) and WeChat (i.e. Zhu et al., 2021), and other online contexts such as trading platforms like eBay (i.e. Dholakia et al., 2009), music platforms (Cova et al., 2021), dedicated brand community websites (i.e. Casaló et al., 2007; Cova et al., 2015a; 2015b) and online forums (i.e. Cova & White, 2010; Cooper et al., 2019). Recent research has started incorporating some online environment characteristics (Morgan-Thomas et al., 2020), such as interactivity (Huang et al., 2021), in brand communities research.

The current focus on the online context generates at least two groups of questions and opportunities in relation to brand community research. The first relates to choosing online brand communities research, rather than communities existing in offline contexts. Given that the online environment is just one environment that brand communities can operate in (Fournier & Lee, 2009; Veloutsou & Black, 2020), one can question whether this explosion of research on online brand communities relates to the convenience to identify and approach community members online, or to a representation of a reality that dictates that brand communities primarily operate online. The second relates to the characteristics of the online environment itself. Given that the online platform features can shape the interaction of brand community members (Morgan-Thomas et al., 2020), and given differences in the social media platforms' features (Pelletier et al., 2020), future research should examine brand communities in existing and emerging online contexts, that may provide unique prospects, facilitate, and enrich the development and diversity of brand communities' activities.

Most research in company-initiated and -managed communities

Brand communities may start and be moderated by the companies behind the brands or from their members with no or very limited company involvement (Dholakia & Vianello, 2011). There is also evidence that most brands that have brand communities often have both company-run and consumer-run brand communities (Dholakia & Vianello, 2011; Pedeliento et al., 2020). Despite these characteristics, the vast majority of existing research examines company-initiated and -managed brand communities. The limited studies that actively consider different brand communities' management types, suggest that company-managed communities (Dholakia & Vianello, 2011; Pedeliento et al., 2020) or company-initiated digital content marketing (Bowden & Mirzaei, 2021) are different to consumer-run brand communities.

In reality though, very little is known concerning the differences between consumer-run and company-run brand communities; furthermore, researchers call for more insights into the behavioral outcomes of members of these differently run communities (Roy Bhattacharjee et al., 2022). In addition to the outcomes, the growth and structure of consumer-run brand communities also needs a much deeper investigation. Engagement with consumer-run brand communities is of high interest since these communities come into existence because of the shared members' positive or negative brand passion but operate without the firm's participation.

Emphasis on supportive brand communities

Brand community members' recognized bonds with the brand (Veloutsou & Moutinho, 2009) demonstrate their passion towards it, with the community providing an avenue to express these strong feelings. However, passion can have a supportive (positive) or distractive (negative) nature (Fetscherin et al., 2019). Negative passionate feelings in the form of brand hate fuel the activity in communities against the brand (Rodrigues et al., 2021) commonly called anti-brand communities (Dessart et al., 2020; Popp et al., 2016; Rodrigues et al., 2021). Although negatively valenced brand-related issues are one of the key priorities in branding research (Veloutsou & Guzmán, 2017), brand communities literature focuses on supportive communities rather than anti-brand communities (Veloutsou & Ruiz-Mafe, 2020). Given that some researchers advocate consumers more commonly have negative rather than positive brand feelings (Alvarez & Fournier, 2016), more research is needed in anti-brand communities. The fact that these brand-centric groups are also consumer-run in their totality, makes academic engagement with the topic captivating.

Most research on consumer brands

Most of the research engagement with brand communities is in the business-to-consumer context. The very limited, and mostly dated, output on brand communities in the business-to-business (B2B) context (Andersen, 2005; Bruhn et al., 2014), demonstrates that B2B brand communities exist.

It is unknown if the limited output is due to the difficulties in access or other domain characteristics or challenges, but as recent work also suggests (Roy Bhattacharjee et al., 2022) there is, indeed, a need to learn more about B2B brand communities. The existence, the nature and the way that these groups operate in this context is far from being understood, and their operation and function needs to be explored. It will be interesting to see many different aspects of B2B brand communities, but primarily who their members are, the motives to join them, and whether the shared members' brand passion is a key factor bringing together the community members or these communities are created and operate differently. Brand-related outcomes, such as their role in solving brand-related problems or in the design of new offers, can also be examined.

Geography of the research output

Existing findings from brand communities research in management suggests that contributions from certain geographical areas dominate the research landscape. The results suggest that operating in the USA, all European countries and East Asia (namely China, Taiwan, South Korea and Japan) account respectively for 24.52%, 21.07% and 15.33% of the brand communities researched (Roy Bhattacharjee et al., 2022). Related findings also support that most contributors of the brand-centric relationships work come from the USA, China and the UK (Veloutsou and Ruiz-Mafe, 2020), but without an analysis of the country from which the data were collected. These findings are consistent with the overall production of academic research in marketing, since the top producing countries in terms of academic output are the USA, the UK, China, Australia and Germany (Scimago Journal & Country Rank, 2022).

If these results indeed stand, there might be a need to conduct more studies outside North America, Europe and East Asia, as suggested (Roy Bhattacharjee et al., 2022). However, a good question here is if the online brand communities really have geographic boundaries as such. Given that members join online brand communities virtually, they can be located anywhere on the planet. Recent research appreciates the multicultural nature of brand community members even when they are in one local area (Villegas & Marin, 2022), while many studies do not report the national makeup of the respondents. Therefore, a good research suggestion would be to incorporate in their research instruments questions on the respondents' country of origin and try to establish if national differences exist in brand community issues, as established in many other academic marketing research topics forming the underlying principle of international marketing research.

3.3 Method and focus characteristics

The following four brand communities' academic research method-specific characteristics also introduce room for additional research: (1) possible fragmentation of research; (2) use of a limited number of methods; (3) data from brand community members; and (4) heavy emphasis on brand-related outcomes.

Possible fragmentation of research

There are indications that both marketing and information technology academic journals publish papers in brand communities (Veloutsou & Ruiz-Mafe, 2020), further supported from the list of journals returned in the Scopus search for this work (Figure 8.1). The only bibliometric engagement on the topic (Roy Bhattacharjee et al., 2022) has extracted literature solely from the Scopus area "Business, Management, and Accounting" listed content, which does not incorporate most of the information technology literature. One of the key findings in Veloutsou and Ruiz-Mafe (2020) is the fragmentation of the research, since they note that information technology and marketing researchers in brand-centric relationships primarily cite work in the respective area in which they are publishing.

The fact that the attempts to map the existing body of knowledge are far from being inclusive suggests that a wider, more in-depth engagement with the body of knowledge is needed. In addition, and in line with previous observations (Veloutsou & Ruiz-Mafe, 2020), the possible research fragmentation does not help with the development of an integrated and complete body of knowledge that can reach a wider audience and provide a fuller understanding of the area. To push brand community research understanding and development, researchers should better integrate the relevant outputs reported in various research streams.

Use of a limited number of methods

In terms of qualitative approaches, a variety of qualitative methods were used in the beginning of the brand communities research engagement, and work using qualitative methods is still produced. However, when researchers moved to quantitative approaches in the last 10 years, the research engagement focused on specific methods (Roy Bhattacharjee et al., 2022). Analysis of the brand communities' published work in management suggests that quantitative brand community research heavily depends on surveys and data analyzed using SEM (Roy Bhattacharjee et al., 2022).

Researchers highlight that new methods including big data, text-mining and sentiment analysis collected online (Roy Bhattacharjee et al., 2022; Veloutsou & Ruiz-Mafe, 2020) or eye tracking studies (Roy Bhattacharjee et al., 2022) can provide many opportunities, with a note that big data studies primarily capture behaviors rather than sentiments and focus on online brand communities. Given the need to further investigate brand communities operating in conventional environments, and both online and offline ethnographic data, experimentation can also help in the understanding of deeper brand communities' processes and structures. There is also a need for multi-methods studies, which can produce complementary insights into various operational and functional brand community aspects.

Data from brand community members

Most of the research concentrates on brand community members, leaving the role of their developers and managers unexplored both for consumer- and company-run communities. Although research has identified roles that brand community members play in a community (Veloutsou & Black, 2020), very little is known concerning specifically the behaviors and motives of the initiators or/and moderators involved in the development and moderation of consumer-initiated and -run brand and anti-brand communities. In a similar tone, and given that many companies try to initiate and grow brand communities for their brands, there is very little research on the role and the views of the companies' employees that act as brand community managers (Miliopoulou, 2021), as well as the activities they engage in when aiming to produce the desired stable active membership base (Fournier & Lee, 2009) rather than just members who are primarily promotion seekers. The desired involvement in and role of community managers of company-run brand communities, as seen by brand community members, is also unexplored.

Heavy emphasis on brand-related outcomes

Researchers suggest that brand community research focusing on brand-related outcomes is one of the two main online brand community research streams (Veloutsou & Ruiz-Mafe, 2020), an issue also observed from researchers analyzing the brand communities' body of work in management (Roy Bhattacharjee et al., 2022). Some typical brand-related outcomes include identity co-creation (Black & Veloutsou, 2017), brand tactics co-creation (Cova et al., 2015a; 2015b), brand attitude (Zhu et al., 2021), brand trust (Brodie et al., 2013; Casaló et al., 2007; Dessart, 2017; Habibi et al., 2014), brand evangelism (Sharma et al., 2022), and various behavioral intentions including brand loyalty (Brodie et al., 2013; Casaló et al., 2007; Dessart, 2017; Dessart et al., 2019; Dessart & Veloutsou, 2021; Huang et al., 2021; Ruiz-Mafe et al., 2014), oppositional brand loyalty (Liao et al., 2021) and positive word of mouth (Coelho et al., 2019). Research examines brand-related outcomes such as brand attachment and brand purchase intention for members with different brand-related profiles, even for those who do not own the brand (Kumar & Nayak, 2019a).

Marketing is indeed a business discipline, and the attention of academic research in the brand community on brand-related outcomes, the practical application of marketing techniques and management of business resources, as well as the activities that can bring benefits to firms, is not surprising. However, there is limited work on the way brand communities operate internally, and the ways that can increase the participation of members and help communities grow. In addition, the brand-related outcomes of anti-brand communities seem to have been somewhat overlooked (Veloutsou & Ruiz-Mafe, 2020). There is also room to better understand members' social interaction and personal feelings in brand communities (Zhou et al., 2022). Finally, some suggest that mediating variables in the form of brand-related outcomes should be considered (Roy Bhattacharjee et al., 2022).

4. Concluding remarks

This work presented 12 specific characteristics of existing brand community research, organized in three broad categories (definitional, contexts, and methods and focus), and suggested specific areas where more research is needed. As with all narrative literature reviews, the presented characteristics of the body of knowledge in brand communities and the suggested directions for future research reflect the author's intuition and research experience. However, in addition to the author's observations and views, this work was also heavily informed from two recent bibliometric papers in related areas, one in online brand-centric relationships (Veloutsou & Ruiz-Mafe, 2020) and another on brand communities in management (Roy Bhattacharjee et al., 2022).

This chapter recognizes that most research on brand communities is descriptive. Most of this body of research does not report theories and, when it does, it primarily relies on social identity theory and the uses and gratification theory (Roy Bhattacharjee et al., 2022). The frameworks of brand community behavior often replicate what is already known in different contexts, without significantly advancing our understanding of brand communities and their possible additional functions. Higher informed studies from the literature research and work incorporating aspects that have not been examined in the existing brand communities' literature will enhance our understanding of the field.

Although there are some attempts to engage with the brand community research as a body of knowledge and present its development, the existing outputs fail to focus clearly and exclusively in the specific area, primarily examining the production of knowledge and reporting the network relationships of the identified sources of literature content (Roy Bhattacharjee et al., 2022; Veloutsou & Ruiz-Mafe, 2020). As this body of knowledge expands, more systematic analysis of the brand communities' literature is needed. The systematic literature engagement may take the form of a more in-depth literature analysis aiming to clarify complicated and controversial issues and help in the area-specific theory building, but also the re-approach of the area's full knowledge base and literature's network relationships reporting.

Note

1. The author would like to thank the two book editors Ceridwyn A. King and Enrique Murillo for their support and comments during the process of finalizing this chapter and Ioanna Kontoliou, Xinyu Dong and an anonymous reviewer for providing comments in earlier versions of this work.

References

Algesheimer, R., Dholakia, U.M., & Herrmann, A. (2005). The social influence of brand community: Evidence from European car clubs. *Journal of Marketing*, *69*(3), 19–34.

Alvarez, C., & Fournier, S. (2016). Consumers' relationships with brands. *Current Opinion in Psychology*, *10*, 129–135.

Andersen, P.H. (2005). Relationship marketing and brand involvement of professionals through web-enhanced brand communities: The case of Coloplast. *Industrial Marketing Management*, *34*(1), 39–51.

Baldus, B.J., Voorhees, C., & Calantone, R. (2015). Online brand community engagement: Scale development and validation. *Journal of Business Research*, *68*(5), 978–985.

Black, I., & Veloutsou, C. (2017). Working consumers: Co-creation of brand identity, consumer identity and brand community identity. *Journal of Business Research*, *70*, 416–429.

Bowden, J., & Mirzaei, A. (2021). Consumer engagement within retail communication channels: An examination of online brand communities and digital content marketing initiatives. *European Journal of Marketing*, *55*(5), 1411–1439.

Brodie, R.J., Ilic, A., Juric, B., & Hollebeek, L.D. (2013). Consumer engagement in a virtual brand community: An exploratory analysis. *Journal of Business Research*, *66*(1), 105–114.

Bruhn, M., Schnebelen, S., & Schäfer, D. (2014). Antecedents and consequences of the quality of e-customer-to-customer interactions in B2B brand communities. *Industrial Marketing Management*, *43*(1), 164–176.

Carlson, J., Wyllie, J., Rahman, M., & Voola, R. (2019). Enhancing brand relationship performance through customer participation and value creation in social media brand communities. *Journal of Retailing and Consumer Services*, *50*, 333–341.

Casaló, L., Flavián, C., & Guinalíu, M. (2007). The impact of participation in virtual brand communities on consumer trust and loyalty: The case of free software. *Online Information Review*, *31*(6), 775–792.

Casaló, L.V., Flavián, C., & Guinalíu, M. (2008). Promoting consumer's participation in virtual brand communities: A new paradigm in branding strategy. *Journal of Marketing Communications*, *14*(1), 19–36.

Coelho, A., Bairrada, C., & Peres, F. (2019). Brand communities' relational outcomes, through brand love. *Journal of Product & Brand Management*, *28*(2), 154–165.

Cooper, T., Stavros, C., & Dobele, A.R. (2019). The levers of engagement: An exploration of governance in an online brand community. *Journal of Brand Management*, *26*(3), 240– 254.

Cova, B., & White, T. (2010). Counter-brand and alter-brand communities: The impact of Web 2.0 on tribal marketing approaches. *Journal of Marketing Management*, *26*, 256–270.

Cova, B., Barès, F., & Nemani, A. (2021). Creating a brand community at the bottom of the pyramid: The case of a Cameroonian music platform. *Journal of Marketing Management*, *37*(9–10), 887–913.

Cova, B., Pace, S., & Skålén, P. (2015a). Brand volunteering: Value co-creation with unpaid consumers. *Marketing Theory*, *15*(4), 465–485.

Cova, B., Pace, S., & Skålén, P. (2015b). Marketing with working consumers: The case of a carmaker and its brand community. *Organization*, *22*(5), 682–701.

Dessart, L. (2017). Social media engagement: A model of antecedents and relational outcomes. *Journal of Marketing Management*, *33*(5–6), 1–25.

Dessart, L., & Veloutsou, C. (2021). Augmenting brand community identification online to increase brand loyalty: A uses and gratification perspective. *Journal of Research in Interactive Marketing*, *15*(3), 361–385.

Dessart, L., Aldás-Manzano, J., & Veloutsou, C. (2019). Unveiling heterogeneous engagement-based loyalty in brand communities. *European Journal of Marketing*, *53*(9), 1854–1881.

Dessart, L., Veloutsou, C., & Morgan-Thomas, A. (2015). Consumer engagement in online brand communities: A social media perspective. *Journal of Product & Brand Management*, *24*(1), 28–42.

Dessart, L., Veloutsou, C., & Morgan-Thomas, A. (2016). Capturing consumer engagement: Duality, dimensionality and measurement. *Journal of Marketing Management*, *32*(5/6), 399–426.

Dessart, L., Veloutsou, C., & Morgan-Thomas, A. (2020). Brand negativity: A relational perspective on anti-brand community participation. *European Journal of Marketing*, *54*(7), 1761–1785.

Dholakia, U., & Vianello, S. (2011). Effective brand community management: Lessons from customer enthusiasts. *The IUP Journal of Brand Management*, *8*(1), 7–21.

Dholakia, U.M., Blazevic, V., Wiertz, C., & Algesheimer, R. (2009). Communal service delivery: How customers benefit from participation in firm-hosted virtual P3 communities. *Journal of Service Research*, *12*(2), 208–226.

Fetscherin, M., Guzmán, F., Veloutsou, C., & Roseira Cayolla, R. (2019). Latest research on brand relationships: Introduction to the special issue. *Journal of Product & Brand Management*, *28*(2), 133–139.

Fournier, S., & Lee, L. (2009). Getting brand communities right. *Harvard Business Review*, *87*(4), 105–111.

Gummerus, J., Liljander, V., Weman, E., & Pihlström, M. (2012). Customer engagement in a Facebook brand community. *Management Research Review*, *35*(9), 857–877.

Habibi, M.R., Laroche, M., & Richard, M.O. (2014). The roles of brand community and community engagement in building brand trust on social media. *Computers in Human Behavior, 37*, 152–161.

Halaszovich, T., & Nel, J. (2017). Customer–brand engagement and Facebook fan-page "Like"-intention. *Journal of Product & Brand Management, 26*(2), 120–134.

Hook, M., Baxter, S., & Kulczynsk, A. (2018). Antecedents and consequences of participation in brand communities: A literature review. *Journal of Brand Management, 25*(4), 277–292.

Huang, T.K., Wang, Y.-T., & Lin, K.-Y. (2021). Enhancing brand loyalty through online brand communities: The role of community benefits. *Journal of Product & Brand Management*, ahead-of-print. https://doi.org/10.1108/JPBM-08-2020-3027

Kang, J., Tang, L., & Fiore, A.M. (2014). Enhancing consumer–brand relationships on restaurant Facebook fan pages: Maximizing consumer benefits and increasing active participation. *International Journal of Hospitality Management, 36*, 145–155.

Kumar, J. (2019). How psychological ownership stimulates participation in online brand communities? The moderating role of member type. *Journal of Business Research, 105*(December), 243–257.

Kumar, J., & Kumar, V. (2020). Drivers of brand community engagement. *Journal of Retailing and Consumer Services, 54*, 1–12.

Kumar, J., & Nayak, J.K. (2019a). Brand engagement without brand ownership: A case of non-brand owner community members. *Journal of Product & Brand Management, 28*(2), 216–230.

Kumar, J., & Nayak, J.K. (2019b). Understanding the participation of passive members in online brand communities through the lens of psychological ownership theory. *Electronic Commerce Research and Applications, 36*, 100859.

Liao, J., Dong, X., Luo, Z., & Guo, R. (2021). Oppositional loyalty as a brand identity-driven outcome: A conceptual framework and empirical evidence. *Journal of Product & Brand Management, 30*(8), 1134–1147.

McAlexander, J.H., Schouten, J.W., & Koenig, H.F. (2002). Building brand community. *Journal of Marketing, 66*(1), 38–54.

Miliopoulou, G.Z. (2021). Brand communities, fans or publics? How social media interests and brand management practices define the rules of engagement. *European Journal of Marketing, 55*(12), 3129–3161.

Morgan-Thomas, A., Dessart, L., & Veloutsou, C. (2020). Digital ecosystem and consumer engagement: A socio-technical perspective. *Journal of Business Research, 121*(December), 713–723.

Mousavi, S., Roper, S., & Keeling, K. (2017). Interpreting social identity in online brand communities: Considering posters and lurkers. *Psychology & Marketing, 34*(4), 376–393.

Muñiz, A.M., & O'Guinn, T.C. (2001). Brand community. *Journal of Consumer Research, 27*(4), 412–432.

Özbölük, T., & Dursun, Y. (2017). Online brand communities as heterogeneous gatherings: A netnographic exploration of Apple users. *Journal of Product & Brand Management, 26*(4), 375–385.

Pedeliento, G., Adreini, D., & Veloutsou, C. (2020). Brand community integration, participation and commitment: A comparison between consumer-run and company-managed communities. *Journal of Business Research, 119*(October), 481–494.

Pelletier, M.J., Krallman, A., Adams, F.G., & Hancock, T. (2020). One size doesn't fit all: A uses and gratifications analysis of social media platforms. *Journal of Research in Interactive Marketing, 14*(2), 269–284.

Popp, B., Germelmann, C.C., & Jung, B. (2016). We love to hate them! Social media-based anti-brand communities in professional football. *International Journal of Sports Marketing and Sponsorship, 17*(4), 349–367.

Rabbanee, F.K., Roy, R., & Spence, M.T. (2020). Factors affecting consumer engagement on online social networks: Self-congruity, brand attachment, and self-extension tendency. *European Journal of Marketing, 54*(6), 1407–1431.

Rodrigues, C., Brandão, A., & Rodrigues, P. (2021). I can't stop hating you: An anti-brand-community perspective on Apple brand hate. *Journal of Product & Brand Management, 30*(8), 1115–1133.

Roy Bhattacharjee, D., Pradhan, D., & Swani, K. (2022). Brand communities: A literature review and future research agendas using TCCM approach. *International Journal of Consumer Studies, 46*(1), 3–28.

Ruiz-Mafe, C., Martí-Parreño, J., & Sanz-Blas, S. (2014). Key drivers of consumer loyalty to Facebook fan pages. *Online Information Review, 38*(3), 362–380.

Sanz-Blas, S., Bigné, E., & Buzova, D. (2019). Facebook brand community bonding: The direct and moderating effect of value creation behaviour. *Electronic Commerce Research and Applications, 35*(May–June), 100850.

Scimago Journal & Country Rank. (2022). https://www.scimagojr.com/countryrank.php (accessed April 1, 2022).

Scopus. (2022). https://www.scopus.com/results/results.uri?sort=r-f&src=s&st1=%22brand+communit*%22&nlo=&nlr=&nls=&sid=70531f062373445bf6b2af88627a2b3a&sot=b&sdt=cl&cluster=scopubyr%2c%222022%22%2cf%2bscopubyr%2c%221997%22%2cf&sl=32&s=TITLE-ABS-KEY%28%22brand+communit*%22%29&origin=resultslist&zone=leftSideBar&editSaveSearch=&txGid=ebe37ad99f7f21b429a57d98f3c789a7 (accessed April 1, 2022).

Sharma, P., Sadh, A., Billore, A., & Motiani, M. (2022). Investigating brand community engagement and evangelistic tendencies on social media. *Journal of Product & Brand Management, 31*(1), 16–28.

Snyder, D.G., & Newman, K.P. (2019). Reducing consumer loneliness through brand communities. *Journal of Consumer Marketing, 36*(2), 337–347.

Snyder, H. (2019). Literature review as a research methodology: An overview and guidelines. *Journal of Business Research, 104*(November), 333–339.

Thompson, S.A., Loveland, J.M., & Loveland, K.E. (2019). The impact of switching costs and brand communities on new product adoption: Served-market tyranny or friendship with benefits. *Journal of Product & Brand Management, 28*(2), 140–153.

Torgerson, C. (2003). *Systematic Reviews.* London: Continuum.

Veloutsou, C. (2009). Brands as relationship facilitators in consumer markets. *Marketing Theory, 9*(1), 127–130.

Veloutsou, C., & Black, I. (2020). Creating and managing participative brand communities: The roles members perform. *Journal of Business Research, 117*(September), 73–85.

Veloutsou, C., & Guzmán, F. (2017). The evolution of brand management thinking over the last 25 years as recorded in the *Journal of Product & Brand Management. Journal of Product & Brand Management, 26*(1), 2–12.

Veloutsou, C., & Moutinho, L. (2009). Brand relationships through brand reputation and brand tribalism. *Journal of Business Research, 62*(3), 314–322.

Veloutsou, C., & Ruiz-Mafe, C. (2020). Brands as relationship builders in the virtual world: A bibliometric analysis. *Electronic Commerce Research & Application, 39*(January–February), 1–13.

Villegas, D.A., & Marin, A.M. (2022). Bilingual brand communities? Strategies for targeting Hispanics on social media. *Journal of Product & Brand Management, 31*(4), 586–605.

Zhou, Z., Wang, R., & Zhan, G. (2022). Cultivating consumer subjective well-being through online brand communities: A multidimensional view of social capital. *Journal of Product & Brand Management, 31*(5), 808–822.

Zhu, G., Liu, Y., & Zhou, L. (2021). The red packet interaction and brand attitude in the brand communities on WeChat. *Journal of Product & Brand Management, 30*(2), 335–350.

9 A theoretical framework exploring three foundational benefits of brand attachment

Andreas B. Eisingerich, Deborah J. MacInnis and C. Whan Park

1. Introduction

Many recent papers in marketing have examined the positive benefits that accrue to brands as the strength of consumers' attachments to brands increases (e.g., Batra et al., 2012; Carroll & Ahuvia, 2006; Fedorikhin et al., 2008; Park et al., 2010; Thomson et al., 2005). Indeed, brand attachment, defined as the strength and salience of the bond connecting the brand with the self, is a significant predictor of difficult-to-perform pro-brand behaviors (e.g., brand loyalty behaviors and brand advocacy behaviors; see Park et al., 2013). It has also been noted as a significantly better predictor of these outcomes than are favorable (Thomson et al., 2005) or strong brand attitudes (Park et al., 2010; 2013). When consumers are strongly attached to a brand, it is highly salient in their thoughts and actions, in part by virtue of its autobiographical associations. Moreover, consumers regard the brand as closely connected to the self (Park et al., 2013), so much so that physical, social, psychological, and economic resources associated with the brand are regarded as part of the self (Reimann & Aron, 2009).

Given the strong and positive outcomes to companies from creating customer brand attachment, it is important for marketers to understand *how*, *when*, and *why* brand attachment affects these pro-brand behaviors. Park et al. (2013) identified three broad goal categories that foster brand attachment. Specifically, consumers seek out brands whose benefits provide resources that enable, entice, and enrich the self. Enabling benefits enhance feelings of competence and self-efficacy by solving consumers' problems and making their lives easier (Park et al., 2013). Enticing benefits please consumers' senses (Krishna, 2012), minds (Raju, 1980) or hearts (Hirschman & Holbrook, 1982), and often provide experiential and hedonic gratification (Brakus et al., 2009).

Enriching benefits capture the brand's ability to represent or express an ideal past, present, or future self-identity, thereby enhancing self-esteem.[1] According to Park et al. (2013), the extent to which the brand can simultaneously enable, entice, and enrich consumers enhances brand attachment (vs. brand aversion) and positively predicts brand attachment and difficult-to-perform pro-brand behaviors. Among the three types of benefits, called the 3 Es, enriching benefits showed the strongest contribution to brand attachment.

While these results are noteworthy and significant, several critical issues have yet to be addressed. For instance, the terms enabling, enticing, and enriching are at a relatively high level of abstraction. In this chapter, we aim to provide deeper insight into these three benefit categories by offering a sharper definition, and more in-depth discussion, of the ways in which brands might enable, entice, and enrich consumers. Furthermore, although prior research has identified three broad benefit categories that may enhance brand attachment (Park et al., 2013), the *process* by which benefits that enable, entice, and enrich the self would influence brand attachment is currently obscured. There is a need to develop a theory that explains *how* and *why* the 3 Es enhance attachment. This chapter emphasizes these issues. Rather than recounting what the literature has already covered, we seek to develop a novel perspective.

Before proceeding, we wish to clarify the difference among (a) brand benefits (i.e., what the brand does for consumers), (b) how receiving these benefits makes consumers feel, and (c) emotive beliefs about brands that stem from these benefits. In our conceptual framework (see Figure 9.1), *empowerment, gratification, and self-esteem* are feelings that consumers have in response to brands whose benefits enable, entice, and enrich them, *respectively*. The feelings in Figure 9.1 are not designed to reflect a comprehensive theory of consumer emotions; rather they reflect a cluster of feelings that arise when the brand's benefits satisfy consumption goals. We use the term emotive beliefs (e.g., trust, love, and respect) rather than feelings or emotions to describe how consumers feel *about the brand*. We use the term "emotive belief" to suggest that while these judgments of brand trust, love, and respect derive from feelings about the brand, they are best described as motivational beliefs. For example, our usage of love, and its representation as an emotive belief in this model is consistent with that of Rempel and Burris (2005) who regard love not as an emotion, but as a motivational state that is rooted in formative emotional experiences. In our model, brand trust, love, and respect are motivational drivers that contribute to the formation of strong brand attachment.

In the next section, we discuss a *process* by which enablement, enticement, and enrichment benefits may impact brand attachment. This critical link is missing in previous research on brand attachment; hence its articulation represents a major contribution to the literature.

2. Theory

2.1 How enablement benefits impact brand attachment

We define enablement benefits as the extent to which the brand provides agency and control to protect one (keep one safe) from negative outcomes, or prevent the loss of valued (monetary, time, energy, psychological) resources. The consumer literature has clearly established consumers' desire to have agency (Han et al., 2016) and to exert control over their environments (e.g., Cutright, 2012; Dholakia et al., 2016). As Figure 9.1 indicates, we identify two broad classes of enablement benefits.

Enabling by problem resolution. Enabling benefits empower consumers and give them a greater sense of control over their environment by fostering a sense of agency; helping consumers solve their problems—large and small, at work or at home, in their business relationships or their personal relationships. Benefits that enable consumers enhance feelings of competence when addressing challenges in various life domains (Proksch et al., 2015). Gaining control over our environments, in part through the brands we use (e.g., Uber, Google Maps), is a foundational concept in theories regarding self-efficacy (e.g., Bandura, 1997).

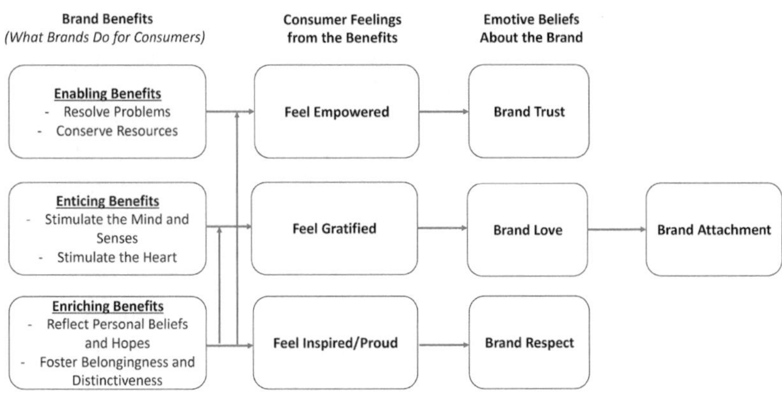

Figure 9.1 Conceptual model of the brand attachment process

Gaining control provides relief through problems being solved and feelings of protection and security from future threats. Enabling benefits thus solve consumers' problems, offering physical, social, psychological, and economic protection and avoiding negative future harm.

Enabling by conserving resources. Benefits can also enable consumers in a different way: by helping consumers conserve scarce time, monetary, psychological, and physical resources (Brinberg & Wood, 1983). Brands that conserve scarce resources (e.g., by minimizing the time or money consumers must spend to own and use them) and/or allow consumers to acquire them (e.g., by earning more money via better investment options, or gaining physical energy from sleeping on a supportive mattress) make consumers feel less mentally taxed, less physically tired, and less emotionally anxious.

Enablement benefits affect brand attachment through feelings of empowerment and brand trust. We posit that brand benefits that enable consumers, contribute to brand attachment by making consumers feel empowered, enhancing their trust in the brand. We define empowerment as the extent to which consumers feel equipped with the resources needed to control (i.e., avoid or redress) negative outcomes. When empowered, one feels more capable, efficacious, resourceful, and less anxious. Brands that empower consumers by their consistent ability to effectively address consumer problems or conserve their resources may be judged as "competent" (Aaker et al., 2012; Kervyn et al., 2012).

To the extent that brands offer enabling benefits and make consumers feel empowered, consumers should come to trust the brand. When a brand consistently helps consumers solve problems and conserve scarce time, money, and physical/psychological resources, consumers come to believe that the brand is acting in their best interests. We define brand trust as the extent to which consumers can count on the brand to consistently act in the customer's best interest (Delgado-Ballester, 2004). Consumers are more willing to establish a connection between the self and the brand because they know they can depend on (trust) the brand. Considerable research supports the idea that consumers develop stronger attachment and greater loyalty/commitment to brands that they trust (Chaudhuri & Holbrook, 2001; Japutra et al., 2014; Palmatier et al., 2013). Based on this logic, we predict that enabling benefits enhance brand attachment via the mediating influence of feelings of empowerment and the emotive belief of brand trust.

2.2 How enticement benefits impact brand attachment

We define enticement benefits as the extent to which the brand provides sensory, cognitive, or emotional stimulation at a level that is psychologically pleasant. Enticing benefits make purely functional products much more interesting, engaging, and exciting. As Figure 9.1 indicates, we identify several classes of enticement benefits.

Enticing by arousing cognitive and sensory experiences. Brands can please the senses when they provide cognitive stimulation arousing curiosity, imagination, and creativity, creating flow, or making people think (Csikszentmihalyi, 1997). Brands can also arouse sensory experiences activating pleasant sights, sounds, tastes, smells, and tactile sensations (Brakus et al., 2009). Consistent with recent emphasis on the importance of sensory experiences in marketing (Alba & Williams, 2013; Krishna, 2012; Peck & Childers, 2008), enticement benefits encompass, but are not limited to, the term experiential marketing. They are critical elements of consumer aesthetics (Hagtvedt & Patrick, 2008) and the concept of design that today differentiates the truly great brands from mediocre ones (Norman, 2013). Enticement benefits arouse the mind and senses, preempt boredom, and hence are powerful drivers of behavior when consumers feel deprived of stimulation and yearn for novelty and arousal (Orth et al., 2010; Raju, 1980).

Enticing by arousing the heart. Beyond stimulating the mind and the senses, brands can provide enticing benefits by stimulating and warming the heart (Hirschman & Holbrook, 1982). They can induce feelings of fun (Hirschman & Holbrook, 1982), sentimentality (Holbrook, 1993a), poignancy (Ersner-Hershfield et al., 2008), humor (McGraw & Warren, 2010), empathy (Escalas & Stern, 2003), gratitude (Palmatier et al., 2009), and/or nostalgia (Holbrook, 1993b).

Enticement benefits affect brand attachment through feelings of gratification and brand love. We propose that brand benefits that entice consumers also contribute to brand attachment. Some prior research beyond that of Park et al. (2013) links enticement benefits to brand attachment. For example, Merchant and Rose (2013) find that the greater the vicarious nostalgia consumers feel toward brands, the stronger the consumers' brand attachment.

But what is the process by which enticement benefits create brand attachment? We examine two critical mediating states; the extent to which consumers feel gratified and the extent to which they come to love the brand. We define gratification as the extent to which the brand and its usage make one feel stimulated, pleased, and warm. As a result of these feelings, consumers come to love the brand. We define love more narrowly than is true of prior research (e.g., Batra et al., 2012), defining it as the extent to which consumers feel a strong degree of affection for the brand. Consistent with the notion that enticing benefits stimulate the mind, senses and heart, Ismail and Spinelli (2012) find that brands that evoke feelings of excitement predict love for a brand. Also consistent with our perspective, Carroll and Ahuvia (2006) show that hedonic brands (which are bought for their strong enticing benefits, such as Hello Kitty or Ben & Jerry's ice-cream) are more likely to evoke feelings of love than utilitarian brands, which are bought for their enabling benefits (such as the reliable Miele washing machine or dependable Pampers diapers). Taken together, we posit that enticing benefits enhance brand attachment via the mediating influence of feelings of gratification and brand love.

2.3 How enrichment benefits impact brand attachment

We define enrichment benefits as the extent to which the brand positively reflects or augments one's sense of self and place in the world. Consumers feel good as people (i.e., their sense of "self" is augmented) when they have a secure (vs. threatened) self-concept, when they act on their values and beliefs, when they are secure in their connection to others, and when they feel that they are valued and respected members of a social system. Brands are instrumental in the development of one's self-concept (Belk, 1988; Eichinger et al., 2021; Escalas & Bettman, 2005). As Figure 9.1 indicates, we identify two ways in which brands can provide enriching benefits: (1) by reflecting personal beliefs and hopes, or what might be called "internal self-enhancement", and (2) by fostering belongingness and distinctiveness, or what might be called "external self-enhancement".

Enriching by reflecting personal beliefs and hopes. One's sense of self is, in part, affected by the extent to which individuals think they are acting in belief (value)-consistent ways that also align with what is good, right, moral, and just. We all want to feel that we are good people and that we are contributing to something larger than ourselves. In marketing, this notion has been studied as self-transcendence (Torelli et al., 2012), morality (Bhattacharya & Sen, 2003; Luedicke et al., 2010), and the desire to act pro-socially toward others (e.g., Cavanaugh et al., 2015; Small & Simonsohn, 2008). Consumers feel true to themselves (authentic) and have a sense of self-respect when the brands they buy and use have principles that converge with their own (brand–self-identification). Consumers identify more with brands whose values are consistent with their own. They become more committed to such brands and are more likely to develop attachments to such brands (Malär et al., 2011).

Enriching by fostering belongingness and distinctiveness. Consumers' self-esteem is also impacted by the extent to which they feel accepted by others and are part of a group. They want to feel like they belong to a family, group, location, or community that accepts them (Eichinger et al., 2021; McAlexander et al., 2002; Schau et al., 2009). Feelings of belongingness and connectedness to others provide meaning to life and enhance self-esteem and well-being. Beyond the desire for belongingness, consumers also have the external desire to signal their unique and special identity to others (i.e., social signaling; Bellezza et al., 2014; Berger & Heath, 2007). People would like to believe that others evaluate and look up to them for who they are (e.g., their style, their independent minds, their beauty or their knowledge) or what they have accomplished (e.g., their wealth, professional successes, musical talents, athletic accomplishments).

Enriching benefits affect brand attachment by affecting self-esteem and brand respect. Research about the linkage among brand-inducing self-esteem, brand respect, and brand attachment is limited. We, thus, develop a novel perspective regarding this linkage. Specifically, we propose that a brand's enriching benefits reflect consumers' cherished values and principles, allowing them to act in ways that build their self-esteem and sense of self. Because the brand resonates with them and builds their own self-esteem it is respected for its integrity and/or benevolence to the customers and their values and identity. Based on this logic, we predict that enriching benefits enhance brand attachment via the mediating influence of feelings of self-esteem and brand respect.

2.4 The roles of brand trust, love, and respect in impacting brand attachment

The fact that the 3 Es represent critical human needs suggests that combined, they should augment and deepen brand–self connection and brand attachment by making consumers feel more empowered, gratified, and esteemed than before. As such, consumers should be motivated to develop and continue to build on their relationship with the brand. We posit that a brand relationship based on trust or feelings of empowerment alone lacks strong hedonic brand desire, which limits the degree of consumers' brand attachment. Likewise, gratification without trust or empowerment makes relationships precarious, both in terms of strength and stability. Finally, there is no close and intimate brand relationship when one merely respects a brand. However, when a brand with highly enabling and enticing benefits also has strong enriching benefits, consumers' attachment to the brand should be strongest.

2.5 The critical role of enriching benefits

Park et al. (2013) observed that relative to enabling and enticing benefits, enriching benefits had the strongest effect in predicting brand attachment. It is important to explain *why* this might be the case. Below, we explore several potential explanations. In the discussion section, we will also explore *how* enriching benefits may have the strongest effect in predicting brand attachment.

Expectations perspective. Consumers may expect little more of a brand than its ability to adequately perform product functions in a pleasing fashion (Mano & Oliver, 1993). Whereas the lack of enriching benefits may not be a source of major disappointment, their presence might delight consumers, making their impact stronger. Moreover, their effects may be easier to sustain over time. This is so since enriching benefits speak to higher-level beliefs and hopes. They reflect one's sense of belongingness and distinctiveness; one's sense of "self" in a social context, and things that are meaningful in one's life.

Identity perspective. Moreover, to the extent that enriching benefits expand the self by bolstering one's identity and fostering identity expression to others, they can more effectively create brand–self connections and influence consumers' sense of the brand as part of the self. The fact that enriching benefits expand the self by bolstering one's identity and fostering identity expression to others means that they may have the greatest impact on reducing the distance between the brand and the self. Switching to other brands might be difficult because the brand's enriching benefits speak to consumers' sense of identity and the values they hold.

Life challenge perspective. Individuals' self-concepts and self-esteem are frequently challenged in daily life. Such challenges to one's identity are psychologically threatening (Gao et al., 2009). The media (e.g., images of the good life) and life experiences (e.g., stepping on the scale to find one is overweight) frequently remind consumers they are not the people they aspire to be. Moreover, consumers often find themselves behaving in value-inconsistent ways (e.g., using disposable diapers even though one values being "green"). They might feel left out of groups to which they wish to belong or feel that there is nothing that makes them distinctive and special. Thus, consumers may be highly sensitive to enriching benefits.

3. Discussion

The strongest brand attachment occurs when managers offer benefits that map each of the 3 Es (enabling, enticing, enriching), not just one or two. Offering benefits that appeal to these diverse goal categories has a greater potential to fully resonate with consumers, motivating them to build strong brand–self connections and making the brand prominent in their lives.

We proposed earlier the critical importance of enriching benefits on the strength of brand attachment. Interestingly, past research has been silent on the roles of enriching benefits and their emotive belief, brand respect, on customer–brand relationships. The important issue is to account for *why* and *how* enriching benefits most strongly influence brand attachment. We suspect that in contrast to enabling and enticing benefits, enriching benefits moderate the impact of the other two benefits on brand attachment. Strong (weak) enriching benefits might significantly enhance (lower) the impact of strong enabling and enticing benefits on brand attachment.

In addition, we suspect that the 3 Es tap different types of motivations, affecting consumers' pro-brand behaviors in different ways. Specifically, enticing benefits motivate consumers to approach the brand, which provides opportunities for the types of interactions necessary for the formation of brand love. Enabling benefits, by virtue of their problem-solving and resource conserving nature, motivate consumers to purchase and use the brand, with consistent usage providing opportunities to form trusting relationships over time. However, the role of enriching benefits is unique and critical in accounting for consumers' willingness to perform difficult-to-perform pro-brand behaviors.

To the extent that strong enriching benefits enhance the impact of enabling and enticing benefits on consumers (their attachment), they further enhance consumers' desire to approach and own the brand. Because of this heightened desire to approach and own the brand, consumers should be highly motivated to overcome barriers that interfere with brand ownership (e.g., brand stock-outs, or long lines at the point of purchase). Given their strong self-implications and unanticipated delight, enriching benefits seem to be particularly potent in driving consumers' difficult-to-perform pro-brand behaviors.

An urgent question for firms is which benefit type should be improved for the more efficient return among three types of benefits under two different situations. First, if all three benefits are unsatisfactory to customers, what should a firm do? We suspect that the enabling benefit should be improved first to get the more efficient return from customers, followed by the enticing benefit and enriching benefit. This is because the absence of the satisfactory enabling and enticing benefits hurts customers more than the absence of the enriching benefits.

Second, which benefit type should be enhanced first to the delighted performance level if all of three benefits are satisfactory from the customers' perspective? For instance, should a firm invest to improve the enabling side, enticing side or enriching side? This order issue is a very important managerial question that has not been addressed before. There may be diminishing returns for enabling benefits. Whereas consumers will likely appreciate it when a brand moves from an unsatisfactory to a satisfactory level of enabling benefits, additional investments in enabling benefits may yield only moderate levels of appreciation. In contrast, there may be an increasing return for enriching benefits when a brand moves from offering an unsatisfactory level to a satisfactory level of enriching benefits, added enriching benefits may move consumers from feeling satisfied to feeling delighted.

How strong is the real impact of brand attachment on customers' brand loyalty relative to its competitors? Will brand attachment deter consumers from acquiring a brand that is competitively superior? Do enriching benefits play a special role? We have proposed that enriching benefits play a powerful role in impacting brand attachment. Extending this logic, when one is attached to a brand that offers strong (vs. weak) enriching benefits, consumers may find it difficult to develop an equally strong attachment to another brand. In part, this is due to discomfort from self-inconsistent behavior. We expect that enriching benefits play an important role in creating loyalty to a brand even in the face of competitively superior alternatives. Specifically, brands with strong enriching benefits are more difficult to abandon given their strong self-relevance and self-augmentation (Ahuvia, 2005; Belk, 1988). By abandoning a brand with strong enriching benefits, one is acting in ways that are inconsistent with the self. It is also possible that consumers might engage in motivated reasoning to convince themselves that the brand to which they are attached is the better option (Bhattacharjee et al., 2013; De Mello & MacInnis, 2005). Moreover, since attached consumers have already invested psychological, financial, and social resources in the brand they may regard switching as a loss of resources, resembling the sunk-cost phenomenon. This sunk-cost phenomenon is supported by Rusbult et al.'s (1998) investment model of relationships. The more one has invested in the relationship, the harder (costlier) it is to leave.

How should the 3 E's be measured? We have identified two sources for each of the 3 E's. Enabling benefits comprise two sub-factors: (1) by problem resolution and (2) by conserving resources. Enticing benefits emanate from two sources: (1) by arousing cognitive and sensory experiences and (2) by arousing the heart. Enriching benefits come from two sources: (1) by reflecting personal beliefs and hopes and (2) by fostering belongingness and distinctiveness. We further decomposed each source for each E into multiple factors (e.g., for enabling by problem resolution there are multiple types of problems such as physical, social, psychological, and economic problems). Therefore, each E was identified in terms of two sources and additional factors associated with each source. This two-source multiple factor-based conceptualization of each of 3 E's has important implications for measurement. The possible number of items from each factor for each source for each E and across 3 E's are expected to be considerable and should be reduced to a parsimonious number to capture the core meaning of each E. The entire process of construct validation needs to be conducted to form a set of a meaningful construct-faithful measurement instrument for each E.

The concept of brand attachment also ties nicely with the concepts of minimalism and sustainability (Hornstein et al., 2005; Sharif & Eisingerich, 2022). That is, wouldn't it be positive for the world we live in, when consumers appreciate what they consume, regardless of how much it costs? And what if we became more attached to, and appreciative of, what we consume on a daily basis? Wouldn't attachment to the brands we use in our daily life add to our overall happiness as people? These are all fundamental questions that deserve further research. Furthermore, as artificial intelligence (AI) and virtual reality solutions evolve, answers to how they may play in the relationships that people have with the various business offerings they use (including digital and access-based service solutions as well as leisure and tourism) may take on added significance (Fritze et al., 2020; Liu et al., 2020). Can humans become even more attached to a virtual representation of themselves and others, say in an online game, than products? Which role do enriching benefits vis-à-vis enticing and enabling benefits play for different consumer groups across virtual reality settings (e.g., financial advice, gaming, dating, caretaking, retailing, etc.)? Future work that continues to build on and extend what we know about consumers' attachment to brands is richly deserving.

Note

1. The benefits a brand offers have been classified in various ways including functional, experiential/ hedonic and symbolic (see Khan et al., 2005; Park et al., 1986; Richins, 1994, to name a few). Park et al. (2013) use the terms enabling, enticing and enriching as opposed to the terms functional, hedonic/experiential and symbolic because the former emphasizes less what benefits the brand *has*, than how these benefits *relate to consumers' self-relevant goals*.

References

Aaker, J., Garbinsky, E. N., & Vohs, K. (2012). Cultivating admiration in brands: Warmth, competence, and landing in the 'golden quadrant'. *Journal of Consumer Psychology, 22*(2), 191–194.

Ahuvia, A. C. (2005). Beyond the extended self: Loved objects and consumers' identity narratives. *Journal of Consumer Research, 32*(1), 171–184.

Alba, J. W., & Williams, E. F. (2013). Pleasure principles: A review of research on hedonic consumption. *Journal of Consumer Psychology, 23*(1), 2–18.

Bandura, A. (1997). *Self-efficacy: The exercise of control*. W.H. Freeman.

Batra, R., Ahuvia, A., & Bagozzi, R. P. (2012). Brand love. *Journal of Marketing, 76*(2), 1–16.

Belk, R. W. (1988). Possessions and the extended self. *Journal of Consumer Research, 15*(2), 139–168.

Bellezza, S., Gino, F., & Keinan, A. (2014). The red sneakers effect: Inferring status and competence from signals of nonconformity. *Journal of Consumer Research, 41*(1), 35–54.

Berger, J., & Heath, C. (2007). Where consumers diverge from others: Identity signaling and product domains. *Journal of Consumer Research, 34*(2), 121–134.

Bhattacharjee, A., Berman, J. Z., & Reed II, A. (2013). Tip of the hat, wag of the finger: How moral decoupling enables consumers to admire and admonish. *Journal of Consumer Research, 39*(6), 1167–1184.

Bhattacharya, C. B., & Sen, S. (2003). Consumer-company identification: A framework for understanding consumers' relationships with companies. *Journal of Marketing, 67*(2), 76–88.

Brakus, J. J., Schmitt, B. H., & Zarantonello, L. (2009). Brand experience: What is it? How is it measured? Does it affect loyalty? *Journal of Marketing, 73*(3), 52–68.

Brinberg, D., & Wood, R. (1983). A resource exchange theory analysis of consumer behavior. *Journal of Consumer Research, 10*(3), 330–338.

Carroll, B. A., & Ahuvia, A. C. (2006). Some antecedents and outcomes of brand love. *Marketing Letters, 17*(2), 79–89.

Cavanaugh, L. A., Bettman, J. R., & Luce, M. F. (2015). Feeling love and doing more for distant others: Specific positive emotions differentially affect prosocial consumption. *Journal of Marketing Research, 52*(5), 657–673.

Chaudhuri, A., & Holbrook, M. B. (2001). The chain of effects from brand trust and brand affect to brand performance: The role of brand loyalty. *Journal of Marketing, 65*(2), 81–93.

Csikszentmihalyi, M. (1997). *Finding flow: The psychology of engagement with everyday life*. Basic Books.

Cutright, K. M. (2012). The beauty of boundaries: When and why we seek structure in consumption. *Journal of Consumer Research, 38*(5), 775-790.

Delgado-Ballester, E. (2004). Applicability of a brand trust scale across product categories. *European Journal of Marketing, 38*(5/6), 573–592.

De Mello, G. E., & MacInnis, D. J. (2005). Why and how consumers hope: Motivated reasoning and the marketplace. In Ratneshwar, S., & Mick, D. G. (Eds.) *Inside consumption*. Routledge, 66-88.

Dholakia, U., Tam, L., Yoon, S., & Wong, N. (2016). The ant and the grasshopper: Understanding personal saving orientation of consumers. *Journal of Consumer Research, 43*(1), 134-155.

Eichinger, I., Schreier, M., & van Osselaer, S. M. J. (2021). Connecting to place, people, and past: How products make us feel grounded. *Journal of Marketing*, 1-16.

Ersner-Hershfield, H., Mikels, J. A., Sullivan, S. J., & Carstensen, L. L. (2008). Poignancy: Mixed emotional experience in the face of meaningful endings. *Journal of Personality and Social Psychology, 94*(1), 158-167.

Escalas, J. E., & Bettman, J. R. (2005). Self-construal, reference groups, and brand meaning. *Journal of Consumer Research, 32*(3), 378-389.

Escalas, J. E., & Stern, B. B. (2003). Sympathy and empathy: Emotional responses to advertising dramas. *Journal of Consumer Research, 29*(4), 566-578.

Fedorikhin, A., Park, C. W., & Thomson, M. (2008). Beyond fit and attitude: The effect of emotional attachment on consumer responses to brand extensions. *Journal of Consumer Psychology, 18*(4), 281-291.

Fritze, M. P., Marchand, A., Eisingerich, A. B., & Benkenstein, M. (2020). Access-based services as substitutes for material possessions: The role of psychological ownership. *Journal of Service Research, 23*(3), 368-385.

Gao, L., Wheeler, C., & Shiv, B. (2009). The 'shaken self': Product choices as a means of restoring self-view confidence. *Journal of Consumer Research, 36*(1), 29–38.

Hagtvedt, H., & Patrick, V. M. (2008). Art infusion: The influence of visual art on the perception and evaluation of consumer products. *Journal of Marketing Research, 45*(3), 379-389.

Han, D., Duhachek, A., & Agrawal, N. (2016). Coping and construal level matching drives health message effectiveness via response efficacy or self-efficacy enhancement. *Journal of Consumer Research, 43*(3), 429-447.

Hirschman, E., & Holbrook, M. B. (1982). Hedonic consumption: Emerging concepts, methods and propositions. *Journal of Marketing, 46*, 92-101.

Holbrook, M. B. (1993a). Romanticism and sentimentality in consumer behavior: A literary approach to the joys and sorrows of consumption. In Holbrook, M. B., & Hirschman, E. C. (Eds.) *The semiotics of consumption: Interpreting symbolic consumer behaviour in popular culture and works of art*. Mouton de Gruyter, 151-228.

Holbrook, M. B. (1993b). Nostalgia and consumption preferences: Some emerging patterns of consumer tastes. *Journal of Consumer Research, 20*(2), 245-256.

Hornstein, N., Nunes, J., & Grohmann, K. K. (2005). *Understanding minimalism*. Cambridge University Press.

Ismail, A. R., & Spinelli, G. (2012). Effects of brand love, personality and image on word of mouth: The case of fashion brands among young consumers. *Journal of Fashion Marketing and Management: An International Journal, 16*(4), 386-398.

Japutra, A., Ekinci, Y., & Simkin, L. (2014). Exploring brand attachment, its determinants and outcomes. *Journal of Strategic Marketing, 22*(7), 616-630.

Kervyn, N., Fiske, S. T., & Malone, C. (2012). Brands as intentional agents framework: How perceived intentions and ability can map brand perception. *Journal of Consumer Psychology, 22*(2), 166–176.

Khan, U., Dhar, R., & Wertenbroch, K. (2005). A behavioral decision theoretic perspective on hedonic and utilitarian choice. In Ratneshwar, S., & Glen, D. (Eds.) *Inside consumption: Frontiers of research on consumer motives, goals, and desires.* Routledge, 144–165.

Krishna, A. (2012). An integrative review of sensory marketing: Engaging the senses to affect perception, judgment and behavior. *Journal of Consumer Psychology, 22*(3), 332–351.

Liu, Y., Hultman, M., Eisingerich, A. B., & Wei, X. (2020). How does brand loyalty interact with tourism destination? Exploring the effect of brand loyalty on place attachment. *Annals of Tourism Research, 81*, 102879.

Luedicke, M. K., Thompson, C. J., & Giesler, M. (2010). Consumer identity work as moral protagonism: How myth and ideology animate a brand-mediated moral conflict. *Journal of Consumer Research, 36*(6), 1016–1032.

Malär, L., Krohmer, H., Hoyer, W. D., & Nyffenegger, B. (2011). Emotional brand attachment and brand personality: The relative importance of the actual and the ideal self. *Journal of Marketing, 75*(July), 35–52.

Mano, H., & Oliver, R. L. (1993). Assessing the dimensionality and structure of the consumption experience: Evaluation, feeling, and satisfaction. *Journal of Consumer Research, 20*(December), 451–66.

McAlexander, J. H., Schouten, J. W., & Koenig, H. F. (2002). Building brand community. *Journal of Marketing, 66*(1), 38–54.

McGraw, A. P., & Warren, C. (2010). Benign violations: Making immoral behavior funny. *Psychological Science, 21*(8), 1141–1149.

Merchant, A., & Rose, G. M. (2013). Effects of advertising-evoked vicarious nostalgia on brand heritage. *Journal of Business Research, 66*(12), 2619–2625.

Norman, D. A. (2013). *The design of everyday things.* Basic Books.

Orth, U. R., Limon, Y. & Rose, G. (2010). Store-evoked affect, personalities, and consumer emotional attachments to brands. *Journal of Business Research, 63*(11), 1202–1208.

Palmatier, R. W., Houston, M. B., Dant, R. P., & Grewal, D. (2013). Relationship velocity: Toward a theory of relationship dynamics. *Journal of Marketing, 77*(1), 13–30.

Palmatier, R. W., Jarvis, C. B., Bechkoff, J. R., & Kardes, F. R. (2009). The role of customer gratitude in relationship marketing. *Journal of Marketing, 73*(5), 1–18.

Park, C. W., Eisingerich, A. B., & Park, J. W. (2013). Attachment–aversion (AA) model of customer–brand relationships. *Journal of Consumer Psychology, 23*(2), 229–248.

Park, C. W., Jaworski, B. J., & MacInnis, D. J. (1986). Strategic brand concept–image management. *Journal of Marketing, 50*(October), 135–145.

Park, C. W., MacInnis, D. J., Priester, J., Eisingerich A. B., & Iacobucci, D. (2010). Brand attachment and brand attitude strength: Conceptual and empirical differentiation of two critical brand equity drivers. *Journal of Marketing, 74*(6), 1–17.

Peck, J., & Childers, T. L. (2008). Effects of sensory factors on consumer behaviors. In Haugtvedt, C. P., Herr, P. M., & Kardes, F. R. (Eds.) *Handbook of consumer psychology.* Erlbaum, 193–220.

Proksch, M., Orth, U. R., & Cornwell, T. B. (2015). Competence enhancement and anticipated emotion as motivational drivers of brand attachment. *Psychology & Marketing, 32*(9), 934–949.

Raju, P. S. (1980). Optimum stimulation level: Its relationship to personality, demographics, and exploratory behavior. *Journal of Consumer Research*, *7*(3), 272-282.

Reimann, M., & Aron, A. (2009). Self-expansion motivation and inclusion of close brands in self: Towards a theory of brand relationships. In Priester, J., MacInnis, D. J., & Park, C. W. (Eds.) *Handbook of brand relationships*. M.E. Sharpe, 65–81.

Rempel, J. K., & Burris, C. T. (2005). Let me count the ways: An integrative theory of love and hate. *Personal Relationships*, *12*(2), 297-313.

Richins, M. L. (1994). Valuing things: The public and private meanings of possessions. *Journal of Consumer Research*, *21*(December), 504-521.

Rusbult, C. E., Martz, J. M., & Agnew, C. R. (1998). The investment model scale: Measuring commitment level, satisfaction level, quality of alternatives, and investment size. *Personal Relationships*, *5*(4), 357-387.

Schau, H. J., Muñiz, A. M., & Arnould, E. J. (2009). How brand community practices create value. *Journal of Marketing*, *73*(5), 30-51.

Sharif, V., & Eisingerich, A. B. (2022). A road to biodiversity: Understanding psychological demand drivers of illegal wildlife products. In George, G., Haas, M. R., Joshi, H., McGahan, A. M., & Tracey, P. (Eds.) *Handbook on the business of sustainability: The organization, implementation and practice of sustainable growth*. Edward Elgar Publishing, 390-404.

Small, D. A., & Simonsohn, U. (2008). Friends of victims: Personal experience and prosocial behavior. *Journal of Consumer Research*, *35*(3), 532-542.

Thomson, M., MacInnis, D. J., & Park, C. W. (2005). The ties that bind: Measuring the strength of consumers' emotional attachments to brands. *Journal of Consumer Psychology*, *15*(1), 77-91.

Torelli, C. J., Monga, A. B., & Kaikati, A. M. (2012). Doing poorly by doing good: Corporate social responsibility and brand concepts. *Journal of Consumer Research*, *38*(5), 948-963.

10 The coming of age of internal brand management research: looking back to look forward

Ceridwyn King, Enrique Murillo and Lina Xiong

1. Introduction

In the last two decades, internal brand management (IBM), which emphasizes aligning employee attitudes and behavior with the organization's brand values to deliver the brand promise to customers (e.g., King & Grace, 2012), has received growing research attention. Also known as internal branding, IBM includes practices that promote employees' brand-consistent attitudes and behavior so that customers' brand expectations can be fulfilled. This research area is primarily studied in service industries, where employees are critical in bringing the unique brand values to life because of the intangibility and heterogeneity characteristics of service products. In short, 'the benefits of having a unique service brand to achieve a competitive advantage can only be realized to the extent that employees are knowledgeable and capable of demonstrating those brand values in their thoughts and actions during service encounters' (Xiong & King, 2015, p. 58).

Internal branding is by no means a new phenomenon. Brand training in prominent hospitality organizations such as Ritz Carlton Hotels (Yeung, 2006) and Singapore Airlines (Chong, 2007) are historic examples of the significance of employee brand-aligned service performance. Since 1999, there has been a growing number of IBM studies that recognize and establish it as an important research area under the umbrella of branding research. As a sign of the phenomenon coming of age, there are, as of this writing, over 240 articles in Scopus-indexed journals that explore a variety of contexts, theories and methods, providing valuable insights with respect to growing brand equity via employees' thoughts and actions.

Considering the time elapsed since the first IBM research publication, as well as the body of work that has subsequently amassed, IBM studies from more recent years appear to have reached a bottleneck, where newer studies are often repetitions of previous studies but in different contexts or under different terms. For example, brand citizenship behavior which denotes employees' extra-role behaviors to advance the brand, was first coined as the desired outcome for IBM (Burmann & Zeplin, 2005). However, its conceptual intent has since been measured by constructs labeled as employees' branding behavior (Uen et al., 2012), employee brand performance (Xiong & King, 2018), brand-supporting/supportive behavior (Erkmen & Hancer, 2015), employee brand equity (King et al., 2012), extra-role brand-building behavior (Morhart et al., 2009), etc. While all these constructs have their nuances, it is questionable whether they are in fact adding to our understanding, or rather just contributing to a perception of fragmentation that previous reviews of this literature have critiqued (Saleem & Iglesias, 2016).

Therefore, to ensure that future studies are forging new ground in IBM research, this chapter provides a comprehensive and systematic review of current research as well as clear and meaningful directions for future research. In doing so it summarizes main theories, methods and contexts in IBM research through a systematic literature review as well as a bibliometric analysis that, unlike other reviews (Saini et al., 2022), is focused on IBM literature exclusively. Guidance for future IBM research that can significantly contribute to both academic research and industry practices through theory building and innovative method adoption is also presented, along with novel research directions that address current trends, such as the gig/sharing economy and the great resignation.

2. Systematic literature review

The quality of a literature review is heavily influenced by methodological decisions such as the inclusion/exclusion criteria of articles to be reviewed. The bibliographic data for this review was obtained in January 2022 from the dominant Social Science article databases, Web of Science (WoS) and Scopus (Wang & Waltman, 2016). A third database, Dimensions by Digital Science, was used to cross-check, identify and correct for missing articles. Identical search strings were used to obtain the data from both sources. Using the proprietary search engine in each database, the search was 'internal branding' OR 'internal brand management' OR 'employee branding', with results limited to English-language journal articles. Two complete IBM datasets were prepared. First, a Scopus dataset, augmented with articles from Dimensions which had better coverage of the 1995–2009 period. This Scopus–Dimensions dataset, comprising 240 records, was used to perform the systematic literature review. However, this dataset was not suitable for bibliometric analysis because important IBM references, and their citation links to other Scopus records are currently missing from the Scopus database, and could not be manually repaired (e.g., Burmann & Zeplin, 2005). Therefore, a 162-record WoS dataset was built exclusively to perform the bibliometric cluster analysis. This was imported into VOSviewer, the bibliometric software adopted for this study.

2.1 Theories applied in IBM research

The 240 articles in the Scopus dataset were content analyzed to reveal how IBM research has evolved over the years as regards the theories that it has applied (see Table 10.1) and the research methods that have been employed (Table 10.2). As to the former, only 50% clearly identify one or more theoretical frameworks to address the articulated research objectives. An additional 31% of publications utilize the term 'theory' or 'theoretical framework', however, upon close inspection these references to theory relate to the cognate area or field of study (e.g., IBM theory). This contrasts with an established theory that is not confined to a context but rather broadly describes a phenomenon, makes predictions about the phenomenon in the future and can be tested. Fifteen percent of publications reviewed do not refer to any theory.

Table 10.1 Theoretical frameworks applied in IBM research

Theories Applied	*n*	%
Social Psychology Theories	**57**	**48%**
Social Identity Theory	25	
Social Exchange Theory	20	
Construal Level Theory	3	
Social Influence Theory	3	
Consumer Culture Theory	1	
Emotional Contagion	1	
Generational Theory	1	
Relational Cohesion Theory	1	
Self-categorization Theory	1	
Social Cognitive Theory	1	

Cognitive/Motivational Theories	**37**	**31%**
Job Characteristics Theory	5	
Self-determination Theory - Organismic Integration Theory	5	
Balance Theory	4	
Organizational Identification Theory	4	
Value Congruence Theory	3	
Organizational Commitment Theory	3	
Commitment Trust Theory	2	
Equity Theory	2	
Person-Environment/Organization Fit Theory	2	
Activation Theory	1	
Attitude Theory	1	
Users and Gratification Theory	1	
Job-demands Resources Theory	1	
Job Design Theory	1	
SOR Theory	1	
Theory of Planned Behavior	1	
Behavioral/Learning Theories	**14**	**12%**
Social Learning Theory	3	
Dilemma Theory	2	
Information Processing Theory	2	
Signaling Theory	2	
Attribution Theory	1	
Conceptual Metaphor Theory	1	
Dual Process Theory	1	
Organizational Learning Theory	1	
Situated Learning Theory	1	
Organizational Management Theories	**10**	**8%**
Stakeholder Theory	3	
Agency Theory	2	
Transformational/Transactional Leadership Theory	1	

Contingency Theory	1
Corporate Image Theory	1
Organization Support Theory (Organizational Management)	1
Resource Based View (Organizational Management)	1
Cognate Area*	**73**
Internal Brand Management (48) Brand Management (brand equity, branding theory, corporate branding etc.) (24) B2B branding (1)	
No theoretical framework/theories applied	**47**

Note: Articles may have applied more than one theory * Cognate area/field of study labeled as a theory in the publication (e.g., internal brand management theory).

Of the 42 theories identified in the examined IBM publications, 48% reflect an interest in understanding the social dynamics that affect employee attitudes and behavior. For example, the application of either social identity theory or social exchange theory are dominant frameworks employed to understand how and why employees bring the brand promise to life. In recognition that such employee behavior is often volitional, requiring them to go above and beyond, there is also a significant body of work (i.e., 31%) that explores the intrinsic perspective, in consideration of the cognitive and motivational effort that is required (e.g., job characteristics theory, self-determination theory, organizational identification theory, value congruence theory). With an emphasis on influencing employee behavior, IBM research is also examined through a learning theoretical lens (e.g., signaling theory, social learning theory, situated learning theory, dual processing theory) with 12% of publications adopting this approach. Consideration of theories that reflect the organizational perspective (e.g., agency theory, stakeholder theory) are explored to a lesser extent (8%), which is in line with the extant IBM literature overwhelmingly being focused on the individual employee level.

2.2 IBM research methods

Table 10.2 summarizes the methodological approaches adopted in the reviewed IBM publications. Overwhelmingly, IBM publications adopt an empirical lens to examine the phenomenon, with 83.6% of publications reflecting quantitative (68.0%), qualitative (24.2%) or mixed methods (7.7%) methodological approaches. Survey methods, at 65.5%, dominate the preferred data collection method, with interviews being second by a significant margin with less than 20% of the publications adopting this procedure. The more contemporary methodologies, such as meta-analyses and experimental design have rarely been applied to IBM studies. Interestingly, given that IBM research reveals the importance of the social/coworker context in employees understanding the brand, it is surprising that focus groups have not been used extensively in IBM research to date.

Table 10.2 Methodological approaches applied in IBM research

Category	Subcategory	*n*	%
Type of Study	Empirical	194	83.6
	Conceptual/Review	31/7	16.4
Research Methodology	Quantitative	132	68.0
	Qualitative	47	24.2
	Mixed Methods	15	7.7
Data Collection Method	Survey	127	65.5
	Interviews	38	19.6
	Mixed Data Collection	21	10.8
	Literature Review/Document Analysis	4	2.1
	Focus Groups	2	1.0
	Experiment	1	0.5
	Meta-Analysis	1	0.5

3. Bibliometric analysis

The cluster analysis performed in VOSviewer is based on a direct citation analysis, using 'documents' as the level of analysis. The source is the WoS dataset. Only articles with four cites or more were included to focus on the most influential references; this resulted in 119 connected documents. The VOSviewer clustering algorithm identified five distinct IBM research clusters; given space limitations, Table 10.3 displays only the top ten cited articles from each cluster.

Table 10.3 Top IBM articles within each research cluster

VOSviewer Label	Title	Cluster	Total Cites
Burmann (2005)	Building brand commitment: A behavioural approach to internal brand management	1	288
Morhart (2009)	Brand-specific leadership: Turning employees into brand champions	1	247
Punjaisri (2007)	The role of internal branding in the delivery of employee brand promise	1	171
Punjaisri (2011)	Internal branding process: Key mechanisms, outcomes and moderating factors	1	128
Foster (2010)	Exploring the relationship between corporate, internal and employer branding	1	124
Punjaisri (2009a)	Internal branding: An enabler of employees' brand-supporting behaviours	1	119
Baumgarth (2010)	How strong is the business-to-business brand in the workforce? An empirically tested model of 'internal brand equity' in a business-to-business setting	1	118
Santos-Vijande (2013)	The brand management system and service firm competitiveness	1	66
King (2010)	'One size doesn't fit all': Tourism and hospitality employees' response to internal brand management	1	59
Mäläskä (2011)	Network actors' participation in B2B SME branding	1	52
Burmann (2009)	Key determinants of internal brand management success: An exploratory empirical analysis	2	159
Chang (2012)	A multilevel investigation of relationships among brand-centered HRM, brand psychological ownership, brand citizenship behaviors, and customer satisfaction	2	78
Xiong (2013)	'That's not my job': Exploring the employee perspective in the development of brand ambassadors	2	67
King (2012)	Employee brand equity: Scale development and validation	2	48

VOSviewer Label	Title	Cluster	Total Cites
Du Preez (2015)	The impact of internal brand management on employee job satisfaction, brand commitment and intention to stay	2	42
Xiong (2015)	Motivational drivers that fuel employees to champion the hospitality brand	2	41
Devasagayam (2010)	Building brand community membership within organizations: A viable internal branding alternative?	2	28
Uen (2012)	Transformational leadership and branding behavior in Taiwanese hotels	2	25
King (2015)	Enhancing hotel employees' brand understanding and brand-building behavior in China	2	23
King (2017)	The effects of generational work values on employee brand attitude and behavior: A multi-group analysis	2	23
King (2008)	Internal branding: Exploring the employee's perspective	3	126
Aurand (2005)	Human resource management's role in internal branding: An opportunity for cross-functional brand message synergy	3	106
Buil (2016)	From internal brand management to organizational citizenship behaviours: Evidence from frontline employees in the hotel industry	3	59
Whisman (2009)	Internal branding: A university's most valuable intangible asset	3	57
Piehler (2016)	The importance of employee brand understanding, brand identification, and brand commitment in realizing brand citizenship behaviour	3	57
Judson (2006)	Building a university brand from within: A comparison of coaches' perspectives of internal branding	3	49
Dean (2016)	Internal brand co-creation: The experiential brand meaning cycle in higher education	3	40
Simmons (2009)	'Both sides now': Aligning external and internal branding for a socially responsible era	3	30

VOSviewer Label	Title	Cluster	Total Cites
Du Preez (2017)	The behavioral consequences of internal brand management among frontline employees	3	25
Burmann (2011)	Does internal brand management really drive brand commitment in shared-service call centers?	3	24
King (2010)	Building and measuring employee-based brand equity	4	142
Kimpakorn (2009)	Employees' commitment to brands in the service sector: Luxury hotel chains in Thailand	4	78
King (2012)	Examining the antecedents of positive employee brand-related attitudes and behaviours	4	75
de Chernatony (2003)	Building a services brand: Stages, people and orientations	4	67
Terglav (2016)	Internal branding process: Exploring the role of mediators in top management's leadership-commitment relationship	4	67
Baker (2014)	The role of brand communications on front line service employee beliefs, behaviors, and performance	4	52
Porricelli (2014)	Antecedents of brand citizenship behavior in retailing	4	23
Dechawatanapaisal (2018)	Employee retention: The effects of internal branding and brand attitudes in sales organizations	4	22
Yang (2015)	Effect of internal branding on employee brand commitment and behavior in hospitality	4	19
Piehler (2018)	Employees' brand understanding, brand commitment, and brand citizenship behaviour: A closer look at the relationships among construct dimensions	4	19
Löhndorf (2014)	Internal branding: Social identity and social exchange perspectives on turning employees into brand champions	5	102
Yaniv (2005)	The impact of person-organization fit on the corporate brand perception of employees and of customers	5	52

VOSviewer Label	Title	Cluster	Total Cites
Gapp (2006)	Important factors to consider when using internal branding as a management strategy: A healthcare case study	5	48
Harris (2007)	We the people: The importance of employees in the process of building customer experience	5	42
Matanda (2013)	Internal marketing, internal branding, and organisational outcomes: The moderating role of perceived goal congruence	5	41
Helm (2016)	Exploring the impact of employees' self-concept, brand identification and brand pride on brand citizenship behaviors	5	37
Iyer (2018)	Determinants of brand performance: The role of internal branding	5	24
Boukis (2017)	Internal market orientation determinants of employee brand enactment	5	22
Piehler (2018)	Internal brand management: Introduction to the special issue and directions for future research	5	20
Morokane (2016)	Drivers of employee propensity to endorse their corporate brand	5	19

Cluster 1 – the ignition of IBM research from corporate branding

The first and largest cluster includes 37 articles that reflect the ignition of IBM research with a strong underpinning of corporate branding. Most of the articles are published in marketing or branding journals and advocate the importance of IBM for organizational performance and positive customer attitudes and behaviors. The seminal internal branding articles are positioned in this cluster, notably the articles by Burmann and Zeplin (2005), Punjaisri et al. (2009a; 2009b; 2013; Punjaisri & Wilson, 2007, 2011), Morhart et al. (2009) and King (2010). Most empirical studies in this cluster examine the effect of IBM processes on employee cognitions and attitudes toward the brand, and their visible manifestation in brand-supportive behaviors. The most cited article is Burmann and Zeplin (2005) which is arguably the foundational paper that brings serious attention from mainstream corporate branding research to IBM. As a conceptual paper, it coined the term employee brand commitment and brand citizenship behavior as the most important outcomes in IBM and proposed likely organizational antecedents, which propelled the series of empirical studies that seek to build a nomological network of IBM research. Punjaisri and Wilson (2007, 2011) followed suit and emphasized the role of IBM in corporate branding, especially for customer-facing employees in service branding.

The employee perspective of internal branding is also reflected in this cluster. A prime example is Morhart et al. (2009), which emphasized how employees' role identity internalization and sense of community mediate organizational influences (e.g., brand-specific transformational leadership and brand-specific transactional leadership) in achieving IBM outcomes. Another focus of this cluster is linking well-established organizational behavioral and corporate branding constructs to IBM, such as brand equity (M'zungu et al., 2010), work engagement (Park et al., 2019), and customer relationship (Kang, 2016). In summary, this cluster primarily exists in mainstream branding literature and regards IBM as an auxiliary research area of corporate branding. Readers of publications in this cluster can generally see the start of IBM research, with a narrowing focus on service branding and the employee perspective.

Cluster 2 – psychological drivers in IBM and applications in the hospitality industry

The second cluster reflects an emphasis of the employee psychological drivers in IBM. There are 24 articles in this cluster with the most prominent characteristics being research grounded in a hospitality industry context and a high percentage (about 60%) of hospitality and tourism journals as the publication outlet. Burmann et al. (2009) is the most cited and the earliest article in this cluster. The central positioning of this paper is likely due to its exploration of applying IBM in the travel and hospitality industry out of the six industries examined. With strong and significant results from this study, a series of IBM studies grew in the hospitality literature. In particular, the cluster reflects the extensive work of King in this domain, with three articles (King et al., 2012; King & So, 2015; King et al., 2017) as first author, and six more as coauthor with Xiong (Xiong et al., 2013; Xiong & King, 2015, 2018, 2019; Xiong et al., 2019) and Murillo (Murillo & King, 2019b).

Another advancement shown in Cluster 2 is the focus on the utility of IBM in hospitality management by proposing and testing relevant constructs and measurements. For example, King et al. (2012) were the first to propose employee-based brand equity as an IBM outcome as well as developing and validating the corresponding measurement. In a similar manner, Xiong et al. (2013) were the first to explore the nuance of employee brand understanding as an IBM antecedent, emphasizing the importance of perceived brand relevance and meaningfulness to achieve brand commitment and brand-supporting behaviors. Chang et al. (2012) and Uen et al. (2012) examined how organizational practices can contribute to employee branding behavior and customer satisfaction. Conditions that may affect the effectiveness of IBM are also explored, such as intrinsic motivation (Xiong & King, 2015), personalities (Kang et al., 2019) and generational values (King et al., 2017). Through the research reflected in this cluster, readers gain an appreciation of the psychological drivers in IBM, with an emphasis on employee responses to IBM practices.

Cluster 3 – a horizontal expansion of IBM to other service-related contexts

Cluster 3, with 21 articles, showcased a variety of service-related contexts in which IBM has been applied. Overall, the conceptual frameworks in this cluster are often drawn from studies in other clusters. The distinction is that there is an emphasis on exploring IBM practices in other service-related contexts, such as banks, healthcare and the public sector. There are two early internal branding articles (Aurand et al., 2005; King & Grace, 2008) near the center of the cluster diagram. Both are of an exploring nature that seeks to explain the importance of human capital and the involvement of HR management in IBM. Most studies in this cluster concentrate on examining IBM in universities, with a total of ten studies. The cluster also includes the two extant studies of employees working in contact centers, the seminal study by Burmann and König (2011) and the more recent piece by Du Preez and Bendixen (2019). This IBM context expansion is also reflected in the publication dates as fewer articles were published in the earlier years (five articles between 2005 and 2010) while more articles were published in recent years (13 articles between 2016 and 2020).

Cluster 4 – IBM process

Cluster 4 reflects work that details the process of IBM. There are 20 articles in this cluster, with a variety of authors and journal outlets. Overall, there seems to be an emphasis on a closer look at the links among different stages of employee brand perception development and subsequent brand attitudes and behavior outcomes. A recurring theme in these articles is examining the role of employee brand commitment as a mediating variable between internal branding practices and employee brand performance. King and Grace (2010) is the most cited article in this cluster. It is one of the first articles that proposed and tested a holistic framework to explain how to achieve employee-based brand equity. They consider factors that include organizational practice, employee factors, process factors and outcomes. Similarly, many articles in this cluster are devoted to articulating the IBM process including Terglav et al. (2016) and Kaur et al. (2020). Research in this cluster also examines a few external factors that may affect employee brand perceptions, such as brand signaling (Karanges et al., 2018), external brand communication (Piehler et al., 2019), and brand image (Hoppe, 2018). Overall, compared to other clusters, this cluster illuminates research that takes a holistic approach to examining IBM.

Cluster 5 - anchoring IBM research with theories

Cluster 5 includes 17 articles with a strong theoretical underpinning. Several studies draw on theories of organizational identification and person–organization fit with the aim of enhancing employee identification with the corporate brand and/or the brand values. Published mostly in brand and marketing journals, articles in this cluster have an emphasis on adopting overarching theories to explain links in IBM, especially regarding how employees respond to corporate practices. For example, the most cited article is Löhndorf and Diamantopoulos (2014), which adopted social identity and social exchange theories that suggest employee brand-aligned performance results from employees' perceived organizational support, enhancing their social identity as well as propels their intention to reciprocate. Vatankhah and Darvishi (2018) adopted social influence theory to explain the strong mediating role of IBM between management commitment and employee in-role and extra-role work performance. Yaniv and Farkas (2005) suggested employee Person–Organization Fit (POF) contributes to their perceived consistency between employee brand perception and management-communicated brand values, which further contributes to coveted IBM outcomes. Although this cluster also shares some characteristics of other clusters in terms of examining moderating and mediating mechanisms in IBM and examining IBM in multiple fields, it shows a stronger theory underpinning when proposing these relationships.

4. Looking forward: future internal brand management research

With over 20 years of sustained research and practitioner effort and interest in this field, there is a need to look to new avenues of meaningful research, which is afforded as a result of the systematic literature review and bibliometric analysis. Such an emphasis prevents falling into a trap of replication or 'slicing the onion too thin' that really does not advance the field but rather enables both academics and practitioners to tread water. A common theme with previous IBM review papers is the observation that the field, because of its nascent stage, is fragmented (Saleem & Iglesias, 2016). While such an observation is not unique to this field, nor is it unexpected given the proliferation of research over a relatively short time frame, often on a simultaneous basis, in reality, at least from our interpretation of the results, the field is not that fragmented. Rather, while there may be a plethora of definitions in the literature that have been ascribed to IBM, all the definitions capture the same essence: living the brand/delivering the brand promise, with the target of such efforts being predominantly the employee (King & Murillo, 2022). Hence it is not that internal brand management has been approached from divergent perspectives that leads to the fragmentation perception, but rather perhaps that researchers, in their quest to make contributions to the field, modify previously established concepts without really making substantive advances (e.g., the case of many variations of 'brand citizenship behavior').

Along the same line, the research clusters suggest that IBM researchers tend to draw from studies in their own 'silos', ignoring work in other related areas. As evidenced in cluster 2, most of the articles are published in hospitality journals, while articles in other clusters were published in mainstream business journals. This might be due to the personal preferences or institutional expectations of the main contributing authors. However, literature reviews on branding that are restricted to specific fields (e.g., the general business management literature or hospitality management literature) may inadvertently lead to repeating work already published in different journal outlets. Through articulating comprehensively what has been done before in this review, the hope is that future research builds on, as opposed to renaming, constructs and relationships that have already been established in the field. For example, research that examines the boundary conditions of well-established relationships is barely reflected in the extant literature (e.g., Dechawatanapaisal, 2019; Murillo, 2022), representing a clear research opportunity. In addition, when seeking to solidify the field and/or break new ground, future research is encouraged to develop a sound theoretical underpinning. The summarized theories adopted in IBM in Table 10.2 as well as the theory-rich cluster 5 should provide valuable insights for this endeavor.

Previous reviews of IBM research have also revealed the plethora of work focused on employee psychological constructs that capture the effects of IBM in pursuit of a brand-aligned workforce, an observation that bears out in our analysis. While this clearly underscores the importance of influencing the employee mindset, the levers in which to do this have enjoyed far less attention. Future research would benefit from a deeper dive into the nuances of what it means for organizations to embrace IBM principles. For example, King (2022) emphasizes that despite the established role of brand orientation in IBM, there is currently no clear and detailed consensus of how an organization can create such an outcome.

Additionally, there is a lack of variety of research methods in current IBM research (Table 10.2). Considering IBM research takes the employee perspective, and the effectiveness of IBM relies on the social environment in the organization as well, focus groups and interviews are highly valuable in gaining employee insights relating to IBM, in addition to surveys. Experiments are also encouraged to further strengthen the link between IBM practices and the coveted outcomes. In fact, IBM research has yet to reveal the extent, and nuance, to which the more implicit influencers impact the process of winning the hearts and minds of brand-engaged employees. Recently the work of Xiong and King (2020) explored the role that an employee's sense of brand community plays when informing their brand-related attitudes and behavior. Evidence from Murillo and King's (2019a) longitudinal study clearly reveals that the implicit environment plays an influential role in one's ability to understand the brand. More work is thus needed to account for these social influences.

The importance of addressing this paucity is underscored by the growing dialogue in the IBM literature around the concept of co-creation. So far, limited insight has focused on employees as being quasi-independent actors that can shape the brand through their thoughts and actions, possibly in a way that the organization does not intend. While there is a plethora of research that shows IBM efforts have been successful, and that employee brand engagement can be nurtured and is a powerful attraction and retention strategy, the extant IBM literature has rarely considered what the employees themselves bring to the table. This is an important oversight. Without consideration of what the employee wants or expects from the brand, or actively involving them in the brand's development, any IBM practices may be rendered ineffective if they are not addressing employee needs. While the IBM literature is not completely void of the examination of factors that seek to account for employees' needs beyond the brand (e.g., generational influences – King et al., 2017), the changing workforce landscape, that has been amplified as a result of the global health pandemic, needs to be reflected in future IBM work.

It is not a new phenomenon that younger generations of workers seek to align themselves with organizations that espouse values reflecting tolerance, sustainability and altruism (Seligman & Csikszentmihalyi, 2014). However, evidence from the 'great resignation/reshuffle' driven by the pandemic suggests these factors, along with an increased desire for greater flexibility, opportunities for personal growth and skill development along with a greater dialogue within the organization (Schleicher & Baumann, 2020), are less likely to be negotiable for the contemporary workforce (King et al., 2021). Employees' expectations of the brands they work for are increasingly becoming aligned with those of the brand's customers. They demand brand authenticity, transparency/consistency, values-based decision making and a brand purpose that resonates (Allredge et al., 2021), however IBM research to date has not accounted for such expectations. With the role of the employee in a brand's success undisputed, the rapidly changing expectation of the workforce suggests that exploration of the intersection of the work being done in the employer branding (Saini et al., 2022) and IBM literatures may be necessary to sustain the intended outcomes of effective brand management.

The changes to the contemporary workforce also illuminate the need to expand how we think about the target of IBM. For example, given the growing transactional nature of employment which has given rise to the 'gig' economy, there can be no disputing that the way organizations/brands interact with those that deliver the brand promise has fundamentally changed. As employees seek diversity through regular changes in employment relationships, as well as increasingly engaging in multiple roles or 'gigs', not as an employee but as an independent contractor (Veen et al., 2020), future research needs to consider that those responsible for delivering the brand may not respond in a manner that aligns with traditional employee management. The utility of expanding the target market for IBM is evident in the literature with examination of such practices for effective destination management (Cox et al., 2014) as well as franchisees (King et al., 2013) and volunteers (Liu et al., 2015). With such examinations predicated on the principal–agent relationship, future research could also consider how IBM manifests in the sharing or gig economy whereby there is a different relationship between the brand and its providers from a traditional employee sense.

5. Conclusion

Internal branding has received growing interest in the last two decades. This review of current IBM research presents the evolution of the topic, deficiencies (e.g., a lack of method varieties, repeating work published in different fields, etc.), and meaningful and relevant future research areas. Anticipating the changing landscape of the labor market in a gig economy, it is expected that IBM research and practices will both deepen in the knowledge of the underlying drivers and expand into new contexts. The brand will not only serve as a necessary element in strategic management that attracts and retains customers, but also as a beacon that enlists, inspires and motivates the employees of future generations. With this in mind, we advocate for the consideration of the employee perspective in all brand management studies.

References

Allredge, K., Jacobs, J., & Teichner, W. (2021). Great expectations: Navigating challenging stakeholder expectations of brand. *McKinsey & Company* (December). https:// www .mckinsey .com/ industries/ consumer -packaged -goods/ our -insights/ great-expectations-navigating-challenging-stakeholder-expectations-of-brands

Aurand, T. W., Gorchels, L., & Bishop, T. R. (2005). Human resource management's role in internal branding: An opportunity for cross-functional brand message synergy. *Journal of Product and Brand Management, 14*(3), 163–169.

Baker, T. L., Rapp, A., Meyer, T., & Mullins, R. (2014). The role of brand communications on front line service employee beliefs, behaviors, and performance. *Journal of the Academy of Marketing Science, 6*(42), 642-657.

Baumgarth, C., & Schmidt, M. (2010). How strong is the business-to-business brand in the workforce? An empirically-tested model of 'internal brand equity' in a business-to-business setting. *Industrial Marketing Management, 39*(8), 1250-1260.

Boukis, A., Gounaris, S., & Lings, I. (2017). Internal market orientation determinants of employee brand enactment. *Journal of Services Marketing, 31*(7), 690-703.

Buil, I., Martínez, E., & Matute, J. (2016). From internal brand management to organizational citizenship behaviours: Evidence from frontline employees in the hotel industry. *Tourism Management, 57*, 256-271.

Burmann, C., & König, V. (2011). Does internal brand management really drive brand commitment in shared-service call centers? *Journal of Brand Management, 18*(6), 374–393.

Burmann, C., & Zeplin, S. (2005). Building brand commitment: A behavioural approach to internal brand management. *Journal of Brand Management, 12*(4), 279–300.

Burmann, C., Zeplin, S., & Riley, N. (2009). Key determinants of internal brand management success: An exploratory empirical analysis. *Journal of Brand Management, 16*(4), 264–284.

Chang, A., Chiang, H. H., & Han, T. S. (2012). A multilevel investigation of relationships among brand-centered HRM, brand psychological ownership, brand citizenship behaviors, and customer satisfaction. *European Journal of Marketing, 46*(5), 626–662.

Chong, M. (2007). The role of internal communication and training in infusing corporate values and delivering brand promise: Singapore Airlines' experience. *Corporate Reputation Review, 10*(3), 201–212.

Cox, N., Gyrd-Jones, R., & Gardiner, S. (2014). Internal brand management of destination brands: Destination management organisations and operators. *Journal of Destination Marketing & Management, 3*(2), 85–95.

de Chernatony, L., Drury, S., & Segal-Horn, S. (2003). Building a services brand: Stages, people and orientations. *Service Industries Journal, 23*(3), 1-21.

Dean, D., Arroyo-Gamez, R. E., Punjaisri, K., & Pich, C. (2016). Internal brand co-creation: The experiential brand meaning cycle in higher education. *Journal of Business Research*, *69*(8), 3041-3048.

Dechawatanapaisal, D. (2018). Employee retention: The effects of internal branding and brand attitudes in sales organizations. *Personnel Review*, *47*(3), 675–693.

Dechawatanapaisal, D. (2019). Internal branding and employees' brand outcomes: Do generational differences and organizational tenure matter? *Industrial and Commercial Training*, *51*(4), 209–227.

Devasagayam, P. R., Buff, C. L., Aurand, T. W., & Judson, K. M. (2010). Building brand community membership within organizations: A viable internal branding alternative? *Journal of Product & Brand Management*, *19*(3), 210-217.

Du Preez, R., & Bendixen, M. T. (2015). The impact of internal brand management on employee job satisfaction, brand commitment and intention to stay. *International Journal of Bank Marketing*, *33*(1), 78–91.

Du Preez, R., & Bendixen, M. (2019). Outsourcing contact centers: Internal branding challenges and consequences. *Journal of Business & Industrial Marketing*, *34*(5), 921–930.

Du Preez, R., Bendixen, M., & Abratt, R. (2017). The behavioral consequences of internal brand management among frontline employees. *Journal of Product & Brand Management*, *26*(3), 251–261.

Erkmen, E., & Hancer, M. (2015). 'Do your internal branding efforts measure up?': Consumers' response to brand supporting behaviors of hospitality employees. *International Journal of Contemporary Hospitality Management*, *27*(5), 878–895.

Foster, C., Punjaisri, K., & Cheng, R. (2010). Exploring the relationship between corporate, internal and employer branding. *Journal of Product & Brand Management*, *19*(6), 401-409.

Gapp, R., & Merrilees, B. (2006). Important factors to consider when using internal branding as a management strategy: A healthcare case study. *Journal of Brand Management*, *14*(1/2), 162-176.

Harris, P. (2007). We the people: The importance of employees in the process of building customer experience. *Journal of Brand Management*, *15*(2), 102-114.

Helm, S. V., Renk, U., & Mishra, A. (2016). Exploring the impact of employees' self-concept, brand identification and brand pride on brand citizenship behaviors. *European Journal of Marketing*, *50*(1/2), 58-77.

Hoppe, D. (2018). Linking employer branding and internal branding: Establishing perceived employer brand image as an antecedent of favourable employee brand attitudes and behaviours. *Journal of Product & Brand Management*, *27*(4), 452–467.

Iyer, P., Davari, A., & Paswan, A. (2018). Determinants of brand performance: The role of internal branding. *Journal of Brand Management*, *25*(3), 202-216.

Judson, K. M., Gorchels, L., & Aurand, T. W. (2006). Building a university brand from within: A comparison of coaches' perspectives of internal branding. *Journal of Marketing for Higher Education*, *16*(1), 97-114.

Kang, A. Y., Legendre, T. S., & Cartier, E. A. (2019). Personality congruence among brands, recruiters, and applicants during the anticipatory socialization process. *Journal of Hospitality & Tourism Research*, *43*(8), 1302–1325.

Kang, D. S. (2016). Turning inside out: Perceived internal branding in customer–firm relationship building. *Journal of Services Marketing*, *30*(4), 462–475.

Karanges, E., Johnston, K. A., Lings, I., & Beatson, A. T. (2018). Brand signalling: An antecedent of employee brand understanding. *Journal of Brand Management*, *25*(3), 235–249.

Kaur, P., Malhotra, K., & Sharma, S. K. (2020). Moderation-mediation framework connecting internal branding, affective commitment, employee engagement and job satisfaction: An empirical study of BPO employees in Indian context. *Asia-Pacific Journal of Business Administration, 12*(3–4), 327–348.

Kimpakorn, N., & Tocquer, G. (2009). Employees' commitment to brands in the service sector: Luxury hotel chains in Thailand. *Journal of Brand Management, 16*(8), 532-544.

King, C. (2010). 'One size doesn't fit all': Tourism and hospitality employees' response to internal brand management. *International Journal of Contemporary Hospitality Management, 22*(4), 517–534.

King, C. (2022). Branding inside-out: Corporate culture and internal branding. In Iglesias, O., Ind, N., & Schultz, M. (Eds.), *The Routledge Companion to Corporate Branding* (pp. 496–504). Abingdon: Routledge.

King, C., & Grace, D. (2008). Internal branding: Exploring the employee's perspective. *Journal of Brand Management, 15*(5), 358-372.

King, C., & Grace, D. (2010). Building and measuring employee-based brand equity. *European Journal of Marketing, 44*(7–8), 938–971.

King, C., & Grace, D. (2012). Examining the antecedents of positive employee brand-related attitudes and behaviours. *European Journal of Marketing, 46*(3–4), 469–488.

King, C., & Murillo, E. (2022). Hire dirtbags: Three tools to help employees become brand champions with a purpose. *Fox Business Review, 1*(4), 15–21.

King, C., & So, K. K. F. (2015). Enhancing hotel employees' brand understanding and brand-building behavior in China. *Journal of Hospitality & Tourism Research, 39*(4), 492–516. https://doi.org/10.1177/1096348013491602

King, C., Grace, D., & Weaven, S. (2013). Developing brand champions: A franchisee perspective. *Journal of Marketing Management, 29*(11-12), 1308-1336.

King, C., Grace, D., & Funk, D. C. (2012). Employee brand equity: Scale development and validation. *Journal of Brand Management, 19*(4), 268–288.

King, C., Madera, J. M., Lee, L., Murillo, E., Baum, T., & Solnet, D. (2021). Reimagining attraction and retention of hospitality management talent: A multilevel identity perspective. *Journal of Business Research, 136*, 251–262. https://doi.org/10.1016/j.jbusres.2021.07.044

King, C., Murillo, E., & Lee, H. (2017). The effects of generational work values on employee brand attitude and behavior: A multi-group analysis. *International Journal of Hospitality Management, 66*, 92–105.

Liu, G., Eng, T. Y., & Takeda, S. (2015). An investigation of marketing capabilities and social enterprise performance in the UK and Japan. *Entrepreneurship Theory and Practice, 39*(2), 267–298.

Löhndorf, B., & Diamantopoulos, A. (2014). Internal branding: Social identity and social exchange perspectives on turning employees into brand champions. *Journal of Service Research, 17*(3), 310–325.

Mäläskä, M., Saraniemi, S., & Tähtinen, J. (2011). Network actors' participation in B2B SME branding. *Industrial Marketing Management, 40*(7), 1144-1152.

Matanda, M. J., & Ndubisi, N. O. (2013). Internal marketing, internal branding, and organisational outcomes: The moderating role of perceived goal congruence. *Journal of Marketing Management, 29*(9-10), 1030-1055.

Morhart, F. M., Herzog, W., & Tomczak, T. (2009). Brand-specific leadership: Turning employees into brand champions. *Journal of Marketing, 73*(5), 122–142. https://doi.org/10.1509/jmkg.73.5.122

Morokane, P., Chiba, M., & Kleyn, N. (2016). Drivers of employee propensity to endorse their corporate brand. *Journal of Brand Management, 23*(1), 55-66.

Murillo, E. (2022). Enhancing brand understanding through brand training: A conditional process analysis of recent hires at an airline. *Review of Business Management, 24*(2), 312–331. https://doi.org/10.7819/rbgn.v24i2.4170

Murillo, E., & King, C. (2019a). Examining the drivers of employee brand understanding: A longitudinal study. *Journal of Product and Brand Management, 28*(7), 892–907. https://doi.org/10.1108/JPBM-09-2018-2007

Murillo, E., & King, C. (2019b). Why do employees respond to hospitality talent management? An examination of a Latin American restaurant chain. *International Journal of Contemporary Hospitality Management, 31*(10), 4021–4042. https://doi.org/10.1108/IJCHM-10-2018-0871

M'zungu, S. D., Merrilees, B., & Miller, D. (2010). Brand management to protect brand equity: A conceptual model. *Journal of Brand Management, 17*(8), 605–617.

Park, S., Johnson, K. R., & Chaudhuri, S. (2019). Promoting work engagement in the hotel sector: Review and analysis. *Management Research Review, 42*(8), 971–990.

Piehler, R. (2018). Employees' brand understanding, brand commitment, and brand citizenship behaviour: A closer look at the relationships among construct dimensions. *Journal of Brand Management, 25*(3), 217–234.

Piehler, R., Grace, D., & Burmann, C. (2018). Internal brand management: Introduction to the special issue and directions for future research. *Journal of Brand Management, 25*(3), 197–201.

Piehler, R., King, C., Burmann, C., & Xiong, L. (2016). The importance of employee brand understanding, brand identification, and brand commitment in realizing brand citizenship behaviour. *European Journal of Marketing, 50*(9/10), 1575–1601.

Piehler, R., Schade, M., & Burmann, C. (2019). Employees as a second audience: The effect of external communication on internal brand management outcomes. *Journal of Brand Management, 26*(4), 445–460.

Porricelli, M. S., Yurova, Y., Abratt, R., & Bendixen, M. (2014). Antecedents of brand citizenship behavior in retailing. *Journal of Retailing and Consumer Services, 5*(21), 745-752.

Punjaisri, K., & Wilson, A. (2007). The role of internal branding in the delivery of employee brand promise. *Journal of Brand Management, 15*(1), 57–70.

Punjaisri, K., & Wilson, A. (2011). Internal branding process: Key mechanisms, outcomes and moderating factors. *European Journal of Marketing, 45*(9–10), 1521–1537.

Punjaisri, K., Evanschitzky, H., & Rudd, J. (2013). Aligning employee service recovery performance with brand values: The role of brand-specific leadership. *Journal of Marketing Management, 29*(9–10), 981–1006.

Punjaisri, K., Evanschitzky, H., & Wilson, A. (2009a). Internal branding: An enabler of employees' brand-supporting behaviours. *Journal of Service Management, 20*(42), 209–226.

Punjaisri, K., Wilson, A., & Evanschitzky, H. (2009b). Internal branding to influence employees' brand promise delivery: A case study in Thailand. *Journal of Service Management, 20*(5), 561–579.

Saini, G. K., Lievens, F., & Srivastava, M. (2022). Employer and internal branding research: A bibliometric analysis of 25 years. *Journal of Product & Brand Management*, ahead-of-print.

Saleem, F. Z., & Iglesias, O. (2016). Mapping the domain of the fragmented field of internal branding. *The Journal of Product and Brand Management, 25*(1), 43–57.

Santos-Vijande, M. L., del Río-Lanza, A. B., Suárez-Álvarez, L., & Díaz-Martín, A. M. (2013). The brand management system and service firm competitiveness. *Journal of Business Research, 66*(2), 148-157.

Schleicher, D. J., & Baumann, H. M. (2020). Performance management and the changing nature of work. In Hoffman, B. J., Shoss, M. K., & Wegman, L. A. (Eds.), *The Cambridge Handbook of the Changing Nature of Work* (pp. 340–363). Cambridge: Cambridge University Press.

Seligman, M. D., & Csikszentmihalyi, M. (2014). *Positive Psychology: An Introduction.* Heidelberg: Springer.

Simmons, J. A. (2009). 'Both sides now': Aligning external and internal branding for a socially responsible era. *Marketing Intelligence & Planning, 27*(5), 681-697.

Terglav, K., Ruzzier, M. K., & Kaše, R. (2016). Internal branding process: Exploring the role of mediators in top management's leadership–commitment relationship. *International Journal of Hospitality Management, 54*, 1–11.

Uen, J. F., Wu, T., Teng, H. C., & Liu, Y. S. (2012). Transformational leadership and branding behavior in Taiwanese hotels. *International Journal of Contemporary Hospitality Management, 24*(1), 26–43.

Vatankhah, S., & Darvishi, M. (2018). An empirical investigation of antecedent and consequences of internal brand equity: Evidence from the airline industry. *Journal of Air Transport Management, 69*(1), 49–58.

Veen, A., Kaine, S., Goods, C. and Barratt, T. (2020). The 'gigification' of work in the 21st century. In Holland, P., & Brewster, C. (Eds.), *Contemporary Work and the Future of Employment in Developed Countries* (pp. 15–32). New York: Routledge-Cavendish.

Wang, Q., & Waltman, L. (2016). Large-scale analysis of the accuracy of the journal classification systems of Web of Science and Scopus. *Journal of Informetrics, 10*(2), 347–364.

Whisman, R. (2009). Internal branding: A university's most valuable intangible asset. *The Journal of Product and Brand Management, 18*(5), 367-370.

Xiong, L., & King, C. (2015). Motivational drivers that fuel employees to champion the hospitality brand. *International Journal of Hospitality Management, 44*, 58–69. https://doi.org/10.1016/j.ijhm.2014.10.009

Xiong, L., & King, C. (2018). Too much of a good thing? Examining how proactive personality affects employee brand performance under formal and informal organizational support. *International Journal of Hospitality Management, 100*(68), 12–22.

Xiong, L., & King, C. (2019). Aligning employees' attitudes and behavior with hospitality brands: The role of employee brand internalization. *Journal of Hospitality and Tourism Management, 40*, 67–76.

Xiong, L., & King, C. (2020). Exploring how employee sense of brand community affects their attitudes and behavior. *Journal of Hospitality & Tourism Research, 44*(4), 567–596.

Xiong, L., King, C., & Piehler, R. (2013). 'That's not my job': Exploring the employee perspective in the development of brand ambassadors. *International Journal of Hospitality Management, 35*, 348–359. https://doi.org/10.1016/j.ijhm.2013.07.009

Xiong, L., So, K. K. F., Wu, L., & King, C. (2019). Speaking up because it's my brand: Examining employee brand psychological ownership and voice behavior in hospitality organizations. *International Journal of Hospitality Management, 83*, 274–282.

Yang, J. T., Wan, C. S., & Wu, C. W. (2015). Effect of internal branding on employee brand commitment and behavior in hospitality. *Tourism and Hospitality Research, 15*(4), 267-280.

Yaniv, E., & Farkas, F. (2005). The impact of person–organization fit on the corporate brand perception of employees and of customers. *Journal of Change Management, 5*(4), 447–461.

Yeung, A. (2006). Setting people up for success: How the Portman Ritz-Carlton hotel gets the best from its people. *Human Resource Management, 45*(2), 267–275.

PART II

Special interest branding research

11 B2B branding: a review and research agenda for turbulent times

Susan M. Mudambi

1. Introduction

Business-to-business (B2B) branding research is phenomenon-based. That may be a controversial statement, as phenomenon-based research goes in and out of fashion in academia. Calls for translational business research, actionable research, and engaged scholarship are currently prominent and persuasive (Shin, 2022; Hanna, 2021), but in other times have been muted. Over the decades, the tone and justification of appeals for applied business research have varied due to current events, changes in university and research funding, and other incentives. Sometimes intellectual curiosity is high about how and why businesses do what they do, and under what conditions these practices are effective and societally beneficial. In academic research, intellectual curiosity about branding and other business practices is inevitably intertwined with intellectual curiosity about the underlying theories and concepts. That higher level of abstraction of theory adds richness and depth to the discussions about business practice. When turbulent and uncertain times push a rethinking of previous assumptions, new academic research is especially needed. Curiosity about branding practice shows little sign of slowing (e.g., Kenney, 2022). Future research on B2B branding can and will take many paths, and the dynamic realities of the business environment will energize the research journeys.

The main objective of this chapter is to provide a roadmap or travel suggestions for future B2B branding research journeys. In the first section, the context and motivation are established. The case is made for the relevance and importance of B2B brands and the practice of B2B branding, and the need for ongoing attention and academic research. In the second section, the goal is to examine and summarize past research on B2B branding. This builds on previous reviews of the literature and highlights key topics and insights. The third section brings together several different future research paths. Some of the research paths are well-established, while others lead to less well-charted destinations. The fourth and final section provides concluding insights regarding B2B branding and future research opportunities.

2. B2B branding in context

B2B branding strategies enable businesses to identify their purpose, build relationships, and differentiate themselves from competitors in ways that are meaningful to their stakeholders. Business-to-business branding, B2B branding, industrial branding, business branding – these terms are often considered interchangeable. All apply to the practice of branding companies and products in industrial, technology, business, and financial markets that do not primarily sell directly to consumers. Most B2B branding strategies focus on highly successful companies that are unknown to the general public, and sometimes not well known within their own broader target markets.

Branding strategies can be at the corporate level or product level, and finding the right balance is challenging. Much depends on the level of merger and acquisition activity, the degree of company diversification, and the potential for appealing to the consumer end user. A merger or acquisition can lead to a loss of corporate identity. This can reduce the return on prior investment in corporate brands, but brand value can also improve (Bahadir et al., 2008). Industrial conglomerates operating across many industry verticals with hundreds or thousands of products tend to focus more on building the corporate brand. However, a McKinsey study (Di Giovacchino et al., 2001) found that 80% of industrial companies only participate in one or two very narrow vertical market segments. That level of product specialization lends itself to a product-level branding strategy. Yet, if the firm offers only a few products in a narrow marketplace, sometimes there is no practical difference between a corporate branding strategy and a product-level branding strategy. Another direction of brand strategy is ingredient branding (Kotler & Pfoertsch, 2010). B2B components can be a source of differentiation or competitive advantage in the end consumer market, as evidenced by the consumer demand for end products that contain GoreTex, Intel (or Intel's Pentium), or DuPont brands such as Tyvek and Kevlar. B2B branding is multifaceted and complex and requires investment in dynamic capabilities.

B2B branding consultants often joke about working with multibillion-dollar companies you never heard of. AmerisourceBergen, United Health Group, McKesson, Anthem, Centene, StoneX, and AbbVie made the *Fortune* 100 list (*Fortune*, 2021), based on their annual revenues, but they are not household names. On the annual lists of top brands or most popular brands, few B2B brands have appeared in the past. Back in 2009, as noted by Homburg, Klarmann, and Schmitt (2010), only 17 B2B brands made the list of the top 100 brands.

Yet, perceptions seem to be changing. The 2021 FutureBrand Index reorders PwC's list of the top 100 companies by market capitalization by "perception strength" rather than financial strength (FutureBrand, 2021). In 2021, four of the top five companies are B2B, namely, ASML Holdings, Prosus NV, Danaher Corporation, and NextEra Energy. Apple is the only B2C company in the top five. The list's methodology incorporates perceptions of the future strength of firms, based on factors such as technology adoption, innovation pipeline, ability to adapt to changing customer tastes and expectations, reputation and trust, and ability to engage diverse audiences and talent. To make the list, companies are expected to be able to make a positive impact on the environment, society, and social justice.

Similarly, *Fortune*'s annual Blue Ribbon list includes many B2B companies, including AbbVie, Accenture, AMD, Anthem, Archer Daniels Midland, Cisco Systems, Northrop Grumman, Nvidia, Salesforce, and Stryker. Companies on *Fortune*'s Blue Ribbon list must appear on at least four of *Fortune*'s nine annual rankings, including: *Fortune* 500, Global 500, 100 Best Companies to Work For, Change the World, Future 50, World's Most Admired Companies, Fastest-Growing Companies, Most Powerful Women, and Most Powerful Women International (*Fortune*, 2021). The publicity regarding these lists indicates some shifts in how customers and other stakeholders evaluate firm reputation. Expert advice on reputation management, corporate communications, and public relations is often given at the firm level. Since, in many B2B markets, branding initiatives also occur primarily at the firm level, the higher prominence of B2B brands in the public eye can be an impetus for rethinking B2B branding strategies.

B2B companies are shaping business practices in many sectors, including technology, health care, financial services, and energy. The technology sector has many companies that are consumer facing, such as Apple and Amazon. Yet, they rely on innovations from B2B companies, such as Cisco Systems, Google, and Shopify. The lines between B2B and B2C can be blurry in technology, as illustrated by brands such as Adobe, Intuit, Microsoft, and Zoom. IBM transformed itself back to a B2B company decades ago, and Facebook and Google are transforming themselves under the umbrella of the B2B brands of Meta Platforms and Alphabet. Branding is likely to continue to be very relevant and important in technology sectors. Excellent and affordable health care and health insurance are ongoing concerns for millions of consumers, and the marketplace realities are often shaped by B2B companies that drive biopharma innovation (e.g., AbbVie), develop and manage health insurance programs for other companies (e.g., Anthem), and manage hospitals (e.g., Hospital Corporation of America). Technology, health care, financial services, and energy are essential to economic prosperity, and they justify research to gain an improved understanding of success factors within these and other sectors.

The increased prominence of B2B companies on prestigious, forward-looking lists could be a fluke of methodology, but more likely this reflects either a disillusionment with familiar consumer brands or an optimism about less known business brands, especially in technology sectors. Either way, a new interest in business brands can motivate future B2B research. However, to better justify new research topics and approaches, a fresh look at the extant body of B2B research is necessary. It is timely to review what researchers previously examined and concluded.

3. B2B branding literature foundation

Branding in business markets started capturing the attention of researchers in the late 1970s (Saunders & Watt, 1979). Since then, researchers have taken various practical, conceptual, and empirical approaches. The body of literature has become substantial, although much less comprehensive than the consumer branding literature. Several comprehensive reviews have chronicled and categorized the literature and developed important insights and research agendas (e.g., Leek & Christodoulides, 2011; Keränen et al., 2012; Seyedghorban et al., 2016). The reviews point to what researchers have been curious about over the decades, the areas of consensus, and the questions that persist.

Explorations of the role of branding in B2B markets have shed light on effective branding strategies and have at least partially ruled out superficial explanations for success. It has long been established that although brand names can matter within business markets, empirical evidence of this is difficult to establish (Saunders & Watt, 1979; Shipley & Howard, 1993). Brand names are useful memory aids (Ballantyne & Aitken, 2007), but names, logos, and slogans alone do not account for financial performance, especially in markets that are less influenced by advertising to customers than in traditional consumer brand markets. Instead, B2B brand value involves the development and communication of value and benefits through multiple channels.

3.1 Sources of brand value

A fundamental question is over the source of B2B brand value. Consumer brand researchers in the 1990s often built on Aaker's identification of three sources of brand value: functional, emotional, and self-expressive. This influenced and provided a contrast to B2B branding perspectives. B2B branding researchers have taken several positions on brand value, as summarized in Table 11.1.

Table 11.1 Sources of brand value in the B2B literature

Authors & Year	Sources of Brand Value	Conceptual Only or Empirical	Key Insights
Aaker (1991)	Functional Emotional Self-expressive	Conceptual	Branding offers three categories of benefits in consumer markets
Montgomery & Wernerfelt (1992)	Quality guaranteeing Risk reduction	Empirical	Risk reduction is more valued than quality guarantees
Mudambi, Doyle, & Wong (1997)	Product Company Distribution services Support services	Empirical, qualitative	Intangible and tangible attributes are both valued by customers
Mudambi (2002)	Tangible attributes (physical properties, price) Services (technical, ordering, and delivery) Intangible (working relationship, how well known, reputation)	Empirical, bearings	There are three clusters of buyers: highly tangible, branding receptive, and low interest
Bendixen, Bukasa, & Abratt (2004)	Brand name, price, delivery, technology used, spare part lead times	Empirical, conjoint, circuit breakers	51% of the purchase decision was due to price and delivery and 16% due to the brand
Chitturi & Mudambi (2009)	Differentiation Relationship building	Empirical, choice based conjoint	Differentiation is more valued by customers

Authors & Year	Sources of Brand Value	Conceptual Only or Empirical	Key Insights
Homburg, Klarmann, & Schmitt (2010)	Reduction of information costs Reduction of perceived risk of decision makers	Empirical	Brand visibility is important to financial performance as it reduces information costs and decision risk
Leek & Christodoulides (2012)	Functional (technology, infrastructure, innovation) Emotional (risk, trust, reassurance, credibility)	Empirical, qualitative	Functional and emotional aspects lead to brand value, and can develop into relationship value

Montgomery and Wernerfelt (1992) identified two sources of value, quality guarantees and risk reduction. The physical product quality of brands is expected to be higher and more consistent. Reduced risk can take the form of product performance or financial risk, but Montgomery and Wernerfelt (1992) highlighted an emotional aspect, with a strong theoretical foundation of risk reduction. They noted how brands can reduce the personal risk for the purchasing agent. Corporate procurement practices are often risk averse, with bias towards incumbent suppliers. Although their insights have been extended primarily within the B2C literature, their findings remain a relevant foundation for future research on B2B brand value.

In industrial product markets that offer relatively comparable physical products, such as bearings, adhesives, and circuit breakers, buyers have many options among large corporations. In this context, Mudambi, Doyle, and Wong (1997) identified intangible and tangible attributes in four areas: product, company, distribution services, and support services. A cluster analysis (Mudambi, 2002) identified three clusters of buyers according to how relevant branding is to them. Highly tangible buyers focused on physical properties and prices, branding receptive buyers also considered intangibles such as services, how well known the company is, quality of the work relationship, and the third cluster of buyers showed low interest in all attributes. In one industrial product market, Bendixen, Bukasa, and Abratt (2004) found that the company brand accounted for 16% of the buyers' purchase decision. In an experiment involving a decision amongst brand offers, Chitturi and Mudambi (2009) offered two sources of B2B brand value, differentiation and relationship building, and found differentiation attributes to be more valued than relationship attributes.

The sources of brand value for business services have also been examined. Keränen, Piirainen and Salminen (2012) identified nine articles on B2B services, but not all explicitly examined the sources of brand value. B2B service brand value depends in part on whether the firm uses a corporate or multi-branding strategy, and the type of business service (Guenther & Guenther, 2019). Research on one B2B services area, logistics services, reaffirms that brand image is more important than simply having a well-known brand name (Davis et al., 2008). Yet, it remains challenging to find meaningful ways to differentiate logistics service quality (Marquardt et al., 2011). Relationship building is key, delivered through both responsive interactions and through relevant and timely communications. Brand value is at the core of success, but value must also be linked to visibility and communication. Di Giovacchino, Queirolo, Santhanam, and Varanasi (2001) examined brand voice and found that 5% of companies capture 95% of brand mentions in publications and media in 2020. These mentions may be more relevant for stakeholders and employees but can still influence purchasing and procurement decisions. Value must be communicated.

3.2 Theoretical perspectives

The perception of sources of value can be connected to the underlying theory foundation. Much of the early work in B2B branding drew heavily on branding theory developed in consumer markets (Seyedghorban et al., 2016). Several other studies rely more on economic theory, rather than theories from psychology. Similar to the risk-reduction perspective of Montgomery and Wernerfelt (1992), the reduction of both information costs and the perceived risk of decision makers are the main sources of brand value in the study by Homburg, Klarmann, and Schmitt (2010). Their perception of value drew on information economics as the theory foundation.

Ballantyne and Aitken (2007) applied service-dominant logic (Vargo & Lusch, 2004) to explain B2B brand value by emphasizing the value-in-use and interactions over time. This approach emphasized services and relationships. Leek and Christodoulides (2012) draw more closely on theories of relationship marketing. They highlighted two sources of brand value that can lead to lasting relationship value, namely functional (technology, infrastructure, innovation) and emotional (risk, trust, reassurance, credibility). The sources of functional and emotional value reflect a consistent theme in B2B branding research and in organizational buyer behavior.

These examples of theoretical perspectives point to the diversity of ways theory has been applied to explain B2B branding value. Research in this area is heavily phenomenon-based, but theory enriches the insights, as it connects to broader themes. Theory can also provide a simplifying framework that can be useful in increasingly complex business environments. Firms have never fully been in control of their brand image, as brand image is also shaped by the word of mouth of customers, employees, other stakeholders, and the interactions within brand communities (Schau et al., 2009). Brand image can be disrupted by customer posts on social media, problems with suppliers, external shocks, and changing social norms. Recent disruptions from trade wars, the COVID-19 pandemic, and other external shocks indicate that B2B brand management must consider ongoing turbulence as the new reality. Fresh applications of established theories of service-dominant logic (Vargo & Lusch, 2004), relationship marketing (Palmatier et al., 2006), and dynamic capabilities (Wilden & Gudergan, 2015) can enhance the understanding of effective B2B brand management in turbulent environments.

4. New paths for B2B branding research

After looking to the past, the question arises: has academic research on branding kept up with business trends? The business environment underwent many shocks between 2020 and 2022, and ongoing turbulence has short-term consequences and long-term uncertainty. The pandemic turned the focus to digital platforms, supply chains, and broader social concerns and questions about justice, environmental sustainability, work–life balance, and world peace. B2B brands must adjust to these new phenomena. Market turbulence may continue to disrupt previous conceptualizations about what is important to purchase decisions, and to job seekers, employers, and researchers.

4.1 Digital platforms

B2B branding and digital platforms has been an area of research since 2000, encompassing e-commerce platforms and social media platforms. B2B procurement platforms were surrounded with hype and with solid-sounding theories of disintermediation and info-mediation (Mahadevan, 2000), before the bursting of the internet bubble in 2002. For example, VerticalNet was a B2B e-marketplace with high brand recognition and promise (Prial, 1999). Its IPO attracted more than $10 billion in investment in 1999, but the value spectacularly crashed a few years later. Now that digital practicality has replaced hype, research is needed to examine to what extent corporate branding efforts matter on newer generations of e-commerce platforms and portals for physical products and services.

Scholars have begun to examine differences in B2B social media usage (see Tiwary et al., 2021 for a recent comprehensive literature review). Swani and colleagues (Swani et al., 2014; Swani et al., 2017) developed multiple insights, including the observation that B2B companies utilize emotional appeals more on Twitter than B2C companies do. This epitomizes how thinking about B2B brands has changed over the decades. B2B branding no longer is expected to stay solely in the lane of functional and rational appeals about tangible attributes. These results find a continuing B2B emphasis on corporate rather than product brands. They also found that on Facebook, posts received more likes and comments when information search cues were included. B2B companies on Facebook were more likely than B2C companies to disseminate product information using links and hashtags. Research has also started to recognize that social media usage in brand building is not just about what companies post about themselves. Unofficial Tweets from employees and others play a role in amplifying, maintaining, and mitigating official Tweets from B2B companies (Pardo et al., 2022). This can influence the creation of the shared meaning of B2B brands. Social networks can play an important role in B2B brand management (Cawsey & Rowley, 2016).

Studies of Twitter and Facebook usage provide a good base for future research that can dive deeper into differences among B2B brands, rather than into the differences between B2B and B2C practices. Research is also needed for the platforms with a fast growth in B2B usage, such as YouTube, TikTok, and LinkedIn. YouTube has long been popular for communicating product information and customer testimonials for a wide range of business, but there is little research on how best to use LinkedIn for branding. TikTok's popularity boomed during the pandemic, first among the young and tech savvy. Its ease of use has also attracted many older users and well established B2B companies. To date, there is no research on the relative effectiveness of different video platforms for building customer perception of B2B brand value.

Visibility decreases over time unless brands have something fresh to say, as media attention focuses on the new (Di Giovacchino et al., 2001). Visibility is difficult to gain. Future research could more closely examine how customers search online for suppliers. Brand-related keywords are a component of search engine optimization (SEO) and lead generation and affect order placement on firm websites and on third-party e-commerce platforms. Similarly, visibility and familiarity are challenges in the pursuit of thought leadership. Firms and CEOs desire to be considered thought leaders, and the savvy utilization of social media plays a big role in who is perceived a thought leader (Taylor et al., 2022).

Social and political polarization have become associated with Twitter and Facebook. Consequently, many B2B businesses and their customers have taken refuge in the less controversial space of LinkedIn. LinkedIn's business networking purpose narrows the focus of blog posts and articles and encourages content sharing. Academic research includes some examinations of the role of LinkedIn in personal brand building (e.g., van Dijck, 2013). This can be relevant for employees and executives, but more research would be beneficial on B2B employee–employer relationships on LinkedIn (e.g., Cervellon & Lirio, 2017). In addition, more research is needed on the use of LinkedIn for developing and implementing effective B2B product and corporate brand strategy.

Even less explored is the context of B2B branding and online reviews. This area is highly relevant to practice but with little academic attention. Some academic research has examined employer reviews by employees on Glassdoor (Pitt et al., 2019), and their insights and approach can be extended to other sites with employee reviews. This approach builds on and connects well with the important literature on internal brand management (Piehler et al., 2018), as employee commitment to the company brand facilitates organizational success (King & Grace, 2008). Yet, despite the thousands of journal articles on B2C online reviews on Amazon and Yelp (e.g., Rocklage & Fazio, 2020; Mudambi & Schuff, 2010), there is almost no research on the influence of online review sites for B2B products and services. For example, multiple sites provide reviews of software as a service (SaaS), including Capterra, GetApp, and G2, and general sites such as Google Reviews provide insights on a wide range of B2B products. These and other review sites attract millions of visitors, but it is unclear in what ways they affect the B2B brand attitudes of professional buyers. It is likely that professional buyers utilize online reviews of B2B products differently than well-informed consumers use B2C reviews, but future research is needed to examine this in a systematic way.

4.2 Supply chains

High up on the list of current business concerns is supply chain resilience and effectiveness. These concerns involve substantial relevance to B2B branding. The pandemic elevated attention to supply chain resilience, or the reliability of delivery during shocks and turbulence. Branding relates to the critical question of can a supplier be trusted? Ordering efficiency and delivery service ease and reliability have long been recognized as sources of B2B brand value, and their importance has skyrocketed in recent years. Ordering via digital platforms has become even more essential, and customers increasingly prefer to communicate with sales personnel via live online chat, not via in-person meetings (Bages-Amat et al., 2020). These new trends may shape B2B brand relationships indefinitely, with the implications not yet fully understood.

The effects of e-commerce and internet technology on B2B brand perceptions are especially relevant for logistics providers (Marquardt et al., 2011), and other supply chain partners. Industrial distributors are key players, and they build their brand relationships through customer relationship management, production and operations management, and knowledge management (Mudambi & Aggarwal, 2003). As technology evolves, the nature of relationship management and other brand-building processes must also continue to change. Brand building requires the effective use of information technology such as video and live chat, and research can help to guide effective relationship management in logistics and other B2B areas.

The change from a supplier selection, procurement emphasis to a supply chain emphasis underscores the shift to building redundancy and new capabilities to avert disruption (Pettit et al., 2019). If one supplier fails, an alternative is essential. It is no longer just the selection of the first supplier that matters. The links to the secondary and tertiary supplier are also crucial. This moves the question to a broader conceptualization, from a single brand to a network of suppliers. Trust in the full network of suppliers is the ideal, although difficult to achieve.

4.3 Social concerns

For a supply chain to be truly resilient, transparency is needed to identify any potential sources of risk and disruption. That necessity motivates the interest in blockchain and its potential to identify all the steps in the journey commodities and products take through the supply chain. Blockchain can play a role (Venkatesh et al., 2020) in increasing the transparency to address multiple considerations. More research is needed to determine under what conditions blockchain is a practical approach for supply chain sustainability and brand transparency.

The new interest in supply chain transparency relates back to an old topic in B2B branding, namely, ingredient branding, what Kotler and Pfoertsch (2010) called making the invisible visible. Some business customers and end consumers seek reassurances that components are not produced by slave labor, and that manufacturing processes do not destroy the environment. There is a substantial literature on the connection between B2B marketing and branding and higher sustainability goals (Voola et al., 2022). That literature review facilitates many new ideas for future research in this area. In times of war and political unrest, an additional brand-related concern is that production does not take place in pariah nation states. With the Russian invasion of Ukraine, many firms had to scramble to ascertain the extent of their sourcing in the region, to avoid negative brand associations. Improvements in supply chain transparency are useful for evaluating resilience and efficiency, for evaluating social desires for sustainability and social concerns about slave labor, and to ensure that corporate claims about their socially responsible behavior are legitimate.

More broadly, corporate social responsibility (CSR) is connected in many ways to B2B brand image, brand equity and brand performance, and to corporate reputation. Research on corporate reputation management (e.g., Barnett et al., 2006) and research on B2B branding have often developed in relatively separate academic bubbles. Moving forward, synergy between the fields could provide important insights. Corporate brand image is multifaceted, and customer segments can differ in their perceptions. Also, it is not just about customer perception of the corporate brand. Employees, suppliers, and other stakeholders can and do weigh in on social concerns. Given the polarization of views and the suddenness that brand "cancellations" arise when fueled by social media, brand management is becoming increasingly dynamic and complex. B2B brands can fall into a brand crisis for multiple reasons, from the COVID pandemic (Cankurtaran & Beverland, 2020) to product failures, and to leadership or employee missteps. Proactive B2B branding strategies will inevitably become broader in their scope, and so the scope of academic research will need to keep up.

5. Concluding insights

Past research has demonstrated the importance of intangible assets in B2B brand management. Looking to the future, it is instructive to identify what intangible assets are currently most relevant, and what is likely to increase in relevance. Current business phenomena and market turbulence have raised the relevance of digital platforms and supply chain effectiveness. These contemporary issues are driving the interest in B2B branding strategies and effectiveness. Modern realities also raise conceptual or abstract questions about the reasons underlying purchase and usage decisions, and for the resistance to change. The nature of B2B branding is broadening in ways that have not been fully captured in past research.

The fundamental focus remains on the sources of brand value. Physical product characteristics and other tangible sources of value will always be important but are not often viable points of differentiation. Intangible sources of value and emotional appeals will continue to increase in relevance to brand development and communications. According to Shah (2021), emotions may be the new B2B tool. These areas are under-researched. Also, there is considerable potential synergy between intangible assets of brands and the risk-reduction role of brands.

Discussions about intangible assets focus on the positive, while discussions about risk reduction focus on what can go wrong, and how brands can avoid the big negatives, the big downsides. Past research has highlighted the role of branding in risk reduction. The mechanisms of how brands reduce risk can be further clarified. There are many areas of risk reduction, including physical product or service risk, sourcing risk, financial risk, reputation risk, and personal risk to the buyer. Although a brand may command a price premium, the total cost of ownership may be less, due to lower expenses from product or delivery failures. Reputation risk can emerge from multiple areas, such as unethical sourcing, rogue employees, or an outspoken CEO. The downsides of bad press can outweigh the upside of a long history of good news about the brand. Procurement managers can be very risk averse. To better understand under what conditions it is worthwhile to pay more to avoid the big downsides or to increase the upsides, prospect theory can be tapped. Researchers have applied prospect theory to a multitude of choices in more than 40 years of research (see Barberis, 2013 for a review), yet there is considerable potential for new insights in the B2B purchase context. Theoretical frameworks can provide insights on the dynamics of business brand perceptions and choices.

Broader social and political concerns have rarely been addressed in prior research on B2B branding but seem inevitable moving forward. B2B CEOs are edging more into the spotlight. Political activism of companies and their employees is becoming more commonplace. Companies are expected to have a positive impact on the environment and society, and on social justice and equity (FutureBrand, 2021). That is a big ask. These phenomena certainly complicate the process of B2B branding. However, many of these issues are important to Millennials, and they are becoming key purchase decision makers and sought-after employees in the current period of labor shortages. B2B branding can help firms attract and keep talent. Overall, ongoing innovative research in B2B branding is needed to enable firms in turbulent times to reduce risks and develop differentiation that is meaningful to customers, employees, and other stakeholders.

References

Aaker, D. (1991). *Managing Brand Equity*. New York: Free Press.

Bages-Amat, A., Harrison, L., Spillecke, D., & Stanley, J. (2020). These eight charts show how COVID-19 has changed B2B sales forever. McKinsey & Company, October. https://www.mckinsey.com/business-functions/growth-marketing-and-sales/our-insights/these-eight-charts-show-how-covid-19-has-changed-b2b-sales-forever

Bahadir, S.C., Bharadwaj, S.G., & Srivastava, R.K. (2008). Financial value of brands in mergers and acquisitions: Is value in the eye of the beholder? *Journal of Marketing*, *72*(6), 49–64.

Ballantyne, D., & Aitken, R. (2007). Branding in B2B markets: Insights from the service-dominant logic of marketing. *Journal of Business & Industrial Marketing*, *22*(6), 363–371.

Barberis, N.C. (2013). Thirty years of prospect theory in economics: A review and assessment. *Journal of Economic Perspectives*, *27*(1), 173–196.

Barnett, M.L., Jermier, J.M., & Lafferty, B.A. (2006). Corporate reputation: The definitional landscape. *Corporate Reputation Review*, *9*(1), 26–38.

Bendixen, M., Bukasa, K.A., & Abratt, R. (2004). Brand equity in the business-to-business market. *Industrial Marketing Management*, *33*(5), 371–380.

Cankurtaran, P., & Beverland, M.B. (2020). Using design thinking to respond to crises: B2B lessons from the 2020 COVID-19 pandemic. *Industrial Marketing Management*, *88*, 255–260.

Cawsey, T., & Rowley, J. (2016). Social media brand building strategies in B2B companies. *Marketing Intelligence & Planning*, *34*(6), 754–776.

Cervellon, M-C, & Lirio, P. (2017). When employees don't "like" their employers on social media. *MIT Sloan Management Review*, *58*(2), 63–70.

Chitturi, P., & Mudambi, S.M. (2009). Building brand value in business markets, in C. Baumgarth (Ed.), *B-to-B Brand Management: Fundamentals, Concepts, and Best Practices*. Istanbul: Gabler Verlag Publishing, pp. 223-239.

Davis, D.F., Golicic, S.L., & Marquardt, A.J. (2008). Branding a B2B service: Does a brand differentiate a logistics service provider? *Industrial Marketing Management*, *37*(2), 218–227.

Di Giovacchino, M., Queirolo, A., Santhanam, N., & Varanasi, S. (2001). The rising value of industrial brands. McKinsey & Company, January 25. https://www.mckinsey.com/industries/advanced-electronics/our-insights/the-rising-value-of-industrial-brands#

Fortune (2021). The Blue Ribbon list. https://fortune.com/2021/12/15/blue-ribbon-companies-2022/

FutureBrand (2021). FutureBrand Index 2021. https://www.futurebrand.com/futurebrand-index-2021

Guenther, M., & Guenther, P. (2019). The value of branding for B2B service firms: The shareholders' perspective. *Industrial Marketing Management*, *78*, 88–101.

Hanna, G. (2021). Four ways translational research applies to leadership in every industry. *Forbes Business Development Council* blog, November 17. https://www.forbes.com/sites/forbesbusinessdevelopmentcouncil/2021/11/16/four-ways-translational-research-applies-to-leadership-in-every-industry/?sh=17f492d5cbc8

Homburg, C., Klarmann, M., & Schmitt, J. (2010). Brand awareness in business markets: When is it related to firm performance? *International Journal of Research in Marketing*, *27*(3), 201–212.

Kenney, B. (2022). B2B branding: How to get it right in the modern world. *Fast Company*, March 8. https://www.fastcompany.com/90725936/b2b-branding-how-to-get-it-right-in-the-modern-world

Keränen, J., Piirainen, K.A., & Salminen, R. (2012). Systematic review on B2B branding: Research issues and avenues for future research. *Journal of Product & Brand Management*, *21*(6), 404–417.

King, C., & Grace, D. (2008). Internal branding: Exploring the employee's perspective. *Journal of Brand Management*, *15*, 358–372.

Kotler, P., & Pfoertsch, W.A. (2010). *Ingredient Branding: Making the Invisible Visible*. Berlin: Springer.

Leek, S., & Christodoulides, G. (2011). A literature review and future agenda for B2B branding: Challenges of branding in a B2B context. *Industrial Marketing Management*, *40*(6), 830–837.

Leek, S., & Christodoulides, G. (2012). A framework of brand value in B2B markets: The contributing role of functional and emotional components. *Industrial Marketing Management*, *41*(1), 106–114.

Mahadevan, B. (2000). Business models for internet-based e-commerce: An anatomy. *California Management Review*, *42*(4), 55–69.

Marquardt, A.J., Golicic, S.L., & Davis, D.F. (2011). B2B services branding in the logistics services industry. *Journal of Services Marketing*, *25*(1), 47–57.

Montgomery, C.A., & Wernerfelt, B. (1992). Risk reduction and umbrella branding. *Journal of Business*, *65*(1), 31–50.

Mudambi, S.M. (2002). Branding importance in business-to-business markets: Three buyer clusters. *Industrial Marketing Management*, *31*, 525–533.

Mudambi, S.M., & Aggarwal, R. (2003). Industrial distributors: Can they survive in the new economy? *Industrial Marketing Management*, *32*(4), 317–325.

Mudambi, S.M., & Schuff, D. (2010). What makes a helpful review? A study of customer reviews on Amazon.com. *MIS Quarterly*, *34*(1), 185–200.

Mudambi, S.M., Doyle, P., & Wong, V. (1997). An exploration of branding in industrial markets. *Industrial Marketing Management*, *26*(5), 433–446.

Palmatier, R.W., Dant, R.P., Grewal, D., & Evans, K.R. (2006). Factors influencing the effectiveness of relationship marketing: A meta-analysis. *Journal of Marketing*, *70*(4), 136–153.

Pardo, C., Pagani, M., & Savinien, J. (2022). The strategic role of social media in business-to-business contexts. *Industrial Marketing Management*, *101*, 82–97.

Pettit, T.J., Croxton, K.L., & Fiksel, J. (2019). The evolution of resilience in supply chain management: A retrospective on ensuring supply chain resilience. *Journal of Business Logistics*, *40*(1), 56–65.

Piehler, R., Grace, D., & Burmann, C. (2018). Internal brand management: Introduction to the special issue and directions for future research. *Journal of Brand Management*, *25*(3), 197–201.

Pitt, C.S., Plangger, K.A., Botha, E., Kietzmann, J., & Pitt, L. (2019). How employees engage with B2B brands on social media: Word choice and verbal tone. *Industrial Marketing Management*, *81*(August), 130–137.

Prial, D. (1999). IPO outlook: VerticalNet poised to lead next wave of internet-related offerings. *Wall Street Journal*, February 8.

Rocklage, M.D., & Fazio, R.H. (2020). The enhancing versus backfiring effects of positive emotion in consumer reviews. *Journal of Marketing Research*, *57*(2), 332–352.

Saunders, J., & Watt, F.A.W. (1979). Do brand names differentiate identical industrial products? *Industrial Marketing Management*, *8*(2), 114–121.

Schau, H.J., Muniz, A.M., & Arnould, E.J. (2009). How brand community practices create value. *Journal of Marketing, 73*(September), 30–51.

Seyedghorban, Z., Matanda, M.J., & LaPlaca, P. (2016), Advancing theory and knowledge in the business-to-business branding literature. *Journal of Business Research, 69*(8), 2664–2677.

Shah, Y. (2021). How to best connect on a human level: Are emotions the new B2B marketing tool? *Forbes Agency Council* post, November 22. https://www.forbes.com/sites/forbesagencycouncil/2021/11/22/how-to-best-connect-on-a-human-level-are-emotions-the-new-b2b-marketing-tool/?sh=33f848de2bf5

Shin, S. (2022). What's wrong with business schools today. *AACSB Insights*, February 14. https://www.aacsb.edu/insights/articles/2022/02/whats-wrong-with-business-schools-today

Shipley, D., & Howard, P. (1993). Brand-naming industrial products. *Industrial Marketing Management, 22*(1), 59-66.

Swani, K., Brown, B.P., & Milne, G.R. (2014). Should tweets differ for B2B and B2C? An analysis of *Fortune* 500 companies' Twitter communications. *Industrial Marketing Management, 43*(5), 873–881.

Swani, K., Milne, G.R., Brown, B.P., Assaf, A.G., & Donthu, N. (2017). What messages to post? Evaluating the popularity of social media communications in business versus consumer markets. *Industrial Marketing Management, 62*(April), 77–87.

Taylor, S., Chitturi, P., & Mudambi, S.M. (2022). #ThoughtLeader: Tradeoffs in social media strategies for B2B CEOs. *Fox Business Review* (forthcoming).

Tiwary, N.K., Kumar, R.K., Sarraf, S., Kumar, P., & Rana, N.P. (2021). Impact assessment of social media usage in B2B marketing: A review of the literature and a way forward. *Journal of Business Research, 131*(July), 121–139.

van Dijck, J. (2013). "You have one identity": Performing the self on Facebook and LinkedIn. *Media, Culture & Society, 35*(2), 199–215.

Vargo, S.L., & Lusch, R.F. (2004). Evolving to a new dominant logic in marketing. *Journal of Marketing, 68*(1), 1–17.

Venkatesh, V.G., Kang, K., Wang, B., Zhong, R.Y., & Zhang, A. (2020). System architecture for blockchain based transparency of supply chain social sustainability. *Robotics and Computer-Integrated Manufacturing, 63*, 101896.

Voola, R., Bandyopadhyay, C., Voola, A., Ray, S., & Carlson, J. (2022). B2B marketing scholarship and the UN sustainable development goals (SDGs): A systematic literature review. *Industrial Marketing Management, 101*(February), 12–32.

Wilden, R., & Gudergan, S.P. (2015). The impact of dynamic capabilities on operational marketing and technological capabilities: Investigating the role of environmental turbulence. *Journal of the Academy of Marketing Science, 43*(2), 181–199.

12 Destination branding

Asli D.A. Tasci and Ady Milman

1. From destination image to destination branding

Destination marketing and management is a complicated subject matter for both researchers and practitioners. Destinations are complex with tangible and intangible products and services that are marked by the heritage and culture of the locality which are modified by both local and global popular cultures. Starting in the 1970s, researchers argued that successful destination marketing and management depends on the creation of a positive destination image. This concept includes three dimensions of human psychology: cognition (thoughts, opinions, beliefs), affect (emotions, feelings), and conation (action in actual behavior, intention to act, likelihood to act, or willingness to act) (Tasci & Gartner, 2007; Tasci, Gartner, & Cavusgil, 2007). Reflective of this presumed structure with its cognitive, affective, and conative components, destination image is summarized as: "an interactive system of thoughts, opinions, feelings, visualizations, and intentions toward a destination" (Tasci, Gartner & Cavusgil 2007, p. 200).

The interactive and dynamic nature of destination image is studied extensively to determine what it is, how it is formed, what affects it, and what are its influences on other visitor behaviors. Until the late 1990s, image was everything and thus tourism marketing literature was dominated by destination image research; it was one of the most studied subjects and it continues to receive attention from both researchers and practitioners. However, in the first decade of the 21st century, increased competition in tourism harbingered the necessity of a more complex concept as the indicator of successful destination marketing and management, thus destination branding became the focal point (Tasci, 2020a).

Destination branding is the *purposeful actions of destination authorities manifested in consistent marketing communications to differentiate and position their destination against their competitors in their target markets.* Ultimately, however, a destination brand is not solely the product of these purposeful actions of authorities. Similar to destination image, diverse influencers affect a destination's branding including the media, word-of-mouth, and even competitors' branding activities. Additionally, individual attractions and businesses in the destination also conduct their own branding, which ends up influencing the destination brand in target markets. Therefore, a destination brand, namely *a destination with a differentiated position compared to its competitors in its target markets*, can never be fully controlled by destination authorities. Nonetheless, the cumulative effect of branding a destination can be boiled down to the destination's brand equity, either in financial or perceptual domains. As the perceptual metrics of brand equity are expected to translate into financial metrics, it is critical to understand what contributes to these perceptual metrics of brand equity to justify the branding activities of Destination Marketing Organizations (DMOs). To this end, the chapter provides a succinct summary of destination brand equity and its indicators explored in past research to guide destination authorities in navigating the trials and tribulations of destination branding. As a result, gaps in the destination brand equity literature are revealed, highlighting fruitful areas for future research exploration.

2. Destination brand equity

Destination brand equity refers to *the worth of a destination, measured objectively through financial and numeric metrics indicating the market demand as in visitor numbers and spending, or subjectively through the perception and attitude of the target markets toward the destination*. Both measures were first used to measure the brand equity of conventional consumer product brands. Subjective measures of conventional consumer product brands involve perceptions, sentiments, and predispositions toward a brand. Essentially, diverse benefits of branding, inclusive of the perceived image of a brand, were distilled into the concept of brand equity by Aaker (1991, 1992, 1996) and Keller (1993, 2003). This multidimensional concept is termed consumer-based brand equity (when assessed from general consumers' point of view) or customer-based brand equity (when assessed from actual customers' point of view) and was used extensively in marketing research. On the other hand, objectively, the worth of conventional consumer product brands is estimated from financial values such as cash flow, profits, stock value, and so on, which is termed financial-based brand equity. Both objective and subjective measures of brand equity have also been proposed to apply for destination brands.

As conglomerate and complex products, destination brands' worth can also be determined objectively or subjectively. Similar to conventional product brands, the subjective worth of a destination brand can also be determined by assessing perceptions, sentiments, and predispositions toward a destination brand; this is termed consumer-based brand equity (when assessed from the general consumers' point of view) or customer-based brand equity (when assessed from the actual visitors' point of view). However, the financial metrics used for conventional product brands do not easily apply to destination brands, because a destination is a conglomerate of independent yet related multiple products, services, and experiences. Nonetheless, a destination brand's objective worth can be defined by assessing common tourism statistics such as visitor numbers and revenues as suggested by Tasci and Denizci (2009). However, potentially due to the lack of reliable statistics, there is a scarcity of empirical studies focusing on financial-based brand equity of destinations while a plethora of studies examine the components and relationship among the components of consumer or customer-based brand equity of destinations. Table 12.1 reflects the dimensions of consumer-based brand equity suggested by Aaker and Keller as well as studies that applied the concept in a destination context. Since brand equity offers a more comprehensive assessment of the success of a destination brand, some destination image researchers have shifted their focus toward this more holistic perspective, with destination image being only one aspect of the consumer-based brand equity.

Generally speaking, consumer/customer-based brand equity of a destination brand is proposed to include:

- Awareness and familiarity with the destination,
- Associations and images comprising knowledge about the destination's attributes and feelings generated by this knowledge,
- Quality of service and tangible aspects of the destination,
- Value in terms of the difference between costs and benefits of visiting the destination,
- Loyalty as manifested not only by behavioral indicators such as repeat visitation but also by attitudinal indicators such as desire and intention to revisit the destination, word-of-mouth, and recommendation (Gartner, Tasci, & So, 2007; Tasci, 2018, 2020a).

Even though awareness, familiarity, associations, image/imagery, perceived quality, and loyalty are the original dimensions suggested by Aaker and Keller, destination researchers have used additional dimensions that reflect the complexity of destination brands. Many researchers suggest consumer value as an additional dimension (e.g., Chekalina, Fuchs, & Lexhagen, 2018; Bianchi,

Pike, & Lings, 2014; Tasci, 2018). Others also suggest brand value, namely the perception of price premiums at a destination or consumers' willingness to pay higher prices for a destination (e.g., Tasci & Denizci, 2009; Tasci, 2018). Further, salience (Pike, Bianchi, Kerr, & Patti, 2010), satisfaction (San Martín, Herrero, & García de los Salmones, 2018), assets (Kladou & Kehagias, 2014), destination resources (Chekalina, Fuchs, & Lexhagen, 2018), value in use (Chekalina, Fuchs, & Lexhagen, 2018), brand performance, attachment, emotions/feelings, and brand judgment (Duman, Ozbal, & Duerod, 2018) have all been explored as being relevant dimensions of a destination's brand equity. Researchers use these dimensions, in different cause and effect relationship structures, to measure the worth or meaning of destinations for different stakeholders ranging from country level to smaller city-level, and even attraction levels such as a museum (Liu, Liu, & Lin, 2015).

As destination image researchers now accept that image is only one component of the more holistic construct of destination brand equity, recent studies on destination image usually address inquiries about image with one or more of the other brand-equity dimensions such as quality, value, and loyalty. As can be seen from Table 12.1, some image dimensions that were included as scale items in destination image measurement scales (e.g., quality of restaurants, good value for money) are being scrutinized deeper by measuring them as multidimensional constructs in the more recent studies following the consumer-based brand equity framework. Thus, conceptual as well as empirical research related to destination brands via a consumer/customer-based brand equity lens has gained acceleration. This holistic measure was instrumental in highlighting the benefits of branding to rationalize the high costs of conducting destination branding (de Chernatony & Riley, 1999; D'Hauteserre, 2001; Morgan, Pritchard, & Piggott, 2002; Pritchard & Morgan, 2001; Williams, Gill, & Chura, 2004).

3. Voids in the destination brand equity literature

Recently, Tasci (2020a) conducted a literature review on consumer-based brand equity research in tourism and hospitality and advanced a few recommendations for better theory development in this domain. These recommendations included using a uniform dimensional and relational structure of the brand equity concept, measuring and comparing brand equity from visitors' as well as other stakeholder perspectives such as residents, and investigating the relationship between objective or financial brand equity indicators and subjective or perception-based brand equity indicators. To see the relation-

Table 12.1 Different consumer/customer-based brand equity indicators and the number of scale items used by researchers

Author(s)	Study Subject	Study Population	Awareness	Familiarity	Associations	Image	Perceived Quality	Loyalty	Consumer Value	Brand Value	Salience	Satisfaction	Destination Resources Assets	Brand Performance Value in Use	Brand Judgment Emotions/ Feelings Attachment
Aaker (1991, 1992)	Brands in general	Conceptual	X		X		X	X							
Keller (1993, 2003)	Brands in general	Conceptual	X			X									
Aaker (1996)	Brands in general	Conceptual	4		8		3	4							
Gartner, Tasci, & So (2007)	Destination-Macau	Visitors		Y		15	9	7	4						
Roth, Diamantopoulos, & Montesinos (2008) applied Yoo & Donthu (2001)	Country-Spain	Students in Spain	4		7		2	2							
Boo, Busser, & Baloglu (2009)	Las Vegas & Atlantic City	Past visitors	4			4	4	4	5						
Pike, Bianchi, Kerr, & Patti (2010)	Australia	Chilean consumers				4	4	4			5				

Author(s)	Study Subject	Study Population	Awareness	Familiarity	Associations	Image	Perceived Quality	Loyalty	Consumer Value	Brand Value	Salience	Satisfaction	Assets	Destination Resources	Brand Performance Value in Use	Brand Judgment Emotions/ Feelings Attachment
Zanfardini, Tamagni, & Gutauskas (2011)	Destinations in Argentina	General consumers	X			X	X	X								
Tasci (2011)	Destination brands in general	Conceptual	X	X	X	X	X	X	X	X						
Horng, Liu, Chou, & Tsai (2012)	Taiwan	Foreign visitors	3			12	9	3								
Yuwo, Ford & Purwanegara (2013) applied Konecnik & Gartner (2007)	Bandung City, Indonesia	Visitors	3			6	9	4								
Bianchi, Pike, & Lings (2014)	Chile, Brazil, and Argentina	Australian tourists				4	4	3	4		4					
Kladou & Kehagias (2014)	Rome	Travelers	3		3		3	4					5			
Kashif, Samsi, & Sarifuddin (2015)	Lahore Fort, Pakistan	Visitors	3		4	17		3								

Author(s)	Study Subject	Study Population	Awareness	Familiarity	Associations	Image	Perceived Quality	Loyalty	Consumer Value	Brand Value	Salience	Satisfaction	Destination Resources Assets	Brand Performance Value in Use	Brand Judgment Emotions/ Feelings Attachment
Vinh & Nga (2015)	Danang City, Vietnam	Domestic and international visitors	4			4	4	4							
Gómez, Lopez, & Molina (2015)	Wineries in Spain	visitors	4					4	4						
Liu, Liu, & Lin (2015)	National Museum of Natural Sciences in Taiwan	Visitors	4			4	12	4	3						
Yang, Liu, & Li (2015)	United States, Europe, Hong Kong, Macau, and Taiwan	Mainland Chinese travelers	3			3	4	3							
Pike & Bianchi (2016)	Australia	Consumers in New Zealand and Chile				4	4	3	4		4				
Frias Jamilena, Polo Pena, & Rodriguez Molina (2017)	Spain	British tourists	3			2	3	4	5						

Author(s)	Study Subject	Study Population	Awareness	Familiarity	Associations	Image	Perceived Quality	Loyalty	Consumer Value	Brand Value	Salience	Satisfaction	Assets	Destination Resources	Value in Use	Brand Performance	Attachment	Emotions/ Feelings	Brand Judgment
Tasci (2016)	City brands in the US	General consumers		1		1	1	1	1	1									
Tasci, Hahm, & Breiter (2016)	Orlando, USA	General US consumers				15	7	7	3	3									
Herrero, San Martín, & Collado (2017)	Cantabria region, Spain	International visitors	3			6	3	3											
Tasci (2018)	City brands in the US	General US and multinational consumers		1		1	1	1	1	1									
Chekalina, Fuchs, & Lexhagen (2018)	Swedish ski destination Åre	International visitors	3					3	2					15	4				
San Martín, Herrero, & García de los Salmones (2018)	A destination in Spain	Domestic and international visitors	3			9	3	3				3							
Duman, Ozbal, & Duerod (2018)	Sarajevo	Visitors				8		2								7	3	4	4

Notes: The numbers reflect the number of dimensions retained after the purification of scales. X is placed for conceptual studies. Y is placed for studies measuring a component without a scale. Table adapted from Tasci (2020b).

ship between objective and subjective brand equity indicators, Tasci (2020b) empirically investigated if perception-based brand equity is in line with the financial brand equity indicators such as visitor numbers for several popular city-level destinations in the U.S.A. The study revealed a lack of comparable tourism statistics for different destinations. As such, Tasci (2020b) recommended collaborative efforts between researchers and practitioners for more uniform data collection to investigate the relationship between financial and perception-based brand equity of destinations in the future.

Tasci's (2020b) study also revealed two different streams of branding studies in the context of geographical entities (i.e., a destination or a place) as a product. The first is *destination branding* which is typically focused on the visitors to a location as a place to visit; this is contrasted to the second perspective of *place branding* which is typically concerned with locals/residents of the location as a place to move and live in. These two streams of research are conducted by scholars with different academic backgrounds who publish in different journals by using entirely different indicators of brand equity as reflected in Table 12.2. Even though the two streams of research are related, researchers typically focus on their domain, destination, or place, without covering the literature on the other stream. Destination branding research is mostly focused on larger-scale locations such as countries and states, while place branding studies mostly focus on smaller-scale locations such as cities. Place branding research includes brand equity indicators such as identity (Lucarelli, 2012), socio-political aspects (Lucarelli, 2012), economic investment, business contracts, quality and quantity of media coverage, the quantity of viewers and visitors of different information sources of the brand, rankings (Jørgensen, 2015), foreign direct investment (Jacobsen, 2009; 2012), residents' cumulative cash flows over the time of residency (Zenker & Martin, 2011) and economic improvement or decrease (Lucarelli, 2012). As mentioned above and listed in Table 12.1, destination branding researchers use perception-based indicators, the most common being awareness or familiarity, image, consumer value, perceived quality, and consumer loyalty. This difference comes from the study populations that researchers focus on, destination researchers focusing on visitors, and place researchers focusing on residents, who have different interests and goals regarding a geographical entity. Nonetheless, Tasci (2020b) recommended the integration of these two streams of branding research for a more comprehensive understanding of the brand equity of a location.

As identified by Tasci (2020a, 2020b), destination and place branding research is conducted in silos without integrating the views of the other, even though both contexts are highly relevant to both visitors and residents of a geographical entity. In addition, destination branding researchers use different

Table 12.2 Place/destination brand equity indicators/metrics listed in the literature

Subjective brand equity indicators	Objective brand equity indicators
From all stakeholder perspectives: industry, businesses, investors, residents, workers, and visitors	**From a tourism destination brand perspective**
• Awareness (Boo, Busser, & Baloglu, 2009; Jacobsen, 2012; Kladou & Kehagias, 2014; Tasci & Gartner, 2009; Yang, Liu, & Li, 2015) • Familiarity (Gartner, Tasci, & So, 2007; Tasci, 2018) • Associations (Kashif, Samsi, & Sarifuddin, 2015; Kladou & Kehagias, 2014; Roth, Diamantopoulos, & Montesinos, 2008) • Image (Florek, 2012; Gartner, Tasci, & So, 2007; Horng, Liu, Chou, & Tsai, 2012; Jacobsen, 2012; Lucarelli, 2012; Pike & Bianchi, 2016; San Martín, Herrero, & García de los Salmones, 2018; Tasci, 2018; Tasci & Gartner, 2009; Tasci, Hahm, & Breiter, 2016; Zenker & Martin, 2011) • Perceived Quality (Gartner, Tasci, & So, 2007; Herrero, San Martín, & Collado, 2017; Jacobsen, 2012; Kladou & Kehagias, 2014; Pike & Bianchi, 2016; Tasci, 2018; Tasci & Gartner, 2009; Tasci, Hahm, & Breiter, 2016) • Consumer Value (Bianchi, Pike, & Lings, 2014; Boo, Busser, & Baloglu, 2009; Gartner, Tasci, & So, 2007; Tasci & Gartner, 2009; Tasci, 2018; Tasci, Hahm, & Breiter, 2016)	• Tourist numbers (Tasci & Denizci, 2009) • Tourism revenues (Tasci & Denizci, 2009) • Market share (Tasci & Denizci, 2009) • Tourism taxes (Tasci & Denizci, 2009) • Tourism-related jobs (Tasci & Denizci, 2009) • Prices – Hotel room rates, restaurant meal prices, and attraction entry fees (Tasci & Denizci, 2009) • Consumers' willingness to pay higher prices (Tasci & Denizci, 2009) • Hotel night sales (Jørgensen, 2015) • Revenues from branding activities such as events (Jørgensen, 2015) • Economic investment (Jørgensen, 2015)

Subjective brand equity indicators	Objective brand equity indicators
• Brand Value (Tasci, 2018; Tasci, Hahm, & Breiter; 2016)	• Sponsorships for branding activities such as events (Jørgensen, 2015)
• Loyalty (Chekalina, Fuchs, & Lexhagen, 2018; Gartner, Tasci, & So, 2007; Kladou & Kehagias, 2014; Pike & Bianchi, 2016; Tasci, 2018; Tasci & Gartner, 2009; Tasci, Hahm, & Breiter, 2016)	• Business contracts (Jørgensen, 2015)
• Salience (Bianchi, Pike, & Lings, 2014; Pike & Bianchi, 2016; Pike, Bianchi, Kerr, & Patti, 2010)	• Growth in private businesses (Jørgensen, 2015)
• Satisfaction (San Martín, Herrero, & García de los Salmones, 2018; Zenker & Martin, 2011)	• Quality and quantity of media coverage (Jørgensen, 2015)
• Assets (Kladou & Kehagias, 2014)	• Quantity of viewers and visitors of different information sources of the brand (Jørgensen, 2015)
• Destination resources (Chekalina, Fuchs, & Lexhagen, 2018)	• Rankings (Jørgensen, 2015)
• Value in use (Chekalina, Fuchs, & Lexhagen, 2018)	• Foreign direct investment (Jacobsen, 2009; 2012)

Subjective brand equity indicators	Objective brand equity indicators
• Brand performance (Duman, Ozbal, & Duerod, 2018) • Attachment (Duman, Ozbal, & Duerod, 2018) • Emotions/feelings (Duman, Ozbal, & Duerod, 2018) • Brand judgment (Duman, Ozbal, & Duerod, 2018) • Brand adoption by stakeholders (Baker, 2007) • Brand consistency (Baker, 2007) • Media coverage (Baker, 2007) • Stakeholders' attitudes (Baker, 2007) • Place brand assets – quality, impression, promotion, awareness, heritage, personality, reputation, and trust (Jacobsen, 2012) • Place brand values – function, distinction, prestige, and identity (Jacobsen, 2012) • Identity (Lucarelli, 2012) • Socio-political aspects – social, cultural, and political outcomes of branding (Lucarelli, 2012) • Willingness to pay (Florek, 2012) • Patents and trademarks (Tasci & Gartner, 2009)	

Subjective brand equity indicators	Objective brand equity indicators
From residents' perspective	**From a place brand perspective**
• Community pride and support for branding (Baker, 2007)	• Residents' cumulative cash flows over the time of residency (Zenker & Martin, 2011)
	• Resident growth due to branding (Jørgensen, 2015)
	• Employment (Jørgensen, 2015)
	• Taxes (Jørgensen, 2015)
	• Economic improvement or decrease (Lucarelli, 2012)
	• Talents' willingness to sacrifice the percentage of wages for the destination brand (Zenker, Eggers, & Farsky, 2013)
	• Revenues from branding activities such as events (Jørgensen, 2015)

Subjective brand equity indicators	Objective brand equity indicators
	• Economic investment (Jørgensen, 2015) • Sponsorships for branding activities such as events (Jørgensen, 2015) • Business contracts (Jørgensen, 2015) • Growth in private businesses (Jørgensen, 2015) • Quality and quantity of media coverage (Jørgensen, 2015) • Quantity of viewers and visitors of different information sources of the brand (Jørgensen, 2015) • Rankings (Jørgensen, 2015) • Foreign direct investment (Jacobsen, 2009; 2012)

Source: The table was adopted from Tasci (2020b).

sets of indicators, thus making comparison difficult or unlikely. Also, even if researchers use the same indicators, they propose and test different cause and effect relationships among those indicators. Furthermore, while the assumption is that the better the perception-based brand equity, the higher the financial-based brand equity, this relationship is rarely investigated. Identifying this relationship is critical for justifying the branding practices of DMOs and other local authorities. These deficiencies in destination and place branding research still await attention in future research. Besides those, there are other areas that branding researchers need to investigate in future research. Past research on brand equity does not address the measurement of specific attractions and experiences' brand equity, and the relative contribution of these attractions and experiences to the overall destination or place brand equity. Rather, empirical research on destinations and places has proposed measuring brand equity with the geographical entity as a holistic product, without addressing the contribution of specific attractions to the destination's overall brand equity. For example, it would be interesting to unveil the brand equity of the Palace Museum and the Forbidden City, the Great Wall of China, Tiananmen Square, the Temple of Heaven, or Wangfujing Snack Street (Dearsley, 2021; Smith, 2019) and their contribution to the collective brand equity of the city of Beijing. Also, there is a lack of studies investigating the influence of negative socio-cultural and environmental factors such as crime, political unrest, earthquakes, and storms on brand equity, even though these factors are studied extensively in destination image research. Assessing this influence on perception-based as well as financial-based brand equity of a destination might move local authorities to adopt remedial actions. Since individual attractions such as Disney in Orlando or the Eiffel Tower in Paris are critical drivers of visitors and thus potential drivers of the overall brand equity of the destination, the following section focuses on this subject for more attention in future research.

4. The role of attractions and experiences in a destination brand equity

Leiper's (1990) cognitive classification approach to tourist attractions suggests that attractions have different levels of importance when tourists go through the decision-making process, where they develop a hierarchical classification that distinguishes between primary, secondary, and tertiary attractions. The primary attraction guides the destination choice consistent with the purpose of travel. The role of secondary and tertiary attractions depends on whether the tourist knew about the attraction (or not) before arriving at the destination (Ćorluka, Vitezic, & Peronja , 2021). Depending on their knowledge of these attractions, tourists may develop different perceptions of a destination, thus affecting its brand equity.

Therefore, future research on destination brand equity needs to look at the brand equity of primary, secondary, and tertiary attractions and their relative contribution to the destination's or place's overall brand equity. For example, Paris is one of the world's well-known cities and among the most popular tourist destinations worldwide. It has been a global hub for history, architecture, culture, art, culinary experience, fashion, technology, and commerce (TPDO, 2020). However, its positive brand image has been developed from a collection of different attractions and experiences, each with its brand equity that contributes collectively to the overall brand equity of the city. The French capital's touristic attractions include many iconic buildings, structures, or bridges that were not purposely built as tourist attractions such as the Notre Dame Cathedral, the Louvre Museum, the Eiffel Tower, Père Lachaise Cemetery, or the Conciergerie (former prison) (Alexander, 2022), but throughout the years these attractions have become the key components of the city's overall brand equity. These iconic structures have necessitated the continual adoption of business operation strategies to address the attractions' appearance, marketing, organization, human resources, finance, and more (Milman, 2022). For example, the Louvre Pyramid, completed in 1988, is a large glass and metal structure located in the Louvre Palace's main courtyard and was built to serve as the main entrance to the Louvre Museum to accommodate an increasing number of visitors and to avoid crowding. The pyramid is surrounded by three smaller pyramids and has become a landmark and attraction by itself, adding to the brand equity of the museum (Paris Vision, 2022).

Other touristic attractions and experiences may also contribute to a destination's overall brand equity like markets such as the Grand Bazaar in Istanbul or Camden Market in London, cultural events and festivals such as the Harbin International Ice & Snow Sculpture Festival (China), the ancient Hindu Holi Festival (India/Pakistan), Día De Los Muertos (Mexico), or the two-week Oktoberfest (Germany), the largest folk festival in the world that attracts annually over six million people to Munich's Fairground and contributes to the city's brand equity (Green Global Travel, 2022).

As an example, a study conducted by the Monza and Brianza Chamber of Commerce (Italy) declared the Eiffel Tower to be the world's most valuable monument at 435 billion euros (Simpson, 2012). The attraction's financial brand equity includes the overall economic benefit that the monument brings to the French economy, including ticket sales, tours, and incremental revenue such as transportation, hotels, restaurants, souvenirs, other attractions, and more (Kanodia, 2022). The Monza and Brianza study also recognized the brand equity of other attractions located within destinations such as Rome's Coliseum valued at 91 billion euros, and Gaudi's unfinished cathedral La Sagrada Familia in Barcelona valued at 90 billion euros. However, the relationship of the economic benefit to the subjective brand equity indicators, namely consumer or customer-based brand equity, has not been identified for any attraction thus far and awaits future research.

5. Conclusion

Destination branding has received much attention during the past decade due to its presumed advantages in the fiercely competitive tourism marketplace. Branding is expected to provide tangible benefits such as increased tourists and tourist spending as well as intangible benefits such as a strong image, high consumer value, strong perceived quality, and thus strong brand loyalty, which then are expected to lead to increased visitors and spending. Therefore, consumer/customer-based brand equity has been studied conceptually and empirically over two decades. However, several areas still await attention from researchers. Brand equity needs to be studied with more uniformity in its indicators and the cause and effect relationships among the indicators for more robust theory development. Also, brand equity needs to be studied from diverse stakeholder viewpoints including tourists, locals, the media, and the local industry for a more holistic understanding of the worth of the destination. Additionally, the relationship between tangible and intangible benefits of branding, namely, the relationship between consumer/customer-based brand equity and financial-based brand equity needs to be studied to substantiate this presumed relationship and to justify the branding activities. Besides, the two streams of research about geographical areas, namely destination branding and place branding studies, need to be integrated for a more comprehensive understanding of branding a place for different interests of different stakeholders. Finally, considering that every destination has primary attractions driving tourists who then sample other secondary attractions and events while at a destination, the contribution of these individual components of the complex destination product on its brand equity needs to be identified to guide destination authorities to allocate their resources in branding accordingly.

References

Aaker, D.A. (1991). *Managing Brand Equity: Capitalizing on the Value of a Brand Name*. New York: The Free Press.

Aaker, D.A. (1992). The value of brand equity. *Journal of Business Strategy*, *13*(4), 27–32.

Aaker, D.A. (1996). Measuring brand equity across products and markets. *California Management Review*, *38*(3), 102–120.

Alexander, L. (2022, March 22). Top-rated tourist attractions in Paris. Retrieved on 4/6/2022 from https://www.planetware.com/tourist-attractions-/paris-f-p-paris.htm

Baker, B. (2007). *Destination Branding for Small Cities: The Essentials for Successful Place Branding*. Portland, OH: Creative Leap Books.

Bianchi, C., Pike, S., & Lings, I. (2014). Investigating attitudes towards three South American destinations in an emerging long haul market using a model of consumer-based brand equity (CBBE). *Tourism Management*, *42*, 215–223.

Boo, S., Busser, J., & Baloglu, S. (2009). A model of customer-based brand equity and its application to multiple destinations. *Tourism Management*, *30*, 219–231.

Chekalina, T., Fuchs, M., & Lexhagen, M. (2018). Customer-based destination brand equity modeling: The role of destination resources, value for money, and value in use. *Journal of Travel Research*, *57*(1), 31–51.

Ćorluka, G., Vitezić, V., & Peronja, I. (2021). The temporal dimension of tourist attraction. *Tourism*, *69*(3), 443–453. doi:10.37741/t.69.3.9.

D'Hauteserre, A.M. (2001). Destination branding in a hostile environment. *Journal of Travel Research*, *39*(February), 300–307.

de Chernatony, L., & Riley, F.D.O. (1999). Experts' views about defining services brands and the principles of services branding. *Journal of Business Research*, *46*, 181–192.

Dearsley, B. (2021, March 9). 17 top-rated tourist attractions in Beijing. Retrieved on 4/6/2022 from https://www.planetware.com/tourist-attractions-/beijing-peking-chn-bj-bj.htm

Duman, T., Ozbal, O., & Duerod, M. (2018). The role of affective factors on brand resonance: Measuring customer-based brand equity for the Sarajevo brand. *Journal of Destination Marketing & Management*, *8*, 359–372.

Florek, M. (2012). Measuring of city brand equity. *Actual Problems of Economics*, *2*(7), 130–139.

Frias Jamilena, D.M., Polo Pena, A.I., & Rodriguez Molina, M.A. (2017). The effect of value-creation on consumer-based destination brand equity. *Journal of Travel Research*, *56*(8), 1011–1031.

Gartner, W.C., Tasci, A.D.A., & So, S.I.A. (2007). Branding Macao: An application of strategic branding for destinations. *Proceedings for the 2nd International Conference on Destination Branding and Marketing: New Advances and Challenges for Practice*, December 17–19, 2007, Macao, China, pp. 133–142.

Gómez, M., Lopez, C., & Molina, A. (2015). A model of tourism destination brand equity: The case of wine tourism destinations in Spain. *Tourism Management*, *51*, 210–222. doi:10.1016/j.tourman.2015.05.019.

Green Global Travel (2022). The 20 best cultural festivals around the world. Retrieved on 4/6/2022 from https://greenglobaltravel.com/best-cultural-festivals-around-the-world/.

Herrero, A., San Martín, H., & Collado, J. (2017). Examining the hierarchy of destination brands and the chain of effects between brand equity dimensions. *Journal of Destination Marketing & Management*, 6, 353–362.

Horng, J.-S., Liu, C.-H., Chou, H.-Y., & Tsai, C.-Y. (2012). Understanding the impact of culinary brand equity and destination familiarity on travel intentions. *Tourism Management*, *33*, 815–824.

Jacobsen, B.P. (2009). Investor-based place brand equity: A theoretical framework. *Journal of Place Management and Development*, *2*(1), 70–84.

Jacobsen, B.P. (2012). Place brand equity: A model for establishing the effectiveness of place brands. *Journal of Place Management and Development*, *5*(3), 253–271. https://doi.org/10.1108/17538331211269657.

Jørgensen, O.H. (2015). Developing a city brand balance sheet: Using the case of Horsens, Denmark. *Place Branding and Public Diplomacy*, *11*(2), 148–160.

Kanodia, B. (2022, February 22). What's the Eiffel Tower worth? Inc. Retrieved on 4/6/2022 from https://www.inc.com/bharat-kanodia/whats-eiffel-tower-worth.html.

Kashif, M., Samsi, S.Z.M., & Sarifuddin, S. (2015). Brand equity of Lahore Fort as a tourism destination brand. *RAE – Revista de Administração de Empresas*, *55*(4), 432–443.

Keller, K.L. (1993). Conceptualizing, measuring, and managing customer-based brand equity. *Journal of Marketing*, *57*(1), 1–22.

Keller, K.L. (2003). *Strategic Brand Management: Building, Measuring, and Managing Brand Equity* (2nd ed.). Boston, MA: Pearson Education.

Kladou, S., & Kehagias, J. (2014). Assessing destination brand equity: An integrated approach. *Journal of Destination Marketing and Management*, *3*(1), 2–10.

Konecnik, M. & Gartner, W.C. (2007). Customer-based brand equity for destination. *Annals of Tourism Research*, *34*(2), 400–421.

Leiper, N. (1990). Tourist attraction systems. *Annals of Tourism Research*, *17*, 367–384.

Liu, C.R., Liu, H.K., & Lin, W.R. (2015). Constructing customer-based museums brand equity model: The mediating role of brand value. *International Journal of Tourism Research*, *17*(3), 229–238.

Lucarelli, A. (2012). Unraveling the complexity of "city brand equity": A three-dimensional framework. *Journal of Place Management and Development*, *5*(3), 231–252. https://doi.org/10.1108/17538331211269648.

Milman, A. (2022). Attraction marketing strategies. In Fyall, A., Garrod, B., Leask, A., & Wanhill, S. (Eds.) *Managing Visitor Attractions* (3rd ed.). Milton Park, Abingdon-on-Thames, UK: Routledge, Chapter 15.

Morgan, N., Pritchard, A., & Piggott, R. (2002). New Zealand, 100% pure: The creation of a powerful niche destination brand. *Journal of Brand Management*, *9*(4/5), 335–354.

Paris Vision (2022). The Louvre Pyramid: History architecture, and legend. Retrieved on 4/6/2022 from https:// www .pariscityvision .com/ en/ paris/ museums/ louvre -museum/the-louvre-pyramid-history-architecture-legend.

Pike, S., & Bianchi, C. (2016). Destination brand equity for Australia: Testing a model of CBBE in short-haul and long-haul markets. *Journal of Hospitality and Tourism Research*, *40*(1), 114–134.

Pike, S., Bianchi, C., Kerr, G., & Patti, C. (2010). Consumer-based brand equity for Australia as a long-haul tourism destination in an emerging market. *International Marketing Review*, *27*(4), 434–449.

Pritchard, A., & Morgan, N.J. (2001). Culture, identity and tourism representation: Marketing Cymru or Wales? *Tourism Management*, *22*, 167–179.

Roth, K.P., Diamantopoulos, A., & Montesinos, M.A. (2008). Home country image, country brand equity, and consumers' product preferences: An empirical study. *Management International Review*, *48*(5), 577–602.

San Martín, H., Herrero, A., & García de los Salmones, M.D.M. (2018). An integrative model of destination brand equity and tourist satisfaction. *Current Issues in Tourism*, 1–22.

Simpson, P.V. (2012, August 22). Eiffel Tower worth €434 billion: Study. *The Local.* Retrieved on 4/6/2022 from https://www.thelocal.fr/20120822/eiffel-tower-worth-434-billion-euros-study/.

Smith, T. (2019, June 18). Unusual things to do in Beijing. *Culture Trip*. Retrieved on 4/6/2022 from https://theculturetrip.com/asia/china/articles/top-10-unusual-things-to-do-in-beijing/.

Tasci, A.D.A. (2011). Destination branding and positioning. In Wang, Y., & Pizam, A. (Eds.) *Destination Marketing and Management: Theories and Applications*. CABI, pp. 113–129.

Tasci, A.D.A. (2016). Added value of a destination brand name by Crimmins' method. *Tourism Analysis*, *21*, 669–673.

Tasci, A.D.A. (2018). Testing the cross-brand and cross-market validity of a consumer-based brand equity model. *Tourism Management*, *65*, 143–159. https://doi.org/10.1016/j.tourman.2017.09.020.

Tasci, A.D.A. (2020a). A critical review and reconstruction of perceptual brand equity. *International Journal of Contemporary Hospitality Management*, *33*(1), 166–198.

Tasci, A.D.A. (2020b). Exploring the analytics for linking consumer-based brand equity (CBBE) and financial-based brand equity (FBBE) of destination or place brands. *Place Branding and Public Diplomacy*, *16*(1), 36–59.

Tasci, A.D.A., & Denizci, B. (2009). Destination branding input–output analysis: A method for evaluating productivity. *Tourism Analysis*, *14*(1), 65–83.

Tasci, A.D.A., & Gartner, W.C. (2007). Destination image and its functional relationships. *Journal of Travel Research*, *45*, 413–425.

Tasci, A.D.A., & Gartner, W.C. (2009). A practical framework for destination branding. In Cai, L., Gartner, W.C., & Munar, A.M. (Eds.) *Tourism Branding: Communities in Action*. Cognizant Communications, pp. 149–158.

Tasci, A.D.A., Gartner, W.C., & Cavusgil, S.T. (2007). Conceptualization and operationalization of destination image. *Journal of Hospitality and Tourism Research*, *31*, 194–223.

Tasci, A.D.A., Hahm, J., & Breiter, D. (2016). Consumer-based brand equity of a destination for sport tourists versus non-sport tourists. *Journal of Vacation Marketing*. doi:10.1177/1356766716679485.

TPDO (2020, February). Paris city performance, brand strength and reputation. Retrieved on 5/4/2023 from https://placebrandobserver.com/paris-city-performance-brand-image-reputation/.

Vinh, T.T., & Nga, V.T.Q. (2015). The relationship between components of customer-based brand equity for destination: Conceptual framework and preliminary testing for scales. *South East Asia Journal of Contemporary Business, Economics and Law*, *7*(20), 47–53.

Williams, P.W., Gill, A.M., & Chura, N. (2004). Branding mountain destinations: The battle for "peacefulness". *Tourism Review*, *59*(1), 6–15.

Yang, Y., Liu, X., & Li, J. (2015). How customer experience affects the customer-based brand equity for tourism destinations. *Journal of Travel and Tourism Marketing*, *32*(sup1), S97–S113.

Yoo, B., & Donthu, N. (2001). Developing and validating a multidimensional consumer based brand equity scale. *Journal of Business Research*, *52*(1), 1–14.

Yuwo, H., Ford, J.B., & Purwanegara, M.S. (2013). Customer-based brand equity for tourism destination (CBBETD): The specific case of Bundung City Indonesia. *Organizations and Markets in Emerging Economies*, *4–1*(7), 8–22.

Zanfardini, M., Tamagni, L., & Gutauskas, A. (2011). Customer-based brand equity for tourism destinations in Patagonia. *Catalan Journal of Communication and Cultural Studies*, *3*(2), 253–271.

Zenker, S., Eggers, F., & Farsky, M. (2013). Putting a price tag on cities: Insights into the competitive environment of places. *Cities*, *30*, 133–139.

Zenker, S., & Martin, N. (2011). Measuring success in place marketing and branding. *Place Branding and Public Diplomacy*, *7*(1), 32–41.

13 Third-party employment branding: current status and future directions

Filip Lievens, Mukta Srivastava and Gordhan K. Saini

1. Introduction

"The War for Talent," "The Great Resignation," ... Despite the ever-changing employee recruitment and retention landscape, one adage seems to stand the test of time: "There is always demand for good people!" To deal with this challenge, employer branding (i.e., "internally and externally promoting a clear view of what makes a firm different and desirable as an employer"; Backhaus & Tikoo, 2004, p. 501) has been a valuable strategy for companies. Companies brand themselves as good employers via their webpage, job ads, events, website testimonials, career fairs, site visits, and social media presence. Such company-controlled approaches help them convey a carefully crafted brand message to prospective applicants, employees, and the general public. Like the growing interest in employer branding in organizations, research on employer branding has also mushroomed (for reviews, see Lievens & Slaughter, 2016; Saini et al., 2022; Theurer et al., 2018).

However, over the last years, there has been increased recognition that the employer brand is not a property described and controlled by the company alone. Today, the employer brand is increasingly defined and shaped outside of a company's direct control by current/former employees and other external stakeholders (e.g., applicants and customers). A company's employer image results from a co-creation of company-controlled employer branding and third-party employment branding (TPEB).

Given that TPEB (for a full definition, see below) is getting increasingly popular, is quite varied, and comes from different sources, scientific research on TPEB is also growing. Therefore, this chapter aims to take stock of TPEB research. We aim to understand the current status of TPEB research better and delineate impactful avenues for future research. We do this in a systematic manner. We start by defining TPEB and describing the different types of TPEB. Next, we conduct a bibliometric study of 734 articles on TPEB. Compared to traditional literature reviews, in the bibliometric approach, massive amounts of scientific data such as citation counts and occurrences of keywords (instead of the scholars) take center stage. A bibliometric analysis complements traditional literature reviews because it serves as a more objective and less biased analytical approach (Baumgartner & Pieters, 2003) for revealing the current and evolutionary nuances of a specific discipline.

In particular, a bibliometric approach is well suited for better understanding the TPEB field for several reasons. First, it allows uncovering its intellectual structure by pinpointing the influential authors, countries, institutions, potential collaborations, and networking patterns. Second, it detects dominant research themes by identifying clusters within a field. Third, a bibliometric approach that deals with several years of academic research might offer insights into the evolution of the domain. Finally, besides revealing the current status, themes, and developments in a field, bibliometric analysis enables building foundations for the future by delineating research gaps and avenues.

In sum, our bibliometric analysis of 734 articles on TPEB seeks to answer the following questions:

(i) Who or which are the most dominant authors, articles, and journals that contributed to TPEB research?
(ii) What are the current themes in TPEB research? How can these themes develop further?
(iii) What are the significant keywords in TPEB research, and have they changed over time?
(iv) What are the future research avenues in TPEB?

2. Third-party employment branding: definition and types

TPEB is defined as "communications, claims, or status-based classifications generated by parties outside of direct company control that shape, enhance, and differentiate organizations' images as favorable or unfavorable employers" (Dineen et al., 2019, p. 173). TPEB is an umbrella term that consists of various types of branding that occur outside the control of companies. Dineen et al. (2019) distinguished among four forms. First, interpersonal word-of-mouth represents the most traditional form of TPEB. In this case, company employment information is transmitted and communicated face-to-face from one person to another person. So, this information does not come from the company itself.

Second, traditional word-of-mouth has been overtaken by “word-of-mouse” (electronic word-of-mouth, Van Hoye & Lievens, 2007a) in the social media era. Current/former employees, job seekers, and customers then provide company employment information via Facebook, Twitter, or Instagram. However, company review websites such as Glassdoor, Kununu, Indeed, and so on, have become the most crucial sources of third-party employment information. According to Dineen et al. (2019), about 80 percent of job seekers today vet a company online via Glassdoor before applying. It is striking because job seekers do not know whether the information on these company review websites is overly optimistic (because it is being “gamed” by the company) or excessively negative (because of the anonymity of the source).

Apart from traditional face-to-face word-of-mouth and word-of-mouse (mostly on company review websites), Dineen et al. (2019) categorized best employer competitions as a third type of TPEB. Here, a formal entity (i.e., certifying body that organizes these competitions) “brands” the company. Examples are ranking lists such as “Great Place to Work for” or “Fortune 100 Best Companies to Work For.” Such lists, certifications, and competitions make it easy for job seekers to compare organizations to each other. Although such lists are independent of a company’s branding, companies can often decide which best employer competition to enter and which employees to contact for providing company ratings for the list.

Finally, media coverage constitutes the fourth manifestation of TPEB (Dineen et al., 2019). Again, a formal entity (news outlet) puts out a news story that informs about a company’s employment practices. Examples are print and digital media, radio, podcasts, television, and so on. Although traditionally, media news stories provide credible information given the media’s aura of impartiality and neutrality, some companies might also “leak” stories to broadcast critical information at strategic times (e.g., crisis management).

In order to offer a comprehensive review of the TPEB research, our review includes articles related to any of the above four manifestations of TPEB. It may be noted that TPEB was practiced even before the discipline was recognized formally in academic literature in the last few years (Dineen et al., 2019). For example, the influence of traditional face-to-face word-of-mouth on several outcomes is well documented in several earlier studies (e.g., Van Hoye

& Lievens, 2007b). Similarly, different employer brand certifications such as "The 100 Best Companies" and "Best Companies to Work For" have been in existence for more than two decades (Joo and Mclean, 2006). Even electronic word-of-mouth is not a new phenomenon in the employment context (e.g., Van Hoye & Lievens, 2007a). Focusing only on the studies which specifically used TPEB terminology or the studies which considered TPEB as their focal research issue would have underrepresented the TPEB phenomenon. Therefore, we deliberately selected a wide range of articles that studied one or more of the four manifestations of TPEB. This is also consistent with the key elements included in the broader definition of TPEB (i.e., "communications, claims, or status-based classifications generated by parties outside of direct company control…") presented above.

3. Methodology

To conduct the bibliometric analysis of third-party employment branding, we systematically followed the detailed suggestions outlined by Donthu et al. (2021). First, we decided to use Elsevier's Scopus database, covering 25,100 journals with 1.7 billion citations (Elsevier, 2020). Second, we created the search formula to identify the TPEB literature. Along with "employer," "employment," "job-seeker," and "recruitment," the following keywords were included in the search formula: "third-party employment branding" (Dineen et al., 2019), "best employer surveys" (Saini et al., 2014), "best employer ranking" (Saini et al., 2015), "best companies to work for" (Hinkin & Tracey, 2010), "great places to work for" (Fulmer et al., 2003), "most attractive employers" (Saini & Jawahar, 2021), "crowdsourced employer branding" (Dabirian et al., 2017), "Glassdoor reviews" (Green et al., 2019), "employer of choice" (Saini & Jawahar, 2019), "employer rankings," "Universum ranks," "Fortune best employer rank" (Bernardi et al., 2006), "word-of-mouth" and "electronic word-of-mouth" (Van Hoye & Lievens, 2009). Third, we shortlisted 734 articles that appeared in journals, books, and book series related to the "Business, Management, and Accounting" field. Fourth, we ran the main analysis (i.e., performance analysis and science mapping) and enrichment analysis (i.e., visualization techniques) using *Biblioshiny* and *VOSviewer* tools. Fifth, we performed bibliographic coupling using *VOSviewer* to identify various evolving themes/clusters of the domain. Later, we used the output of keyword analyses, cluster analysis, and content analysis to propose unexplored future research directions under each theme.

4. Results and discussion

4.1 Results of performance and citation analyses

Between 1996 and 2021, 734 documents (including four book chapters, and six review papers) were published in 129 sources with 7,563 references. An article-wise analysis resulted in 95 articles with a minimum of three citations. Collins and Stevens (2002) received the highest citation (280 citations). The second most cited (234 citations) document is Fulmer et al. (2003). Collins and Stevens (2002) revealed that early recruitment-related activities influenced job seekers' intentions and decisions through employer brand image dimensions using a brand equity framework. In contrast, the latter article found that the "companies on the 100 Best list enjoy not only stable and highly positive workforce attitudes, but also performance advantage" (Fulmer et al., 2003, p. 965). Among the top 10 articles, Van Hoye and Lievens (2007a; 2007b; 2009) contributed three significant articles related to employee testimonials and employee word-of-mouth in the recruitment context. The authors establish that company-independent recruitment sources (such as word-of-mouth) were associated with higher organizational attractiveness than company-dependent information sources (such as web-based employee testimonials).

An author-wise analysis revealed 27 authors with at least two documents with a minimum of two citations. *Van Hoye G.* is the most influential author with ten documents and 454 citations, followed by *Lievens F.* with seven documents and 397 citations. Next, we performed a source-wise analysis, resulting in 17 sources with at least two documents and two citations. *Journal of Applied Psychology* topped the list with two documents and 403 citations, followed by the *International Journal of Selection and Assessment* (3 documents, 178 citations) and *Human Resource Management* (4 documents, 159 citations).

4.2 Results of science mapping and visualization

These results revealed "employer branding," "recruitment," "Glassdoor," and "word-of-mouth" as the major keywords. "Employer branding" has 21 percent occurrences, while "recruitment" has 17 percent, followed by "Glassdoor" with 13 percent, and "word-of-mouth" with 9 percent occurrences. Interestingly, among all salient keywords, only "Glassdoor" and "employee satisfaction" have been growing in the past two years (2019–2021) while others are declining. During the past five years (2015–2020), keywords such as "employer branding," "social media," "human resource management," "employee engagement," and "content analysis" were all growing before declining. While "human resource management" and "employee engagement" are common keywords in this field, scholars have extensively used "social media" and "content analysis" keywords as these terms (to indicate either "data source" or "analysis method") are closely related to the third-party employment branding. Higher usage of the "Glassdoor" keyword may be attributed to the ready availability of employee experience data from the Glassdoor website and the importance of such reviews by HR professionals (Saini & Jawahar, 2019).

We then conducted a thematic map analysis to obtain the domain's emerging themes, which resulted in six clusters on the map (Figure 13.1). Centrality and density are the two dimensions of the map. The centrality is a measure of "the intensity of its links with other clusters" (Callon et al., 1991, p. 164). It, therefore, denotes the importance of a theme in developing a particular domain (Cobo et al., 2011). On the other hand, *Density* denotes "the strength of the links that tie the words making up the cluster together" (Callon et al., 1991, p. 165). It is a measure of the theme's capability to sustain and develop itself over a period (Callon et al., 1991; Cobo et al., 2011). From Figure 13.1, it is evident that "employer branding" emerged as the most prominent cluster with eight independent keywords, the theme is well connected with other themes in the domain, and the keywords belonging to this cluster are closely tied up with each other. The keywords of this theme are "employer branding," "employee satisfaction," "employee engagement," and "human resource management." Conversely, the theme "awards" depicts low density and centrality, and hence this theme can be considered a declining theme. We also see that the theme "recruitment" has high centrality but low density. It means that the theme is well connected with the other themes of the domain, but they seem to be loosely tied to the keywords falling within this theme. A deeper look at the keywords falling within this cluster proves this. Some keywords include "employee attitudes," "recruitment," "reputation," and "retention." Hence, the theme has played a crucial role in developing the domain. However, more research is needed to investigate these keywords together.

4.3 Cluster analysis

We obtained three clusters using the bibliographic coupling method, the recommended technique for identifying current trends and future themes in the literature (Donthu et al., 2021). The minimum threshold for the number of citations was set to 15, which resulted in 43 documents[1] (36 linked). These clusters are described below.

Cluster 1: Best employer status and its outcomes: This cluster comprises 13 articles that studied the best employer status and its outcomes. Fulmer et al.'s (2003) article that assessed the relationship between a great place to work

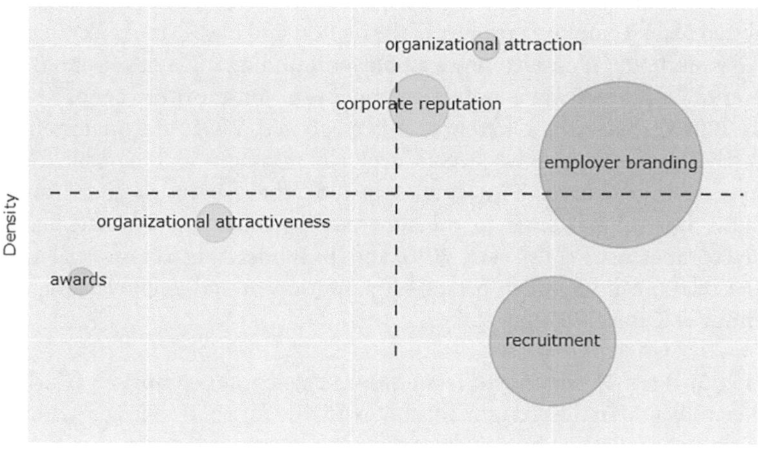

Figure 13.1 Thematic map analysis

status and firm performance received the highest citations (234 citations), followed by Edmans' (2012) paper (182 citations). Other seminal papers are Bernardi et al. (2006) (97 citations), Hinkin and Tracey (2010) (90 citations), and Love and Singh (2011) (80 citations). The papers of this cluster deal with the best employer status outcomes related to different aspects such as HR outcomes (Dineen & Allen, 2016), job seekers' attractiveness toward prospective employers (Saini et al., 2014), and customer satisfaction (Simon & DeVaro, 2006). Dineen and Allen (2016) found that the best employer certifications are associated with lower turnover rates and better applicant pool quality. In contrast, Saini et al. (2014, p. 95) revealed that "firms with a consistent or recent listing in best employer surveys (BES) receive a significantly higher intention to apply than firms present only in one or an older BES." Hinkin and Tracey (2010) and Love and Singh (2011) analyzed the best employers and identified common HR practices among the best employers.

Cluster 2: Antecedents and consequences of third-party employment branding: This cluster included ten articles that broadly dealt with the antecedents and consequences of third-party employment branding. Green et al. (1999) examined whether racial and ethnic groups varied in their job-search strategies and received the highest citations (126 citations), followed by Arasli and Tumer (2008) with 79 citations. Some papers have used data from crowdsourced-based websites such as Glassdoor (Dabirian et al., 2017; Green et al., 2019), while some other studies have examined antecedences (Uen et al., 2015) and consequences (Keeling et al., 2013) of WOM. Dabirian et al. (2017) analyzed 38,000 employee reviews of the highest and lowest-ranked employers on Glassdoor and identified seven employer branding value propositions that matter to employees when evaluating employers. On the other hand, Keeling et al. (2013) found the differential effects of staff WOM on organizational attractiveness with positive versus negative messages and tangible versus intangible information. Two studies include the aspects of social media: a multi-dimensional scale to measure employees' company-related social media competence (Walsh et al., 2016) and the moderating role of social media in the relationship between person–organization fit and employer of choice (Tanwar & Kumar, 2019).

Cluster 3: Word-of-mouth and recruitment: This cluster comprises 12 articles related to WOM in the recruitment context. Van Hoye and colleagues contributed six articles to this cluster. The authors studied various topics such as comparison of employee testimonials with WOM in the recruitment context (Van Hoye & Lievens, 2007a), WOM as a recruitment source (Van Hoye & Lievens, 2009), and social influences on organizational attractiveness and recruitment (Van Hoye & Lievens, 2007a; Van Hoye et al., 2016). Studies show that WOM generates higher organizational attractiveness than web-based employee testimonials (Van Hoye & Lievens, 2007a). Further, a favorable WOM is positively related to organizational attractiveness and job seekers' intention to apply compared to other recruitment sources (Van Hoye & Lievens, 2009). Also, job seekers are attracted to the potential employer when WOM is provided by a more experienced source (e.g., an employee) and by a stronger tie (e.g., a friend) (Van Hoye et al., 2016).

5. Future research directions

After identifying the cluster themes, all articles within each cluster were carefully read, with special attention to their recommendations for future research. The process generated a list of future research questions based on the suggestions given in the clustered articles. Next, we filtered this list using keyword search to verify that subsequent researchers had not already addressed the research question. Thus, using this procedure, we obtained a list of unaddressed future research questions for each cluster theme reported in Table 13.1. It may be noted that the papers retained in Table 13.1 represent the most influential articles under a particular theme. For example, cluster one has articles by Carvalho and Areal (2016), Dineen and Allen (2016) and Saini et al. (2014) on the theme – best employer status. Similarly, cluster three has articles on word-of-mouth and recruitment by top scholars such as Carpentier, Lievens and Van Hoye.

Although the classification of articles into the cluster themes was based on homogeneity of topics covered by the articles, authors of these papers (e.g., Dineen, Lievens, Saini, Tanwar and Van Hoye) sometimes proposed future research directions on a range of topics for employer branding research that were not always aligned with the cluster theme to which the paper belonged (see Table 13.1).

Apart from the above research agenda generated from the bibliometric analysis, we also sketch our suggestions for future research below. Some of them build further on those mentioned in Table 13.1. As "Third-party employment branding" is an umbrella term for different third-party employment branding strategies (e.g., media releases vs. company employer reviews), we especially list directions for future research that go beyond the specific types and generally apply to third-party employment branding. First, we reiterate a common thread running through the avenues for future research mentioned in the articles in our bibliometric analysis. We need more research on how third-party employment branding (e.g., best places to work certifications, employer reviews) affects outcomes in the long run, such as longer-term financial metrics (see Fulmer et al., 2003 for a good example). We also need to know whether the benefits spill over to other domains like effects on product marketing or corporate social performance. Such research is needed to demonstrate that third-party employment branding "matters."

Second, we recommend methodologically going beyond surveys and self-reports. Companies can automatically scrape third-party employment information (e.g., social media websites, employer review websites) via artificial intelligence (AI). Different domains within AI are computer vision (image recognition), machine learning, and language processing (Kaplan & Haenlein, 2019; Paschen et al., 2020). Interestingly, AI applications transform the qualitative reports into quantifiable information, which can then be used in subsequent analyses to document the impact of third-party employment branding. At a practical level, AI applications enable organizations to monitor how their employer brand is perceived among various stakeholders at regular intervals or after specific events (e.g., a media release). Similarly, these applications allow them to monitor how third parties perceive competitors' employer brands. All of this then fits into a broader "brand intelligence" framework.

Table 13.1 Future research directions

Cluster No.	Article	Future Research Questions
(1) Best employer status and its outcomes	Carvalho and Areal (2016)	• What are the effects of dropping out of the best employer status list? How the absence from "great place to work for list" influences financial performance?
	Cycyota et al. (2016)	• What is the value of employee volunteerism? Does it add any value to the business? What role does employee volunteerism play for best companies to work for?
	Arikan et al. (2016)	• Whether corporate reputation mediates the relationship between CSR and multi-stakeholder (customer, employees, investors) outcomes for less reputable firms (i.e., companies ranked low in best employer surveys)? • How does CSR influence stakeholder outcomes through different mediators such as higher brand equity, favorable corporate image?
	Dineen and Allen (2016)	• What are the attributions about positive third-party employment branding, particularly among employees who have unfavorable views of company employment practices? • How best places to work certifications affect outcomes such as longer-term financial metrics, product marketing benefits? • How rank-level effects (5th vs. 45th rank out of top 50 best employers) influence current and potential employees and other stakeholders?
	Saini et al. (2014)	• How intention to apply to best employers is influenced by factors such as applicant characteristics (such as fresh graduates and experienced), firm characteristics (such as firm size, product/services offered, firm reputation) and industry sector (such as manufacturing and services)?

Cluster No.	Article	Future Research Questions
(2) *Antecedents and consequences of third-party employment branding*	Dabirian et al. (2017)	• How the employer characteristics (size, industry, growth, etc.) and job characteristics (skill requirement, job demand, etc.) shape the expectations of current and potential employees about employee value proposition? • What motivates employees to provide feedback on crowdsourced employer branding sites? How smaller firms can motivate employees to write reviews on crowdsourced based sites and generate favorable word-of-mouth?
	Tanwar and Prasad (2016)	• How does employee commitment contribute to building brand advocates? Can brand advocates directly be developed by employer branding efforts?
	Tanwar and Kumar (2019)	• What is the mediating role of anticipatory psychological contract, social identity, salary expectations and corporate reputation in influencing relationship between employer brand and employer of choice status? • What is the relationship between the person–organization fit and the employer of choice status for employees with limited work experience? And how does this relationship change over time?
	Uen et al. (2015)	• What is the role of word-of-mouth in recruitment in societies/geographies where personal relations and informal communication are valued heavily? And how does it vary across several cultures or geographies? • How individual-level outcome variables such as organizational identification and job satisfaction influence employees' word-of-mouth? • How are employer brand management (EBM) practices related to employees' word-of-mouth referrals? • What are the possible negative consequences of the influence of EBM practices on employees' word-of-mouth referrals?

Cluster No.	Article	Future Research Questions
	Keeling et al. (2013)	• In the context of employee word-of-mouth as a recruitment source, how does information valence and type of information influence organizational attractiveness in different job roles, conditions, and sectors?
(3) *Word-of-mouth and recruitment*	Van Hoye and Lievens (2009)	• How variations in the medium (such as face-to-face versus electronic) through which word-of-mouth is received affect its prevalence and effects? • How different motives for providing positive and negative word-of-mouth about employment information influence job seekers and organizational attractiveness? • What is the relative efficacy of various strategies used by organizations to influence word-of-mouth such as employee referral programs and internships? Also, what is their impact on the outcomes of word-of-mouth?
	Carpentier et al. (2019)	• How do different social media platforms affect job applicants' attitudes and intention? • How does social media compare with other recruitment channels such as job ads and recruitment websites in attracting applicants? • What kind of content (e.g., social media page characteristics) is considered socially present or informative? For example, the influence of the number of pictures displayed and the specific content (e.g., people or not) on perceptions of social presence. • How social media influences actual word-of-mouth. For example, word-of-mouth behaviors on social media platforms themselves (such as sharing an organization's vacancies) as these platforms increase the possibility for actors outside the organization to share information about their experience with the organization.

Cluster No.	Article	Future Research Questions
	Melián-González and Bulchand-Gidumal (2016)	• What are the consequences of employees' electronic WOM and how does it compare with internal aspects of companies, such as work environment or organizational climate? • What is the relationship between employees' electronic WOM and human resource management?
	Van Hoye (2012)	• What is the differential effect of recruitment advertising (e.g., print – job advertisements in national magazines, regional papers; and internet advertising – corporate websites, job boards, and social network sites) on organizational attractiveness? • What are different mediators between word-of-mouth and organizational attractiveness and how do they influence the relationship between these two variables?
	Van Hoye et al. (2016)	• What is the impact of incentives in increasing word-of-mouth effectiveness without reducing its credibility and impact? What is the relative effectiveness of different strategies to stimulate positive word-of-mouth such as employer branding, corporate social responsibility, campus recruitment, internships or sponsorship? Also, what is the effects of these practices on the frequency of word-of-mouth, what are possible unintended effects on the credibility and impact of word-of-mouth? How negative information (WOM) affects organizational attractiveness and how it might best be addressed?

Source: Prepared by authors.

For example, applying AI and especially natural language processing methods on 1.4 million employee reviews from Glassdoor,[2] CultureX has proposed nine dimensions of corporate culture – agility, collaboration, customer, diversity, execution, innovation, integrity, performance, and respect. The project provides free data on nine cultural dimensions for 500 companies (including the company ranking). It would be interesting to explore how cultural dimensions correlate with employer branding outcomes such as employer attractiveness, employee engagement, intention to leave, and firms' financial performance. Similarly, how do cultural dimensions such as "customer" and "innovation" influence a firm's "consumer-based brand equity"? And how is the "performance" dimension (i.e., the company rewards results through compensation, informal recognition, and promotions, and deals effectively with underperforming employees) related to psychological contract fulfillment and turnover intentions? We believe these are exciting areas for future exploration.

Third, future researchers should examine how companies can best deal with negative information that appears via third-party employment branding (e.g., media stories, social media). Examples are economic scandals, environmental disasters, and diversity and inclusion issues. To this end, image repair theory (Benoit, 1995) might be used to inspire remedying actions. It might result in "unbranding" and "rebranding" interventions. We also know little about the effectiveness of such rebranding efforts and the accompanying specific actions (e.g., use of online communities, social media presence).

Fourth and relatedly, current third-party employment branding typically examines effects at one point in time. Therefore, it is crucial to investigate trajectories in third-party employment branding. A good example is Dineen and Allen (2016), who demonstrated that the effects of being included in the best employer competition on turnover were strongest after the first certification. However, this effect weakened with subsequent certifications, showing thus some novelty effect. Building on this, we need to determine the impact of dropping out from such lists (and reappearing again on them) on stakeholders' perceptions and hard financial metrics.

Fifth, related to the above points, it would be helpful to understand the counter-productive effects of (i) simultaneous participation in multiple certifications/surveys and (ii) lower ranks in a survey. Different certification agencies use diverse methodologies and produce divergent rankings. For example, in the first case, an employer may be ranked very differently in two surveys (5th rank out of 50 employers in one survey; and 35th rank out of 50 employers in the second survey). Such divergence may lead to confusion and lack of trust in these rankings, primarily when most stakeholders focus on outcomes rather than processes. In the second case, the knowledge of a lower rank in a survey may generate an unfavorable evaluation of an employer by different stakeholders. Perhaps the employer is better off if it is absent from that specific list (Saini & Jawahar, 2021). So, these likely counter-productive effects need to be studied empirically. At a practical level, these counter-productive effects are also a concern given most certification agencies charge a significant participation fee.

Sixth, most certifications focus on white-collar employees because of their skewed sample selection and lack of inclusiveness. Questions may be raised whether a given empoyer status truly represents the voices of different segments of employees such as blue-collar workers, shopfloor workers, gig workers (associated with that employer)? and can be labeled as "the best" or "the great"? Such questions need more attention from scholars if "the great" companies are prone to labor rights violations and exploitative HR practices for shopfloor workers, and the reported cases of industrial accidents. While it may be methodologically challenging to do such studies, the theme offers a fertile ground for relevant and vital research.

Seventh, it is still unknown how the effects of different types of company-independent sources vary on job seekers and employees. Information from different media platforms such as Facebook, Glassdoor, and LinkedIn may have an unequal effect on potential job seekers because of the varying effectiveness of platforms. Also, the nature of content characteristics (i.e., informative, interactive, and entertaining) and the potential applicants' attitudes about various platforms may contribute to this differential effect. This requires empirical testing.

Finally, we call for more cross-fertilization between employer branding, internal branding, and third-party employment branding research. These domains have evolved separately (Saini et al., 2022). Such more integrative research that focuses on spill-overs between different perspectives is necessary because it reflects the reality in which organizations are working. This research might illuminate which source of information employees attend to most. In a similar vein, it sheds light on employees' attributions (how do they deal with conflicting information from different sources?).

Notes

1. This number is less than the total articles reviewed in this chapter as we intended to include impactful papers (measured in terms of citations) and linked papers for better cluster formation. This is a standard and recommended approach in a bibliometric analysis.
2. Founded by the faculties of MIT Sloan School of Management, CultureX conducted a rigorous large-scale research project to measure corporate culture in top companies, using a data set of 1.4 million employee reviews from Glassdoor.

References

Arasli, H., & Tumer, M. (2008). Nepotism, favoritism and cronyism: A study of their effects on job stress and job satisfaction in the banking industry of north Cyprus. *Social Behavior and Personality: An International Journal, 36*(9), 1237–1250.

Arikan, E., Kantur, D., Maden, C., & Telci, E.E. (2016). Investigating the mediating role of corporate reputation on the relationship between corporate social responsibility and multiple stakeholder outcomes. *Quality & Quantity, 50*(1), 129–149.

Backhaus, K.B., & Tikoo, S. (2004). Conceptualizing and researching employer branding. *Career Development International, 9*(5), 501–517.

Baumgartner, H., & Pieters, R. (2003). The structural influence of marketing journals: A citation analysis of the discipline and its subareas over time. *Journal of Marketing, 67*(2), 123–139.

Benoit, W.L. (1995). Sears' repair of its auto service image: Image restoration discourse in the corporate sector. *Communication Studies, 46*(1–2), 89–105.

Bernardi, R.A., Bosco, S.M., & Vassill, K.M. (2006). Does female representation on boards of directors associate with Fortune's "100 best companies to work for" list? *Business & Society, 45*(2), 235–248.

Callon, M., Courtial, J.P., & Laville, F. (1991). Co-word analysis as a tool for describing the network of interactions between basic and technological research: The case of polymer chemistry. *Scientometrics, 22*(1), 155–205.

Carpentier, M., Van Hoye, G., & Weijters, B. (2019). Attracting applicants through the organization's social media page: Signaling employer brand personality. *Journal of Vocational Behavior, 115*, 103326.

Carvalho, A., & Areal, N. (2016). Great Places to Work®: Resilience in times of crisis. *Human Resource Management, 55*(3), 479–498.

Cobo, M.J., López-Herrera, A.G., Herrera-Viedma, E., & Herrera, F. (2011). An approach for detecting, quantifying, and visualizing the evolution of a research field: A practical application to the Fuzzy Sets Theory field. *Journal of Infometrics, 5*(1), 146–166.

Collins, C.J., & Stevens, C.K. (2002). The relationship between early recruitment-related activities and the application decisions of new labor-market entrants: A brand-equity approach to recruitment. *Journal of Applied Psychology, 87*(6), 1121–1133.

Cycyota, C.S., Ferrante, C.J., & Schroeder, J.M. (2016). Corporate social responsibility and employee volunteerism: What do the best companies do? *Business Horizons, 59*(3), 321–329.

Dabirian, A., Kietzmann, J., & Diba, H. (2017). A great place to work!? Understanding crowdsourced employer branding. *Business Horizons, 60*(2), 197–205.

Dineen, B.R., & Allen, D.G. (2016). Third party employment branding: Human capital inflows and outflows following "best places to work" certifications. *Academy of Management Journal, 59*(1), 90–112.

Dineen, B.R., Van Hoye, G., Lievens, F., & Rosokha, L.M. (2019). Third party employment branding: What are its signaling dimensions, mechanisms, and sources? *Research in Personnel and Human Resources Management*, 173-226. Research Collection Lee Kong Chian School of Business.

Donthu, N., Kumar, S., Mukherjee, D., Pandey, N., & Lim, W.M. (2021). How to conduct a bibliometric analysis: An overview and guidelines. *Journal of Business Research, 133*(April), 285–296. https://doi.org/10.1016/j.jbusres.2021.04.070

Edmans, A. (2012). The link between job satisfaction and firm value, with implications for corporate social responsibility. *Academy of Management Perspectives, 26*(4), 1-19.

Elsevier. (2020). *Content Coverage Guide.* https://www.elsevier.com/__data/assets/pdf_file/0017/114533/Scopus_GlobalResearch_Factsheet2019_FINAL_WEB.pdf

Fulmer, I.S., Gerhart, B., & Scott, K.S. (2003). Are the 100 best better? An empirical investigation of the relationship between being a "great place to work" and firm performance. *Personnel Psychology, 56*(4), 965-993.

Green, G.P., Tigges, L.M., & Diaz, D. (1999). Racial and ethnic differences in job-search strategies in Atlanta, Boston, and Los Angeles. *Social Science Quarterly, 80*(2), 263-278.

Green, T.C., Huang, R., Wen, Q., & Zhou, D. (2019). Crowdsourced employer reviews and stock returns. *Journal of Financial Economics, 134*(1), 236-251.

Hinkin, T.R., & Tracey, J.B. (2010). What makes it so great? An analysis of human resources practices among Fortune's best companies to work for. *Cornell Hospitality Quarterly, 51*(2), 158-170.

Joo, B.K.B., & Mclean, G.N. (2006). Best employer studies: A conceptual model from a literature review and a case study. *Human Resource Development Review, 5*(2), 228-257.

Kaplan, A., & Haenlein, M. (2019). Siri, Siri, in my hand: who's the fairest in the land? On the interpretations, illustrations, and implications of artificial intelligence. *Business Horizons, 62*(1), 15-25.

Keeling, K.A., McGoldrick, P.J., & Sadhu, H. (2013). Staff word-of-mouth (SWOM) and retail employee recruitment. *Journal of Retailing, 89*(1), 88-104.

Lievens, F., & Slaughter, J.E. (2016). Employer image and employer branding: What we know and what we need to know. *Annual Review of Organizational Psychology and Organizational Behavior, 3*, 407–440.

Love, L.F., & Singh, P. (2011). Workplace branding: Leveraging human resources management practices for competitive advantage through "Best Employer" surveys. *Journal of Business and Psychology, 26*(2), 175-181.

Melián-González, S., & Bulchand-Gidumal, J. (2016). Worker word of mouth on the internet: Influence on human resource image, job seekers and employees. *International Journal of Manpower, 37*(4), 709-723.

Paschen, U., Pitt, C., & Kietzmann, J. (2020). Artificial intelligence: Building blocks and an innovation typology. *Business Horizons, 63*(2), 147-155.

Saini, G.K., & Jawahar, J. (2019). The influence of employer rankings, employment experience, and employee characteristics on employer branding as an employer of choice. *Career Development International, 24*(7), 636-657.

Saini, G.K., & Jawahar, J. (2021). Do employment experience and attractiveness rankings matter in employee recommendation? A firm-level analysis of employers. *Management and Labour Studies*, *46*(2), 175-191.

Saini, G.K., Gopal, A., & Kumari, N. (2015). Employer brand and job application decisions: Insights from the best employers. *Management and Labour Studies*, *40*(1-2), 1–19.

Saini, G.K., Lievens, F., & Srivastava, M. (2022). Employer and internal branding research: A bibliometric analysis of 25 years. *Journal of Product and Brand Management* (ahead-of-print). https://doi.org/10.1108/JPBM-06-2021-3526.

Saini, G.K., Rai, P., & Chaudhary, M.K. (2014). What do best employer surveys reveal about employer branding and intention to apply. *Journal of Brand Management*, *21*(2), 95-111.

Simon, D.H., & DeVaro, J. (2006). Do the best companies to work for provide better customer satisfaction? *Managerial and Decision Economics*, *27*(8), 667-683.

Tanwar, K., & Kumar, A. (2019). Employer brand, person–organisation fit and employer of choice: Investigating the moderating effect of social media. *Personnel Review*, *48*(3), 799-823. https://doi.org/10.1108/PR-10-2017-0299

Tanwar, K., & Prasad, A. (2016). Exploring the relationship between employer branding and employee retention. *Global Business Review*, *17*(3_suppl), 186S-206S.

Theurer, C.P., Tumasjan, A., Welpe, I.M., & Lievens, F. (2018). Employer branding: A brand equity-based literature review and research agenda. *International Journal of Management Reviews*, *20*(1), 155-179.

Uen, J.F., Ahlstrom, D., Chen, S., & Liu, J. (2015). Employer brand management, organizational prestige and employees' word-of-mouth referrals in Taiwan. *Asia Pacific Journal of Human Resources*, *53*(1), 104-123.

Van Hoye, G. (2012). Recruitment sources and organizational attraction: A field study of Belgian nurses. *European Journal of Work and Organizational Psychology*, *21*(3), 376–391.

Van Hoye, G., & Lievens, F. (2007a). Investigating web-based recruitment sources: Employee testimonials vs word-of-mouse. *International Journal of Selection and Assessment*, *15*(4), 372-382. https://doi.org/10.1111/j.1468-2389.2007.00396.x

Van Hoye, G., & Lievens, F. (2007b). Social influences on organizational attractiveness: Investigating if and when word of mouth matters. *Journal of Applied Social Psychology*, *37*(9), 2024-2047. https://doi.org/10.1037/a0014066.

Van Hoye, G., & Lievens, F. (2009). Tapping the grapevine: A closer look at word-of-mouth as a recruitment source. *Journal of Applied Psychology*, *94*(2), 341–352.

Van Hoye, G., Weijters, B., Lievens, F., & Stockman, S. (2016). Social influences in recruitment: When is word-of-mouth most effective? *International Journal of Selection and Assessment*, *24*(1), 42-53.

Walsh, G., Schaarschmidt, M., & Von Kortzfleisch, H. (2016). Employees' company reputation-related social media competence: Scale development and validation. *Journal of Interactive Marketing*, *36*, 46-59.

14 Building brands for nonprofit organisations: a review of current themes and future research directions

Zoe Lee

1. Introduction

Nonprofit organisations play a key role in addressing global societal challenges. They also occupy a significant economic role in societies, for example, by collecting over £18.2 billion in donations annually in the UK. The UK has approximately 168,000 active nonprofits (Charity Commission, 2020) and the US is home to over 1.5 million nonprofits (National Center for Charitable Statistics, 2019). Despite the massive number of charities, nonprofit practitioners are slow to leverage their brands to stand out to, and retain top-of-mind recall for donors. Why?

One factor in their reluctance to adopt branding strategies has been the debate about the relevance of using for-profit branding tools and practices in this sector (Bennett & Sargeant, 2005; Fajardo et al., 2018; Lee, 2013; Wymer et al., 2021). Branding is often seen as too commercialised and profit-driven, and not in keeping with the altruistic nature of nonprofit organisations. This attitude overlooks the potential of branding in furthering their social missions. For example, Macmillan Cancer Support, a household nonprofit brand, has been able to leverage the power of its brand to co-partner with Boots (the UK's leading pharmacy retailer) to increase awareness around cancer support and living with cancer. Consequently, this partnership provides additional income to the charity as well as building a positive reputation. So branding bolsters the efforts of nonprofits to provide more services to their beneficiaries by increasing visibility and driving income growth.

Branding also helps organisations to distinguish themselves from one another. This factor is important for nonprofits because they compete with other nonprofit organisations, as well as businesses and social enterprises, to attract donor funds. More companies are incorporating social purpose into their business and embracing the vision of being 'net positive' (Polman & Winston, 2021); and worryingly, for nonprofits, recent reports show that businesses are regarded as more trusted to carry out social goals than other kinds of organisations (Edelman, 2022). In addition, the challenge is intensified when commercial brands are engaging in prosocial positioning by adopting activism such as taking a stand on antislavery, inequality and injustice causes (Lee et al., 2023).

Given these challenges, it is unsurprising that marketing scholars are increasingly interested in the topic of branding in nonprofit organisations to understand how a brand can actively steer these nonprofits in a purpose-driven era (Gregg et al., 2020). Both research and practice strongly demonstrate that brands have considerable influence on charitable giving. There are two groups of scholars writing about how donors choose charities, and they have little apparent interaction (Fajardo et al., 2018). The first, composed primarily of philanthropic and consumer behaviour academics (e.g., Bekkers & Wiepking, 2011; Breeze, 2013; Sneddon et al., 2020; Winterich et al., 2012), focus on why individuals give to charities in general (e.g., the role of the individual – related factors and the various appeals). The second group is composed largely of branding and communication researchers (e.g., Boenigk & Becker, 2016; Hankinson, 2001; Lee, 2013; Wymer et al., 2021) who focus on how individuals choose a specific charity, paying attention to distinctive characteristics of these organisations and their brands.

We note a shifting paradigm towards organisational-level research guided by the notion that brands are increasingly socially constructed and co-created (Campbell & Price, 2021; Ind et al., 2013; Lee & Bourne, 2017). Most nonprofit research is silent about the dynamic and strategic nature of the nonprofit brand (Lee & Davies, 2021). Instead, brand leaders should expect to manage and react to forces of continuity and change in brand meaning that emerge from empowered and dispersed networks of donors, partners, volunteers and other actors. In a recently published bibliometric analysis of nonprofit branding, Sepulcri et al. (2020) called for more research at the organisational level to understand how organisations' character and meaning shape donors' choice.

In sum, this chapter addresses current and emerging issues in nonprofit branding that provide both opportunities and challenges for researchers and PhD students.

2. Nonprofit branding: what are they and what are the theoretical perspectives?

Nonprofit branding refers to a set of tools developed for fundraising purposes as well as driving broad, long-term social goals while strengthening internal identity, cohesion and capacity (Kylander & Stone, 2012). These tools help to encourage donations by developing trust, effectively communicating the values and beliefs of an organisational, stimulating engagement and acting to reduce the perceived risk to a donor of offering a donation. Interestingly, much of the early work in nonprofit branding adopted a narrow approach to brand management, focused heavily on donors' giving behaviour and fundraising issues (Tapp, 1996). These studies tend to use multiple theories from economics (e.g., agency theory, strategic altruism), sociology (e.g., normative influence, social comparison) and psychology (e.g., social impact theory, reactance theory) to identify factors that affect giving behaviours and subsequently what this means for managing nonprofit brands (Bendapudi et al., 1996). However, such a narrow view of nonprofit branding has a short-term time perspective, because the primary focus for the nonprofit marketers is the next transaction rather than relationship building.

More recently, there has been a progression to a different perspective on nonprofit branding by shifting away from a highly rationalist prescriptive to a social constructionist, reflective approach. Vallaster and von Wallpach (2018) applied nonprofit brand strategy co-creation from a strategy as practice theory (Reckwitz, 2002). This approach highlights that the value of brands emerges through continuous social interactions and practices among multiple, networked stakeholders (Merz et al., 2009), beyond the dyadic relationship between nonprofit managers and supporters. The rise of the social constructionist approach is linked to the societal transition where consumers and other stakeholders are empowered through technology; and expect access to and transparency of information on company-internal processes and structure (Hatch & Schultz, 2010; Prahalad & Ramaswamy, 2004). This suggests that nonprofit managers are no longer the sole author and custodian of brand identity. More open practice of embracing interactions with multiple stakeholders in shaping the meanings of nonprofit brands is necessary to ensure the survival of nonprofit organisations.

So, have nonprofit branding concepts kept up with this progression? The changing dynamics of consumption in the neoliberal era had led to brand cultures that encourage consumers and donors alike to be an active contributor to brand mechanisms and meaning-making (Heding et al., 2020). Through these actions, nonprofit managers acts as facilitators in this process. The next section will identify and elaborate on these various concepts in nonprofit branding research.

3. Nonprofit branding concepts and strategies

There has been considerable fluidity concerning nonprofit branding research. In addition to debates about what for-profit concepts could be used in the non-profit sector, other concepts have been proposed as alternative or improved versions for capturing the essence of nonprofits in addressing societal challenges. Among the major themes are brand image, brand personality, brand stereotypes, brand equity, brand orientation and rebranding strategies at an organisational level (see Figure 14.1). A brief consideration of each concept will point out both the broadening and blurring of branding boundaries such as going beyond seeing the role of brands as cultural symbols in both the for-profit and nonprofit sectors; and examine them as agents of social change (Swaminathan et al., 2020).

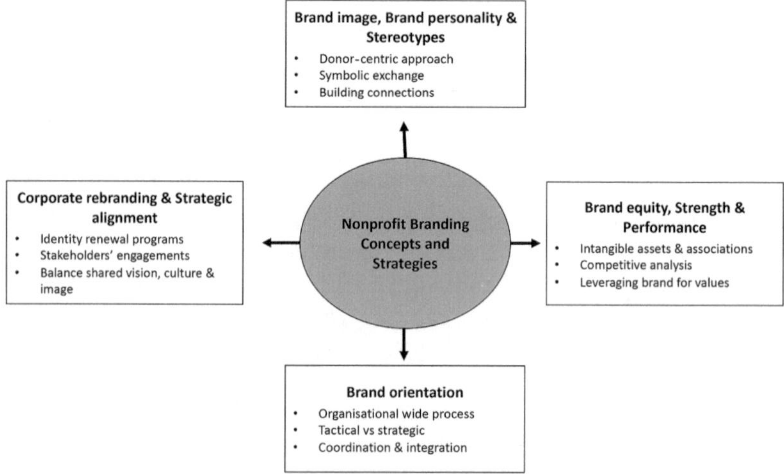

Figure 14.1 Nonprofit branding concepts and strategies

3.1 Brand image, brand personality and stereotyping in nonprofit organisations

The existing research on nonprofit branding is dominated by a donor-centric approach, with a focus on the concept of brand image and brand personality and its influence on giving behaviours (Bennett & Gabriel, 2003; Michaelidou et al., 2015; Stride & Lee, 2007). This is unsurprising as extant research shows that donors tend to give following their taste, rather than need (Breeze, 2013). Hence, a strong brand image is crucial for attracting the right supporters and customers. The concept of brand image is associated with consumers' perception of a brand reflected by the brand associations held in consumers' memory (Keller, 1993). It is how these potential donors think about the charities that matters. However, there are inconsistencies in terms of how nonprofit brand image is measured. Bennett and Gabriel (2003) conceptualised the concept as having five dimensions (compassion, dynamism, idealism, focus on beneficiaries and non-political image), whereas Michel and Rieunier (2012) use four dimensions (usefulness, efficiency, affect and dynamism). Despite such differences, these studies emphasise that an attractive brand image is crucial for nonprofit brands to differentiate themselves in such a competitive marketplace, and be perceived as credible (Liu et al., 2018).

As an image is something that is reimagined (Campbell & Price, 2021), nonprofit managers need to reflect on and revisit their brand image, as other sources, especially on social media, could jeopardise their carefully crafted image and meaning. In addition to understanding donors' behaviours, the concept of brand image has also been applied at a strategic level. For instance, Randle et al. (2013) found that depending on brand image, a nonprofit organisation could consider adopting competitive or collaborative strategies when recruiting volunteers. In addition, Lee and Davies (2021) question the stickiness of nonprofit brand image whereby it can be perceived as useful to appeal to core supporters, but could also be a hindrance in appealing to younger audiences. Taking the example of Macmillan Cancer Support, this nonprofit's brand image has a strong association with Macmillan Coffee mornings – a very successful fundraising event that appeals to older supporters. However, it can be tricky to make such an image appeal to a younger audience on the nonprofit's growth journey.

Brand personality refers to the human characteristics associated with a brand (Aaker et al., 2010). Firms typically use marketing communications to influence individuals to attribute human characteristics to their brands. When there is a fit between an individual's self and the brand's personality, it can help to create deeper differentiation and elevate relationships. Hence, brand personality tends to serve and fulfil symbolic or self-expressive functions for consumers (Malär et al., 2011). Sargeant et al. (2008) argue that brand personality manifests differently in the nonprofit sector than in the for-profit sector. For consumer brands, Aaker et al. (2010) outlined a brand personality scale composed of five dimensions: sincerity, excitement, competence, sophistication and ruggedness. For the nonprofit context, Venable et al. (2005) and Sargeant et al. (2008) adopt brand personality traits to conceptualise nonprofit brand image and suggest that 'integrity' and nurturance' are better measures relative to 'sincerity', 'excitement' and 'competence'.

An interesting application of these concepts is the theory of brand stereotyping (Kolbl et al., 2020). Brand stereotypes refer to consumers' oversimplified and generalised beliefs about brands as intentional agents (Greenwald & Banaji, 1995; Kervyn et al., 2012). For instance, consumers perceive nonprofits as being warmer than for-profits but less competent (Aaker et al., 2010), which implies that nonprofit brands are perceived as having good intentions (e.g., caring for animals, children and the vulnerable) but as unable to enact key actions (e.g., lacking ability and accountability). Despite the perceived incompetence, Kolbl et al. (2020) show that brand warmth has a stronger impact on behavioural outcomes than brand competence. As such, nonprofit managers need to manage their image and personality to cement their reputation around warmth, and subsequently increase their brand's remarkability (Wymer & Casidy, 2019).

3.2 Building brand equity, strength and performance

The next concept relates to brand equity. Interest in the topic of brand equity has expanded to many domains including the nonprofit sector. Researchers agree that brand equity refers to the added value that a given brand lends to a firm's product (Yoo et al., 2000) and hence, it is "the differential effect of brand knowledge on consumer response to the marketing of the brand" (Keller, 1993, p.2). In a review of three decades of brand equity research, Rojas-Lamorena et al. (2022) show that brand equity scholarship can be studied using three main perspectives: financial, consumer, or both. Concerning the nonprofit sector, however, researchers have noted that there are still unanswered questions regarding what makes up a strong nonprofit brand, despite the recent work on conceptualising and measuring nonprofit brand equity (Boenigk & Becker, 2016; Juntunen et al., 2013; Wymer et al., 2016). This poses a significant gap in this field of research.

Researchers agree that strong nonprofit brands have a positive effect on donations, reputation and loyalty. Wymer et al. (2016) suggested new dimensions such as brand remarkability, meaning being extraordinary in comparison with other peer brands. Despite the growing number of studies, researchers still hold on to the assumption that brand assets and meanings are static and controlled by managers. What tends to be overlooked is the growing notion that brands can be co-created. An exception is the work carried out by Juntunen et al. (2013), who measured the differential effect of internal and external stakeholders' brand equity. What appears to be a strong nonprofit brand for one audience may be seen as weak for another audience. For example, the commercial interests of a nonprofit organisation in a co-branding exercise with a business partner that can push the brand in a certain direction, can come into conflict with donors' identification.

3.3 Brand orientation in the nonprofit sector

In the marketing literature, the concept of brand orientation appears to be an important strategic orientation that impacts organisational success (Baumgarth et al., 2013; Piha et al., 2021). Urde (1999) was the first to show that brand orientation is a process of ongoing creation, development, and protection of brand identity in interaction with customers. Since then, several approaches have emerged, in particular the view that brand orientation is a shared sense of brand meaning that offers added value to stakeholders and superior performance to companies (Ewing & Napoli, 2005). In addition, scholars have emphasised managers' mindset in terms of prioritising branding in their organisational strategy (Wong & Merrilees, 2007), and hence have focused on the significance of brand identity (mission, vision and values) as a hub for organisational culture, behaviours and strategy (Urde et al., 2013). As such, brand orientation provides the guiding principles that influence a firm's marketing and brand strategy activities, especially in shaping managers' efforts to create powerful brands.

In the nonprofit sector, the work of Hankinson (2001) is pivotal in providing the foundations of brand orientation in nonprofit organisations and its impact on nonprofits' performance. A strong nonprofit brand and its management are important for managing consistency in terms of both internal and external stakeholders' perceptions aligning with the nonprofit's values. Ewing and Napoli (2005) further developed nonprofit brand orientation scales consisting of three main dimensions: orchestration, interaction and affect, to capture the degree of brand orientation in organisations. The orchestration dimension captures the capacity of nonprofits to develop a consistent image amongst their stakeholders. The interaction dimension facilitates the creation of a meaningful dialogue with stakeholders where their needs are met. Finally, the affect dimension allows the development of detailed knowledge about what stakeholders like, or do not like, about their brands.

Although nonprofit brand orientation is linked to better performance, not all nonprofits are brand oriented. Larger charities appear to have sufficient resources and a more deliberate approach of using brands as their strategic platforms for all of the functions in the organisation (Wallace & Rutherford, 2021). More importantly, commitment from the senior management team is necessary to align the direction of brand orientation with the organisational strategy. As different stakeholders have different opinions and identification with the same nonprofit brand, the senior management team needs to be able to embrace different perspectives. And to cultivate a culture that could foster brand orientation mindsets across the whole organisation, not just within the branding and communication domains.

3.4 Corporate rebranding and strategic alignment

Beyond brand-related attributes and the donor perspective, the final concept relates to organisational brand strategy as an interesting pillar that should be considered in this field of research. Swaminathan et al. (2020) recently urged scholars to rethink the boundaries of the brand in a hyperconnected world, especially in rethinking organisations as a brand. In the nonprofit sector, charities as organisational brands have a responsibility to their missions, to the communities, to the environment, and even to their employees. Many nonprofits increasingly use corporate rebranding strategies to refresh their brand, generate value, and achieve internal efficiency (Lee, 2013; Melewar et al., 2012; Miller et al., 2014). A growing stream of research is documenting the effect of building a strong organisational brand to achieve greater social impact and tighter organisational cohesion (Ewing & Napoli, 2005; Kylander & Stone, 2012). Other studies have also related rebranding strategies to organisation-wide processes, where, to be successful, it is necessary to achieve strong alignment between the vision, image and culture (Hatch & Schultz, 2003; Miller & Merrilees, 2013). A recent review of the challenges to rebranding for UK charities appeared in a book by Hyde and Mitchell (2021) called *Charity Marketing*, which provides a rich overview of the benchmarks in charity rebranding, and the strategies for effectively managing the rebranding exercise.

Branding in the nonprofit sector is highly emotive, as people care deeply about charity causes and brands. As such, people may be more resistant to the rebranding exercise, and view it as a waste of resources which could have been used to benefit the vulnerable. In analysing the distinct characteristics of nonprofit rebranding, Lee and Bourne (2017) stress the risk of a dual perspective that affects strategic decision making in several ways. On the one hand, nonprofit organisations need to leverage their brand to generate awareness, and reach out to relevant beneficiaries to serve their missions. On the other hand, the organisational brand must appeal to potential supporters and partners in order to drive income growth. Such a dual perspective is significantly more complex and hence creates tensions. This creates various opportunities and challenges for nonprofit branding researchers to understand how to bridge these tensions.

4. Future research directions

4.1 Brand activism, being woke and changing donors' expectations

In recent years, much academic research has focused on 'brands doing good', highlighting the positive contributions of for-profit firms to societal challenges (e.g., Iglesias & Ind, 2020; Moorman, 2020; Spry et al., 2021). New research streams in for-profit branding, such as brand activism and being woke, have potential to advance nonprofit branding research (Bhagwat et al., 2020; Moorman, 2020; Mukherjee & Althuizen, 2020; Schmidt et al., 2021). For example, Shelter, a homeless national UK charity, recently used an activist-driven campaign called *Fight for Home*, in which they took a public stand in support of the human right to safe housing. More recently, Barnardo's, a leading British children's charity introduced a controversy when they published a guide on white privilege to spotlight their commitment to advocating anti-racism and protecting vulnerable children (Dufour, 2021). These examples represent trends towards brand activism in the nonprofit sector.

While calls for brand activism have increased, this is a polarising strategy because taking a stance on a divisive issue risks alienating customers and investors (Bhagwat et al., 2020). Research has shown that one way to reduce the reputational risk is to be authentic (Mirzaei et al., 2022), where firms' promises must be followed through. However, brands tend to struggle to convince the public that their virtue-signalling efforts are authentic. In some cases, this may be associated with the practice of 'woke washing' (Vredenburg et al., 2020). Hence, it is important for activism strategy to align with the organisation's values, which can then lead to a stronger emotional attachment with the brand (Schmidt et al., 2021).

Reflecting on the nonprofit sector, naturally, nonprofits as *higher purpose natives* are expected to take a stand on sociopolitical issues to cement their reputation as moral leaders, and align with their social missions (Mirzaei et al., 2021). However, we argue that this is even more risky, because we know that they are stereotyped as 'warm' and 'compassionate', which is seen as rising above a political cause. Even though warmth can raise donations, this can be a hindrance in reaching the social mission, especially when the charities are striving to change systemic structures (Robson & Hart, 2020). Hence, depending on the types of causes (e.g., immigration, military, international aids, etc.), and the projected brand image, nonprofit managers need to think carefully about how multiple audiences would react when they engage in sociopolitical issues.

In sum, the concept of activism offers the opportunity for both theoretical development (e.g., co-creation) and continued debate, as brand researchers attempt to answer the question: to what extent can/should nonprofits use activist-driven brand positioning in fulfilling their missions and avoiding the 'woke washing' typically associated with businesses trying to be more purpose-driven?

4.2 Heritage in nonprofit brands

Much of the branding literature has focused on the positive impact of for-profit firms' heritage (Hakala et al., 2011; Pecot & Merchant, 2022). Yet, with the ongoing changing times and crises, recent research shows that certain forms of heritage branding can also have negative outcomes (Han et al., 2021) by leading consumers to reject the good changes made to the brand's original, flagship product. In their study, the authors highlight two key forms: brands can emphasise their longevity (e.g., their flagship product) or their core values. In the first approach regarding longevity, consumers think about lasting heritage traits over time. As such, consumers can resist even positive changes to the product as they attach authenticity to integrity over time. To avoid such negativity, brands must reframe product changes as being in line with the brand's origin in order to improve consumers' evaluation (Han et al., 2021). Although this study was done using a for-profit brand, the question remains as to how nonprofit brand heritage would work.

The notion of brand heritage appears to have now spread to the nonprofit context (Curran et al., 2016), with many charities engaged in rebranding exercises as a way to return to their roots and hence staying authentic to their brands. For example, Scope (a UK disability charity) and Shelter (UK homelessness charity) rebranded to return to their roots as social advocates and campaigning organisations in order to champion policy change. Similarly, those with a strong history such as the Royal British Legion which also leverages its track records to connect with supporters with the latest rebrand program by fronting the poppy symbol in their new visual identity – honouring the service and sacrifice of the Armed Forces community. However, there are unique challenges of nonprofit brand heritage to consider – for instance, younger supporters may not have a strong association with the history as compared to the older supporters. Internally, nonprofit employees may reject the positive change to brand heritage identity due to strong attachment. Lee and Davies (2021) showed that these employees can be seen as *corporate heritage identity defenders*, who feel a sense of ownership of the brand, and are keen to protect its legacy.

These developments raise several interesting research questions worthy of investigation by branding researchers. For instance, what types of nonprofit organisations engage in heritage branding and are there discernible differences in terms of causes, region and reputation. In addition, future research can focus on the management of brand heritage in nonprofit brands, to what extent changes to nonprofit brand heritage help to address its mission, how to reduce a sense of alienation felt by different stakeholders especially those who have supported the nonprofit for a long time (Lee & Davies, 2021). Other research can also tap into the use of technology and heritage in the revitalisation exercise to reach wider audiences. Hence, there is much to gain in nonprofit organisations to consider the role of heritage in managing their brands.

5. Conclusion

In conclusion, a strong brand is important for nonprofit organisations in attracting and engaging both the internal and external stakeholders. More specifically, a strong nonprofit brand has a remarkable impact in contributing to its mission, revolutionise an organisation and the way people view and support it. As pressures continues to grow, innovative branding strategies and creative communications that are relevant to specific audiences, are crucial in ensuring the relevance of these organisations. For example, in engaging in a powerful story-telling program (Mitchell & Clark, 2021) to be perceived as authentic. Whilst many for-profit businesses are stepping up to address their social responsibilities, nonprofit organisations must leverage their history and brand connection to embrace change.

Finally, are there any dark sides to nonprofit branding? For example, could concerns for building a strong brand jeopardise its mission (e.g., over-commercialisation) and hinder the ability to address societal challenges? Could concerns around accountability shift young donors' preferences to consider other alternatives to give? Indeed, the ability of nonprofit organisations to be agile around identity is often subject to question. How might nonprofit organisations reinvent their branding strategies to align with a new social reality (e.g., activism), and what role will different stakeholders play in this exercise? Nonprofit managers need to adapt to an agenda of paradigm shift discussed earlier and get ready for a rather complicated work method. Insights from this discussion can also be used to become aware of the importance of monitoring if the nonprofit brand is being subjected to criticism or backlash. This can be an early warning sign of a nonprofit brand becoming irrelevant. Nonprofit managers can figure out how to harness multiple stakeholders' passion and commitment that will drive the nonprofit forwards in doing better for the society.

References

Aaker, J., Vohs, K.D. & Mogilner, C. (2010). Nonprofits are seen as warm and for-profits as competent: Firm stereotypes matter. *Journal of Consumer Research, 37*(2), 224–237.

Baumgarth, C., Merrilees, B. & Urde, M. (2013). Brand orientation: Past, present, and future. *Journal of Marketing Management, 29*(9–10), 973–980.

Bekkers, R. & Wiepking, P. (2011). A literature review of empirical studies of philanthropy: Eight mechanisms that drive charitable giving. *Nonprofit and Voluntary Sector Quarterly, 40*(5), 924–973.

Bendapudi, N., Singh, S.N. & Bendapudi, V. (1996). Enhancing helping behavior: An integrative framework for promotion planning. *Journal of Marketing, 60*(3), 33–49.

Bennett, R. & Gabriel, H. (2003). Image and reputational characteristics of UK charitable organizations: An empirical study. *Corporate Reputation Review, 6*(3), 276–289.

Bennett, R. & Sargeant, A. (2005). The nonprofit marketing landscape: Guest editors' introduction to a special section. *Journal of Business Research, 58*(6), 797–805.

Bhagwat, Y., Warren, N.L., Beck, J.T. & Watson IV, G.F. (2020). Corporate sociopolitical activism and firm value. *Journal of Marketing, 84*(5), 1–21.

Boenigk, S. & Becker, A. (2016). Toward the importance of nonprofit brand equity: Results from a study of German nonprofit organizations. *Nonprofit Management and Leadership, 27*(2), 181–198.

Breeze, B. (2013). How donors choose charities: The role of personal taste and experiences in giving decisions. *Voluntary Sector Review, 4*(2), 165–183.

Campbell, M.C. & Price, L.L. (2021). Three themes for the future of brands in a changing consumer marketplace. *Journal of Consumer Research, 48*(4), 517–526.

Charity Commission (2020). Annual report and accounts. Accessed 15 April 2022, https:// assets .publishing .service .gov .uk/ government/ uploads/ system/ uploads/

attachment _data/ file/ 1025877/ Charity _Commission _Annual _Report _and _Accounts_2020_to_2021.pdf

Curran, R., Taheri, B., MacIntosh, R. & O'Gorman, K. (2016). Nonprofit brand heritage: Its ability to influence volunteer retention, engagement, and satisfaction. *Nonprofit and Voluntary Sector Quarterly*, *45*(6), 1234–1257.

Dufour, D. (2021). The changing face of charity branding. Accessed 15 March 2022, https://www.charitycomms.org.uk/the-changing-face-of-charity-branding.

Edelman (2022). Accessed 10 January 2022, https:// www.edelman.com/ sites/ g/ files/ aatuss191/files/2022-01/Trust 22_Top10.pdf.

Ewing, M.T. & Napoli, J. (2005). Developing and validating a multidimensional nonprofit brand orientation scale. *Journal of Business Research*, *58*(6), 841–853.

Fajardo, T.M., Townsend, C. & Bolander, W. (2018). Toward an optimal donation solicitation: Evidence from the field of the differential influence of donor-related and organization-related information on donation choice and amount. *Journal of Marketing*, *82*(2), 142–152.

Greenwald, A.G. & Banaji, M.R. (1995). Implicit social cognition: Attitudes, self-esteem, and stereotypes. *Psychological Review*, *102*(1), 4–27.

Gregg, B., Kim, A. & Perrey, J. (2020). Leading with purpose: How marketing and sales leaders can shape the next normal. *McKinsey Report*, April, 1–10.

Hakala, U., Lätti, S. & Sandberg, B. (2011). Operationalising brand heritage and cultural heritage. *Journal of Product & Brand Management*, *20*, 447–456.

Han, M., Newman, G.E., Smith, R.K. & Dhar, R. (2021). The curse of the original: How and when heritage branding reduces consumer evaluations of enhanced products. *Journal of Consumer Research*, *48*(4), 709–730.

Hankinson, P. (2001). Brand orientation in the charity sector: A framework for discussion and research. *International Journal of Nonprofit and Voluntary Sector Marketing*, *6*(3), 231–242.

Hatch, M.J. & Schultz, M. (2003). Bringing the corporation into corporate branding. *European Journal of Marketing*, *37*(7/8), 1041–1064.

Hatch, M.J. & Schultz, M. (2010). Toward a theory of brand co-creation with implications for brand governance. *Journal of Brand Management*, *17*, 590–604.

Heding, T., Knudtzen, C.F. & Bjerre, M. (2020). *Brand Management: Mastering Research, Theory and Practice*. London: Routledge.

Hyde, F. & Mitchell, S.L. (eds) (2021). *Charity Marketing: Contemporary Issues, Research and Practice*. London: Routledge.

Iglesias, O. & Ind, N. (2020). Towards a theory of conscientious corporate brand co-creation: The next key challenge in brand management. *Journal of Brand Management*, *27*(6), 710–720.

Ind, N., Iglesias, O. & Schultz, M. (2013). Building brands together: Emergence and outcomes of co-creation. *California Management Review*, *55*(3), 5–26.

Juntunen, M., Juntunen, J. & Autere, V. (2013). Co-creating nonprofit brand equity. *International Journal of Nonprofit and Voluntary Sector Marketing*, *18*(2), 122–132.

Keller, K.L. (1993). Conceptualizing, measuring, and managing customer-based brand equity. *Journal of Marketing*, *57*(1), 1–22.

Kervyn, N., Fiske, S.T. & Malone, C. (2012). Brands as intentional agents framework: How perceived intentions and ability can map brand perception. *Journal of Consumer Psychology*, *22*(2), 166–176.

Kolbl, Ž., Diamantopoulos, A., Arslanagic-Kalajdzic, M. & Zabkar, V. (2020). Do brand warmth and brand competence add value to consumers? A stereotyping perspective. *Journal of Business Research*, *118*, 346–362.

Kylander, N. & Stone, C. (2012). The role of brand in the nonprofit sector. *Stanford Social Innovation Review*, Spring, 1-32.

Lee, Z. (2013). Rebranding in brand-oriented organisations: Exploring tensions in the nonprofit sector. *Journal of Marketing Management, 29*(9–10), 1124–1142.

Lee, Z. & Bourne, H. (2017). Managing dual identities in nonprofit rebranding: An exploratory study. *Nonprofit and Voluntary Sector Quarterly, 46*(4), 794–816.

Lee, Z. & Davies, I. (2021). Navigating relative invariance: Perspectives on corporate heritage identity and organizational heritage identity in an evolving nonprofit institution. *Journal of Business Research, 129*(May), 813-825.

Lee, Z., Spry, A., Ekinci, Y. & Vredenburg, J. (2023). From warmth to warrior: Impacts of non-profit brand activism on brand bravery, brand hypocrisy and brand equity. *Journal of Brand Management,* 1–19.

Liu, L., Suh, A. & Wagner, C. (2018). Empathy or perceived credibility? An empirical study on individual donation behaviour in charitable crowdfunding. *Internet Research, 28*(3), 623-651.

Malär, L., Krohmer, H., Hoyer, W.D. & Nyffenegger, B. (2011). Emotional brand attachment and brand personality: The relative importance of the actual and the ideal self. *Journal of Marketing, 75*(4), 35–52.

Melewar, T.C., Gotsi, M. & Andriopoulos, C. (2012). Shaping the research agenda for corporate branding: Avenues for future research. *European Journal of Marketing, 46*(5), 600-608.

Merz, M., He, Y. & Vargo, S. (2009). The evolving brand logic: A service-dominant logic perspective. *Journal of the Academy of Marketing Science, 37*, 328–344.

Michaelidou, N., Micevski, M. & Cadogan, J.W. (2015). An evaluation of nonprofit brand image: Towards a better conceptualization and measurement. *Journal of Business Research, 68*(8), 1657-1666.

Michel, G. & Rieunier, S. (2012). Nonprofit brand image and typicality influences on charitable giving. *Journal of Business Research, 65*(5), 701-707.

Miller, D. & Merrilees, B. (2013). Rebuilding community corporate brands: A total stakeholder involvement approach. *Journal of Business Research, 66*(2), 172–179.

Miller, D., Merrilees, B. & Yakimova, R. (2014). Corporate rebranding: An integrative review of major enablers and barriers to the rebranding process. *International Journal of Management Reviews, 16*(3), 265-289.

Mirzaei, A., Webster, C.M. & Siuki, H. (2021). Exploring brand purpose dimensions for non-profit organizations. *Journal of Brand Management, 28*(2), 186–198.

Mirzaei, A., Wilkie, D.C. & Siuki, H. (2022). Woke brand activism authenticity or the lack of it. *Journal of Business Research, 139*, 1-12.

Mitchell, S.L. & Clark, M. (2021). Telling a different story: How nonprofit organizations reveal strategic purpose through storytelling. *Psychology & Marketing, 38*(1), 142-158.

Moorman, C. (2020). Commentary: Brand activism in a political world. *Journal of Public Policy & Marketing, 39*(4), 388–392.

Mukherjee, S. & Althuizen, N. (2020). Brand activism: Does courting controversy help or hurt a brand? *International Journal of Research in Marketing, 37*(4), 772–788.

National Center for Charitable Statistics (2019). The nonprofit sector in brief. Accessed 15 April 2022, https://nccs.urban.org/publication/nonprofit-sector-brief-2019.

Pecot, F. & Merchant, A. (2022). Why and when is older better? The role of brand heritage and of the product category in the evaluation of brand longevity. *Journal of Business Research, 140*, 533–545.

Piha, L., Papadas, K. & Davvetas, V. (2021). Brand orientation: Conceptual extension, scale development and validation. *Journal of Business Research, 134*, 203-222.

Polman, P. & Winston, A. (2021). The net positive manifesto. *Harvard Business Review*, September to October, 2021.

Prahalad, C.K. & Ramaswamy, V. (2004). Co-creation experiences: The next practice in value creation. *Journal of Interactive Marketing, 18*(3), 5-14.

Randle, M., Leisch, F. & Dolnicar, S. (2013). Competition or collaboration? The effect of non-profit brand image on volunteer recruitment strategy. *Journal of Brand Management, 20*(8), 689-704.

Reckwitz, A. (2002). Toward a theory of social practices: A development in culturalist theorizing. *European Journal of Social Theory, 5*, 243-263.

Robson, A. & Hart, D.J. (2020). Feed the world or help the heroes? Exploring how political attitudes influence charitable choice. *Journal of Marketing Management, 36* (17-18), 1680-1706.

Rojas-Lamorena, Á.J., Del Barrio-García, S. & Alcántara-Pilar, J.M. (2022). A review of three decades of academic research on brand equity: A bibliometric approach using co-word analysis and bibliographic coupling. *Journal of Business Research, 139*, 1067-1083.

Sargeant, A., Ford, J.B. & Hudson, J. (2008). Charity brand personality: The relationship with giving behaviour. *Nonprofit and Voluntary Sector Quarterly, 37*(3), 468–491.

Schmidt, H.J., Ind, N., Guzmán, F. & Kennedy, E. (2021). Sociopolitical activist brands. *Journal of Product & Brand Management, 31*(1), 40-55.

Sepulcri, L.M.C.B., Mainardes, E.W. & Belchior, C.C. (2020). Nonprofit branding: A bibliometric analysis. *Journal of Product & Brand Management, 29*(5), 655-673.

Sneddon, J.N., Evers, U. & Lee, J.A. (2020). Personal values and choice of charitable cause: An exploration of donors' giving behaviour. *Nonprofit and Voluntary Sector Quarterly, 49*(4), 803-826.

Spry, A., Figueiredo, B., Gurrieri, L., Kemper, J.A. & Vredenburg, J. (2021). Transformative branding: A dynamic capability to challenge the dominant social paradigm. *Journal of Macromarketing, 41*(4), 531-546.

Stride, H. & Lee, S. (2007). No logo? No way. Branding in the non-profit sector. *Journal of Marketing Management, 23*(1–2), 107–122.

Swaminathan, V., Sorescu, A., Steenkamp, J.B.E., O'Guinn, T.C.G. & Schmitt, B. (2020). Branding in a hyperconnected world: Refocusing theories and rethinking boundaries. *Journal of Marketing, 84*(2), 24-46.

Tapp, A. (1996). Charity brands: A qualitative study of current practice. *International Journal of Nonprofit and Voluntary Sector Marketing, 1*(4), 327-336.

Urde, M. (1999). Brand orientation: A mindset for building brands into strategic resources. *Journal of Marketing Management, 15*(1-3), 117-133.

Urde, M., Baumgarth, C. & Merrilees, B. (2013). Brand orientation and market orientation: From alternatives to synergy. *Journal of Business Research, 66*(1), 13-20.

Vallaster, C. & von Wallpach, S. (2018). Brand strategy co-creation in a nonprofit context: A strategy-as-practice approach. *Nonprofit and Voluntary Sector Quarterly, 47*(5), 984-1006.

Venable, B.T., Rose, G.M., Bush, V.D. & Gilbert, F.W. (2005). The role of brand personality in charitable giving: An assessment and validation. *Journal of the Academy of Marketing Science, 33*(3), 295–312.

Vredenburg, J., Kapitan, S., Spry, A. & Kemper, J.A. (2020). Brands taking a stand: Authentic brand activism or woke washing? *Journal of Public Policy & Marketing, 39*(4), 444-460.

Wallace, T. & Rutherford, A.C. (2021). The big bird gets the worm? How size influences social networking by charitable organizations. *Nonprofit and Voluntary Sector Quarterly*, *50*(3), 626–646.

Winterich, K.P., Zhang, Y. & Mittal, V. (2012). How political identity and charity positioning increase donations: Insights from moral foundations theory. *International Journal of Research in Marketing*, *29*(4), 346–354.

Wong, H.Y. & Merrilees, B. (2007). Multiple roles for branding in international marketing. *International Marketing Review*, *24*(4), 384–408.

Wymer, W. & Casidy, R. (2019). Exploring brand strength's nomological net and its dimensional dynamics. *Journal of Retailing and Consumer Services*, *49*, 11–22.

Wymer, W., Becker, A. & Boenigk, S. (2021). The antecedents of charity trust and its influence on charity supportive behaviour. *Journal of Philanthropy and Marketing*, *26*(2), 1690–1701.

Wymer, W., Gross, H.P. & Helmig, B. (2016). Nonprofit brand strength: What is it? How is it measured? What are its outcomes? *Voluntas: International Journal of Voluntary and Nonprofit Organizations*, *27*(3), 1448–1471.

Yoo, B., Donthu, N. & Lee, S. (2000). An examination of selected marketing mix elements and brand equity. *Journal of the Academy of Marketing Science*, *28*(2), 195–211.

15 Luxury brand research: four decades of innovation

Charles Aaron Lawry

1. Introduction

Luxury brand research is a thought-provoking topic that has rapidly evolved into a significant domain of research inquiry and managerial interest. For this reason, luxury brand research is ever-changing and intertwined with global market shifts. These shifts relate to four phases of luxury research (Luxury 1.0, 2.0, 3.0, and 4.0):

- *Luxury 1.0* (1990~2000) represents an attempt to define luxury brand identities and identify the drivers of luxury consumption due to the codification of luxury brand management as a research topic.
- *Luxury 2.0* (2000~2010) refers to the emergence of research on global branding, brand extensions, and brand experiences during the democratization of luxury through the rise of global luxury conglomerates and the Great Recession.
- *Luxury 3.0* (2010~2020) research examines the mediatization and artification of luxury during the post-recession years due to brand fatigue, digital disruption, and the new spending power of Millennials.
- *Luxury 4.0* (2020–present) is the next phase of luxury research characterized by new luxury, sustainability, emerging markets, phygital strategies, and luxury talent due to the global pandemic, Industry 4.0, and new generational cohorts.

This chapter will chronologically review these industry shifts and analyze downstream effects on luxury brand research. These decade-long themes are rough estimates, spilling from one phase to the next. Therefore, we aim to provide jumping-off points for exploration rather than discuss the evolution of each topic. In doing so, we will provide students, professors, and managers with much-needed context and tools to push the envelope in luxury brand research.

2. Luxury 1.0

Luxury research can be traced to the global propagation of department stores and shopping arcades during the nineteenth and twentieth centuries. Early heavy hitters in social science such as Veblen, Benjamin, Leibenstein, Goffman, and Bourdieu deeply analyzed these phenomena, disseminating theoretical work on luxury consumption. They discovered that luxury brands are not merely logos, like Baccarat, Moët-Chandon, Schiaparelli, or the Ritz-Carlton. Instead, they are expressive devices that reflect social classes and identity projects. Within this chapter, we refer to this theoretical work as Luxury 1.0, which defined luxury and identified the drivers of luxury consumption. Early researchers developed working definitions by analyzing the semantics of luxury. For example, "lux" and "luxus" are the origins of luxury in Latin, which translates into "light" and "excess" (Mortelmans, 1998). Nevertheless, luxury researchers craved scientific legitimacy and developed empirical evidence for this wordplay through perceptual maps and factor analyses (Dubois & Paternault, 1995; Kapferer, 1998; Kemp, 1998).

Findings revealed three major traits of luxury brands: desirability, polysensoriality, and temporality. First, *desirability* means that many people desire luxury brands, but they are exclusive and reserved for the well-heeled (Dubois & Duquesne, 1993). According to this logic, luxury brands must be revered to encourage consumers to dream about them. As such, consumers often perceive luxury brands as the crown jewels of fashion, automotive, hospitality, or food and beverage categories (Bernstein, 1999; Dubois & Paternault, 1995). Second, *polysensoriality* was another theme that emerged from this research. This theme refers to the ability of luxury brands to stimulate multiple senses through creative strategies often involving exquisite storytelling and unique offerings that differentiate luxury brands from ordinary experiences (Dubois & Laurent, 1994; Kapferer, 1998). Third, consumers perceive luxury brands as having *temporality* or standing the test of time. In other words, luxury brands should consistently deliver product quality and service excellence.

These foundational studies have since been widely accepted, but early researchers did not fully grasp why people consume luxury brands. For instance, Dubois and Paternault (1995, p. 69) argued that luxury motivations "seem hidden in an impenetrable black box". These unresolved issues encouraged a theoretical shift from conceptualizing luxury to analyzing luxury motivations. Motivational research initially pointed towards status-seeking as the primary driver of luxury brand preferences (Chao & Schor, 1998; Eastman et al., 1999). Such observations supported prevailing ideas about desirability. If luxury brands are unattainable, people will be more inclined to desire them. Yet, findings showed that status-seeking was also related to other motivations, such as materialism (Eastman et al., 1997), self-fulfillment (Holbrook, 1994), and pleasure-seeking (Dubois & Laurent, 1996). This realization led to discovering additional motivations through Vigneron and Johnson's (1999) prestige-seeking consumer behavior (PSCB) framework.

The PSCB framework was pivotal for widening the scope of luxury and understanding why consumers desire luxury brands. Specifically, this framework illustrates that luxury motivations can be extrinsic and intrinsic. *Extrinsic* motivations are interpersonal (i.e., ostentation, non-conformity, and conformity), and they are tied to conspicuousness, uniqueness, and social value. On the other hand, *intrinsic motivations* are personal (i.e., self-actualization and reassurance), and they are tied to emotional value and perceived quality. Overall, this duality between extrinsic vs. intrinsic motivations showed that equating luxury brands with exclusivity was an oversimplification. In reality, luxury motivations are multilayered, and firms must devote vast resources to attract a narrow yet colorful strata of luxury customers. These resources were stress-tested in the next phase due to the democratization of luxury.

3. Luxury 2.0

Luxury brands seemed unstoppable during Luxury 2.0 as global revenue accelerated (1985–2009) from $20 billion to $180 billion annually (Okonkwo, 2009). During this time, luxury CEOs invested heavily in global operations and serialized production to meet demand (Thomas, 2007). Luxury brands also produced masstige lines, expanded into duty-free shops and touristic playgrounds, and extended into adjacent categories, including fragrances, hospitality, and automotives (Nueno & Quelch, 1998; Stankeviciute & Hoffmann, 2010). Therefore, luxury researchers during this phase focused on global branding, brand extensions, and brand experiences. This work was prescient as researchers often expressed fears of brand dilution amid the *democratization of luxury*, exacerbated by the looming Great Recession (2007 to 2009) and the uncertainties of digital disruption (D'Arpizio et al., 2015).

Country of origin (COO) effects and cross-cultural marketing were the theoretical foci of global luxury research. Luxury researchers were interested in COO effects because luxury goods retained made-in labels, such as "Made in Italy" or "Made in France", even though many firms outsourced their production to factories or craftspeople in different countries with cheaper labor

(Thomas, 2007). In all, multi-country studies confirmed that COO effects are vital for brand equity, but they become less potent than brand names at higher levels of brand maturity (Manrai et al., 1998; Aiello et al., 2009; Piron, 2000). Similarly, multiple researchers found that extrinsic/intrinsic motivations underlie brand preferences in East Asia, South Asia, Europe, and the United States (Eng & Bogaert, 2010; Wong & Ahuvia, 1998). Global consumers in every market seemed to use luxury brands to impress others and express themselves. This cross-cultural stability opened up the possibility of global segmentation strategies (e.g., Wiedmann et al., 2009). Even so, several studies added that local consumers express themselves differently with luxury brands even if their motivations are similar (Bian & Forsythe, 2012; Shukla, 2010). Thus, luxury researchers suggested glocalization as an ideal strategy, such as Gucci's special-edition red handbags within the *Bright Bit* collection, which celebrated its equine heritage and commemorated the Year of the Horse in China (Kapferer, 2014).

As luxury brands transformed into global forces, luxury researchers were also curious about the effects of vertical/horizontal extensions on brand stature. First, studies showed that vertical extensions, or masstige lines (e.g., Armani Exchange), increased competitiveness when they preserved the core brand and increased the distance from line extensions (Kim et al., 2001; Riley et al., 2004). Moreover, horizontal extensions were shown to elevate brand stature, streamline operations, and diffuse risks when adding new categories (e.g., Armani/Casa) and forming luxury conglomerates, such as Kering, LVMH, Mercedes-Benz Group, and Aman Group Sarl (Stankeviciute, 2012). However, findings supported that horizontal extensions are constrained by the prestige and hedonic potential of the parent brand (Hagtvedt & Patrick, 2009; Reddy et al., 2009). Second, researchers stressed the importance of differentiating luxury brands through experience design. They moved the searchlight away from cross-cultural marketing onto value co-creation (Atwal & Williams, 2009; Tynan et al., 2010). According to this perspective, luxury branding requires interactivity at multiple levels between consumers, employees, investors, and the media. During the next phase, this interactivity would become essential to sustain luxury brands in the digital age.

4. Luxury 3.0

Luxury brands experienced slow and steady growth during Luxury 3.0. Even though sales slowed throughout the Great Recession, the global luxury market bounced back from 2009 to 2013 (D'Arpizio et al., 2015). This success was owed to democratization, pushing managers to revitalize luxury brands and protect them from brand fatigue. Paradoxically, new technologies entered this conversation due to online competition (e.g., Gilt Groupe and Net-a-porter) and increased purchasing power from Millennials (born between 1981 and 1996). Essentially, luxury brands needed to lasso the digital space and take control of their digital identities. Luxury brands also countermanded brand fatigue through artification, effectively becoming cultural institutions to reestablish their creative roots. Luxury 3.0 research, therefore, was underscored by two major themes: the mediatization and the artification of luxury.

Luxury researchers found that digital luxury audiences have higher socioeconomic status and technological proficiency than mass audiences (Castillan et al., 2017). They also noticed that luxury consumers are not only motivated to seek status or conspicuousness from digital luxury experiences (Hennigs et al., 2012; Jain & Schultz, 2019). They sometimes interact with digital media in pursuit of convenience, self-fulfillment, and emotional gratification (Delpal, 2021; Yoo & Park, 2016). Furthermore, luxury consumers are willing to shop and browse online when they are innovative, younger, and less risk-averse (Fazeli et al., 2020; Liu et al., 2013; Park et al., 2013). Many authors echoed this message and identified best practices for digital luxury branding, such as e-service quality (Kim et al., 2015; Türk et al., 2012) and alluring content (Baker et al., 2018; Rocamora, 2016).

Equally, the rise of social media marketing gained currency within the field. Luxury researchers were especially interested in Burberry's *Art of the Trench,* an award-winning global campaign and closed platform that crowdsourced photos of everyday people from different cultures wearing its iconic trench coats (Phan et al., 2011; Tokatli, 2012). The longevity of this campaign, which lasted from 2009 to 2017, stemmed from an alchemy of interactivity, brand love, and self-expression. This success led researchers to wonder if luxury brands could implement a similar strategy on open platforms like Facebook, Instagram, and Twitter. In turn, luxury researchers discovered that social networks and online forums are powerful forms of brand advocacy (Heine & Berghaus, 2014; Parrott et al., 2015). They also observed that social media participation triggers feelings of elite group membership and self-expression in luxury consumers (Hughes et al., 2016; Quach & Thaichon, 2017).

During the 3.0 phase, luxury brands counterbalanced these digital strategies with the artification of luxury to resist post-recession fatigue. The *artification* of luxury involved revitalizing connections between luxury brands and the art world to rekindle their status as tastemakers in society (Peluso et al., 2017; Vukadin et al., 2019). For example, luxury brands commissioned starchitects to redesign their physical spaces (e.g., Peter Marino), sponsored art installations (e.g., Hugo Boss Prize), and founded museums that exuded their brand legacies alongside iconic artwork (e.g., Fondazione Prada and Fondation Louis Vuitton). Empirical findings supported that luxury brands also reinforced ties to the art world by incorporating status and emotional games into their service strategies (Lawry, 2022b). *Status games* are actions that validate luxury brands and produce a high-stakes atmosphere through social judgment, brand worship, and gatekeeping strategies (Cervellon et al., 2019; Dion & Arnould, 2011; Ward & Dahl, 2014). On the other hand, *emotional games* create feelings of longing and tantalize the senses through elaborate staging and selling techniques borrowed from art galleries and auction houses (Joy et al., 2014; Logkizidou et al., 2018). Cumulatively, this research confirmed that artification could enhance brand images and enliven the key properties of luxury brands (i.e., desirability, polysensoriality, and temporality) during the post-recession years. However, the global pandemic shook things up and challenged its effectiveness during the next research phase.

5. Luxury 4.0

In 2020, the pandemic halted the global luxury market for the first time since the Great Recession. The pace of global luxury revenue dramatically slowed by 20% (year-over-year) due to factory closures, city lockdowns, and cautious spending (de Montgolfier et al., 2021). As a result, luxury brands transformed the home into a new hub for luxury consumers (Beauloye, 2022). For example, Louis Vuitton stocked exquisite caravans with merchandise and traveled to people's homes to boost sales through online bookings (Chikhoune, 2021), and Galeries Lafayette Champs-Élysées launched a mobile platform with virtual stylists (McDowell, 2020). These creative experiments signal a march towards something even more significant than adopting new technologies. Luxury 4.0 (2020–present) represents a time for managers to pause, reflect, and innovate in the face of uncertainty. This chapter follows a similar logic as we wrap up our discussion on luxury branding. That is, what should be the future priorities for luxury brand research? To address this question, we will hit "rewind" and reflect on previous phases to identify gaps, highlight market needs, and set an agenda for the next decade.

First, *Luxury 1.0* was primarily focused on defining luxury and identifying the key drivers of luxury consumption. Critical studies have been published recently, describing luxury as poorly defined and undertheorized within brand management. Nevertheless, the attempt to produce a singular definition of luxury is quixotic. Time would be better served trying to develop a classification system to categorize different types of luxury and explain how multiple luxuries are born from the external environment. After creating this classificatory scheme, luxury researchers can help brand managers identify relevant data points and forecast trends in the luxury market. This chapter and previous studies have laid the groundwork (Miller & Mills, 2012), but there is ample room to explore this topic.

On the other hand, psychosocial motivations for consuming luxury brands have been undertheorized. Many researchers have granted attention to extrinsic motivations, but fewer have probed intrinsic or inner-directed drivers such as self-gifting, self-directed pleasure, escapism, and self-identity. Intrinsic motivations are especially relevant as new trends – digital and ephemeral experiences (e.g., pop-up shops, connected stores, NFT collections, and private events) – allow luxury consumers to become more autonomous and less reliant on salespersons at physical touchpoints (Carta & de Kock, 2019). Furthermore, theoreticians have developed and proposed the idea of *new luxury* or the pursuit of subtler luxury values (e.g., minimalism, self-actualization, and sustainability) (Atkinson & Kang, 2021; Thomsen et al., 2020). New luxury is an emergent property of younger audiences, the experience economy, and the slow movement. These phenomena need to be investigated to see how intrinsic motivations shape the co-creation of new luxury experiences (Holmqvist et al., 2020b; von Wallpach et al., 2020).

Second, *Luxury 2.0* was the inception of global luxury research, highlighting the global diffusion and democratization of luxury. Researchers frequently discussed the ill effects of democratization on brand equity but less often considered how it simultaneously increased waste and a throwaway culture. This gap uncovers the need to probe issues in sustainable luxury. To date, several studies have examined attitudes towards sustainable luxury branding and motivations for seeking green luxury goods and services (Chen & Petersen, 2022; Kumagai & Nagasawa, 2022; Talukdar & Yu, 2020). However, an unrelenting and underexplored issue is that sustainable luxury is a paradox since environmental responsibility implies the mitigation of waste and pollution (Osburg et al., 2021; Wong & Dhanesh, 2017). Yet, the luxury brands can be extractive of natural capital and exploitative of social capital. Future studies will need to reassess how luxury brands can resolve this paradox and analyze consumer perceptions when brands attempt to address it.

For example, researchers have suggested that the durability of luxury goods can encourage responsible and mindful consumer behaviors by increasing satisfaction and reducing product obsolescence (Amatulli et al., 2021). Thus, knowing how luxury consumers interact with repair services will be insightful. Specifically, what factors will (de)motivate luxury consumers to seek repairs or refurbish existing products? Moreover, most luxury brands have adopted carbon trading and supply chain transparency to promote sustainability (Di Leo et al., 2023). These practices raise the following questions: Will carbon trading and supply chain transparency initiatives reaffirm or resolve the sustainable luxury paradox? How will perceptions of these initiatives differ between younger (Millennial and Gen-Z) versus older consumers? What will be the overall impact of these initiatives on brand equity?

In the future, luxury researchers should also address the ethnocentrism derived from Luxury 2.0. Cross-cultural studies have been biased towards existing markets and the home countries of research teams (e.g., Western Europe, the United States, Japan, South Korea, and China). As a result, the voices of consumers in emerging luxury markets with larger middle-class or high-net-worth segments are absent from luxury research, especially in Latin America, Southeast Asia, and sub-Saharan Africa (The Future Laboratory, 2017). Researchers should get ahead of the curve and teach brand managers about the nuances of luxury consumption within these global regions. Meanwhile, luxury researchers have failed to unpack social issues, such as aesthetic and emotional labor within the luxury workforce (Kim & Baker, 2022; Lam et al., 2022) and historical controversies within the luxury industry (e.g., human rights abuses and cultural appropriation) (Gerrie, 2019; Paulicelli, 2022). Recently, several researchers have articulated the value of corporate social responsibility and philanthropy (Amatulli et al., 2018; Sipilä et al., 2021), but these deeper social issues have not been investigated. Specifically, how should luxury brands address past controversies and prevent future occurrences of exploitation? Today, what steps can be taken to cultivate meaningful and empathic relationships between luxury brands, employees, and local communities where they operate businesses?

Third, *Luxury 3.0* was a paradigm-shifting moment when researchers analyzed post-recession luxury strategies from two angles: mediatization and artification. These researchers left the door open to explore new opportunities for luxury brands. E-commerce and social media strategies were top-of-mind during Luxury 3.0, but mobile experiences have since become valuable tools for managing luxury brands (Achille et al., 2018). Due to this growing demand for mobile experiences, luxury researchers are poised to conduct innovative work on m-commerce. So far, researchers have demonstrated how usability, interactivity, and intrinsic motivations increase participation in mobile luxury experiences (Pantano et al., 2018; Rao & Ko, 2021; Rovai, 2018). Equally, it will be essential to understand how mobile experiences align with the broader strategy of luxury brand storytelling. Future studies, therefore, should assess the roles of gamification and narrative transportation within these experiences.

In addition, the widespread adoption of smartphones and tablets is fueling an exciting *phygital* trend in which luxury consumers blend immersive mobile experiences with physical servicescapes (Lawry, 2022a). Phygital strategies allow luxury brands to maximize the benefits of digital experiences and high-touch services (Pangarkar et al., 2022). However, phygital strategies will transform luxury experiences from top-down service models into multi-actor networks as mobile devices can fuse a single service encounter with online communities and social networks (Holmqvist et al., 2020a). This opportunity calls for cutting-edge studies on the customer journey. Specifically, how might luxury researchers analyze data from digital and physical touchpoints to describe these new customer journeys? Over time, luxury brands may also incorporate the Metaverse into journey maps if VR headsets reach a tipping point in the market. Thus, researchers should be prepared to advise managers on best practices for integrating the Metaverse into phygital strategies. To begin with, researchers should find productive ways for luxury brands to interact with customers through the Metaverse to encourage brand activation and deepen their emotional connections to the brand community.

In sum, there has been a sea-change in the viewpoints of luxury managers and researchers on the viability of digital brand strategies. Nevertheless, the threat of extinction is real for luxury brands in the digital age. Currently, artification has sustained luxury brands, but the fragile art of luxury ultimately resides within people. The dwindling of creative leadership and *savoir faire*, the artisans who help create luxury goods (e.g., horology, tailoring, perfumery, winemaking, and leather smithing), has become a pressing concern in the past decade. Creative directors are known for being charismatic and often lack concrete plans for passing the torch even as they grow older because they regard themselves as creative geniuses (Lawry & Helm, 2014). By contrast, younger workers in Western Europe do not wish to carry on artisanal legacies and increasingly seek white-collar professions (Martin, 2014).

In the future, luxury researchers must tackle these issues by helping luxury brands develop effective processes for managing corporate succession and recruiting the next generation of artisans. The following questions should inform research in this new area of inquiry: How can luxury brands document and transmit the iterative thinking and design processes that underlie the strengths of their leadership? Also, what is the most effective approach to assessing the future potential of new luxury talent and developing them to assume leadership roles? Lastly, how can young people worldwide be incentivized and trained to acquire the *savoir faire* that comprises the intricate production of luxury brands?

In closing, innovation is essential for advancing luxury research to the next phase: Luxury 4.0. This new decade will call for thought leadership and studies on the dynamics of new luxury, the paradox of sustainability, emerging luxury markets, phygital luxury strategies, and the future of leadership and *savoir faire* in the luxury industry. These four decades of luxury research demonstrate that students and researchers must keep up with the pace of the industry to stay relevant and develop meaningful work in this fascinating field. Meanwhile, managers need to keep track of research trends to build unique and creative strategies that enhance the desirability, polysensoriality, and temporality of luxury brands. This cross-fertilization of ideas between academia and industry will pave the way towards innovation, again and again, within the ebbs and flows of the luxury market.

References

Achille, A., Remy, N., & Marchessou, S. (2018). *The Age of Digital Darwinism*. McKinsey & Company.

Aiello, G., Donvito, R., Godey, B., Pederzoli, D., Wiedmann, K.-P., Hennigs, N., Siebels, A., Chan, P., Tsuchiya, J., Rabino, S., Ivanovna, S. I., Weitz, B., Oh, H., & Singh, R. (2009). An international perspective on luxury brand and country-of-origin effect. *Journal of Brand Management*, *16*(5), 323–337.

Amatulli, C., De Angelis, M., & Donato, C. (2021). The atypicality of sustainable luxury products. *Psychology & Marketing*, *38*(11), 1990–2005.

Amatulli, C., De Angelis, M., Korschun, D., & Romani, S. (2018). Consumers' perceptions of luxury brands' CSR initiatives: An investigation of the role of status and conspicuous consumption. *Journal of Cleaner Production*, *194*, 277–287.

Atkinson, S. D., & Kang, J. (2021). New luxury: Defining and evaluating emerging luxury trends through the lenses of consumption and personal values. *Journal of Product & Brand Management*, *31*(3), 377–393.

Atwal, G., & Williams, A. (2009). Luxury brand marketing: The experience is everything! *Journal of Brand Management*, *16*(5), 338–346.

Baker, J., Ashill, N., Amer, N., & Diab, E. (2018). The internet dilemma: An exploratory study of luxury firms' usage of internet-based technologies. *Journal of Retailing and Consumer Services*, *41*, 37–47.

Beauloye, F. E. (2022, November 16). *Luxury And The Stay-At-Home Economy: A New Paradigm*. https://luxe.digital/business/digital-luxury-reports/stay-at-home-luxury/

Bernstein, L. (1999). Luxury and the hotel brand: Art, science, or fiction? *Cornell Hotel and Restaurant Administration Quarterly*, *40*(1), 47–53.

Bian, Q., & Forsythe, S. (2012). Purchase intention for luxury brands: A cross-cultural comparison. *Journal of Business Research*, *65*(10), 1443–1451.

Carta, S., & de Kock, P. (2019). Reifying luxury, gold to golden: How the showroom became a digital showreel, from object (gold) to experience (golden) experiencing luxury by abstracting the object. *Journal of Design, Business & Society*, *5*(2), 193–206.

Castillan, L., Chheang, C., Denoux, C., Ferrenbach, C., Gérard, C., Hua, E., Van Holt, J., & Coste Manière, I. (2017). Online luxury: The code breakers of a traditional sector. *Procedia Computer Science*, *122*, 579–586.

Cervellon, M.-C., Poujol, J. F., & Tanner, J. F. (2019). Judging by the wristwatch: Salespersons' responses to status signals and stereotypes of luxury clients. *Journal of Retailing and Consumer Services*, *51*, 191–201.

Chao, A., & Schor, J. B. (1998). Empirical tests of status consumption: Evidence from women's cosmetics. *Journal Of Economic Psychology*, *19*(1), 107–131.

Chen, N., & Petersen, F. E. (2022). Consumers' cooperation with sustainability programs: The role of luxury branding and profit motive attribution. *Journal of Macromarketing*, *42*(4), 655–672.

Chikhoune, R. (2021, February 12). *Louis Vuitton Is Traveling to Homes*. https://wwd.com/fashion-news/fashion-scoops/louis-vuitton-traveling-homes-1234728635

D'Arpizio, C., Levato, F., Zito, D., & Montgolfier, J. (2015). *A Time to Act: How Luxury Brands can Rebuild to Win*. Bain & Company.

Delpal, F. (2021). The different determinants of purchasing luxury goods online: An international comparison. *Journal of Design Business & Society*, *7*(1), 29–48.

de Montgolfier, J., D'Arpizio, C., Levato, F., Prete, F., & Gault, C. (2021). *The Future of Luxury: Bouncing Back from Covid-19*. Bain & Company.

Di Leo, A., Sfodera, F., Cucari, N., Mattia, G., & Dezi, L. (2023). Sustainability reporting practices: An explorative analysis of luxury fashion brands. *Management Decision*. Advance online publication. https://doi.org/10.1108/MD-02-2022-0142

Dion, D., & Arnould, E. (2011). Retail luxury strategy: Assembling charisma through art and magic. *Journal of Retailing*, *87*(4), 502–520.

Dubois, B., & Duquesne, P. (1993). The market for luxury goods: Income versus culture. *European Journal of Marketing*, *27*(1), 35–44.

Dubois, B., & Laurent, G. (1994). Attitudes toward the concept of luxury: An exploratory analysis. *Asian Pacific Advances in Consumer Research*, *1*, 273–278.

Dubois, B., & Laurent, G. (1996). The functions of luxury: A situational approach to excursionism. *ACR North American Advances*. https:// www .acrwebsite .org/ volumes/7875/volumes/v23/NA-23/full

Dubois, B., & Paternault, C. (1995). Understanding the world of international luxury brands and the "Dream Formula". *Journal of Advertising Research*, *35*(4), 69–76.

Eastman, J. K., Fredenberger, B., Campbell, D., & Calvert, S. (1997). The relationship between status consumption and materialism: A cross-cultural comparison of Chinese, Mexican, and American students. *The Journal of Marketing Theory and Practice*, *5*(1), 52–66.

Eastman, J. K., Goldsmith, R. E., & Flynn, L. R. (1999). Status consumption in consumer behavior: Scale development and validation. *Journal of Marketing Theory and Practice*, *7*(3), 41–52.

Eng, T.-Y., & Bogaert, J. (2010). Psychological and cultural insights into consumption of luxury Western brands in India. *Journal of Customer Behaviour*, *9*(1), 55–75.

Fazeli, Z., Shukla, P., & Perks, K. (2020). Digital buying behavior: The role of regulatory fit and self-construal in online luxury goods purchase intentions. *Psychology & Marketing*, *37*(1), 15–26.

Gerrie, V. (2019). The Diet Prada effect: "Call-out culture" in the contemporary fashionscape. *Clothing Cultures*, *6*(1), 97–113.

Hagtvedt, H., & Patrick, V. M. (2009). The broad embrace of luxury: Hedonic potential as a driver of brand extendibility. *Journal of Consumer Psychology, 19*(4), 608–618.
Heine, K., & Berghaus, B. (2014). Luxury goes digital: How to tackle the digital luxury brand–consumer touchpoints. *Journal of Global Fashion Marketing, 5*(3), 223–234.
Hennigs, N., Wiedmann, K.-P., & Klarmann, C. (2012). Luxury brands in the digital age: Exclusivity versus ubiquity. *Marketing Review St. Gallen, 29*(1), 30–34.
Holbrook, M. (1994). *Consumer Value: A Framework for Analysis and Research.* Routledge.
Holmqvist, J., Diaz Ruiz, C., & Peñaloza, L. (2020a). Moments of luxury: Hedonic escapism as a luxury experience. *Journal of Business Research, 116*, 503–513.
Holmqvist, J., Wirtz, J., & Fritze, M. P. (2020b). Luxury in the digital age: A multi-actor service encounter perspective. *Journal of Business Research, 121*, 747–756.
Hughes, M. Ü., Bendoni, W. K., & Pehlivan, E. (2016). Storygiving as a co-creation tool for luxury brands in the age of the Internet: A love story by Tiffany and thousands of lovers. *Journal of Product & Brand Management, 25*(4), 357–364.
Jain, V., & Schultz, D. E. (2019). How digital platforms influence luxury purchase behavior in India? *Journal of Marketing Communications, 25*(1), 41–64.
Joy, A., Wang, J. J., Chan, T.-S., Sherry, J. F., & Cui, G. (2014). M(art)worlds: Consumer perceptions of how luxury brand stores become art institutions. *Journal of Retailing, 90*(3), 347–364.
Kapferer, J.-N. (1998). Why are we seduced by luxury brands? *Journal of Brand Management, 6*(1), 44–49.
Kapferer, J.-N. (2014). The artification of luxury: From artisans to artists. *Business Horizons, 57*(3), 371–380.
Kemp, S. (1998). Perceiving luxury and necessity. *Journal of Economic Psychology, 19*(5), 591–606.
Kim, C. K., Lavack, A. M., & Smith, M. (2001). Consumer evaluation of vertical brand extensions and core brands. *Journal of Business Research, 52*(3), 211–222.
Kim, H., Choi, Y. J., & Lee, Y. (2015). Web atmospheric qualities in luxury fashion brand websites. *Journal of Fashion Marketing and Management, 19*(4), 384–401.
Kim, K., & Baker, M. A. (2022). Luxury branding in the hospitality industry: The impact of employee's luxury appearance and elitism attitude. *Cornell Hospitality Quarterly, 63*(1), 5–18.
Kumagai, K., & Nagasawa, S. (2022). Effects of perceived luxury value and use of sustainable polyester on brand trust, perceived quality risk, and consumers' brand evaluation. *Journal of Global Fashion Marketing.* Advance online publication. https://doi.org/10.1080/20932685.2022.2085594
Lam, R., Cheung, C., & Lugosi, P. (2022). The impacts of cultural intelligence and emotional labor on the job satisfaction of luxury hotel employees. *International Journal of Hospitality Management, 100*, 103084.
Lawry, C. A. (2022a). Blurring luxury: The mediating role of self-gifting in consumer acceptance of phygital shopping experiences. *International Journal of Advertising, 41*(4), 796–822.
Lawry, C. A. (2022b). Futurizing luxury: An activity-centric model of phygital luxury experiences. *Journal of Fashion Marketing and Management.* Advance online publication. https://doi.org/10.1108/JFMM-05-2021-0125
Lawry, C. A., & Helm, S. V. (2014). Curating the creative genius in luxury firms. In B. Berghaus, G. Müller-Stewens, & S. Reinecke (Eds.), *The Management of Luxury: A Practitioner's Handbook* (pp. 114–125). Kogan Page.

Liu, X., Burns, A. C., & Hou, Y. (2013). Comparing online and in-store shopping behavior towards luxury goods. *International Journal of Retail & Distribution Management, 41*(11/12), 885–900.

Logkizidou, M., Bottomley, P., Angell, R., & Evanschitzky, H. (2018). Why museological merchandise displays enhance luxury product evaluations: An extended art infusion effect. *Journal of Retailing, 95*(1), 67–82.

Manrai, L. A., Lascu, D.-N., & Manrai, A. K. (1998). Interactive effects of country of origin and product category on product evaluations. *International Business Review, 7*(6), 591–615.

Martin, J. J. (2014, September 1). *Class Action: The Fashion Brands Training Tomorrow's Artisans.* https:// www .wallpaper .com/ fashion/ class -action -the -fashion -brands -training-tomorrows-artisans

McDowell, M. (2020). *Smartphones are the New Salesfloor.* Vogue Business. https:// www .voguebusiness .com/ technology/ smartphones -are -the -new -salesfloor -e -commerce-chat

Miller, K. W., & Mills, M. K. (2012). Probing brand luxury: A multiple lens approach. *Journal of Brand Management, 20*(1), 41–51.

Mortelmans, D. (1998). Socio-semiotic analysis of print advertisements for luxury products. *Semiotica, 120*(1–2), 181–206.

Nueno, J. L., & Quelch, J. A. (1998). The mass marketing of luxury. *Business Horizons, 41*(6), 61–68.

Okonkwo, U. (2009). The luxury brand strategy challenge. *Journal of Brand Management, 16*(5), 287–289.

Osburg, V.-S., Davies, I., Yoganathan, V., & McLeay, F. (2021). Perspectives, opportunities and tensions in ethical and sustainable luxury: Introduction to the thematic symposium. *Journal of Business Ethics, 169*(2), 201–210.

Pangarkar, A., Arora, V., & Shukla, Y. (2022). Exploring phygital omnichannel luxury retailing for immersive customer experience: The role of rapport and social engagement. *Journal of Retailing and Consumer Services, 68*, 103001.

Pantano, E., Passavanti, R., Priporas, C.-V., & Verteramo, S. (2018). To what extent luxury retailing can be smart? *Journal of Retailing and Consumer Services, 43*, 94–100.

Park, H., Burns, L. D., & Rabolt, N. J. (2013). Fashion innovativeness, materialism, and attitude toward purchasing foreign fashion goods online across national borders. *Journal of Fashion Marketing and Management, 11*(2), 201–214.

Parrott, G., Danbury, A., & Kanthavanich, P. (2015). Online behaviour of luxury fashion brand advocates. *Journal of Fashion Marketing and Management, 19*(4), 360–383.

Paulicelli, E. (2022). Made in Italy: Translating cultures from Gucci to Dapper Dan and back. *Textile, 20*(2), 216–230.

Peluso, A. M., Pino, G., Amatulli, C., & Guido, G. (2017). Luxury advertising and recognizable artworks. *European Journal of Marketing, 51*(11/12), 2192–2206.

Phan, M., Thomas, R., & Heine, K. (2011). Social media and luxury brand management: The case of Burberry. *Journal of Global Fashion Marketing, 2*(4), 213–222.

Piron, F. (2000). Consumers' perceptions of the country-of-origin effect on purchasing intentions of (in)conspicuous products. *Journal of Consumer Marketing, 17*(4), 308–321.

Quach, S., & Thaichon, P. (2017). From connoisseur luxury to mass luxury: Value co-creation and co-destruction in the online environment. *Journal of Business Research, 81*, 163–172.

Rao, Q., & Ko, E. (2021). Impulsive purchasing and luxury brand loyalty in WeChat Mini Program. *Asia Pacific Journal of Marketing and Logistics, 33*(10), 2054–2071.

Reddy, M., Terblanche, N., Pitt, L., & Parent, M. (2009). How far can luxury brands travel? Avoiding the pitfalls of luxury brand extension. *Business Horizons, 52*(2), 187–197.

Riley, F. D., Lomax, W., & Blunden, A. (2004). Dove vs. Dior: Extending the brand extension decision-making process from mass to luxury. *Australasian Marketing Journal, 12*(3), 40–55.

Rocamora, A. (2016). Online luxury: Geographies of production and consumption and the Louis Vuitton website. In J. Armitage & J. Roberts (Eds.), *Critical Luxury Studies: Art, Design, Media* (pp. 199–220). Edinburgh University Press.

Rovai, S. (2018). Digitalisation, luxury fashion and "Chineseness": The influence of the Chinese context for luxury brands and the online luxury consumers experience. *Journal of Global Fashion Marketing, 9*(2), 116–128.

Shukla, P. (2010). Status consumption in cross-national context: Socio-psychological, brand and situational antecedents. *International Marketing Review, 27*(1), 108–129.

Sipilä, J., Alavi, S., Edinger-Schons, L. M., Dörfer, S., & Schmitz, C. (2021). Corporate social responsibility in luxury contexts: Potential pitfalls and how to overcome them. *Journal of the Academy of Marketing Science, 49*(2), 280–303.

Stankeviciute, R. (2012). Brand extensions in the luxury industry. In J. Hoffmann & I. Coste-Manière (Eds.), *Luxury Strategy in Action* (pp. 144–159). Palgrave Macmillan UK.

Stankeviciute, R., & Hoffmann, J. (2010). The impact of brand extension on the parent luxury fashion brand: The cases of Giorgio Armani, Calvin Klein, and Jimmy Choo. *Journal of Global Fashion Marketing, 1*(2), 119–128.

Talukdar, N., & Yu, S. (2020). Do materialists care about sustainable luxury? *Marketing Intelligence & Planning*. Advance online publication. https://doi.org/10.1108/MIP-05-2019-0277

The Future Laboratory. (2017). *Luxury Futures*. https://www.thefuturelaboratory.com/reports/luxury-futures-report-2017

Thomas, D. (2007). *Deluxe: How Luxury Lost its Luster*. Penguin Press.

Thomsen, T. U., Holmqvist, J., von Wallpach, S., Hemetsberger, A., & Belk, R. W. (2020). Conceptualizing unconventional luxury. *Journal of Business Research, 116*, 441–445.

Tokatli, N. (2012). Old firms, new tricks and the quest for profits: Burberry's journey from success to failure and back to success again. *Journal of Economic Geography, 12*(1), 55–77.

Türk, B., Scholz, M., & Berresheim, P. (2012). Measuring service quality in online luxury goods retailing. *Journal of Electronic Commerce Research, 13*(1), 88–103.

Tynan, C., McKechnie, S., & Chhuon, C. (2010). Co-creating value for luxury brands. *Journal of Business Research, 63*(11), 1156–1163.

Vigneron, F., & Johnson, L. W. (1999). A review and a conceptual framework of prestige-seeking consumer behavior. *Academy of Marketing Science Review, 1*(1), 1–15.

von Wallpach, S., Hemetsberger, A., Thomsen, T. U., & Belk, R. W. (2020). Moments of luxury: A qualitative account of the experiential essence of luxury. *Journal of Business Research, 116*, 491–502.

Vukadin, A., Lemoine, J.-F., & Badot, O. (2019). Store artification and retail performance. *Journal of Marketing Management, 35*(7–8), 634–661.

Ward, M. K., & Dahl, D. W. (2014). Should the devil sell Prada? Retail rejection increases aspiring consumers' desire for the brand. *The Journal of Consumer Research, 41*(3), 590–609.

Wiedmann, K.-P., Hennigs, N., & Siebels, A. (2009). Value-based segmentation of luxury consumption behavior. *Psychology & Marketing, 26*(7), 625–651.

Wong, J. Y., & Dhanesh, G. S. (2017). Communicating corporate social responsibility (CSR) in the luxury industry: Managing CSR–luxury paradox online through acceptance strategies of coexistence and convergence. *Management Communication Quarterly, 31*(1), 88–112.

Wong, N. Y., & Ahuvia, A. C. (1998). Personal taste and family face: Luxury consumption in Confucian and Western societies. *Psychology & Marketing, 15*(5), 423–441.

Yoo, J., & Park, M. (2016). The effects of e-mass customization on consumer perceived value, satisfaction, and loyalty toward luxury brands. *Journal of Business Research, 69*(12), 5775–5784.

Index